ADVANCE PRAISE
for *Addressing Anti-Asian Racism with Social Work, Advocacy, and Action*

It is an esteemed privilege to endorse the groundbreaking book titled *Addressing Anti-Asian Racism with Social Work Advocacy and Action*. This seminal work represents a pivotal advancement within the domains of social work and social science literature, profoundly bridging a critical gap in our comprehension of racial inequality, particularly within the context of Asian American experiences.

Amidst our profession's steadfast dedication to combatting racism, a conspicuous void has persisted in scholarly discourse surrounding anti-Asian racism. With unwavering resolve, this book fearlessly confronts this lacuna, embarking on a comprehensive exploration of the historical, social, cultural, and psychological dimensions inherent to anti-Asian racism as experienced by Asian Americans.

Adopting an evidence-based approach of unparalleled rigor, this work compellingly underscores the imperative for social work practitioners, scholars, and students to actively engage with this pressing societal issue. By meticulously illuminating the systemic underpinnings of racism and its profound ramifications upon individuals and communities, this book serves as a clarion call, compelling us to scrutinize and recalibrate our paradigms of social work practice and education.

The evidence marshaled throughout the book is nothing short of sobering, laying bare the persistent marginalization of anti-Asian racism within social work research and literature. In filling this critical lacuna, the book proffers a nuanced analysis of the structural inequities perpetuated by racism, whilst fervently advocating for institutional reforms aimed at engendering social justice and equity.

I commend this formidable tome and the erudite contributions of its authors for their unwavering commitment to amplifying the voices of Asian Americans and advancing our collective comprehension of racial injustice. I wholeheartedly endorse this indispensable resource to social work practitioners, scholars, and professionals across the medical and social services spectrum. It stands as an indispensable beacon for all who espouse the ideals of equality and strive to foster inclusive spaces for Asian Americans and all individuals within our society.

—Ada C. Mui, Professor, Columbia University School of Social Work

Addressing Anti-Asian Racism with Social Work, Advocacy, and Action

Edited by
MEIRONG LIU AND KEITH T. CHAN

OXFORD
UNIVERSITY PRESS

Oxford University Press is a department of the University of Oxford. It furthers
the University's objective of excellence in research, scholarship, and education
by publishing worldwide. Oxford is a registered trade mark of Oxford University
Press in the UK and certain other countries.

Published in the United States of America by Oxford University Press
198 Madison Avenue, New York, NY 10016, United States of America.

© Oxford University Press 2024

All rights reserved. No part of this publication may be reproduced, stored in
a retrieval system, or transmitted, in any form or by any means, without the
prior permission in writing of Oxford University Press, or as expressly permitted
by law, by license, or under terms agreed with the appropriate reproduction
rights organization. Inquiries concerning reproduction outside the scope of the
above should be sent to the Rights Department, Oxford University Press, at the
address above.

You must not circulate this work in any other form
and you must impose this same condition on any acquirer.

Library of Congress Cataloging-in-Publication Data
Names: Liu, Meirong, 1977– editor. | Chan, Keith T., editor.
Title: Addressing anti-Asian racism with social work, advocacy, and action /
edited by Meirong Liu and Keith Chan.
Description: New York, NY : Oxford University Press, [2024] |
Includes bibliographical references and index.
Identifiers: LCCN 2024023361 | ISBN 9780197672242 (hardback) |
ISBN 9780197672266 (epub) | ISBN 9780197672259 | ISBN 9780197672273
Subjects: LCSH: Racism against Asians—United States. |
Asian Americans—Violence against. | Asian Americans—Psychology. |
Anti-racism—United States. | Social work with minorities—United States. |
Asian Americans—Government policy. | United States—Race relations.
Classification: LCC E184.A75 A36 2024 | DDC 305.895/073—dc23/eng/20240705
LC record available at https://lccn.loc.gov/2024023361

DOI: 10.1093/oso/9780197672242.001.0001

The manufacturer's authorised representative in the EU for product safety is
Oxford University Press España S.A. of El Parque Empresarial San Fernando
de Henares, Avenida de Castilla, 2 – 28830 Madrid (www.oup.es/en or
product.safety@oup.com). OUP España S.A. also acts as importer into Spain
of products made by the manufacturer.

Contents

Foreword ix
Acknowledgments xiii
Editors xv
List of Contributors xvii
Introduction xix
    Meirong Liu and Keith T. Chan

SECTION I DECONSTRUCTING ANTI-ASIAN RACISM: UNDERSTANDING HISTORY, SOCIAL CONTEXTS, AND COMPLEXITIES

1. The History of Anti-Asian Racism and Violence in the United States — 3
   Meirong Liu, Nayoun Lee, Zhanjie Si, and Olivia Aquino

2. Racism, Xenophobia, and Violence Against Asian Americans During the COVID-19 Pandemic — 24
   Xiaofang Liu, Kenny Kwong, and Qingwen Xu

3. Acculturation, the Asian American Identity, and the Impact of Anti-Asian Racism on Health and Mental Health — 41
   Keith T. Chan

4. The Intersection of Racism and Marginalized Identities Among Asian Americans — 56
   Jun Sung Hong, Sofie Hana Aaron, Cindy C. Sangalang, Jane J. Lee, and Joong Won Kim

5. Understanding and Dismantling the "Model Minority" Stereotype — 77
   Lalaine Sevillano and Kirin Macagupay

6. Asian American, Racial Solidarity, and Black Lives Matter — 95
   Robert Cosby, Meirong Liu, and Keith T. Chan

SECTION II VOICES OF DIVERSE COMMUNITIES: INTERSECTIONALITIES IN THE EXPERIENCE OF ANTI-ASIAN RACISM

7. The Perceptions of Korean Americans on the Rise of Anti-Asian Racial Discrimination and the Negative Impact on Psychological Distress — 111
   Shinwoo Choi, Joo Young Hong, Catherine Hawkins, and Hyejoon Park

8. Acculturation and Cultural Socialization Practices of Japanese Immigrant and Temporary Resident Families in the United States — 129
   Misa Kayama

9. *Bahaghari*: Visibilizing the Experiences and Resistance of LGBTQ+ Filipinx Americans in the Diaspora — 146
   Dale Dagar Maglalang and Hillary Nicole Peregrina

10. Religion and Spirituality as Buffers Against Islamophobia in the Lives of Asian American Youth — 168
    Altaf Husain, Hannan Hijazi, and Sarah Carlis

11. Coping at the Margins: Managing Loneliness for Hmong Older Adults — 186
    Cindy Vang, Michael Sieng, and Austin Thao

12. The Impact of Anti-Asian Racism on the Psychosocial Well-Being of Older Asian Americans: A Systematic Review — 203
    Fei Sun, Siyu Gao, Ethan Liu, and Yali Feng

SECTION III DISMANTLING ANTI-ASIAN RACISM: MICRO, MEZZO, AND MACRO-LEVEL STRATEGIES

13. The Role of Social Work and Storytelling in Eliminating Anti-Asian Racism and Hate Crimes — 227
    Sofie Hana Aaron, Juliann Li Verdugo, Jane J. Lee, Hye-Kyung Kang, Tam Q. Dinh, and Michael S. Spencer

14. Reflecting on Racism Within the Social Work Profession and Developing an Anti-Racist Workforce — 252
    Kenny Kwong

15. Service Access to Depression Treatment: Mental Health
    Help-Seeking Sources Among Asian Americans   270
    Patrick Leung, Monit Cheung, and Carol A. Leung

16. Promising, Culturally Sensitive Evidence-Based
    Interventions for Asian Americans   296
    Dhrubodhi Mukherjee

17. The Importance of Community-Based Solutions in
    Addressing Anti-Asian Racism   311
    Clifford S. Bersamira, Sophia B. Lau, and Yeonjung Jane Lee

18. Policy Initiatives on Eliminating Anti-Asian Racism   334
    Meirong Liu, Yanfeng Xu, and Zhanjie Si

    Conclusion: Hopes for the Future and Call for Action in
    Addressing Anti-Asian Racism   359
    Keith T. Chan and Meirong Liu

Index   361

Foreword

I am honored to be included in this anthology of action-oriented, thoughtful scholarship on anti-Asian racism edited and produced by Dr. Meirong Liu and Dr. Keith T. Chan. For some time now, I have known and followed the work of Drs. Liu and Chan, who support and influence change at the local and national levels in their respective communities. Thus, it is unsurprising that both of these scholars took the lead in organizing this edited volume, *Addressing Anti-Asian Racism with Social Work Advocacy and Action*, which explicates issues important to various Asian American diaspora groups. Their passion and commitment to this issue come through clearly and impactfully.

Being an immigrant from India, along with being a part of the Asian American community since 1992, I understand the racism and discrimination this population is facing. Over the past 30 years of living, studying, and working in multiple states and universities, I have also observed a pronounced rise in anti-Asian racism, violence, and discrimination nationwide. It has unfortunately become far more commonplace than an exception to label Asian Americans as the "other" whenever people and communities do not understand the Asian diaspora and especially when some people, communities, (and media) show hate to this very diverse population while seeking someone to "blame." Anti-Asian racism has existed for a long time and unfortunately will continue to manifest in many apparent and subtle ways directed at Asian people, communities, and families. Though seldom spoken about due to the intrinsic nature of these collectivist groups where stigma and beliefs in fate, faith, and family values are paramount, it is a scourge that demands our attention, our empathy, and, above all, our actions.

Aware of this increasing hatred and violence, we must stand with knowledge and empathy as well as with a relentless advocacy and action agenda. In a world where diversity must be recognized and variations acknowledged, racism in its numerous forms is a reminder of our collective pain as a way of life. Social justice issues have been under attack lately from persistent injustices in our society. Within the complexities of social justice, the threads of prejudice against Asian Americans run through history and leave scars that suggest that much work is yet to be done. Among them, anti-Asian racism and violence have once again dominated the public consciousness and need immediate action. Addressing the underlying causes of this prejudice requires a multifaceted strategy of recognizing proactive advocacy for and empathy toward anti-Asian racism. This edited volume does that and more. It is timely and relevant to the racism–social justice conversation.

The editors, along with their co-authors, describe the history of anti-Asian racism, its current forms, and its consequences for those it targets. This collection of work highlights false information and ignorance and reveals the complexity of hatred toward Asian Americans and the violence they face. The volume also exposes the "model minority" misconception—the stereotype that perpetuates negative stereotypes of Asian Americans as generally successful, competent, and immune to discrimination—that is based on that prejudice. The authors examine the ways this myth corrodes social norms and individual psyches by destroying an Asian American sense of identity and creating feelings of isolation, invisibility, and otherness.

Anti-Asian racism's impact on mental health is an adversity with a tenacity that deserves our compassion and attention. From the mental health costs of racial microaggressions to the trauma of hate-fueled violence, Asian Americans face multiple complications that impact affective wellness and self-worth. Nevertheless, through this adversity, there is a resilience built on community, solidarity, and a collective will to reclaim our power against oppression of any kind. This volume presents a significant, in-depth discussion of how anti-Asian racial discrimination interacts with other marginalized Asian American identities. Because oppression happens in different ways, the authors talk about just how racism interrelates with factors such as age, sexuality, class, and immigration status to compound problems for Asian Americans.

This volume centers on the experiences of those most affected by discrimination and it tests intersectional advocacy in the struggle for social justice. It is grounded in social work intervention and action concepts. It provides a roadmap for addressing anti-Asian racism and, at the same time, helping with mental health issues in Asian American people and communities. Social workers can address systemic inequalities by promoting marginalized voices, healing, and empowerment through culturally sensitive interventions, trauma-informed care, and community-based initiatives. Social workers tend to be uniquely situated to advocate for marginalized people, to promote their voices, and also to effect change at individual, systemic, and institutional levels. The authors provide suggestions, best practices, and actions that social workers can use to challenge anti-Asian racism and promote social justice using their collective experience and knowledge.

This is a call to action not just for social workers but for us all. Regardless of whether you are a practitioner, a student, an educator, or simply a concerned citizen, there is much to learn from the ideas and viewpoints offered here. We can all learn by being inclusive and equitable, by having difficult conversations and standing with those who are marginalized. Focusing on the voices and experiences of the people most affected by violence and hate can lead to a more inclusive and fair society where everyone is welcomed, valued, and primed to thrive.

As we travel our world, we confront injustices there. Pick up the call to action; speak up for those who are silenced; join forces to make anti-Asian racism (and racism in general) a thing of the past. This edited work is a timely reference for anyone interested in social justice and racial equity. By participating in the ideas and viewpoints presented in this publication, we can understand anti-Asian racism better and work for a just future for all. Starting this process of understanding and transformation, *Addressing Anti-Asian Racism with Social Work, Advocacy, and Action* is a volume that calls for action—and a path forward for those of us who can lead change in our communities.

May this volume usher in hope and change in our fight for a world with no racism, hate, or violence.

—Goutham M. Menon, PhD, MBA, MA
Professor and former Dean
Loyola University Chicago School of Social Work

Acknowledgments

The journey of writing this book has been profoundly inspiring, and was built upon the stories of over 50 social work practitioners, researchers, policy makers, activists, educators and scholars. Their contributions along the way have been invaluable, and we are deeply grateful.

* * *

I had a most rewarding experience working with my collaborators on this book.

To my mentors, your support throughout my PhD program, especially when I came here as an international student, and throughout my career path, has shaped me as a scholar, a teacher, and a person.

I am grateful to my friends and colleagues for standing by me and cheering me on, even through the toughest times.

A heartfelt thank you to Dana Bliss, executive editor; Sarah Ebel, our project editor; and Brady McNamara, our art director, for working closely with us through the publishing process.

To my mother Luying Liu, father Deyao Liu, aunts, uncles, cousins, and grandmother, I am grateful for each of you for believing in me and supporting my dreams.

Meirong Liu

* * *

I dedicate my part of this work to my family by blood and by fate, who are too many to name. The writing of this book was a labor of love, supported by many people and organizations that made this possible.

I wish to extend my gratitude to Dean Mary Cavanaugh, the Silberman School of Social Work at Hunter College, and my funders for supporting my research. These include the Health and Aging Policy Fellows Program, the NIH Loan Repayment Program through the National Institute of Aging Health Disparities Research Award (1L60AG079415-01), the Rutgers University Asian Resource Center for Minority Aging Research Center (P30-AG0059304), the Rutgers-NYU Center for Asian Health Promotion and Equity (1P50MD017356), the Michigan Health Endowment Fund Healthy Aging Grant (R-2108-149060), the John A. Hartford Foundation, and the Council on Social Work Education Minority Fellowship Program.

Also a special thank you to my colleagues at the US House of Representatives, Committee on Ways and Means, Democratic Staff, who shared their wisdom, kindness, and quirkiness with me every day during the 117th and 118th Congress.

Keith T. Chan

Editors

Meirong Liu is Professor and Chair of Research Sequence at Howard University School of Social Work. Her research centers on social welfare policies, health disparities, and multicultural social work. She collaborates with interdisciplinary research teams and has secured multimillion dollars in grants on health disparities from the National Institutes of Health, the Health Resources and Services Administration, the Princeton Alliance for Collaborative Research and Innovation, and the Bezos Earth Fund. Serving as the Chair of the Council on Social Work Education (CSWE) Asian and Pacific Islander Track, she is dedicated to advancing equity and inclusion in the social work field.

Keith Chan is Associate Professor of Social Work at Hunter College. His research examines social determinants of physical and mental health for vulnerable populations, in particular Asian Americans, immigrants, and older adults. He currently also serves as Co-Investigator on the NIMHD/P50-funded Center for Asian Health Promotion and Equity, Community Engagement Core, as well as the NIA/P30-funded RCASIA, Community Liaison and Recruitment Core. Since 2021, he provides his research expertise as Congressional Fellow to the US House Committee on Ways and Means, Subcommittee on Health, Democratic Staff, on issues related to mental health, substance use, disability, and population health data with a focus on health equity for underserved communities.

Contributors

Sofie Hana Aaron, MSW, University of Washington

Olivia Aquino, San Jose State University

Clifford S. Bersamira, PhD, MA, University of Hawaii at Manoa

Sarah Carlis, MSW, MBA, LMSW, Howard University

Monit Cheung, PhD, MA, MSW, University of Houston

Shinwoo Choi, PhD, MSSW, Texas State University

Robert Cosby, PhD, MPhil, MSW, Howard University

Tam Q. Dinh, PhD, MSW, LICSW, Seattle University

Yali Feng, MLIS, University of Illinois Urbana-Champaign Library

Siyu Gao, MSW, School of Social Work, University of Minnesota, Twin Cities

Catherine Hawkins, PhD, MSSW, Texas State University

Hannan Hijazi, MA, LMSW, LGSW, Howard University

Joo Young Hong, MDiv, ThM, Mercer University

Jun Sung Hong, PhD, MSW, Wayne State University & Ewha Womans University

Altaf Husain, PhD, MSW, Howard University

Hye-Kyung Kang, PhD, MA, MSW, LCSW, Seattle University

Misa Kayama, PhD, MS, MSW, University of Mississippi

Joong Won Kim, PhD, MA, University of Tennessee, Knoxville

Kenny Kwong, PhD, LMSW, Touro University

Sophia B. Lau, PhD, MSW, University of Hawaii at Manoa

Jane J. Lee, PhD, MSW, University of Washington

Nayoun Lee, PhD, MIA, MSW, San Jose State University

Yeonjung Jane Lee, PhD, MA, University of Hawaii at Manoa

Carol A. Leung, PhD, LCSW, Azusa Pacific University

Patrick Leung, PhD, MA, MSW, University of Houston

Ethan Liu, Phillips Exeter Academy, Exeter, New Hampshire

Xiaofang Liu, PhD, MSW, Columbia University in the City of New York

Kirin Macapugay, DSW, MSW, San Diego City College

Dale Dagar Maglalang, PhD, MA, MSW, MPH, New York University

Dhrubodhi Mukherjee, PhD, LCSW-S, University of North Texas

Hyejoon Park, PhD, MSW, EdM, Western Michigan University

Hillary Nicole Peregrina, MA, MSW, University of California, Los Angeles

Cindy C. Sangalang, PhD, MSW, University of California, Los Angeles

Lalaine Sevillano, PhD, MSW, Portland State University

Zhanjie Si, PhD, MPA, MSW, Southern Connecticut State University

Michael Sieng, PhD, MS, Arizona State University

Michael S. Spencer, PhD, MS, University of Washington

Fei Sun, PhD, MA, MSW, Michigan State University

Austin Thao, MPH, MSW, Amherst H. Wilder Foundation

Cindy Vang, PhD, MSW, California State University, Chico

Juliann Li Verdugo, MSW, LMSW, University of Washington

Qingwen Xu, PhD, LLM, LLB, New York University

Yanfeng Xu, PhD, MSW, University of South Carolina

Introduction

Meirong Liu and Keith T. Chan

This volume aims to address the pressing need for social workers in the effort to eradicate anti-Asian racism in the current historical and political context. Asian Americans have become the fastest growing population among all racial and ethnic groups in the United States over the past two decades; the population nearly doubled during this period and estimates are projected that it will surpass 46 million by 2060 (Budiman & Ruiz, 2021). In New York, Michigan, Illinois, and Rhode Island, the growth of the Asian American population between 2000 and 2019 exceeded the growth of the overall population in these states (Budiman & Ruiz, 2021). In the wake of the coronavirus pandemic, there has been a spike in hate crimes and racist incidents targeting Asian American communities.

From January 2020 to December 2022, Stop AAPI Hate documented approximately 11,409 hate incidents against the Asian American, Native Hawaiian, and Pacific Islander (AANHPI) community. These incidents, alongside the Atlanta Spa Shooting in the Spring of 2021, are part of a long-standing pattern of anti-Asian racism that dates back to the 18th century. Asian Americans have consistently faced marginalizing stereotyping, microaggressions, verbal and physical assaults, hate crimes, and harassment driven by individual-level racism and xenophobia. Moreover, at the institutional level, the United States has at times implicitly or explicitly reinforced, encouraged, or perpetuated anti-Asian racism. This is evidenced by xenophobic and discriminatory rhetoric as well as by exclusionary immigration policies which specifically targeted Asian populations. We believe it is necessary and timely to edit a volume that systematically examines the history of anti-Asian racism in the United States, its impact on Asian American communities, and, more importantly, the innovative, evidence-based solutions that social work educators, practitioners, and researchers can adopt to dismantle anti-Asian racism.

Meirong Liu and Keith T. Chan, *Introduction* In: *Addressing Anti-Asian Racism with Social Work, Advocacy, and Action*. Edited by: Meirong Liu and Keith T. Chan, Oxford University Press. © Oxford University Press 2024.
DOI: 10.1093/oso/9780197672242.001.0001

Past Response from Social Work Scholarship on Addressing Anti-Asian Racism

Despite social work's stated commitment to combating racism, there is limited literature on anti-Asian racism in our discipline. McMahon and Allen-Meares (1992) conducted a systematic review of articles from 1980 to 1989 in four major social work journals on Asian Americans, Native Americans, African Americans, and Hispanic Americans, finding that fewer than 6% of articles focused on racial and ethnic minorities and recommended social work intervention. Corley and Young (2018) revisited this study and reported that only 7% of articles published between 2005 and 2015 focused on racial and ethnic minorities and included a social work intervention, indicating the profession's ongoing struggle with an institutional response to addressing racism, especially for Asian Americans. Moreover, social work research on race tended to focus specifically on the experiences of African American and, at times, Latinx communities, which excludes many other ethnic groups also experiencing racism and oppression (Choi & Lahey, 2006; Corley & Young, 2018). Furthermore, the number of articles on Asian Americans has declined, from 20 articles in the 1992 study to just 14 articles in the 2018 update (Corley & Young, 2018). This trend is particularly concerning given the increasing population of Asian families in the United States (Choi & Lahey, 2006; Ruiz et al., 2021).

Similarly, as of this writing, there have been no published book focused on social work and anti-Asian racism and only a very limited number of books on social work practice with Asian Americans. No previous scholarship comprehensively and directly addressed how individual- and institutional-level racism, a chronic and acute stressor that elicits psychological, physiological, and behavioral responses within individuals, has operated to marginalize Asian Americans and reproduce inequality. In addition, previous scholarship focused primarily on micro social work practice. Racism and its impact on a minority population's health and mental health operate at both institutional and individual levels; thus, to address these negative impacts of racism and promote the well-being of any ethnic minority, social workers must also look beyond traditional therapy and operate outside academic and healthcare settings to consider interventions at macro and policy levels. It is paramount for social workers to study the roots of racism and engage in institutional changes that address structural inequalities. Furthermore, the current state of literature on this topic is very much in need of an update to address contemporary social work research, education, and practice on eliminating anti-Asian racism.

Audiences for This Volume

Recent events have highlighted incidents of anti-Asian racism, which has a long history tied to various marginalized identities in the United States. The Grand Challenges for Social Work (Teasley et al., 2021) call for eliminating racism; however, there is a lack of literature that systematically examines the racism experienced by Asian American populations. This volume examines the experience and impact of racism from the perspective of Asian Americans and delves into the need to seek out evidence-based micro, meso, and macro solutions. This comprehensive volume intends to serve as a timely resource for social work educators, researchers, and practitioners who urgently need to address racism experienced by this neglected yet rapidly growing population. This volume can also serve as a resource in supporting the curriculum for Social Welfare Policies and Programs, Human Behaviors in Social Environment, Social Work Practice with Diverse Populations, and other courses teaching practice techniques and cultural competence. Due to the lack of literature on Asian American experiences of racism, we believe our volume offers a much-needed resource for this readership that is not available elsewhere. The volume can also serve as essential reading for students and professionals in ethnic studies, psychology, public health, gender studies, and other interdisciplinary programs at colleges and universities.

Structure of the Volume

This volume addresses the imminent needs of social workers in their efforts to eradicate anti-Asian racism in the current historical and political context. We begin with Section I "Deconstructing Anti-Asian Racism: Understanding History, Social Contexts, and Complexities." Chapter 1 provides a review of anti-Asian racism and xenophobia in US history at both individual and institutional levels and how this has operated to marginalize Asian Americans and reproduce inequality. Chapter 2 examines increasing microaggressions, verbal attacks, and physical violence against Asian Americans during the COVID-19 pandemic, with ties to their ethnic background and exacerbated by political rhetoric. The chapter also explores theoretical explanations, including the role of nationalism and White supremacy in scapegoating and escalating racial discrimination and violence. Chapter 3 investigates the impact of anti-Asian racism on the health and mental health of Asian Americans in the context of acculturation and the evolving Asian American identity. The chapter points out that the negative impacts of racism on physical and mental health can be long-lasting and that racial trauma can carry across generations. Chapter 4 highlights the diversity of Asian identities in America and explores how intersecting identities can foster or inhibit racism experienced by Asians in the United States. The chapter explores the intersectional experiences of Asians in the United States, paying attention to immigrant status, racism and sexism, sexual orientation and gender identity, religiosity/spirituality, and multiracial and biracial identities. Chapter 5 examines the origins of the MMS and examples of how the MMS impacts the health and well-being of AANHPI individuals. The chapter also provides a critique of the model minority stereotype (MMS) using critical race theory and recommendations for how social work can disrupt the MMS across micro, meso, and macro levels. Chapter 6 explores powerful and impactful alliances between Asian and Black communities which led to major leaps forward in the pursuit of racial justice and civil rights. Social workers can promote racial solidarity by including the history of interracial solidarity in curriculum, promoting conversation across race, recognizing one's own racial biases, and engaging in anti-racism community and policy initiatives. White supremacy is the root of racism, and efforts to eliminate racism broadly will work toward freeing oppressed populations from the negative effects of White supremacy.

The rapidly growing and diverse Asian American population is composed of individuals and communities originating from more than 20 different countries. Yet data on these groups are often combined, thus obscuring important differences and disparities within the population. Section II, "Voices of Diverse Communities: Intersectionalities in the Experience of Anti-Asian Racism," presents the challenges and manifestation of anti-Asian racism among several major Asian American subgroups. Chapter 7 presents the history, cultural background, mental health challenges, and experiences of racial discrimination among Korean Americans. It also presents Korean Americans' coping strategies against racial discrimination and their implications for practice, policy, and research. Chapter 8 discusses the experiences of new Japanese immigrant families in the United States as they acculturate to US local communities and schools, as well as implications to support the acculturation of immigrant children and their families. Chapter 9 discusses the precolonial and colonial history of the conceptualization of the Filipino and Filipinx American LGBTQ+ identity and how these identities are further shaped by and in contention with religion, familism, race and ethnicity, immigration, and education that influence Filipinx LGBTQ+'s contemporary experiences and issues, and their implications on research and services. Chapter 10 focuses on Asian American Muslims and specifically on the impact of anti-Islamic bigotry on youth who self-identify as Muslim. The chapter highlights the impact of anti-Islamic bigotry on youth and how religion and spirituality serve as buffers against the impact of such bigotry. Chapter 11 examines how community-dwelling Hmong older adults experience loneliness and construct four coping mechanisms to minimize loneliness amid challenges and losses including finding greater power, seeking support and community, escaping through activity, and avoidance and control. The chapter recommends culturally sensitive approaches informed by Hmong elders' experiences to guide practice, policy, and research. Chapter 12 critically examines empirical evidence pertaining to the impact of racism on the psychosocial well-being of older Asian Americans and summarizes research, practice, and policy recommendations for mitigating racism and discrimination among this demographic. The findings also suggest that a variety of individual, family, community, and societal contextual factors can moderate the effects of racism on older Asians' psychosocial well-being.

Section III, "Dismantling Anti-Asian Racism: Micro, Mezzo, and Macro-level Strategies," focuses on multilevel strategies that social work educators, practitioners, and researchers can adopt to eliminate anti-Asian racism in the United States. Chapter 13 provides personal narratives of AANHPI social workers' own lived experiences of witnessing and navigating hate and oppressive systems as AANHPI individuals and social workers. It concludes with a collaborative discussion on the implications for social work practice, policy, and research and discusses a call to action and forward steps in countering anti-Asian racism and hate. Chapter 14 initiates a reflection on racism within the social work profession and on developing an anti-Asian racism workforce. It introduces both the cultural humility framework and social justice perspective for social work educators to effectively teach, model, and evaluate anti-racist and anti-oppressive practice. Chapter 15 investigates studies on mental health challenges and service utilizations among six Asian American ethnicities in Houston, Texas. The findings highlight limited access to mental health care but also the supportive roles of family and personal networks. This work underscores the significance of understanding mental health disparities and calls for equitable care that addresses the unique needs of culturally diverse Asian American communities. Chapter 16 focuses on assessment techniques and intervention strategies that are culturally attuned and responsive to the unique needs of Asian American individuals. It serves as a crucial resource for mental health practitioners seeking to adopt best practices and develop a deeper understanding of the specific mental health challenges and needs of the Asian American community. Chapter 17 highlights the importance of community-based solutions in addressing anti-Asian racism. It overviews the history and context of Asian American community advocacy, discusses the challenges and considerations when doing advocacy work with the Asian American community, and recommends action steps for social workers engaging in community-based advocacy work. Last but not the least, Chapter 18 discusses macro practice methods to address racial injustice through advocacy efforts such as fostering policies to eliminate anti-Asian hate and violence, improving language access, campaigning for narrative change, building coalitions, improving civic engagement, and promoting policies and programs regarding AANHPI history education and awareness. We conclude this volume by calling for urgent institutional changes through advocacy and legislative action.

References

Budiman, A., & Ruiz, N. (2021). Key facts about Asian Americans, a diverse and growing population. *Pew Research Center.* https://www.pewresearch.org/fact-tank/2021/04/29/key-facts-about-Asian Americans/

Choi, Y. & Lahey, B. (2006). Testing the model minority stereotype: Youth behaviors across racial and ethnic groups. *Social Service Review, 80*(3), 419–452. doi:10.1086/505288

Corley, N. A., & Young, S. M. (2018). Is social work still racist? A content analysis of recent literature. *Social Work (New York), 63*(4), 317–326. doi:10.1093/sw/swy042

McMahon, A., & Allen-Meares, P. (1992). Is social work racist? A content analysis of recent literature. *Social Work, 37,* 533–539. doi:10.1093/sw/37.6.533

Ruiz, N., Edwards, K., & Lopez, M. (2021). One-third of Asian Americans fear threats, physical attacks and most say violence against them is rising. *Pew Research Center.* https://www.pewresearch.org/fact-tank/2021/04/21/one-third-of-Asian Americans-fear-threats-physical-attacks-and-most-say-violence-against-them-is-rising/

Teasley, M., McCarter, S., Woo, B., Conner, L., Spencer, M. & Green, T. (2021). Eliminate Racism. *Grand Challenges for Social Work Initiative Working Paper.* https://grandchallengesforsocialwork.org/wp-content/uploads/2021/05/Eliminate-Racism-Concept-Paper.pdf

SECTION I
DECONSTRUCTING ANTI-ASIAN RACISM: UNDERSTANDING HISTORY, SOCIAL CONTEXTS, AND COMPLEXITIES

1
The History of Anti-Asian Racism and Violence in the United States

Meirong Liu, Nayoun Lee, Zhanjie Si, and Olivia Aquino

Introduction

On May 20, 2021, President Biden signed the COVID-19 Hate Crimes Act (Publ. L. No. 117-13). Responding to a surge in violence against Asian Americans, the law aims to improve the reporting and review of hate crimes by setting up hotlines at the local and state levels, providing training to law enforcement officers, and educating the public through outreach and in multiple languages (COVID-19 Hate Crimes Act, 2021). While the intense racist and xenophobic backlash against persons of Asian descent during the pandemic shocked the world, scholars and activists point out that the scapegoating of Asian communities in the United States is nothing new, with deep historical roots to the 19th-century "yellow peril" stereotype that persists and reinforces the notion that Asian Americans are "perpetual foreigners," "unfit" for full acceptance into American society (Chang, 2023; Chen et al., 2020; Li & Nicholson, 2020; US Commission on Civil Rights, 2023).

The COVID-19 pandemic was a rude awakening for Asian Americans as they were reminded of the precarious position they hold in the US racial hierarchy (Lee, 2021). On one hand, Asian Americans are valorized as model minorities (i.e., minorities with high achievement and upward social mobility consistent with the "American Dream"; Kim, 1999); on the other, they are the unassimilable "perpetual foreigners" who are inherently different from the rest of America (Tuan, 1998). With a new wave of immigrants since the 1965 Immigration and Naturalization Act, which abolished the old quota system favoring Western Europeans, not only has the Asian immigrant population dramatically increased, but more Asian immigrants with higher

Meirong Liu, Nayoun Lee, Zhanjie Si, and Olivia Aquino, *The History of Anti-Asian Racism and Violence in the United States* In: *Addressing Anti-Asian Racism with Social Work, Advocacy, and Action.* Edited by: Meirong Liu and Keith T. Chan, Oxford University Press. © Oxford University Press 2024. DOI: 10.1093/oso/9780197672242.003.0001 education and skill levels also were admitted to the United States—described as "hyperselectivity" by Lee and Zhou (2015). This hyperselectivity of highly skilled professionals such as engineers, doctors, and scientists seemingly made the "model minority" stereotype more prominent than the "perpetual foreigner" stereotype prior to the pandemic-fueled anti-Asian racism (Chen et al., 2020).

However, as Li and Nicholson (2020) note in their reevaluation of the Asian American assimilation theory in the wake of the COVID-19 pandemic, the more insidious stereotype of the "perpetual foreigner" prevails in times of crisis, revealing the "perpetual marginalized and conditional status of Asian Americans" (p. 1). Thus, the racial triangulation theory of Asian Americans by Claire Kim (1999), which argues that both the model minority and perpetual foreigner stereotypes restrict full incorporation of Asian Americans into mainstream society, stands as true today as it did decades ago.

The COVID-19 pandemic confirmed once again how elusive the goal of a post-racial America was to achieve, from the murder of George Floyd and countless other Black and Brown persons by law enforcement to the relentless xenophobic attacks on the Asian American community. Hence, researchers have taken the moment to review the historical context of Asian American discrimination and racism (Chang, 2023; Chen et al., 2020; Li & Nicholson, 2020; US Commission on Civil Rights, 2023).

Similarly, in this chapter, we review the history of anti-Asian racism in the United States through an in-depth analysis of anti-Chinese sentiments and institutional oppression. We focus on Chinese immigrants for a couple of reasons: the first large-scale immigration of Asians to the United States that incited mass racial violence involved Chinese laborers during the gold rush and westward expansion of the nineteenth century; and anti-Chinese racism tends to indiscriminately spread to other groups in the Asian American community due to "racial/ethnic lumping" (i.e., the notion that all Asians look alike). While the focus is on Chinese Americans, major events involving other Asian groups illustrating systemic oppression and bias are also discussed, such as the Asian Exclusion Act of 1924, the Japanese American incarceration during World War II, and the Ku Klux Klan mob violence against Filipino Americans. We illustrate how a long legacy of systemic racism and xenophobia, particularly pronounced during periods of economic recession, disease outbreak, or war, has marginalized Asian American communities and reproduced inequalities despite the vital roles Asian Americans played in the development of the country.

Anti-Asian Racism and Violence During the COVID-19 Pandemic

At the start of the COVID-19 pandemic, anti-Asian racism and hate incidents, including hate crimes, spiked. According to Stop AAPI Hate (2023), a coalition founded in response to rising anti-Asian hate and violence in 2020, 11,409 hate incidents against the Asian American and Pacific Islander community were reported from January 2020 to December 2022. The main type of offense was harassment (88%), while physical and property harm constituted 23% and 6%, respectively (Stop AAPI Hate, 2023). Hate crime data collected by the Federal Bureau of Investigation (FBI) from more than 15,000 local law enforcement agencies across the nation show that anti-Asian hate crimes increased from 188 cases in 2019 to 334 in 2020 (78% increase), which then jumped to 753 cases in 2021 (125% increase) before decreasing to 499 in 2022 (FBI, n.d.). New York City alone reported a 361% increase in anti-Asian hate crimes between 2020 and 2021 (Yam, 2021).

On top of the stress and anxiety caused by the COVID-19 pandemic, Asian Americans were now fearful of becoming targets of random and brutal violence due to their race. While the following series of tragic events in 2021 are only a small sample of the COVID-19-related anti-Asian hate violence and xenophobia, they show the random, callous, and ubiquitous nature of such racialized violence.

On March 14, 2021, in Midland, Texas, a Burmese American family, including a 2-year-old and a 6-year-old, was stabbed during grocery shopping because the suspect thought they were Chinese (Melendez, 2020). Two days later, the nation was faced with a somber watershed moment in anti-Asian hate violence: eight people were fatally shot at three different spas in Atlanta, Georgia, six of whom were Asian American women. The Atlanta spa murders galvanized nationwide support from a broad coalition of activists, local and national leaders, and the public to do more to recognize and stem the violence against the Asian American community, which led to the historic passing of the COVID-19 federal hate crimes legislation two months later (Chang, 2023).

However, only a day later, on March 17, even before the Asian American community could absorb the shock of the Atlanta spa killings, two older adults, an 83-year-old male and 76-year-old female, were attacked in back-to-back separate assaults in San Francisco. The xenophobic attacks on Asian American seniors had been occurring at alarming rates prior to March 2021 (Smith, 2021) and continued throughout the pandemic.

Seeking Answers to Pandemic-Fueled Asian Hate

There are several explanations for the uptick in anti-Asian hate events during the COVID-19 pandemic. First, Chinese Americans were blamed for spreading the coronavirus to the United States after it was reported by the media that Chinese authorities first identified the virus in Wuhan, China (Ng, 2021). Next, due to the false stereotypes that Asians "look alike," not only Chinese immigrants but also other Asian Americans perceived as having a connection to China were targeted and attacked (Tessler et al., 2020).

Third, powerful institutions, such as the media and government, racialized the pandemic (Li & Nicholson, 2020). For example, on March 16, 2020, former US President Donald J. Trump referred to the coronavirus as the "Chinese virus" or "kung flu" in his Twitter account. Subsequently, there was a significant surge in anti-Asian hashtags on the platform, with increases of 797% for #covid19 and 17,400% for #chinesevirus within just one week (Hswen et al., 2021). Similarly, then Secretary of State Mike Pompeo used the term "Wuhan virus," and major news media including the *New York Times*, *Washington Times*, *Forbes*, *Fox News*, and the *Wall Street Journal* reinforced the association between China, Chinatown, and the coronavirus (Li & Nicholson, 2020). Some politicians and media outlets went so far as to accuse China of deliberately manufacturing the coronavirus as a bio-terrorism weapon (Sharma, 2020).

All in all, the growing chorus of hateful words and fearmongering from authorities, the media, and the public via social media contributed to the rise in anti-Asian hate incidents. Attacks on Asians in 16 of America's largest cities soared by an unprecedented 164% during the first quarter of 2021 compared with 2020 (Levin, 2021).

Theory of "Othering"

To many, the surge in anti-Asian violence may seem like an anomaly or an isolated racist backlash during a globally unprecedented health crisis. However, the scapegoating of Asian Americans as a monolith group, especially during times of economic, health, and political crises, is a replay of an all-too-familiar scenario to Asian Americans. Throughout US history, they have faced exclusion and discrimination, which remains a persistent challenge.

To contextualize the rise in racialized hate and violence against the Asian American community during the COVID-19 pandemic, we need to

(1) acknowledge and review the US history of Asian American discrimination and institutional marginalization, especially that of government-sanctioned discrimination via anti-Asian laws and policies and (2) adopt the framework of "othering" to analyze these historical events.

"Othering" is a process that "serves to mark and name those thought to be different from oneself" (Weis, 1995, p. 18). "Othering" reinforces one's own normality and stigmatizes the differences observed in others; also, to secure one's own identity, one has to maintain their distance from other groups (Grove & Zwi, 2006; Kim & Sundstrom, 2014). Those who are considered different and deviant, such as immigrants, are subjected to an ongoing process of marginalization, disempowerment, and social exclusion (Grove & Zwi, 2006; Gover et al., 2020). In times of crisis, such as during a pandemic, war, or economic downturn, "othering" intensifies as the dominant racial group dissociates themselves from the threatening environment and blames "others," which can be other countries, immigrants, or minorities, to mitigate their feelings of powerlessness (Eichelberger, 2007).

As for Asian Americans, there are at least two main stereotypes—the aforementioned model minority and perpetual foreigner stereotypes—that differently marginalize and exclude them depending on the socioeconomic and political climate (Chen et al., 2020; Gover et al., 2020; Lee, 2021; Li & Nicholson, 2020). In times of peace and economic security, Asian Americans are "othered" by the model minority myth; conversely, in times of economic adversity, war, or pandemic, they are "othered" as the "yellow peril" or "perpetual foreigners" (Gover et al., 2020). In the latter case, the state, as an institution, has frequently reinforced, endorsed, and perpetuated racialized violence and oppression through prejudiced rhetoric and exclusionary policies (Gover et al., 2020).

In the following sections, we examine this "othering" of Asian Americans in historical detail due to their perceived threat to White supremacy in three domains: economic, public health, and civic-political engagement.

An Economic Threat: "Chinese Are Taking Away Our Jobs"

By the early 1850s, more than 25,000 Chinese workers had immigrated to the United States following the Gold Rush of 1849 (McClain, 1988; Rotondi, 2023). While gold mining and the Central Pacific Railway were the pull factors for mass Chinese immigration during the 1850s and 1860s (McClain,

1988), push factors such as the dire economic consequences of the Opium Wars and an ensuing series of floods and droughts drove members of the lower classes to leave their farms and seek new work opportunities abroad (Rotondi, 2023). These Chinese immigrants joined a growing wave of Irish settlers fleeing the Irish Potato Famine and increasing numbers of German settlers seeking a new life alongside other groups from Europe.

From 1863 to 1869, more than 10,000 Chinese laborers were employed by the Central Pacific Railroad—one of the transcontinental railroad companies that would link the East Coast to the West Coast, speeding up westward expansion and facilitating the movement of troops during the Civil War (Rotondi, 2023). By 1870, the Chinese represented 20% of California's labor force, working as miners, railroad builders, domestic workers, farmers, factory workers, and fishermen, even though they constituted only 0.002% of the entire US population (Asia Society, n.d.; History.com Staff, 2022). They labored and lived under harsh conditions, were paid less than their White counterparts toiling in dangerous mining operations and railroad construction, and were generally kept apart from mainstream society (Kang, 2022; Yung et al., 2006).

While both European and Asian immigrants came to the United States seeking to improve their economic well-being, Chinese immigrants were regarded as a larger threat to the nation and were subject to intense nativist backlash (Rotondi, 2023). Chinese laborers were cast as scapegoats for White migrants' employment frustration and were viewed as "coming to steal white jobs" (Yung et al., 2006). Hence, during the latter half of the 19th century, a series of organized actions against Chinese immigrants and exclusionary policies took hold, especially on the West Coast (addressed later in this chapter).

A Public Health Threat: Leprosy Stigma

The United States has a long history of associating immigrants with diseases and using them as public health scapegoats (Mallapragada, 2021; Markel & Stern, 1999, 2002; Trauner, 1978). In the late 1800s, the rhetoric of a public health threat also played a significant role in fueling the anti-Chinese movement (Tresch, 2020). Chinese immigrants were depicted as carriers of infectious diseases, presenting a risk to public health in the United States (Leung, 2009).

For instance, on May 26, 1882, the cover of *The Wasp*, a widely circulated weekly magazine on the West Coast at the time, vividly portrayed this fear by linking malaria, smallpox, and leprosy to Chinese laborers (The Wasp, 1882). Leprosy, in particular, was labeled a "Chinese disease," and it was falsely claimed that all Chinese laborers were leprous, threatening both the moral and physical well-being of Anglo-Americans. While Chinese laborers were neither the first nor the only population that brought leprosy to the United States (Gussow, 2021), the fear and agitation of the public were used to justify halting Chinese immigration.

Underlying the perceived disease and economic threats is the idea that the Chinese as a race is unassimilable, inferior, and immoral (Lee, 2007). Rotondi (2023) describes it as follows:

> They were seen as a racial threat to a pure White America. They were seen as an economic threat to free White labor. They were depicted as a disease threat—a lot of anti-Chinese rhetoric hinged on portraying Chinese people as filthy and disease-ridden. They were also seen as a religious and moral threat as heathens who threatened a Christian America.

Government Sanctions: Economic and Public Health Domains

The economic and public health scapegoating of Chinese immigrants led to racially exclusionary and oppressive policies at the local and national levels. Seen as an economic threat, Chinese immigrants were banned from operating laundry businesses and selling fresh produce as vendors in certain areas of San Francisco and Los Angeles under the guise of public health and safety, namely the bubonic plague and building fires, respectively. However, the real motive of White political and business stakeholders behind these local ordinances was to confine Chinese businesses to Chinatowns (McClain, 1994; Molina, 2006).

Another profound example of an economic exclusionary law is the Coolie Trade Prohibition Act of 1862. During the pre-Civil War debates on slavery, the Chinese immigrants were characterized as "coolies," or indentured laborers, even though they were not involuntary laborers. They were portrayed either as an industrious labor force that would make slavery unnecessary or as an(other) inferior race that was vulnerable to cruel exploitation, as the African American slaves were (Lee, 2007). The 1862 Act banned American ships from transporting "unfree" Chinese workers and limited the competition between White and Asian laborers by imposing a tax on Chinese migrant workers in manufacturing factories as well as on their employers.

Following the landmark case of *In re: Ah Yup* (1878), which ruled Asians ineligible for citizenship due to their non-White status, the California Constitution in 1879 further restricted Chinese immigration by prohibiting corporations from employing them.

As for health sanctions, Chinese patients were segregated and required to go to a separate quarter of the hospital, one reserved for the quarantine of infectious diseases (Trauner, 1978). Furthermore, during an outbreak of the bubonic plague from 1900 to 1904, Chinese immigrants in San Francisco's Chinatown were forced to quarantine, and Chinese and Japanese Americans were not allowed to leave California without bearing a vaccine certificate despite little scientific evidence for the vaccine (McClain, 1988). The South Pacific Railroad also stopped selling tickets to Asians to restrict their travel. The plague then was used to permanently extend the 1882 Chinese Exclusion Act (CEA).

Similarly, Takai's (2020) case study of Hawai'i during the bubonic plague shows how the government arbitrarily made decisions to burn houses on an unsubstantiated belief that, to control the plague, the measure was needed. Moreover, the enforcement of the policy was based on racial background and not on medical test results of those infected (Takai, 2020). The Board of Health of Honolulu went on to burn houses, which tragically ended in an uncontrolled fire burning down the whole Chinatown. Armed guards, police officers, and White residents forced the residents of Chinatown to stay in the area even during conflagration. About 8,000 Chinese, Japanese, and Kanakas were made homeless and then placed in detention camps (Takai, 2020).

A Civic-Political Threat

Dominant racial groups with civic belonging (i.e., those who are formally and informally eligible to participate in the sociopolitical sphere and have the social capital and resources to do so) in the United States have long perceived new immigrants with some degree of mistrust and resentment (Fussell, 2014). Historically, all immigrant groups who differ from the existing White,

English-speaking, Protestant American majority have endured high degrees of suspicion as they fought to gradually establish their foothold on American soil (Alba & Foner, 2006). This nativism, intricately tied to xenophobia, reflects institutional racism, including discriminative and exclusionary immigration policies and legal racial restrictions, some of which have specifically targeted Asian immigrants (Kil, 2012).

Media, medical journals, and government officials propagated the false ideas that Asians were "dirty, diseased, sinister, sexually depraved, invasive, and perpetually foreign." These stereotypes have fueled violence against Asian communities. In the late 1800s, a proliferation of "Chinese invasion" rhetoric in the media further activated or exacerbated anti-Asian hatred.

For instance, on August 27, 1873, the *San Francisco Chronicle* published a headline that reads in bold "The Chinese invasion! They are Coming, 900,000 STRONG!" In 1881, George Frederick Keller crafted an impactful image central to the exclusion fight. The cartoon "A Statue for Our Harbor" symbolized the anti-Chinese sentiment of the era. It portrayed the Statue of Liberty as a Chinese man dressed in rags, standing on a skull. In radiating points of light surrounding his head, were the words "ruin to White labor," "diseases," "immorality," and "filth," highlighting the xenophobic attitudes of the period (Kang, 2021). More recent examples include the 1980s "Dotbusters" attacks on South Asians in New Jersey and the post-9/11 hate crimes in New York City, which marked one of FBI's highest reported hate crime numbers since 1992.

Although Chinese laborers were initially welcomed into the country to work, such rhetoric reflected the popular ideology that they were to be seen as threats to the "true Americans" (specifically those who were White), which in turn threatened the Western way of life (Zimmer, 2019). This type of rhetoric is an illustration of the enduring narrative in US history of the "hordes of immigrant invaders," which serves to support varying political agendas (Zimmer, 2019). These laws and media rhetoric in the 1870s paved the way for the passing of the CEA.

Government Sanctions: Neutralizing the Threat via Civic-Political Ostracism

In 1854, in the landmark case *People v. George Hall*, the California Supreme Court reinforced that people of Asian descent, like African Americans and

Native Americans, could not testify against a White person in court, virtually guaranteeing that White individuals could escape punishment for anti-Asian violence (Brockell, 2021). Additionally, the 1870 Naturalization Act granted naturalized citizenship to African Americans while still denying naturalization to other non-White persons.

In 1875, the Page Act, one of the earliest federal legislations to restrict Asian immigration to the United States, was passed. It prohibited the recruitment of laborers from "China, Japan or any Oriental country" who were not brought to the United States of their own will or who were brought for "lewd and immoral purposes." It severely restricted Chinese women from entering the country to discourage Chinese workers from starting families (Kang, 2021), thus reinforcing the idea that Asians are racially immoral, inferior, and unassimilable and should not be allowed to grow their US-born population.

In re: Ah Yup (1878) was another landmark case that ruled Asians ineligible for naturalized citizenship. Ah Yup tried to convince the court that individuals of the Mongolian race should be seen as "White" and therefore eligible for naturalization. The court ruled that because Mongolians were born in China, they could not be deemed as "White" and were thus ineligible for citizenship.

The Chinese Exclusion Act of 1882

Due to racist and xenophobic fears among the White working class (Gover et al., 2020), a series of exclusionary laws were passed that barred Chinese from citizenship and restricted Chinese economic activity by levying excessive taxes (Yung et al., 2006). These laws culminated in the passing of the 1882 CEA. The CEA prohibited new immigration of Chinese laborers, allowed only a few select classes of Chinese immigrants to apply for admission, and affirmed the principle that all Chinese immigrants were prohibited from naturalizing to citizens. It was the only US law that prevented immigration and naturalization on the basis of race and country of origin, and it restricted Chinese immigration for the next 60 years (Fisher & Fisher, 2010).

A Chinese student, Saum Song Bo, pointed out the irony of erecting a Statue of Liberty shortly after passing legislation to exclude Chinese immigrants in his letter to the *New York Sun*.

That statue represents Liberty holding a torch which lights the passage of those of all nations who come into this country. But are the Chinese allowed to come? As for the Chinese who are here, are they allowed to enjoy liberty as men of all other nationalities enjoy it? Are they allowed to go about everywhere free from the insults, abuse, assaults, wrongs and injuries from which men of other nationalities are free? (Bo, 1885)

Discrimination and exclusion intensified with legislations that followed the CEA. For example, the Scott Act of 1888 built on the CEA and prohibited most Chinese, even long-term legal residents, from reentering the United States. The Geary Act of 1892 extended the CEA by mandating that all Chinese residents in the United States carry a resident permit; those who failed to carry the permit at all times were subjected to deportation or a year of hard labor.

The Exclusion of Other Asians Post-CEA

The CEA represented just the first stage in a series of restrictions targeting Asian immigrants. The xenophobic ban also spread to include migrants from Japan, India, Korea, and the Philippines as their numbers increased dramatically to fill the labor shortages after the CEA (Lee, 2007). These groups, often collectively viewed as "inassimilable Orientals," faced the same racial stereotypes and discrimination as the Chinese before them (Lee, 2007). When many Japanese immigrants arrived to work in agriculture, railroad work, logging, mining, and the service sector (Aoki, 2010), White resentment and calls for Japanese exclusion laws soon followed. The debates over the new "problem" of Japanese immigration, in particular, including the characterization of Japan and Japanese as the "yellow peril," intensified by the early 1900s (Aoki, 2010).

Legislative barriers to land ownership, citizenship, and education had to be erected for these new Asian groups (Gover et al., 2020). Specifically, the Gentleman's Agreement in 1907 restricted Japanese immigration to the United States (Aoki, 2010; Cullinane, 2014; Kang, 2021). The California Alien Land Law of 1913 prohibited "aliens ineligible for citizenship" from owning agricultural land or holding long-term leases for it, which forced farmers of Asian descent, especially Japanese immigrants, to relinquish their farms and move elsewhere. Moreover, the Immigration Act of 1917 created a "barred zone" extending from the Middle East to Southeast Asia, from which no persons were allowed to enter the United States.

In *Takao Ozawa v. United States* (1922), the Supreme Court upheld the naturalization law that declared Japanese and other Asian immigrants ineligible for citizenship. In *United States v. Bhagat Singh Thind* (1923), the Supreme Court further ruled Indians ineligible for US citizenship. At this point, nearly all Asians were ineligible for citizenship. Eventually, a 1924 amendment to the CEA defined an "immigrant" as someone who also had the right to eventual citizenship, and because people from the Orient could not become citizens, the law effectively ended all Asian immigration to the US: namely the Asian Exclusion Act of 1924 (Gover et al., 2020; Kang, 2021; Lee, 2002).

The Incarceration of Japanese Americans During World War II

In February 1942, President Roosevelt signed an executive order that resulted in the forced removal of the entire Japanese American population of the West Coast. Approximately 112,000 persons of Japanese ancestry, among whom nearly 70,000 of the evacuees were American citizens, were sent to concentration camps, where they stayed for the rest of the war (Burton et al., 2011; Howard, 2008). There were no charges of disloyalty against any of them, nor was there any vehicle by which they could appeal their loss of property and personal liberty. Meanwhile, tens of thousands of Asian American soldiers of varying ethnicities defended the nation during World War II. The well-known 442nd regimental combat team was made up entirely of Japanese Americans. Ironically, back at home, the families of these soldiers were detained and denied the basic rights to freedom and property.

In 1988, the US government apologized for the injustice of "internment" via the Civil Liberties Act and provided a $20,000 cash payment to each person who was incarcerated. However, as then President Reagan (1988) said, "no payment can make up for those lost years."

Espionage Charges: Chinese Americans as Untrustworthy

Today, with increasingly intensified US-China competition, the target of blame has shifted back to China. Research indicates that the Department of

Justice has *disproportionately* accused Chinese and other Asian Americans—no matter if guilty or innocent—of espionage (Kim, 2018). Many allegations against Chinese American scientists were later dropped without full explanation and accountability. Yet even after the charges have been dropped, some scientists were still fired (Wang, 2017).

A long-standing prejudice against the people of Chinese heritage has influenced decision-making at the Federal Bureau of Investigation (FBI) and other security agencies in the United States, to the point that even American-born Chinese are perceived as "Chinese at heart" (Bloomberg Businessweek, 2019). The persistent view of Chinese Americans as probable spies instead of loyal citizens echoes the historical "yellow peril" stereotype and the ongoing marginalization of Asian Americans (Li & Nicholson, 2021).

Racialized Violence and Institutional Complicity

In the late 19th century, amid cries of "They're taking away our jobs!," anti-Chinese violence raged throughout the West Coast. In the 1870s to 1880s, growing anti-Chinese prejudice in the United States culminated in a number of expulsions, attacks, and riots. On October 24, 1871, a mob of 500 locals in Los Angeles attacked innocent Chinese residents. Nearly 20 Chinese people were lynched, including a 14-year-old boy. Those killed during the massacre at the time represented 10% of the total Chinese population in LA. Yet discriminatory state legislation prohibited Chinese people from testifying against White people in California courts. Though eight perpetrators of the massacre were convicted of manslaughter, their convictions were overturned by the California Supreme Court.

On September 2, 1885, in Rock Springs, Wyoming, 28 Chinese miners were killed, and all 500 Chinese miners were driven out of town, with no person ever convicted. That same year, in Tacoma, Washington, the entire Chinese community was expelled and the Chinatown was burned down. In 1887, a gang of White men ambushed and murdered 36 Chinese miners in Hells Canyon; no one was found guilty of the crimes. In the late 1890s, Chinese American communities responded to housing segregation policies by forming Chinatowns (Chen, 2000). Yet several of these communities faced deadly attacks by the White majority (Chen, 2000).

These historical examples show how the government is complicit in the oppression of Chinese immigrants through inaction. As such, racialized violence is implicitly condoned to institutionally repress minorities (Gover et al., 2020).

Racial/Ethnic Lumping: Other Asian Ethnic Groups No Longer Exempt From Violence

As mentioned above, Asian Americans are often treated as a monolith. Racially lumped together for "looking alike," what starts out as anti-Chinese sentiments and violence eventually spreads and applies to other Asian ethnic groups and vice versa. Once Chinese immigration was nearly stopped due to the restrictions of the CEA, other Asian groups were subjected to racialized violence.

In 1907, Japanese restaurants and bathhouses in San Francisco were attacked by nativist mobs, and Japanese students were expelled and forced to enroll in already-segregated Chinese schools (Kang, 2021). In the same year, the South Asian community in Bellingham, Washington, was attacked by a mob of 150 White men. The call to "drive out the Hindus" was heard throughout the city, and 125 South Asians were ousted (Lee, 2007).

Between 1927 and 1930, Filipinos across the United States were subjected to extensive intimidation and violence by the Ku Klux Klan and White Americans who cast Filipinos as a source of inexpensive labor and a threat to White women. Amid rising racial tension spurred by the Great Depression and the increased employment of Filipino farm laborers (a result of the barring of Japanese immigration), combined with emerging anti-miscegenation rhetoric, several anti-Filipino riots took place along the West Coast.

In November 1927, 30 men in Washington state stormed the home of Ellis Peregrino, a Filipino man married to a White woman, demanding they leave Yakima County or be hanged (Meyers, 2017). The following day 150 men rode into Toppenish, Washington, to round up Filipinos, ordering them to leave or be killed (Griffey, 2007; Meyers, 2017).

In October 1929, in Exeter, California, 300 men marched on E. J. Firebaugh's ranch and burned down his barn because he employed Filipino laborers and there had been a racial conflict between Filipinos and White individuals at a local carnival (De Witt, 1979). Most notably, the Watsonville Riot of 1930 resulted in the murder of 22-year-old Fermin Tobera after four days of terror, where mobs of 200 to 700 searched the streets for Filipinos, eventually opening fire on a bunkhouse inhabited by Filipinos (De Witt, 1979; Showalter, 1989).

In the 1980s, the perceived economic threat posed by Asian Americans continued. The Ku Klux Klan burned the boats of Vietnamese Americans who were taking up shrimping in Texas in the 1980s (Smith, 2017). In 1982, Vincent Chin, a Chinese American who was mistaken for a Japanese, was beaten to death by two disgruntled, unemployed White autoworkers in Michigan, who harbored resentment against the Japanese for their success in the auto industry that seemingly came at the expense of US automakers (Wu, 2009).

These examples are tragic but typical cases of how all Asian Americans are racially or ethnically lumped together and treated as a monolithic group. The quick association of competition with an Asian nation (Japan) and anti-Asian violence exemplify that Asian Americans have been long regarded as outsiders and potential foes to America (Wu, 2009). This conspicuous anti-Asian racism reflects the sense of entitlement many White individuals have to "defend" what they assume "belongs" to them and to fight against groups who are deemed a threat to White privilege and well-being.

After September 11, 2001, South Asian, Sikh, Muslim, and Arab Americans have been subjected to a wave of hate crimes, harassment, and racial profiling (Hing, 2001). In a notable incident in 2017, an Indian American man was fatally shot by a suspect who shouted, "Get out of my country." Prior to the shooting, the suspect asked the man if he was a legal immigrant (Morey, 2018).

Relative Valorization of Asian Americans as "Honorary Whites" to Maintain White Hegemony

As new waves of East Asian immigrants arrived in the United States during the mid to late 20th century and integrated into society, a new stereotype proliferated alongside them: the myth of the "model minority" (Liu, 2017). A 1966 article in the *New York Times*, "Success Story Japanese American Style" (Petersen, 1966), portrayed Asian Americans as the quintessential American success narrative, one rooted in meritocracy and hard work. It suggested that other minorities, such as Black and Latino communities, could similarly overcome the hurdles of racism to achieve success.

Media, politicians, and scholars portrayed Asian Americans as a model minority whose cultural values of diligence, family solidarity, respect for education, and self-sufficiency propelled it to notable success. This stereotype has been utilized by some conservative groups as a means of undermining civil rights activists' assertions that systematic racism is a significant factor in the challenges faced by people of color by attempting to invalidate the struggle against racial oppression (Museus, 2013).

However, regardless of how successful Asian Americans are in upward mobility, they are still relegated to the status of *minorities* (Lee & Kye, 2016). According to Kim's (1999) racial triangulation theory, the model minority myth attributes Asian American's educational and economic success to their cultural values and hard work. Interestingly, the model minority myth implies that Asian Americans are too busy being successful and making money to worry about politics (Kim, 1999)—which can be interpreted as a carrot approach to civic ostracism. The relative valorization of Asians to Black populations serves as a way to subordinate Black individuals (Kim, 1999) as well as to keep Asians at bay from full civic incorporation.

The perpetual foreigner stereotype, on the other hand, outright reinforces the enduring historical notion that Asian Americans are unassimilable into White society and therefore should be ostracized from politics and civic membership (Kim, 1999). The dual strategy of relative valorization and civic ostracism of Asian Americans helps "protect White privileges from both Black and Asian American encroachment" (Kim, 1999, p. 126) and ensures the domination of White people over the two minority groups. The model minority myth, therefore, is instrumental in racializing and marginalizing Asian Americans (Ancheta, 2006). It also helps divide racial minority groups by pitting Asians and other minorities against each other and leads to discounting the structural and cumulative disadvantages that other minority communities face and to denigrating other racial minorities as "problem" minorities (Kawai, 2005; Kim, 1999; Xu & Lee, 2013).

Conclusion

Both the "yellow peril" and model minority tropes characterize Asian Americans' marginalized status in the United States as the unassimilable "perpetual foreigner" or the preferable "minority." Throughout their history, Asian Americans have confronted a long legacy of exclusion and inequity, particularly during periods of economic recession, disease outbreaks, or war. Unless people actually understand the historic roots of racism in the United States, how can we address present-day racism, including anti-Asian racism, from its most mundane to its most systemic forms?

Therefore, to contextualize the rise in racialized hate and violence against the Asian Americans community during the COVID-19 pandemic, we reviewed the history of anti-Asian racism in the United States through an in-depth analysis of anti-Chinese violence and institutional oppression. We used the lens of "othering" to show how anti-Asian discrimination and xenophobia has manifested itself throughout history in different formal and informal governmental sanctions, such as the 1882 CEA and the inaction of law enforcement when confronting public violence against Asian Americans. These policy outcomes can further be understood in the context of "perceived threat"—that is, how White individuals perceived Asian Americans to be a threat to White hegemony in the economic, public health, and civic-political domains. Finally, we demonstrated how anti-Chinese institutional repression spreads to restrict other Asian groups through ethnic lumping.

It is our hope that a more in-depth understanding of the historical trajectory of anti-Asian racism can help us begin a dialogue toward bridging deeply entrenched racial divisions in the United States and put us on a path to collective healing.

References

Alba, R., & Foner, N. (2006, October 1). The second generation from the last great wave of immigration: Setting the record straight. Migration Policy Institute. https://www.migrationpolicy.org/article/second-generation-last-great-wave-immigration-setting-record-straight

Ancheta, A. N. (2006). *Race, rights, and the Asian American experience.* Rutgers University Press.

Aoki, K. (2010). The yellow Pacific: Transnational identities, diasporic racialization, and myth(s) of the Asian century. *UC Davis Law Review, 44,* 897–951.

Asia Society. (n.d.). Asian Americans then and now linking past to present. *Asia Society.* https://asiasociety.org/education/asian-americans-then-and-now

Bloomberg Businessweek. (2019, December). Mistrust and the hunt for spies among Chinese Americans. https://www.bloombergquint.com/businessweek/the-u-s-government-s-mistrust-of-chinese-americans

Bo, S. (1885). A protest against the Statue of Liberty. *Digital History.* https://www.digitalhistory.uh.edu/disp_textbook_print.cfm?smtid=3&psid=31

Brockell, G. (2021, March 18). The long, ugly history of anti-Asian racism and violence in the U.S. *The Washington Post.* https://www.washingtonpost.com/history/2021/03/18/history-anti-asian-violence-racism/

Burton, J., Farrell, M., Lord, F., & Lord, R. (2011). *Confinement and ethnicity: An overview of World War II Japanese American relocation sites*. University of Washington Press.

Chang, V. (2023, December 13). How Asian Americans fought back against hate—and won. New York State Bar Association (NYSBA). https://nysba.org/how-asian-americans-fought-back-against-hate-and-won/#_edn28

Chen, H. A., Trinh, J., & Yang, G. P. (2020). Anti-Asian sentiment in the United States: COVID-19 and history. *American Journal of Surgery*, 220(3), 556–557. https://doi.org/10.1016/j.amjsurg.2020.05.020

Chen, T. (2000). Hate violence as border patrol: An Asian American theory of hate violence. *Asian Law Journal*, 7, 69–102.

COVID-19 Hate Crimes Act, Publ. L. No. 117-13, 123 Stat. 2835 (2021). https://www.govinfo.gov/app/details/PLAW-117publ13

Cullinane, M. P. (2014). The "Gentlemen's" Agreement: Exclusion by class. *Immigrants & Minorities*, 32(2), 139–161.

De Witt, H. A. (1979). The Watsonville Anti-Filipino Riot of 1930: A case study of the Great Depression and ethnic conflict in California. *Southern California Quarterly*, 61(3), 291–302. https://doi.org/10.2307/41170831

Eichelberger, L. (2007). SARS and New York's Chinatown: The politics of risk and blame during an epidemic of fear. *Social Science & Medicine*, 65(6), 1284–1295.

FBI. (n.d.). Uniform Crime Reporting Program. https://cde.ucr.cjis.gov/LATEST/webapp/#/pages/explorer/crime/hate-crime

Fisher, F., & Fisher, F. (2010). Congressional passage of the Chinese exclusion act of 1882. *Immigrants & Minorities*, 20(2), 58–74. doi:10.1080/02619288.2001.9975015

Fussell, E. (2014). Warmth of the welcome: Attitudes toward immigrants and immigration policy. *Annual Review of Sociology*, 40, 479–498. https://doi.org/10.1146/annurev-soc-071913-043325

Gover, A. R., Harper, S. B., & Langton, L. (2020). Anti-Asian hate crime during the COVID-19 pandemic: Exploring the reproduction of inequality. *American Journal of Criminal Justice*, 45(4), 647–667. https://doi.org/10.1007/s12103-020-09545-1

Griffey, T. (2007). *The Ku Klux Klan and vigilante culture in Yakima Valley*. The Seattle Civil Rights and Labor History Project. https://depts.washington.edu/civilr/kkk_yakima.htm

Grove, N. J., & Zwi, A. B. (2006). Our health and theirs: Forced migration, othering, and public health. *Social Science & Medicine*, 62(8), 1931–1942.

Gussow, Z. (2021). *Leprosy, racism, and public health: Social policy in chronic disease control*. Routledge.

Hing, B. O. (2001). Vigilante racism: The de-Americanization of immigrant America. *Michigan Journal of Race & Law*, 7, 441.

History.com Staff. (2022, August 9). *Chinese Exclusion Act*. History.com. https://www.history.com/topics/19th-century/chinese-exclusion-act-1882

Howard, J. (2008). *Concentration camps on the home front Japanese Americans in the house of Jim Crow*. University of Chicago Press.

Hswen, Y., Xu, X., Hing, A., Hawkins, J. B., Brownstein, J. S., & Gee, G. C. (2021). Association of "covid19" versus "Chinese virus" with anti-Asian sentiments on Twitter: March 9–23, 2020. *American Journal of Public Health*, 111, 956–964. https://doi.org/10.2105/AJPH.2021.306154

Kang, J. C. (2021). *The loneliest Americans*. Crown Publishing Group.

Kawai, Y. (2005). Stereotyping Asian Americans: The dialectic of the model minority and the yellow peril. *Howard Journal of Communications*, 16(2), 109–130. 10.1080/10646170590948974

Kil, S. H. (2012). Fearing yellow, imagining white: Media analysis of the Chinese Exclusion Act of 1882. *Social Identities*, 18, 663–677.

Kim, A. C. (2018). Prosecuting "Chinese Spies": Empirical analysis of economic espionage. *Cardozo Law Review, 40*(2), 749–822. http://cardozolawreview.com/prosecuting-chinese-spies-an-empirical-analysis-of-the-economic-espionage-act/

Kim, C. J. (1999). The racial triangulation of Asian Americans. *Politics & Society, 27*(1), 105–138.

Kim, D. H., & Sundstrom, R. R. (2014). Xenophobia and racism. *Critical Philosophy of Race, 2*(1), 20–44.

Lee, E. (2002). The Chinese exclusion example: Race, immigration, and American gatekeeping, 1882–1924. *Journal of American Ethnic History, 21*(3), 36–62.

Lee, E. (2007). The "yellow peril" and Asian exclusion in the Americas. *Pacific Historical Review, 76*(4), 537–562. https://doi.org/10.1525/phr.2007.76.4.537

Lee, J. (2021). Asian Americans, affirmative action & the rise in anti-Asian hate. *Daedalus, 150*(2), 180–198. https://doi.org/10.1162/daed_a_01854

Lee, J. & Zhou, M. (2015). *The Asian American achievement paradox*. Russell Sage Foundation.

Lee, J. C., & Kye, S. (2016). Racialized assimilation of Asian Americans. *Annual Review of Sociology, 42*(1), 253–273. 10.1146/annurev-soc-081715-074310

Leung, A. K. C. (2009). *Leprosy in China: A history*. Columbia University Press.

Levin, B. (2021). *Report to the nation: Anti-Asian prejudice and hate crime*. Center for the Study of Hate & Extremism, California State University San Bernardino. https://www.csusb.edu/sites/default/files/Report%20to%20the%20Nation%20-%20Anti-Asian%20Hate%202020%20Final%20Draft%20-%20As%20of%20Apr%2030%202021%206%20PM%20corrected.pdf

Li, Y., & Nicholson, H. L., Jr. (2021). When "model minorities" become "yellow peril": Othering and the racialization of Asian Americans in the COVID-19 pandemic. *Sociology Compass, 15*(2), e12849. https://doi.org/10.1111/soc4.12849

Liu, B. (2017). *Solving the mystery of the model minority: The journey of Asian Americans in America*. Cognella Academic Publishing.

Mallapragada, M. (2021). Asian Americans as racial contagion. *Cultural Studies, 35*, 279–290.

Markel, H., & Stern, A. M. (2002). The foreignness of germs: The persistent association of immigrants and disease in American society. *Milbank Quarterly, 80*(4), 757–788. https://doi.org/10.1111/1468-0009.00030

Markel, H., & Stern, A. M. (1999). Which face? Whose nation?: Immigration, public health, and the construction of disease at America's ports and borders, 1891–1928. *American Behavioral Scientist, 42*(9), 1314–1331. https://doi.org/10.1177/00027649921954921

McClain, C. (1988). Of medicine, race, and American law: The bubonic plague outbreak of 1900. *Law and Social Inquiry, 13*(3), 447–513. https://doi.org/10.1111/j.1747-4469.1988.tb01126.x

McClain, C. (1994). *In search of equality: The Chinese struggle against discrimination in nineteenth-century America*. University of California Press.

Melendez, P. (2020, March 31). Stabbing of Asian-American 2-year-old and her family was a virus-fueled hate crime: Feds. *Daily Beast*. https://www.thedailybeast.com/stabbing-of-asian-american-2-year-old-and-her-family-was-a-coronavirus-fueled-hate-crime-feds-say

Meyers, P. (2017, September 18). It happened here: Mobs attack Filipinos in Lower Valley. *Yakima Herald-Republic*. https://www.yakimaherald.com/news/local/it-happened-here-mobs-attack-filipinos-in-lower-valley/article_43b171f2-9c2b-11e7-a071-57c15018e1de.html

Molina, N. (2006). *Fit to be citizens? Public health and race in Los Angeles, 1879–1939*. University of California Press.

Morey, B. N. (2018). Mechanisms by which anti-immigrant stigma exacerbates racial/ethnic health disparities. *American Journal of Public Health, 108*(4), 460–463.

Museus, S. D. (2013). Asian Americans and Pacific Islanders: A national portrait of growth, diversity, and inequality. In Museus, S. D., Maramba, D. C., & Teranishi, R. T. (Eds.), *The

Misrepresented Minority: New Insights on Asian Americans and Pacific Islanders, and Their Implications for Higher Education (pp. 11–41). Stylus.

Ng, R. (2021). Anti-Asian sentiments during the COVID-19 pandemic across 20 countries: Analysis of a 12-billion-word news media database. *Journal of Medical Internet Research, 23*(12), e28305.

Petersen, W. (1966, January 9). Success Story, Japanese American Style. *The New York Times.* https://www.nytimes.com/1966/01/09/archives/success-story-japaneseamerican-style-success-story-japaneseamerican.html

Reagan, R. (1988, August 10). Remarks on signing the bill providing restitution for the wartime internment of Japanese-American civilians. *Ronald Reagan Presidential Library and Museum.* https://www.reaganlibrary.gov/archives/speech/remarks-signing-bill-providing-restitution-wartime-internment-japanese-american

Rotondi, J. P. (2023, September 28,). Before the Chinese Exclusion Act, this anti-immigrant law targeted Asian women. *History.* https://www.history.com/news/chinese-immigration-page-act-women

Sharma, G. (2020, March 5). Why are there so many conspiracy theories around the coronavirus? COVID-19 has been accompanied by a conspiracy theory outbreak, not just on social media, on mainstream outlets, too. *Aljazeera.* https://www.aljazeera.com/news/2020/3/5/why-are-there-so-many-conspiracy-theories-around-the-coronavirus

Showalter, M. P. (1989). The Watsonville Anti-Filipino Riot of 1930: A reconsideration of Fermin Tobera's murder. *Southern California Quarterly, 71*(4), 341–348. https://doi.org/10.2307/41171455

Smith, K. (2021, February 15). Hundreds of people are volunteering to escort elderly Asian Americans to help keep them safe. *CNN.* https://edition.cnn.com/2021/02/15/us/volunteer-group-helps-to-keep-elderly-asian-americans-safe-trnd/index.html

Smith, L. (2017). The war between Vietnamese fishermen and the KKK signaled a new type of white supremacy. *Timeline.* https://timeline.com/kkk-vietnamese-fishermen-beam-43730353df06

Stop AAPI Hate. (2023, November). Community reports to Stop AAPI Hate: 2020–2022 key findings. *Stop AAPI Hate.* https://stopaapihate.org/wp-content/uploads/2023/10/23-SAH-TaxonomyReport-KeyFindings-F.pdf

Takai, Y. (2020, June 12). Epidemics and racism: Honolulu's bubonic plague and the Big Fire, 1899–1900. *Active History.* https://activehistory.ca/blog/2020/06/12/epidemics-and-racism-honolulu-bubonic-plague-and-the-big-fire-1899-1900/

Tessler, H., Choi, M., & Kao, G. (2020). The anxiety of being Asian American: Hate crimes and negative biases during the COVID-19 pandemic. *American Journal of Criminal Justice, 45,* 636–646.

Trauner, J. B. (1978). The Chinese as medical scapegoats in San Francisco, 1870–1905. *California History, 57*(1), 70–87.

Tresch, E. (2020). "They are vile and polluted in a filthy degree": An analysis of health and disease rhetoric during the anti-Chinese movement, 1849–1900. Master's thesis. University of Tulsa. https://www.proquest.com/docview/2407627987/abstract/60511255FB144AD6PQ/1

Tuan, M. (1998). *Forever foreigners or honorary whites? The Asian ethnic experience today.* Rutgers University Press.

US Commission on Civil Rights. (2023). The federal response to anti-Asian racism in the United States. https://www.usccr.gov/files/2023-10/fy-2023-se-report.pdf

Wang, F. K.-H. (2017, March). Government scientist fired after dropped spying charges petitions for reinstatement. *NBC News.* https://www.nbcnews.com/news/asian-america/government-scientist-fired-after-dropped-spying-charges-petitions-reinstatement-n733281

The Wasp. (1882). *San Francisco's three graces.* 8 (304).

Weis, L. (1995). Identity formation and the process of "othering": Unravelling sexual threads. *Educational Foundations, 9,* 17–33.

Wu, F. H. (2009). Embracing mistaken identity: How the Vincent Chin case unified Asian Americans. *Asian American Policy Review, 19*, 17.

Xu, J. & Lee, J. C. (2013). The marginalized "model" minority: An empirical examination of the racial triangulation of Asian Americans. *Social Forces, 91*(4), 1363–1397. 10.1093/sf/sot049

Yam, K. (2021, December 10). NYPD reports 361 percent increase in anti-Asian hate crimes since last year: Officials said anti-Asian incidents in part drove the city's 100 percent overall increase in hate crimes this year. *NBC News.* https://www.nbcnews.com/news/asian-america/nypd-reports-361-percent-increase-anti-asian-hate-crimes-last-%20year-rcna8427

Yung, J., Chang, G., & Lai, H. (Eds.). (2006). *Chinese American voices: From the gold rush to the present.* University of California Press.

Zimmer, B. (2019). Why Trump uses "invasion" to describe immigrants. *The Atlantic*, https://www.theatlantic.com/entertainment/archive/2019/08/trump-immigrant-invasion-language-origins/595579/

2
Racism, Xenophobia, and Violence Against Asian Americans During the COVID-19 Pandemic

Xiaofang Liu, Kenny Kwong, and Qingwen Xu

Introduction

This chapter delves into the unsettling wave of racism and xenophobia that swept through Asian American communities during the COVID-19 pandemic. It examines this deeply concerning issue by following a structured path, beginning with a meticulous examination of empirical evidence that shed light on the stark realities of anti-Asian discrimination, hate incidents, and hate crimes that unfolded across the United States during the COVID-19 pandemic. Subsequently, the chapter unveils the profound toll this discrimination took on the mental health of Asian Americans, underscoring the urgency of addressing this crisis as a pressing public health concern. Furthermore, it navigates through the theoretical explanations, dissecting the phenomenon through the lenses of nationalism and White supremacy, revealing the complex dynamics that underpinned the scapegoating of Asian communities. In conclusion, the chapter distills practice and policy recommendations from our research, providing a roadmap for addressing this pressing social problem. Through rigorous analysis and deep insights, the chapter aims to contribute to the discourse surrounding these critical issues and call for action to combat anti-Asian racism.

The Pandemic and Anti-Asian Violence and Discrimination

The United States has witnessed a significant increase in reported racial discrimination, harassment, and violence against Asian Americans since the onset of the COVID-19 pandemic. As early as late January 2020, when the outbreak was first reported in China, incidents began to emerge in the media. The escalation of such cases coincided with the spread of COVID-19 across the United States, particularly affecting individuals of Chinese origin due to the virus's initial outbreak in Wuhan, China, and the subsequent use of inflammatory terms such as the "China virus" in political rhetoric.

In response to this troubling trend, an online anti-Asian racism incident reporting center called Stop AAPI Hate was established in March 2020 to track acts of hate against Asian American, Native Hawai'ian, and Pacific Islander (AANHPI) individuals nationwide. Over the first two years of its operation, the center recorded 11,467 hate incidents against AANHPI people across the United States. Notably, 43% of these victims were of Chinese descent (Yellow Horse & Chen, 2022). The reported cases encompassed various forms of incidents, including verbal harassment, physical assault, civil rights violations, and online harassment. In addition, government agencies documented a significant increase in anti-Asian hate crimes since the onset of the pandemic, acts of prejudice that go beyond incidents and involve violence, threats, or property damage (US Department of Justice, 2023). While the total number of hate crimes across the nation decreased by 7% from 2019 to 2020, those targeting Asian Americans in the 16 largest US cities rose by nearly 150% during the same period (Levin & Grisham, 2021); there was a subsequent 167% increase from 279 incidents in 2020 to 746 in 2021, with the number remaining elevated at 499 in 2022 (FBI, 2023). It is worth noting that these reported cases likely represent only a fraction of actual occurrences because Asian victims were less likely to report victimization than other population groups (Lantz & Wenger, 2022), suggesting that the true extent of the problem might be even more substantial than reported.

Alongside the surge in anti-Asian violence has been a significant increase in anti-Asian discrimination. Several studies based on national representative data showed that Asians had a significantly greater likelihood of experiencing coronavirus-related discrimination compared to other racial groups (Ha et al., 2020; Liu et al., 2020; Pan et al., 2021; Ruiz et al., 2021). A survey conducted by the Pew Research Center found that a staggering

73% of Asian adults said they "have personally experienced discrimination" or "been treated unfairly because of their race or ethnicity during the coronavirus outbreak"; "people acted as if they were uncomfortable around Asians," and "Asians had been subject to racial slurs or jokes" (Ruiz et al., 2021). Liu and Finch (2020) specified that the odds of reporting perceived discrimination during the pandemic were four times higher for Asians than non-Hispanic White individuals, indicating that the observed surge in discrimination was not a carry-over from respondents' previous day-to-day experiences but rather new and could be attributed to the coronavirus pandemic.

The increase in COVID-19-related anti-Asian racial discrimination, hate incidents, and hate crimes disproportionately affected specific subgroups and geographical areas. Not surprisingly, the surge in anti-Asian violence was particularly pronounced on the East and West coasts, particularly in New York and California, reflecting the concentration of Asian populations in these regions (Gao et al., 2022; Yellow Horse & Chen, 2022). Individuals of Chinese descent, women, youth, immigrants, international students, those with lower levels of education, those with limited English proficiency, healthcare workers, and Chinese business owners and employees faced a higher risk of being targeted and victimized (Dye et al., 2020; Ha et al., 2020; Liu et al., 2020; Ma & Miller, 2020; Yellow Horse & Chen, 2022). Notably, Asian American women were more than twice as likely to be targeted than men, as detailed in the "Report to the Nation: Anti-Asian Prejudice & Hate Crime" (Levin, 2021), suggesting an intersectional dynamic perceiving Asian women as easier targets.

Additionally, more than half of reported hate incidents occurred in public spaces, such as streets, businesses, parks, and public transit. For example, in New York City, since the onset of the pandemic, numerous reports have detailed assaults on Asian individuals in public transportation places as well as incidents where individuals were shoved onto subway tracks in New York City. Tragically, on January 15, 2022, a 40-year-old Asian American woman named Michelle Alyssa Go lost her life after being pushed into the path of an oncoming subway train at the Times Square subway station. The rise in anti-Asian hate crimes, coupled with the alarming frequency of incidents and day-to-day perceived discrimination, is unprecedented, and hate-generated violence against Asian people in the public arena has particularly instilled fear and hypervigilance within Asian American communities. This atmosphere of fear and anxiety has been further exacerbated by the tragic mass shooting that claimed the lives of six Asian American women in Atlanta, Georgia, amid the pandemic. During the COVID-19 pandemic, Asian Americans had to cope with two public health crises: the coronavirus pandemic and anti-Asian racism; indeed, racism, as a key driving force of racial inequities in health and well-being, is also a public health crisis (Mendez et al., 2021). Pandemic-related discrimination affects the spread of the virus by distorting public attitudes toward prevention and restriction, health service procurement, and the establishment of health-related policies (Demirtaş-Madran, 2020). Such crises underscore the urgency of addressing and combating anti-Asian racism in society.

In response to the widespread pandemic-related discrimination nationally, more than 200 declarations of racism as a public health crisis have been passed in 37 states, including by city councils, county boards, governor/mayoral offices, education boards, and health associations or public health departments (American Public Health Association, 2021). In New York State, with a high number of anti-Asian hate incidents reported and the high publicity of anti-Asian hate crimes, Governor Kathy Hochul declared racism as a "public health crisis" and signed new legislation, the Hate Crimes Analysis and Review Act of New York, on December 23, 2021 (Alfonseca, 2021) to address discrimination and racial injustice and the need for comprehensive data collection on victims of violence, specifically Asian American communities that have been targeted by hate crimes during the COVID-19 pandemic. Nationally, President Joe Biden signed into law the COVID-19 Hate Crimes Act. Congress enacted this legislation in response to the rise in hate crimes and hate incidents against Asian Americans and Pacific Islanders. More states are now requiring Asian American history to be taught in their public schools.

Pandemic-Related Mental Health Risks Among Asian Americans

Despite these policy responses, racism against Asian Americans during the outbreak of the coronavirus pandemic has caused mental and emotional imprinting and led to a greater negative societal and mental health impact affecting Asian American populations. Scholars have documented the race-based stress and cumulative trauma that Asian Americans experienced throughout history (Ashby et al., 2022) by being cast as the "enemy" and the cause of national health crises (Carter, 2007). They are frequently taxed with witnessing and experiencing anti-Asian verbal and physical assaults (Ahrens, 2020) and feel unwelcome, not belonging, or endangered in America. This makes Asian Americans vulnerable to developing acute stress or traumatic symptoms such as anxiety, fear, hypervigilance, guilt, shame, or anger (Cheng, 2020).

Framing COVID-19 as a unique traumatic stressor, the time during the pandemic was charged with disease-related stress and potentially traumatic experiences such as being isolated due to pandemic control measures (e.g., social distancing and quarantine), witnessing and caring for those who are severely ill, dealing with bereavement and mortality, and experiencing food and resource insecurity (Shi & Hall, 2020; Shultz et al., 2015). For Asian Americans, studies indicated that anticipating and experiencing race-based stigma and discrimination during disease outbreaks, as well as pandemic politicization and widespread scapegoating accusations against Asians, further increase the risk for mental health problems, can have severe and long-lasting negative impacts, and may result in heightened suicidal ideation (Chen et al., 2020; Shi & Hall, 2020).

Data collected during the pandemic, though not comprehensive, report a high level of mental health concerns. Studies using longitudinal data from a representative sample found that 79% of Chinese New Yorkers experienced high levels of racism-related vigilance in 2020 (e.g., being worried about their or their family's safety from hate crime or harassment, trying to avoid certain social situations or places due to worries about racial discrimination, and feeling unease in public areas or being worried about how other people might look at them; Gao & Liu, 2021); this percentage went up to 85% in 2021 (Gao et al., 2022). Pandemic-related anti-Asian racism is associated with higher levels of reported generalized anxiety and depressive symptoms and has a more pronounced and lasting negative impact, particularly on Asian American youth and young adults, given their important development of sense of self and identity, and self-esteem (Benner et al., 2018; Schmitt et al., 2014). The study by Cheah and colleagues (2020) found that the majority of youth respondents perceived both health-related Sinophobia and media-perpetuated Sinophobia; higher levels of youth-perceived racism and racial discrimination were associated with their poorer mental health.

The mental health impact goes beyond an individual focus. When people of Asian descent collectively experience anti-Asian racism ranging from hate incidents, crimes, and discrimination to hypervigilance, nervousness in public, and anticipated discrimination, they struggle to cope with these experiences and feelings. Asian communities must contend with the ramifications not only of a disease outbreak but also with associated stigma during the pandemic (Misra et al., 2020). These collective psychosocial experiences have transformed Asian communities' behaviors and perceptions. Due to social stigma and self-perceived discrimination, Asian community members during the pandemic were afraid to go outside their own homes, with detrimental impacts on their mental health; were afraid to seek treatment or disclose symptoms in the event of contracting COVID-19; and were less likely to seek mental health care, which led to increased risks during the public health crises and challenges in following preventive measures against the coronavirus (Marchi et al., 2022).

Of note, Asian community-based organizations provided critical resources during the pandemic and became trusted liaisons to connect linguistically isolated community members to care and services (Wong et al., 2022). Meanwhile, gripped by anger and despair, and informed by a greater understanding of racism as well as experiences gained from recent social movements like Black Lives Matter, community advocates and members have been organizing, debating, and building liaisons to respond strongly to the anti-Asian racism; the Stop AAPI Hate Reporting Center that emerged alongside the COVID-19 pandemic is considered a model of such community advocacy (Takasaki, 2020). But stopping the ongoing epidemic of anti-Asian hate and racism during the pandemic needed a deeper examination of the United States' racially structured society.

Psychosociological Perspectives on Scapegoating and Discrimination

Collective fears of coronavirus—and thus collective racism perceived in the forms of health-related Sinophobia, blaming, and scapegoating Asian Americans—fueled anti-Asian hostility and sentiment (Budhwani & Sun, 2020; Cheah et al., 2020; Stechemesser et al., 2020). According to scapegoating theories (Allport, 1954; Glick, 2002), being from a minority group or one with visible differences such as skin color is seen as a vulnerability to being considered a scapegoat. Such explanations became significantly clear during the coronavirus pandemic in the United States, with high levels of social and economic deprivation (e.g., lack of access to masks, vaccines, or healthcare resources) experienced as a form of frustration. Frustration causes aggression and prejudice, and people tend to select some targeted outgroups as a scapegoats for them to blame (Demirtaş-Madran, 2020). Glick (2005) defined scapegoating as "an extreme form of prejudice in which an outgroup is unfairly blamed for having intentionally caused an ingroup's misfortunes" (p. 244). Glick (2002) argued that there are certain key determinants to a group being scapegoated: they are mostly weaker groups that lack the means of self-defense, are currently seen as minority groups, and/or have visible differences such as skin color or gender.

Scapegoating offers a designated villain for an individual aggressor to blame for frustration and deprivation caused by economic or social problems; universally, people also react to the anxious uncertainty of loss of personal control by scapegoating (Alicke, 2000), disproportionately blaming or aggressing against particular viable targets. Blaming is argued to be the outcome of psychological processes and is equally driven by cognitive and motivational biases. More importantly, when an ideology points to a scapegoat to target blame for the deprivation of a resource, blaming meets the dominant group's need for positive social identity. Such dynamics can be further understood from the *Social Identity Approach* (Tajfel, 1978), with group membership being a crucial factor that psychologically and socially predicts each person's pandemic experience. Individuals who discriminate against certain groups aim to strengthen their own social identity and self-esteem as a means of coping with the anxiety of having contracted or been potentially exposed to the disease (Demirtaş-Madran, 2020). Existing prejudices and associating the COVID-19 virus with a sociodemographic group built a false, illusionary relationship, which led to anti-Asian stigmatization and discrimination (Demirtaş-Madran, 2020).

Racism, xenophobia, and violence against Asian Americans during the coronavirus pandemic were caused by a confluence of factors. In times of national crises and in response to health threats derived from an unknown source, there is a tendency to discriminate and blame groups that are perceived as threats. During the early waves of the pandemic, speculation about the origins of the virus and the methods of transmission were widespread. National polls showed that the coronavirus first being reported by China was the top reason for discrimination against the Asian American community (Findling et al., 2022). Thus, not only was the country of origin directly blamed for the pandemic, but also other groups that are proximate to the Chinese subsequently became the targets of collective blame

(Hahm et al., 2021; Ruiz et al., 2021). Following many of these historical patterns, Asian Americans were scapegoated due to being perceived as an "outgroup." Throughout US history, Asian Americans have been subject to various forms of social repression, including the codification of anti-Asian racism in US law in the Chinese Exclusion Act of 1882, the Immigration Act of 1924, Japanese internment camps during World War II, and the treatment of Asian Americans as "perpetual foreigners" resulting in the sense of feeling like "aliens in their own lands" (Chen et al., 2020). Asians are not accepted as "real" Americans regardless of where they were born or how many years they have lived in the United States (Gee et al., 2007; Yoo et al., 2009).

During the pandemic, irrational fear and scapegoating among the general public were also exacerbated when politicians and government officials manipulated the crisis to pursue their own or their political party's agendas and divert public attention from the real causes of the underlying issues. Following former President Donald Trump's referring to COVID-19 as "the China virus," there were immediate spikes in anti-Asian Google searches and tweets (Budhwani & Sun, 2020; Stechemesser et al., 2020). Giving voice to politicians who were increasingly making explicitly racial appeals by singling out marginalized groups and providing incomplete or inaccurate information chosen by politicians reinforced anti-Asian sentiment during the pandemic (Hahm et al., 2021). Meanwhile, the media's role in perpetuating such anti-Asian sentiment has been enormous in today's digitalized society. Within a week of Trump's "China virus" accusation, the number of anti-Asian hashtags on Twitter rose by 797% and 17400% for #covid19 and #chinesevirus, respectively (Hswen et al., 2021). The worrying facts are that hateful tweets were more successful in attracting followers compared to counter-hate ones (Ziems et al., 2020), and most racist tweets were posted by users who had never used racist terms before (Lu & Sheng, 2020). The hate was learned, and the hate was contagious. Anti-Asian hate became a new virus spread online amid the pandemic, and its harmful real-life consequences were suggested by many studies (Costello et al., 2021; Hswen, 2022).

Anti-Asian Racism and the Intensified Nationalism

Targeting and scapegoating Asian Americans as a group to blame for the pandemic was the result of deeply rooted, underlying social, political, or economic tensions (Asian American Bar Association of New York, 2021). Going deeper, increasing anti-Asian racism has been tied to the American context of growing nationalism and the election of Donald Trump in the 21st century. Using the terms "China virus" and "kung flu," as well as making other unsubstantiated claims, the Trump administration's racial scapegoating of China reflects a long history of using "othering" in the construction of international relationships (Dionne & Turkmen, 2020). The foundation on which international relationships are built often goes beyond national security and economic interdependence; in fact, global inequality dynamics across nation-states are shaped by shared ideas—shared goals, threats, fears, identities, and other elements of perceived social reality (Wendt, 1999). These socially shared ideas thus have been deeply fabricated into power relations on local, national, and global scales. Winant (2001) has argued that the foundation of modern nation-states and the construction of the international system were deeply racialized processes; national ideas about racial difference and power hierarchy associated with race were developed through transnational connections and comparisons (Winant, 2001; Yu et al., 2020). In US history, the rising Anti-Asian sentiment and racism in the late 19th and early 20th centuries were closely tied to growing transnational Asian migration, the alleged and public perceived threat that Asian immigrants posed, and globalized race dynamics (Lee, 2007).

Given such a constructionism framework in international relationships, blaming other countries and "othering" people from certain countries has repeatedly been the strategy in the United States to cope with the society's fear of the unknown, loss of control, and crisis; such blames and otherings consistently targeted non-European countries and non-White groups of people. For instance, Chinese immigrants were blamed in the late 1800s and early 1900s during smallpox outbreaks because public health officials believed that the Chinese immigrant community spread urban "filth" and disease; at the same time, regular physicians provided minimal medical care for Chinese immigrants (Klee, 1983). Japan was blamed for US economic downturns in the 1980s and early 1990s, and the perceived threat of this Asian country quickly turned into anti-Asian violence, with one of the most notorious cases being the killing of Chinese American Vincent Chin by two White autoworkers (Tuan, 1998). The connection between economic competition with an Asian nation (Japan) and anti-Asian violence in America suggests the same process of racializing international relations and othering Asian Americans. In recent decades, with the rise of China as a global economic power, the target to blame seems to have shifted to China.

China–US relationships were complex and tense under the Trump administration, and Sinophobia has played an important role in the American national imaginary due to the two country's ideological conflicts and their impacts at both systemic and interpersonal levels (Löfflmann, 2022). On a larger scale, nationalism as a political practice is best understood as a narrow ideology that values the dominant political and social importance of the nation; the promotion of "America First" by the Trump administration at its roots suggests an increase in nationalism that perceives international relationships to be structured and constructed around the interests of America (Bieber, 2022). A major problem with nationalism is the aspect of exclusion; scholars have clearly argued for the interconnection between racism and exclusionary nationalism as a constituent element within nationalism (Bieber, 2022; Elias et al., 2021; Nowrasteh, 2020). The election of Trump signified rising and intensified nationalism in the United States; consequently, it came with repressive and oppressive immigration policies as well as increased hate crimes and discrimination after the election (Williamson & Gelfand, 2019). The Trump administration used historic threats of immigrants, terrorism, or Islam and present threats of transmissible disease from a socialist/communist country during the pandemic to justify the exclusionary nationalism policies at the systemic level and political rhetoric, discriminatory language, and violent behaviors at the interpersonal level.

Exclusionary nationalism can express itself and be reflected in widely held public discourses. Furthermore, it is noted that the Trump's election marked a shift in political appeals to emotion over reason and a disruption in the use of rationality, objectivity, and the value of facts in policymaking and wider public discourse (Crilley, 2018). When the use of racist rhetoric by politicians builds their electoral successes, parties and politicians are likely to maintain such strategies. The terms "China virus" and "kung flu" convey the emotive register for nationalists or White supremacists who felt called upon to act upon the "foreign" threat to the American nation—not so much the virus, but the immigrant-as-"alien" (Louie & Viladrich, 2021; Mallapragada, 2021), or further, the Asian American-as-"alien." Othering and targeting Asian American groups of people during the coronavirus pandemic risked reinforcing preexisting power dynamics based on race, ethnicity, and immigration status, despite the fact that US-centric White-based nationalism is obsolete and antithetical to a shared global experience of solidarity and cooperation.

The Root of Racial Hierarchy: White Supremacism

Asian Americans have been the target of othering from both racist nationalism and nativist racism. The very early 1882 Chinese Exclusion Act, propelled by White labor unrest, and Trump's pre-COVID travel ban policies and associated hate violence against South Asian communities are simply examples of racist nationalism and nativist racism, respectively. The violence against Asian Americans during the coronavirus pandemic, not surprisingly, has followed a historical pattern. Starks (2021) calls it a "double pandemic" of coronavirus and White supremacy; indeed, preexisting racism, xenophobia, nationalism, blaming, othering, and the like, all lie in White supremacism. White supremacism is not limited merely to instances of racism or ethnocentrism; nationality and xenophobia also play a role in the construction of Whiteness. Scholars (see the notable work done by Hall, 2017) have argued that White supremacy has three distinct but interwoven strands, racial, ethnic, and national. In addition to being structured into US institutions and everyday social relations, White supremacy also works in tandem with capitalism and other systems of exclusion, such as patriarchy (Golash-Boza et al., 2019). Speed (2020), based on 10 years of research data, indicated that the changing needs of capitalism had affected discourses of race, nationality, and xenophobia over time yet remained fundamentally underwritten by White supremacist assumptions.

Research analysis suggests that White supremacy principles are deeply rooted in former president Trump's social media posts, speeches, and press releases (Louie & Viladrich, 2021). Some noted that the election of former President Trump marked the resurgence of openly White supremacist discourse and action in the United States, a backlash against the assumed progress of multiculturalism and a response to the changing needs of White capitalist power (Speed, 2020). While this observation is widely agreed upon, the assumption inherent in this perspective—that White supremacism was voted back in and reemerged in American society—is problematic; White superiority thinking, White privileges, and structural racism, in conjunction with capitalism, have been reproducing and reinforcing themselves over time despite the vote and election. What has been alarming is that, when old-fashioned White supremacy was no longer appealing and leading to political success, then a new attempt at stoking fear and hatred, repackaging racist language, and using new social media during the coronavirus pandemic allowed White supremacist ideology much easier access to mainstream public discourses.

History reminds us of the danger of the Trump administration's reignition of the "yellow peril" pathology during the pandemic to intensify anti-Asian xenophobia in the United States. But, on the other side of the racist coin, Asian Americans also have been stereotyped as the "model minority." Scholarship on "yellow peril" and "model minority" stereotypes is abundant, with critical reflections all showing that the existence of both "yellow peril" and "model minority" stereotypes and the characterizing of Asians' marginalized status in the United States as perpetual "outsiders" or unassimilable "others" support White supremacy in the racial hierarchy (Li & Nicholson Jr, 2021; Walker & Daniel Anders, 2022; Wu & Nguyen, 2022). The influential work done by Kim (1999) discusses the manipulation of stereotypes to protect White privilege and ensure the domination of White individuals over other minority groups. The two seemingly opposite stereotypes both have been used to defend the immigrant-receiving country (the United States) and to reduce the threat to White privilege and well-being. To prevent the ongoing amplification of these stereotypes about Asian Americans and to erase the discrimination and violence that Asian groups have experienced during the pandemic, the actual Asian American experience should not be silenced in the newsroom, social media, and general public literature.

Conclusion: Call for Responses From Policy, Practice, and Research

Anti-Asian racial discrimination and hate crimes reached an unprecedented level in the United States during the COVID-19 pandemic; this is indisputable. People of Asian descent, especially Chinese, have been treated as scapegoats based on their race since the coronavirus was first reported in China. This was further exacerbated by politicians' racist rhetoric and has caused substantial distress in larger Asian American communities. The intertwining of the politics of disease, xenophobia, and racism has created a public health crisis more profound than an infectious disease pandemic alone. Anti-Asian racism is nothing new in the United States. Scapegoating people of color for societal misfortunes is also nothing new in the United States. The rise of anti-Asian racism is history repeating itself under current sociopolitical circumstances. It is critical to recognize this pattern consciously and take action collectively to put a stop to this hateful and destructive trend.

Top-down actions from governmental authorities are essential to combat such racism. The step taken in May 2021, the passage of COVID-19 Hate Crime Act, is significant, but not sufficient. The law has a high bar for hate crime charges; many forms of racism or discrimination that do not qualify as hate crimes are primarily unaddressed by this law. To eliminate structural racism as well as racist practices and norms at all levels, a racial equity strategic plan needs to be developed and implemented through the coordination of all governmental entities. This includes, but should not be limited to, reviewing existing policies and programs and then developing policies, programs, and interventions comprehensively and coherently through a racial equity lens; crucially, Asian American communities' voices need to be amplified and Asian Americans need to be included as stakeholders during this process.

The social work profession has an enduring commitment to anti-racism, diversity, equity, and inclusion. As a profession deeply rooted in social justice goals, social work practitioners, educators, and researchers collaborate with community organizations to advocate for anti-racism policies, create additional resources, and develop culturally competent practices and accessible community safety programs for Asian American populations. The uptick in anti-Asian violence during the pandemic serves as a wake-up call to increase Asian American communities' awareness of the fight against racial "othering" and institutional racism. Social work practitioners, educators, and researchers must understand that COVID-19 anti-Asian racism is closely associated with White supremacy notions (Starks, 2021); the development and implementation of evidence-based stigma reduction and/or anti-oppressive programs and initiatives can help dismantle systems of White supremacism. To support community self-determination, we must commit to organizational changes, collaborate with other marginalized groups, and build allyship and solidarity to combat xenophobia, racial discrimination, and violence.

On a final note, anti-Asian racism during the pandemic must be seen in the context of preexisting racism and xenophobia. Such racism and discrimination have significant impacts on physical and mental health. Data on Asian Americans were deficient before the pandemic, and this deficiency has been magnified during the COVID crisis. No data, no equity (Yi et al., 2021). Additional efforts in data collection and research focusing on quality race/ethnicity classifications and attention to Asian Americans' unique situation, culture, and needs in well-being will help drive funding decisions, policy development/reform, intervention responses, and resource allocation. Research and the accumulation of knowledge and practice wisdom are critical to addressing the exponential rise in anti-Asian racism.

References

Ahrens, R. P. (2020). COVID-19 impact on Asian American and Pacific Islander mental and physical health. Statement before the House Ways and Means Committee on "The Disproportionate Impact of COVID-19 on Communities of Color, 26. https://democrats-waysandmeans.house.gov/sites/evo-subsites/democrats-waysandmeans.house.gov/files/documents/OCA%20Testimony.pdf

Alfonseca, K. (2021). New York governor declares racism 'public health emergency' amid new anti-discrimination legislation. https://abcnews.go.com/US/york-governor-declares-racism-public-health-emergency-amid/story?id=82002884

Alicke, M. D. (2000). Culpable control and the psychology of blame. *Psychological Bulletin*, *126*(4), 556.

Allport, G. W. (1954). *The nature of prejudice*. Addison-Wesley.

American Public Health Association. (2021). *Analysis: Declarations of racism as a public health crisis.* https://www.apha.org/-/media/Files/PDF/topics/racism/Racism_Declarations_Analysis.pdf

Ashby, J. S., Rice, K. G., Kira, I. A., & Davari, J. (2022). The relationship of COVID-19 traumatic stress, cumulative trauma, and race to posttraumatic stress disorder symptoms. *Journal of Community Psychology*, *50*(6), 2597–2610. https://doi.org/10.1002/jcop.22762

Asian American Bar Association of New York. (2021). *A rising tide of hate and violence against Asian Americans in New York during COVID-19: Impact, causes, solutions.* https://cdn.ymaws.com/www.aabany.org/resource/resmgr/press_releases/2021/a_rising_tide_of_hate_and_vi.pdf

Benner, A. D., Wang, Y., Shen, Y., Boyle, A. E., Polk, R., & Cheng, Y.-P. (2018). Racial/ethnic discrimination and well-being during adolescence: A meta-analytic review. *American Psychologist*, *73*(7), 855.

Bieber, F. (2022). Global nationalism in times of the COVID-19 pandemic. *Nationalities Papers*, *50*(1), 13–25.

Budhwani, H., & Sun, R. (2020). Creating COVID-19 stigma by referencing the novel coronavirus as the "Chinese virus" on Twitter: Quantitative analysis of social media data. *Journal of Medical Internet Research*, *22*(5), e19301.

Carter, R. T. (2007). Racism and psychological and emotional injury: Recognizing and assessing race-based traumatic stress. *Counseling Psychologist*, *35*(1), 13–105.

Cheah, C. S., Wang, C., Ren, H., Zong, X., Cho, H. S., & Xue, X. (2020). COVID-19 racism and mental health in Chinese American families. *Pediatrics*, *146*(5), e2020021816.

Chen, Z., Poon, K.-T., DeWall, C. N., & Jiang, T. (2020). Life lacks meaning without acceptance: Ostracism triggers suicidal thoughts. *Journal of Personality and Social Psychology*, *119*(6), 1423.

Cheng, H.-L. (2020). Xenophobia and racism against Asian Americans during the COVID-19 pandemic: Mental health implications. *Journal of Interdisciplinary Perspectives and Scholarship, 3*(1), 3.

Costello, M. L. C., Feng Luo, H. H., & Song Liao, N. V. (2021). COVID-19: A pandemic of Anti-Asian cyberhate. *Journal of Hate Studies, 17*(1), 108–118.

Crilley, R. (2018). International relations in the age of "post-truth" politics. *International Affairs, 94*(2), 417–425.

Demirtaş-Madran, H. A. (2020). Exploring the motivation behind discrimination and stigmatization related to COVID-19: A social psychological discussion based on the main theoretical explanations. *Frontiers in Psychology, 11*, 569528.

Dionne, K. Y., & Turkmen, F. F. (2020). The politics of pandemic othering: Putting COVID-19 in global and historical context. *International Organization, 74*(S1), E213–E230.

Dye, T. D., Alcantara, L., Siddiqi, S., Barbosu, M., Sharma, S., Panko, T., & Pressman, E. (2020). Risk of COVID-19-related bullying, harassment and stigma among healthcare workers: An analytical cross-sectional global study. *BMJ Open, 10*(12), e046620.

Elias, A., Ben, J., Mansouri, F., & Paradies, Y. (2021). Racism and nationalism during and beyond the COVID-19 pandemic. *Ethnic and Racial Studies, 44*(5), 783–793.

Federal Bureau of Investigation (FBI). (2023). Federal Bureau of Investigation, Crime Data Explorer. https://cde.ucr.cjis.gov/LATEST/webapp/#/pages/explorer/crime/crime-trend

Findling, M., Blendon, R., Benson, J., & Koh, H. (2022, April 12). COVID-19 has driven racism and violence against Asian Americans: Perspectives from 12 national polls. *Health Affairs Forefront.* https://www.healthaffairs.org/content/forefront/covid-19-has-driven-racism-and-violence-against-asian-americans-perspectives-12

Gao, Q., Jia, X., Shen, A., Xia, X., & Liu, X. (2022). Racial discrimination has changed my daily life. https://www.povertycenter.columbia.edu/publication/racial-discrimination-has-changed-my-daily-life

Gao, Q., & Liu, X. (2021). Double pandemic: Discrimination experiences of New Yorkers of Chinese descent during COVID-19. https://www.povertycenter.columbia.edu/nyc-poverty-tracker/discrimination-experiences-new-yorkers-of-chinese-descent-during-pandemic

Gee, G. C., Spencer, M. S., Chen, J., & Takeuchi, D. (2007). A nationwide study of discrimination and chronic health conditions among Asian Americans. *American Journal of Public Health, 97*(7), 1275–1282.

Glick, P. (2002). Sacrificial lambs dressed in wolves' clothing: Envious prejudice, ideology and the scapegoating of Jews. In L. S. Newman & R. Erber (Eds.), *Understanding genocide: The social psychology of the holocaust* (pp. 113–142). Oxford University.

Glick, P. (2005). Scaling up HIV voluntary counseling and testing in Africa: What can evaluation studies tell us about potential prevention impacts? *Evaluation Review, 29*(4), 331–357.

Golash-Boza, T., Duenas, M. D., & Xiong, C. (2019). White supremacy, patriarchy, and global capitalism in migration studies. *American Behavioral Scientist, 63*(13), 1741–1759.

Ha, S. K., Nguyen, A. T., Sales, C., Chang, R. S., Ta, H., Srinivasan, M., Chung, S., Palaniappan, L., & Lin, B. (2020). Increased self-reported discrimination and concern for physical assault due to the COVID-19 pandemic in Chinese, Vietnamese, Korean, Japanese and Filipino Americans. *medRxiv*, 2020.2009.2015.20194720. https://doi.org/10.1101/2020.09.15.20194720

Hahm, H. C., Xavier Hall, C. D., Garcia, K. T., Cavallino, A., Ha, Y., Cozier, Y. C., & Liu, C. (2021). Experiences of COVID-19-related anti-Asian discrimination and affective reactions in a multiple race sample of US young adults. *BMC Public Health, 21*(1), 1–11.

Hall, S. (2017). *The fateful triangle: Race, ethnicity, nation.* Harvard University Press.

Hswen, Y. (2022). Online hate: The new virus. *American Journal of Public Health, 112*(4), 545–547.

Hswen, Y., Xu, X., Hing, A., Hawkins, J. B., Brownstein, J. S., & Gee, G. C. (2021). Association of "#covid19" versus "#chinesevirus" with anti-Asian sentiments on Twitter: March 9–23, 2020. *American Journal of Public Health, 111*(5), 956–964.

Kim, C. J. (1999). The racial triangulation of Asian Americans. *Politics & Society, 27*(1), 105–138.

Klee, L. (1983). The "regulars" and the Chinese: Ethnicity and public health in 1870s San Francisco. *Urban Anthropology, 12*(2), 181–207.

Lantz, B., & Wenger, M. R. (2022). Are Asian victims less likely to report hate crime victimization to the police? Implications for research and policy in the wake of the COVID-19 pandemic. *Crime & Delinquency, 68*(8), 1292–1319.

Lee, E. (2007). The "yellow peril" and Asian exclusion in the Americas. *Pacific Historical Review, 76*(4), 537–562.

Levin, B. (2021). Report to the nation: Anti-Asian prejudice and hate crime. https://www.csusb.edu/sites/default/files/Report%20to%20the%20Nation%20-%20Anti-Asian%20Hate%202020%20Final%20Draft%20-%20As%20of%20Apr%2028%202021%2010%20AM%20corrected.pdf#:~:text=Anti-Asian%20hate%20crime%20reported%20to%20police%20in%2015,Extremism%20%28CSHE%29%20at%20California%20State%20University%2C%20San%20Bernardino

Levin, B., & Grisham, K. (2021). *Anti-Asian hate crime reported to police in America's largest cities: 2019 & 2020*. Center for the Study of Hate and Extremism CSUSB.

Li, Y., & Nicholson Jr, H. L. (2021). When "model minorities" become "yellow peril": Othering and the racialization of Asian Americans in the COVID-19 pandemic. *Sociology Compass, 15*(2), e12849.

Liu, Y., & Finch, B. K. (2020). Discrimination against Asian, Black Americans more likely amid coronavirus pandemic. *The Evidence Base*. https://healthpolicy.usc.edu/evidence-base/discrimination-against-asian-black-americans-more-likely-amid-coronavirus-pandemic/

Liu, Y., Finch, B. K., Brenneke, S. G., Thomas, K., & Le, P. D. (2020). Perceived discrimination and mental distress amid the COVID-19 pandemic: Evidence from the Understanding America Study. *American Journal of Preventive Medicine, 59*(4), 481–492.

Löfflmann, G. (2022). "Enemies of the people": Donald Trump and the security imaginary of America First. *British Journal of Politics and International Relations, 24*(3), 543–560.

Louie, V., & Viladrich, A. (2021). "Divide, divert, & conquer": Deconstructing the presidential framing of White supremacy in the COVID-19 era. *Social Sciences, 10*(8), 280.

Lu, R., & Sheng, Y. (2020). From fear to hate: How the COVID-19 pandemic sparks racial animus in the United States. arXiv preprint arXiv:2007.01448.

Ma, H., & Miller, C. (2020). Trapped in a double bind: Chinese overseas student anxiety during the COVID-19 pandemic. *Health Communication, 36*(13), 1598–1605.

Mallapragada, M. (2021). Asian Americans as racial contagion. *Cultural Studies, 35*(2–3), 279–290.

Marchi, M., Magarini, F. M., Chiarenza, A., Galeazzi, G. M., Paloma, V., Garrido, R., Ioannidi, E., Vassilikou, K., Gaspar de Matos, M., Gaspar, T., Guedes, F. B., Primdahl, N. L., Skovdal, M., Murphy, R., Durbeej, N., Osman, F., Watters, C., van den Muijsenbergh, M., Sturm, G., ... Derluyn, I. (2022). Experience of discrimination during COVID-19 pandemic: The impact of public health measures and psychological distress among refugees and other migrants in Europe. *BMC Public Health, 22*(1), 1–14.

Mendez, D. D., Scott, J., Adodoadji, L., Toval, C., McNeil, M., & Sindhu, M. (2021). Racism as public health crisis: Assessment and review of municipal declarations and resolutions across the United States. *Frontiers in Public Health, 9*, 686807.

Misra, S., Le, P. D., Goldmann, E., & Yang, L. H. (2020). Psychological impact of anti-Asian stigma due to the COVID-19 pandemic: A call for research, practice, and policy responses. *Psychological Trauma, 12*(5), 461.

Nowrasteh, A. (2020). The case for nationalism: How it made us powerful, united, and free. *The Cato Journal, 40*(2), 574–582.

Pan, S. W., Shen, G. C., Liu, C., & Hsi, J. H. (2021). Coronavirus stigmatization and psychological distress among Asians in the United States. *Ethnicity & Health, 26*(1), 110–125.

Ruiz, N. G., Edwards, K., & Lopez, M. H. (2021). One-third of Asian Americans fear threats, physical attacks and most say violence against them is rising. Pew Research Center. https://www.pewresearch.org/short-reads/2021/04/21/one-third-of-asian-americans-fear-threats-physical-attacks-and-most-say-violence-against-them-is-rising/

Schmitt, M. T., Branscombe, N. R., Postmes, T., & Garcia, A. (2014). The consequences of perceived discrimination for psychological well-being: A meta-analytic review. *Psychological Bulletin, 140*(4), 921.

Shi, W., & Hall, B. J. (2020). What can we do for people exposed to multiple traumatic events during the coronavirus pandemic? *Asian Journal of Psychiatry, 51*, 102065.

Shultz, J. M., Baingana, F., & Neria, Y. (2015). The 2014 Ebola outbreak and mental health: Current status and recommended response. *JAMA, 313*(6), 567–568.

Speed, S. (2020). The persistence of White supremacy: Indigenous women migrants and the structures of settler capitalism. *American Anthropologist, 122*(1), 76–85.

Starks, B. (2021). The double pandemic: Covid-19 and White supremacy. *Qualitative Social Work, 20*(1–2), 222–224.

Stechemesser, A., Wenz, L., & Levermann, A. (2020). Corona crisis fuels racially profiled hate in social media networks. *EClinicalMedicine, 23*, 100372. https://www.thelancet.com/journals/eclinm/article/PIIS2589-5370(20)30116-4/fulltext

Tajfel, H. E. (1978). *Differentiation between social groups: Studies in the social psychology of intergroup relations.* Academic Press.

Takasaki, K. (2020). Stop AAPI hate reporting center: A model of collective leadership and community advocacy. *Journal of Asian American Studies, 23*(3), 341–351.

Tuan, M. (1998). *Forever foreigners or honorary whites? The Asian ethnic experience today.* Rutgers University Press.

US Department of Justice. (2023). Learn about hate crimes. https://www.justice.gov/hatecrimes/learn-about-hate-crimes

Walker, D., & Daniel Anders, A. (2022). "China virus" and "kung-flu": A critical race case study of Asian American journalists' experiences during COVID-19. *Cultural Studies Critical Methodologies, 22*(1), 76–88.

Wendt, A. (1999). *Social theory of international politics* (Vol. 67). Cambridge University Press.

Williamson, V., & Gelfand, I. (2019). Trump and racism: What do the data say. *Brookings Institute.* https://www.brookings.edu/blog/fixgov/2019/08/14/trump-and-racism-what-do-the-data-say/

Winant, H. (2001). *The world is a ghetto: Race and democracy since World War II.* Basic Books.

Wong, J. A., Yi, S. S., Kwon, S. C., Islam, N. S., Trinh-Shevrin, C., & Đoàn, L. N. (2022). COVID-19 and Asian Americans: Reinforcing the role of community-based organizations in providing culturally and linguistically centered care. *Health Equity, 6*(1), 278–290.

Wu, L., & Nguyen, N. (2022). From yellow peril to model minority and back to yellow peril. *Aera Open, 8*, 23328584211067796.

Yellow Horse, A. J., & Chen, T. (2022). Two years and thousands of voices: What community-generated data tells us about Anti-AAPI hate. *Stop AAPI Hate.* https://stopaapihate.org/wp-content/uploads/2022/07/Stop-AAPI-Hate-Year-2-Report.pdf

Yi, S. S., Đoàn, L. N., Choi, J. K., Wong, J. A., Russo, R., Chin, M., . . . Kwon, S. C. (2021). With no data, there's no equity: Addressing the lack of data on COVID-19 for Asian American communities. *eClinicalMedicine, 41*, 101165.

Yoo, H. C., Gee, G. C., & Takeuchi, D. (2009). Discrimination and health among Asian American immigrants: Disentangling racial from language discrimination. *Social Science & Medicine, 68*(4), 726–732.

Yu, N., Pan, S., Yang, C.-c., & Tsai, J.-Y. (2020). Exploring the role of media sources on COVID-19–related discrimination experiences and concerns among Asian people in the United States: Cross-sectional survey study. *Journal of Medical Internet Research, 22*(11), e21684.

Ziems, C., He, B., Soni, S., & Kumar, S. (2020). Racism is a virus: Anti-Asian hate and counterhate in social media during the covid-19 crisis. https://arxiv.org/pdf/2005.12423v2

3
Acculturation, the Asian American Identity, and the Impact of Anti-Asian Racism on Health and Mental Health

Keith T. Chan

Introduction

More than 22 million Asian Americans live in the United States. Asian Americans are one of the fastest growing US populations, at a rate faster than any other major race group in the United States (Ruiz et al., 2023). As other chapters in this volume have highlighted, anti-Asian racism surged during the height of the COVID-19 pandemic. Ever since persons of Asian descent have emigrated to and lived in the United States, anti-Asian racism has existed historically and is intricately tied to the marginalized identities of Asian Americans in the United States.

The Asian American identity is an evolving construct and has been shaped by the immigrant identity of this population. Estimates from the US Census (2020) indicated that more than 57% of Asian Americans are foreign-born, and a majority live in multigenerational households with immigrants in their immediate and extended families (Budiman & Ruiz, 2021). The history and shifting identity of Asian Americans are explored in further detail in Chapters 1 and 4 of this volume. A substantive body of research has examined the complexities found within anti-Asian racism, such as the marginalization of Asian identities in colonial and postcolonial contexts as well as the boundaries of where Asian Americans fit in the dichotomy of whiteness and blackness specifically in the United States (Wu, 2014). While a majority of persons of Asian descent in the United States identify strongly with their culture of origin, approximately 1 in 5 identify as Asian American (Ruiz et al., 2023). This appears to differ based on ethnicity and length of time living in the United States as well as on citizenship status. Past research has investigated the dual nature of the relationship of acculturation and anti-Asian racism, in that acculturation may lead to better outcomes in some cases or worse outcomes in others. For those who are foreign-born, poor language acculturation may be linked to fewer opportunities for workplace advancement and lower economic status, which can lead to the compounding effect of poverty (Takei & Sakamoto, 2011). Acculturation seems to account for the deep bifurcation or multifurcation in health and socioeconomic status (SES), which may be explained by exposure to discrimination and structural inequalities (Viruell-Fuentes et al., 2012). These complexities in the relationship of acculturation with discrimination and health may be based on ethnic variations, differences in immigration pathways, consequences of employment in the United States, and other factors across the life span. In metropolitan areas such as New York City, Asian Americans have the highest poverty rates compared with any other race group (Chan & Marsack-Topolewski, 2022). Scholarship has highlighted that structural factors may explain disparities experienced by immigrants (Portes & Rumbaut, 2006; Viruell-Fuentes et al., 2012), and this can be understood through the examination of discrimination perceived by Asian Americans in the United States. In the context of this framework, understanding the relationship of acculturation with exposure to discrimination may further explain differences in well-being, service utilization, and other health outcomes for Asian Americans across the life span.

Anti-Asian Racism and Impact on Overall Health

Social work scholars and other health-related researchers have highlighted the deleterious impact of racism on physical and mental health directed at persons of Asian descent. For example, past research which examined perceived discrimination among Asian Americans has found that it is negatively associated with health outcomes such as health status (Gee et al., 2009), chronic health conditions (Gee, Spencer, Chen, & Takeuchi, 2007), and mental health (Chau et al., 2018; Gee, Spencer, Chen, Yip et al., 2007; Singh et al., 2017). Furthermore, these effects can differ based on ethnicity, immigrant status, and level of language acculturation, as well as access to medical care and level of support in workplace and social settings.

Research has suggested that Asian Americans who lived longer lengths of time in the United States tend to experience more perceived discrimination, which exacerbates other risk factors on health outcomes (Carlisle & Stone, 2015; Siordia & Covington-Ward, 2016). Higher levels of perceived discrimination were associated with more intergenerational conflict and, in turn, with more depressive symptoms for both US and foreign-born Asian Americans (Cheng et al., 2015). It appears that the effect of perceived discrimination on psychological distress varies according to age and ethnic identity and that ethnic identity increases the negative effects of discrimination on the mental health of older adults (Yip et al., 2008). Perceived discrimination had a stronger effect on psychological distress for Asian Americans with more education, which may be explained by the *exposure hypothesis*, in that those who are educated are more likely to work in sectors with greater exposure to instances of discrimination (Zhang & Hong, 2013). In another study, the relationship between perceived discrimination and psychological distress was also stronger for those educated outside the United States (Zhang & Hong, 2013). It is possible that those who received their education in another country experienced more difficulties in acculturating to different customs and practices, which may lead to more perceived discrimination. A different line of research has suggested that greater acculturation and identifying as Asian American, such as becoming a US citizen, may be associated with greater sensitivity to unfair treatment based on one's own race, as well as greater exposure to instances of anti-Asian racism in places where one lives, works, plays, attends school, and visits places of engagement in everyday activities (Chan, 2020).

Anti-Asian Racism and Physical Health

Research that examined population-level effects of anti-Asian racism on the health outcomes of Asian Americans were primarily based on smaller samples until the early 1990s. Findings from a sample of 1,503 Chinese Americans living in Los Angeles from 1993 to 1994 indicated that racial/ethnic, language, and accent discrimination were associated with poor health status even when controlling for sociodemographic and acculturation variables (Gee, 2002). Analyses on data from 2,241 Filipino Americans living in San Francisco from 1998 to 1999 suggested that reporting unfair treatment was associated with increased illness, even after controlling for SES, acculturation, ethnic identity, and negative life events (Gee et al., 2006).

In 2002 and 2003, the National Latino and Asian American Study (NLAAS) was collected as the first dataset of its kind to examine socioepidemiological factors on health; it included 2,095 Chinese, Filipino, and Vietnamese individuals along with a smaller subgroup described as "other Asians." Since that time, a substantive body of research based on this dataset has identified perceived discrimination, measured by the Williams Everyday Discrimination Scale (EDS), as a risk factor for a multitude of health conditions. The EDS, developed by Williams and colleagues (1997), has been found to be negatively associated with physical health and psychological well-being for all race groups in epidemiological surveys (Kessler et al., 1999; Ryff et al., 2003). For example, perceived discrimination was associated with lower mental health outcomes for both African Americans (Lewis et al., 2015; Schmitt et al., 2014; Williams & Mohammed, 2009) and Asian American populations (Singh et al., 2017; Yip et al., 2008). Measurement validation research has found the EDS to be both reliable and valid for different race groups (Chan et al., 2012; Kim et al., 2014; Lewis et al., 2012), although there is evidence that the measure may be best used as two separate subscales to examine overt and covert forms of discrimination (Barnes et al., 2004; Chan, 2020; Chan et al., 2012).

Research using the National Latino and Asian American Study (NLAAS) data found that for Asian Americans, perceived discrimination was associated with disability domains such as self-care, cognition, mobility, time out of role, and social interactions (Waldman et al., 2022). In terms of chronic illness, perceived discrimination was associated with cardiovascular (heart attack, stroke, heart disease, high blood pressure), respiratory (hay fever, asthma, tuberculosis, emphysema, chronic obstructive pulmonary disease), and pain-related conditions (chronic back or neck problems, headaches, arthritis, ulcers, and other chronic pains issues; Gee et al., 2007). However, the effect of perceived discrimination on chronic illness may be somewhat different across ethnic groups of Asians, where perceived discrimination was associated with cardiovascular conditions for Vietnamese and Chinese but not for Filipinos, and discrimination was associated with pain and respiratory conditions for Vietnamese and Filipinos but not Chinese (Gee et al., 2007). Furthermore, gender differences were found, where perceived discrimination was negatively associated with chronic conditions and mental health issues for Asian women and men, although for Asian women there appears to be a double minority status effect resulting from perceived discrimination due to gender and race (Hahm et al., 2010). Research using the NLAAS data has found that the effects of perceived discrimination on health outcomes operate in interpersonal as well as institutional contexts as psychosocial stressors that have a cumulative effect on health, healthcare quality, and healthcare access. Similarly, population health studies using the California Health Interview Survey (CHIS) and the Population-Based Study of Chinese Elderly (PINE) have found that, among different ethnic subgroups of Asians, perceived discrimination is associated with higher incidences of chronic health conditions and lower overall health status (Dong et al. 2014; Gee et al., 2009; Gee & Ponce, 2010).

Anti-Asian Racism and Mental Health

A robust body of research has established the link between anti-Asian racism and poor mental health outcomes such as depression (Chau et al., 2018; Cheng et al., 2015), anxiety (Singh et al., 2017), symptoms of posttraumatic stress disorder (PTSD) (Spencer et al., 2010), and increased suicidal ideations (Cheng et al., 2010; Dong et al., 2014; Li et al., 2018). Although Asian Americans seem to report lower rates of mental health problems, this may be misleading due to patterns of underreporting and underidentification of mental health problems (Spencer et al., 2010). The reasons for this underreporting and underidentification among Asian American populations are complex, and symptoms related to mental health challenges may sometimes be attributed to chronic conditions (Gee et al., 2007) which may not be recognized by those experiencing these challenges and/or by their providers (Gautam et al., 2011; Ina et al., 2011). Stigma associated with a mental health diagnosis in Asian American communities may also play a role in the underreporting of mental health symptoms and conditions. Overall, it would appear that a culturally specific framework for understanding mental health for Asian American populations is inadequate in the service delivery system, and culturally appropriate treatments continues to be underresourced or unavailable for Asian Americans who need them, which can deter the use of these services (Augsberger et al., 2015; Derr, 2016; Hechanova & Waelde, 2017).

Similar to past research on overall health and physical health, the relationship of anti-Asian racism and mental health has been examined primarily through the lens of perceived discrimination. Findings from a review of evidence on the relationship of racial discrimination and health among Asian

Americans indicated that the majority of studies focused on mental health outcomes such as psychological functioning and depressive disorders along with substance use risk (Gee et al., 2009). The relationship of perceived discrimination with mental health outcomes appeared to operate at multiple ecological levels including family support (Chae et al., 2021), immigration and citizenship status (Chan, 2020), acculturation-related factors (Lueck & Wilson, 2010; Takeuchi, Zane, et al., 2007; Tran et al., 2007), places of school or employment (Hwang & Goto, 2008), and, more recently, bias directed at specific Asian ethnic groups due to public opinion and statements made directly by public officials during the COVID-19 pandemic.

Feeling a sense of support from one's ethnic group and social support network can be protective in managing the impact of anti-Asian racism on one's mental health. Although experiences of discrimination were linked to higher odds for suicidal ideations among Asian Americans, past research has found that identification with one's ethnic group was associated with lower rates of suicidal attempts (Cheng et al., 2010). Similarly, perceived discrimination was linked to higher odds for suicidal ideations among Chinese American seniors, and having positive social relationships from those in their community appeared to buffer against this effect (Li et al., 2018). A strong ethnic/racial identity can be protective because identity development can lead to a better sense of self, which can protect against the negative psychological effects of unfair treatment due to anti-Asian racism. Furthermore, having positive social relationships with others of the same ethnic group may confer culturally specific benefits that can only come from the shared, lived experience of having to cope with anti-Asian racism. However, it seems that the effect of ethnic identity can differ based on ethnicity and other sociodemographic and environmental factors (Ai et al., 2010; Yip, 2018). For example, analysis from NLAAS found that perceived discrimination had a stronger effect for those who identified more strongly with their ethnic group and were middle-aged (31–40) and older (51–75) adults (Yip et al., 2008). The effect of ethnic and racial identity can be complex in that identifying more strongly with one's ethnicity may increase one's sensitivity and awareness of anti-Asian racism, thus serving as a double-edge sword (Yip, 2018). This ambiguity in the effect of ethnic identity may reflect the changing nature of how, developmentally, Asian Americans may feel about their ethnic and racial identity throughout the life course as they navigate adolescence, young adulthood, middle adulthood, and late life. Along the same intersecting lines, the effect of gender discrimination can further exacerbate the impact of anti-Asian racism on mental health, creating a double minority effect for Asian American women (Hahm et al., 2010; Yip, 2018).

Similarly, the impact of acculturation on anti-Asian racism and mental health outcomes appears to be multifaceted and at times contradictory. Lower English proficiency is associated with poorer mental health outcomes, particularly for newer immigrants (Takeuchi, Zane, et al., 2007; Zhang & Ta, 2009), which suggests that those who are less acculturated to American culture may be more vulnerable to anti-Asian racism. Conversely, Asians who are more acculturated may have greater exposure to instances of anti-Asian racism through interactions with others outside of their own cultural groups, in the context of the *exposure hypothesis*. Past research has found that foreign-born Asian older adults who were naturalized reported higher levels of perceived discrimination (Chan, 2020). This may be explained by greater exposure or sensitivity to acts of anti-Asian racism for those who are more acculturated to American culture. By choosing to become an American citizen, foreign-born persons of Asian descent adopt an identity as an American and, by law, forfeit their previous status as a citizen of their country of origin. It is also possible that Asian Americans who naturalize do so in order to participate in civic actions such as voting, as a means to counter acts of anti-Asian racism in their lives and in their communities. Taking personal agency to change the outcomes of anti-Asian racism may lead to more sustainable improvements in one's identity and mental health in the long term.

Anti-Asian Racism and Impact on Mental Health Since the COVID-19 Pandemic

The COVID-19 pandemic increased both the frequency and intensity of anti-Asian racism in the United States, a fact that is well-documented in multiple sources and detailed in other chapters of this volume. Emerging research has provided evidence that anti-Asian racism during the COVID-19 pandemic has led to an increase in psychological distress among Asian Americans due to experienced racial discrimination and perceived racial bias (Shi et al., 2022; Wen et al., 2023). Analysis with disaggregated Asian ethnic groups indicated that, regardless of ethnicity, racial discrimination was associated with psychological distress even when controlling for worries about the pandemic (Okazaki et al., 2022). Among Asian American young adults, vicarious, or second-hand, discrimination such as witnessing racism targeting one's own race group, was associated with race-based stress symptoms even when controlling for having directly experienced discrimination (El Tohamy et al., 2023). Similarly, a study conducted with undergraduate students in the Spring of 2021 indicated that direct and vicarious discrimination was significantly associated with distress among Asian college students in the United States (Macaranas et al., 2023). Vicarious racism was also associated with poorer sleep quality among Asian Americans during the COVID-19 pandemic, which is linked to an overall reduction in mental health status and increase in other health hazards (Yip et al., 2024).

The increase in social media use during COVID-19, which include SMS text messaging, online chats, comments sections, discussion forums, online games, and social networking sites, led to greater exposure to anti-Asian racism, which was associated with higher levels of anxiety, depression, and secondary traumatic stress among a sample of Asian American adults (Layug et al., 2022). Similarly, a separate cross-sectional study of Asians in the United States found that up to a third surveyed experienced some form of discrimination since the start of the pandemic, and stigmatizing cues in social media reports intensified the negative impact of perceived discrimination on mental health (Yu et al., 2020). Vicarious racism also contributed to increased risk of depression and anxiety through heightened vigilance of anti-Asian racism among Asian Americans when they heard about violence and other acts perpetrated against Asian people in the news and on social media (Chae et al., 2021). In a population-based sample of Chinese American families, nearly half of parents and youth reported being directly targeted by COVID-19 racial discrimination online as well as in person, which was associated with poorer mental health outcomes (Cheah et al., 2020).

Anti-Asian Racism and Trauma

Since the start of the COVID-19 pandemic in March 2020, Stop AAPI Hate (2023), as of this writing in November 2023, received more than 11,000 reported hate incidents involving explicit, aggravated violence, harassment, and direct harm such as killings, beatings, and even acid burning. These events, as well as the Atlanta Spa Shooting in the Spring of 2021 and the church shooting in May 2022, represent a continuity in the history of anti-Asian racism, beginning in the 18th century (as outlined in Chapter 1). Asian Americans have experienced persistent racism, marginalizing stereotyping, microaggressions, verbal and physical attacks, hate crimes and harassments motivated by individual-level racism and xenophobia. Furthermore, at the institutional level, the United States has often implicitly or explicitly reinforced, encouraged, or perpetuated anti-Asian racism. This is evidenced by xenophobic and discriminatory rhetoric as well as by exclusionary immigration policies which specifically targeted Asian populations. The effect of anti-Asian racism had a population-level impact on Asians in the United States, one that was exacerbated by the COVID-19 pandemic, and it is not yet known what will be the full extent of its effects on the consciousness and well-being of Asian Americans across the United States.

Although research on the role of anti-Asian racism and its impact on the health and mental health of Asians is limited primarily to the past 30 years, Asian Americans have endured racism since the beginning of our migration and community-building in the United States. This has taken institutionalized forms, such as the various Asian exclusion acts (e.g., Geary Act of 1892) and the internment of Japanese American citizens during World War II, as well as violence committed against Asian American communities throughout periods of xenophobia and anti-Asian fearmongering. Asians Americans have benefited from social reforms and the civil rights movement, gaining legal rights and protections to address racial discrimination in workplace and public settings. In particular, the repeal of various exclusion acts in 1965 ended almost a century of laws prohibiting Asians from immigrating to the United States. Data trends across decades indicate that there was a rise in incomes for Asian Americans after World War II, which may be attributable to lower employment discrimination due to legal protections in the workplace (Hilger, 2016). Driven by waves of mass migration from Asia to the United States beginning in the 1970s, there was a steady growth of ethnic enclaves primarily in urban areas in the Northeast and on the West Coast. For Asian Americans, this change in the circumstances of immigration is intertwined with their experience of racial discrimination. Asians went from racially distinct aliens ineligible for citizenship in the 19th century ("the yellow peril") to "assimilating others" who were not White but definitively not Black (Wu, 2014). The conceptual boundaries of race as White versus non-White were destabilized, and, as Wu (2014) pointed out, the lifting of immigration exclusion for Asians generated new modes of exclusion. It is within the context of these subtle yet profound changes in race-making that anti-Asian racism has affected those Asian Americans who have lived through many of these shifts in their racial and immigration status in the United States.

Explicitly discriminatory laws and policies that enforce unjust, prejudicial treatment of historically disadvantaged minority groups have largely been taken apart since the passage of the Civil Rights Act in 1965. However, racial discrimination appears to have evolved from its overt, violent forms to more subtle, nuanced expressions (Sue, 2010). A growing body of literature has begun to address modern forms of racism as *microaggressions*, which are encoded, everyday messages that are relayed interpersonally and are negative, degrading, or exclusionary (Chau et al., 2018; Sue, 2010). It is in this light that Asians have been controversially referred to as the "model minority." Asian Americans, as an example of definitively non-Black members of the "model minority," were held up as evidence of racial mobility. This simultaneously reinforced a perception of racial liberalization while invalidating the persisting acts of racism and discrimination experienced by Black and Brown people in the United States (Wu, 2014). Specifically, the perceived socioeconomic success of Asian Americans has been used to suggest that laws and policies such as affirmative action, aimed to address past and present discrimination, are no longer needed in this "post-racial" era of the United States. The "model minority" narrative reifies the claim of egalitarianism as a triumph over exclusion while justifying social differences and inequalities. Detrimentally, the model minority stereotype has been used to justify inadequate access to and low utilization of social and health-related services among Asians. Findings from data on Asian Americans in geographically separate neighborhoods indicate persisting health and economic disparities clustered within ethnic and immigrant groups (Vo & Hom, 2018). Although average household incomes have risen for Asian Americans (Pew Research Center, 2013), Asian Americans are the most socioeconomically divided race group in America (Pew Research Center, 2018).

Implication for Advocacy, Policy, and Practice

Before the rise of anti-Asian racism during the COVID-19 pandemic, notably the murder of Vincent Chin in 1982 traumatized the Asian American community into collective action. Various Asian American advocacy organizations and coalitions such as the American Citizens for Justice (ACJ) were formed to advance grassroots advocacy efforts with a national scope that is inclusive of all Asian American ethnic groups (Zia, 2022). Findings from studies outlined earlier in this chapter suggest that there may be long-term effects on the health and mental health of Asian Americans from the rise of anti-Asian hate. It is likely that the memories of these traumatic events will carry into the future as part of the collective memory of Asian Americans, their families, and their communities. Examining the history of Asian Americans from a strength-based perspective, when confronted with racism and collective trauma, there is in response a mobilization and galvanizing of efforts from Asian Americans across different ethnicities, religious beliefs, and political agendas to advocate collectively for our populations. This may include advocacy to address anti-Asian racism as a health-adjacent issue as it relates to the prevention and treatment of chronic health conditions and mental health disorders. A comprehensive, culturally specific framework for understanding health and mental health for Asian American populations is sorely needed, especially in light of ongoing anti-Asian racism in the United States. More funding is needed for culturally and ethnically appropriate treatments which can be made available for Asian Americans and their families in the diverse geographic areas where they reside.

Conclusion

Research findings presented in this chapter indicate that Asian Americans have real needs in terms of health and mental health care due to their unique circumstances as a culturally diverse and ethnically distinct population. Acculturation plays an important role across the life span in health and mental health outcomes for many Asians who arrive as immigrants in the United States, and this may have an intergenerational impact on their children who live and grow in the US communities in which they reside. Healthcare systems can better serve Asian Americans through enhanced engagement, improved identification, and greater awareness of the health and mental health needs of this population.

References

Ai, A. L., Nicdao, E. G., Appel, H. B., & Lee, D. H. J. (2015). Ethnic identity and major depression in Asian American subgroups nationwide: Differential findings in relation to subcultural contexts. *Journal of Clinical Psychology, 71*, 1225–1244. doi:10.1002/jclp.22214

Augsberger, A., Yeung, A., Dougher, M., & Hahm, H. C. (2015). Factors influencing the underutilization of mental health services among Asian American women with a history of depression and suicide. *BMC Health Services Research, 15*(1). https://doi.org/10.1186/s12913-015-1191-7

Barnes, L. L., De Leon, C.F.M., Wilson, R. S., Bienias, J. L., Bennett, D. A., & Evans, D. A. (2004). Racial differences in perceived discrimination in a community population of older blacks and whites. *Journal of Aging and Health, 16*, 315–337. doi: 10.1177/0898264304264202

Budiman, A., & Ruiz, N. (2021). Key facts about Asian Americans, a diverse and growing population. Pew Research Center. https://www.pewresearch.org/short-reads/2021/04/29/key-facts-about-asian-americans/

Carlisle, S. K., & Stone, A. L. (2015). Effects of perceived discrimination and length of residency on the health of foreign-born populations. *Journal of Racial and Ethnic Health Disparities, 2*(4), 434–444.

Chae, D. H., Yip, T., Martz, C. D., Chung, K., Richeson, J. A., Hajat, A., Curtis, D. S., Rogers, L. O., & LaVeist, T. A. (2021). Vicarious racism and vigilance during the COVID-19 pandemic: Mental health implications among Asian and Black Americans. *Public Health Reports (Washington, D.C.: 1974), 136*(4), 508–517. https://doi.org/10.1177/0033354921 1018675

Chan, K. (2020). The association of acculturation with overt and covert perceived discrimination for older Asian Americans. *Social Work Research, 44*(1), 59–71. https://doi.org/10.1093/swr/svz023

Chan, K., & Marsack-Topolewski, C. (2022). Ethnic and neighborhood differences in poverty and disability among older Asian Americans in New York City. *Social Work in Public Health, 37*(30), 258–273. https://doi.org/10.1080/19371918.2021.2000916

Chan, K. T., Tran, T. V., & Nguyen, T. (2012). Cross-cultural equivalence of a measure of perceived discrimination between Chinese-Americans and Vietnamese-Americans. *Journal of Ethnic & Cultural Diversity in Social Work, 21*(1), 20–36. doi:10.1080/15313204.2011.647348

Chau, V., Bowie, J., & Juon, H. (2018). The association of perceived discrimination and depressive symptoms among Chinese, Korean, and Vietnamese Americans. *Cultural Diversity & Ethnic Minority Psychology, 24*, 389–399. doi:10.1037/cdp0000183

Cheah, C. S. L., Wang, C., Ren, H., Zong, X., Cho, H. S., & Xue, X. (2020). COVID-19 racism and mental health in Chinese American families. *Pediatrics, 146*(5), e2020021816. https://doi.org/10.1542/peds.2020-021816

Cheng, H., Cha, C., & Lin, S. (2015). Perceived discrimination, intergenerational family conflicts, and depressive symptoms in foreign-born and U.S.-born Asian American emerging adults. *Asian American Journal of Psychology, 6*, 107–116. doi:10.1037/a0038710

Cheng, J. K. Y., Fancher, T. L., Ratanasen, M., Conner, K. R., Duberstein, P. R., Sue, S., & Takeuchi, D. (2010). Lifetime suicidal ideation and suicide attempts in Asian Americans. *Asian American Journal of Psychology, 1*(1), 18–30. https://doi.org/10.1037/a0018799

Derr, A. S. (2016). Mental health service use among immigrants in the United States: A systematic review. *Psychiatric Services, 67*(3), 265–274. https://doi.org/10.1176/appi.ps.201500004

Dong, X., Chen, R., & Simon, M. A. (2014). Experience of discrimination among U.S. Chinese older adults. *Journals of Gerontology. Series A, Biological Sciences and Medical Sciences, 69*(Suppl 2), S76–S81. https://doi.org/10.1093/gerona/glu150

El Tohamy, A., Hyun, S., Rastogi, R., Finneas Wong, G. T., Kim, G. S., Chae, D. H., Hahm, H. C., & Liu, C. H. (2023). Effect of vicarious discrimination on race-based stress symptoms among Asian American young adults during the COVID-19 pandemic. *Psychological Trauma*, 10.1037/tra0001480. Advance online publication. https://doi.org/10.1037/tra 0001480

Gautam, R., Saito, T., Houde, S. C., & Kai, I. (2011). Social interactions and depressive symptoms among community dwelling older adults in Nepal: A synergic effect model. *Archives of Gerontology and Geriatrics, 53*(1), 24–30. https://doi.org/10.1016/j.arch ger.2010.06.007

Gee, G. C. (2002). A multilevel analysis of the relationship between institutional and individual racial discrimination and health status. *American Journal of Public Health, 92*(4), 615–623. https://doi.org/10.2105/ajph.92.4.615

Gee, G. C., Chen, J., Spencer, M. S., See, S., Kuester, O. A., Tran, D., & Takeuchi, D. (2006). Social support as a buffer for perceived unfair treatment among Filipino Americans: Differences between San Francisco and Honolulu. *American Journal of Public Health, 96*(4), 677–684. https://doi.org/10.2105/AJPH.2004.060442

Gee, G. C., & Ponce, N. (2010). Associations between racial discrimination, limited English proficiency, and health-related quality of life among 6 Asian ethnic groups in California. *American Journal of Public Health, 100*(5), 888–895. 10.2105/AJPH.2009.178012

Gee, G. C., Ro, A., Shariff-Marco, S., & Chae, D. (2009). Racial discrimination and health among Asian Americans: Evidence, assessment, and directions for future research. *Epidemiologic Reviews, 31*, 130–151. 10.1093/epirev/mxp009

Gee, G. C., Spencer, M. S., Chen, J., & Takeuchi, D. (2007). A nationwide study of discrimination and chronic health conditions among Asian Americans. *American Journal of Public Health, 97*(7), 1275–1282. 10.2105/AJPH.2006.091827

Gee, G. C., Spencer, M., Chen, J., Yip, T., & Takeuchi, D. (2007). The association between self-reported racial discrimination and 12-month DSM-IV mental disorders among Asian Americans nationwide. *Social Science & Medicine, 64*, 1984–1996. https://10.1016/j.socscimed.2007.02.013

Hahm, H. C., Ozonoff, A., Gaumond, J., & Sue, S. (2010). Perceived discrimination and health outcomes a gender comparison among Asian-Americans nationwide. *Women's Health Issues, 20*(5), 350–358. https://doi.org/10.1016/j.whi.2010.05.002

Hechanova, R., & Waelde, L. C. (2017). The influence of culture on disaster mental health and psychosocial support interventions in Southeast Asia. *Mental Health, Religion & Culture, 20*(1), 31–44. https://doi.org/10.1080/13674676.2017.1322048

Hilger, N. (2016). *Upward mobility and discrimination: The case of Asian Americans* (NBER Working Paper No. w22748). National Bureau of Economic Research. https://www.nber.org/papers/w22748

Hwang, W.-C., & Goto, S. (2008). The impact of perceived racial discrimination on the mental health of Asian American and Latino college students. *Cultural Diversity and Ethnic Minority Psychology, 14*(4), 326–335. https://doi.org/10.1037/1099-9809.14.4.326

Ina, K., Hayashi, T., Nomura, H., Ishitsuka, A., Hirai, H., & Iguchi, A. (2011). Depression, quality of life (QoL) and will to live of community-dwelling postmenopausal women in three Asian countries: Korea, China and Japan. *Archives of Gerontology and Geriatrics, 53*(1), 8–12. https://doi.org/10.1016/j.archger.2010.05.010

Kessler, R. C., Mickelson, K. D., & Williams, D. R. (1999). The prevalence, distribution, and mental health correlates of perceived discrimination in the United States. *Journal of Health and Social Behavior, 40*, 208–230.

Kim, J., & Choi, N. G. (2010). Twelve-month prevalence of DSM-IV mental disorders among older Asian Americans: Comparison with younger groups. *Aging & Mental Health, 14*(1), 90–99.

Layug, A., Krishnamurthy, S., McKenzie, R., & Feng, B. (2022). The impacts of social media use and online racial discrimination on Asian American mental health: Cross-sectional survey in the United States During COVID-19. *JMIR Formative Research, 6*(9), e38589. https://doi.org/10.2196/38589

Lewis, T. T., Cogburn, C. D., & Williams, D. R. (2015). Self-reported experiences of discrimination and health: Scientific advances, ongoing controversies, and emerging issues. *Annual Review of Clinical Psychology, 11*, 407–440.

Lewis, T. T., Yang, F. M., Jacobs, E. A., & Fitchett, G. (2012). Racial/ethnic differences in responses to the Everyday Discrimination Scale: A differential item functioning analysis. *American Journal of Epidemiology, 175*, 391–401. doi:10.1093/aje/kwr287

Li, L. W., Gee, G. C., & Dong, X. (2018). Association of self-reported discrimination and suicide ideation in older Chinese Americans. *American Journal of Geriatric Psychiatry, 26*(1), 42–51. 10.1016/j.jagp.2017.08.006

Lueck, K., & Wilson, M. (2010). Acculturative stress in Asian immigrants: The impact of social and linguistic factors. *International Journal of Intercultural Relations, 34*(1), 47–57. doi:10.1016/j.ijintrel.2009.10.004

Macaranas, A. R., El Tohamy, A., Hyun, S., Chae, D. H., Stevens, C., Chen, J. A., & Liu, C. H. (2023). COVID-19-related direct and vicarious racial discrimination: Associations with psychological distress among U.S. college students. *Journal of Affective Disorders, 325,* 747–754. https://doi.org/10.1016/j.jad.2023.01.009

Okazaki, S., Lee, C. S., Prasai, A., Chang, D. F., & Yoo, N. (2022). Disaggregating the data: Diversity of COVID-19 stressors, discrimination, and mental health among Asian American communities. *Frontiers in Public Health, 10,* 956076. https://doi.org/10.3389/fpubh.2022.956076

Pew Research Center. (2013). *The rise of Asian Americans.* http://www.pewsocialtrends.org/2012/06/19/the-rise-of-asian-americans/

Pew Research Center. (2018). *Income inequality in the U.S. is rising most rapidly among Asians: Asians displace blacks as the most economically divided group in the U.S.* https://www.pewsocialtrends.org/2018/07/12/income-inequality-in-the-u-s-is-rising-most-rapidly-among-asians/

Portes, A., & Rumbaut, R. G. (2006). *Immigrant America: A portrait* (3rd, revised, expanded and updated). University of California Press.

Ruiz, N. G., Noe-Bustamante, L., Shah, S., & Klein, H. (2023). *Diverse cultures and shared experiences shape Asian American identities.* Pew Research Center. https://www.pewresearch.org/wp-content/uploads/sites/20/2023/05/RE_2023.05.08_Asian-American-Identity_Report.pdf

Ryff, C. D., Keyes, C. L., & Hughes, D. L. (2003). Status inequalities, perceived discrimination, and eudaimonic well-being: Do the challenges of minority life hone purpose and growth? *Journal of Health and Social Behavior, 44,* 275–291.

Schmitt, M. T., Branscombe, N. R., Postmes, T., & Garcia, A. (2014). The consequences of perceived discrimination for psychological well-being: A meta-analytic review. *Psychological Bulletin, 140,* 921–948.

Shi, L., Zhang, D., Martin, E., Chen, Z., Li, H., Han, X., Wen, M., Chen, L., Li, Y., Li, J., Chen, B., Ramos, A. K., King, K. M., Michaud, T., & Su, D. (2022). Racial discrimination, mental health and behavioral health during the COVID-19 pandemic: A national survey in the United States. *Journal of General Internal Medicine, 37*(10), 2496–2504. https://doi.org/10.1007/s11606-022-07540-2

Singh, S., Schulz, A. J., Neighbors, H. W., & Griffith, D. M. (2017). Interactive effect of immigration-related factors with legal and discrimination acculturative stress in predicting depression among Asian American immigrants. *Community Mental Health Journal, 53,* 638–646. doi:10.1007/s10597-016-0064-9

Siordia, C., & Covington-Ward, Y. D. (2016). Association between perceived ethnic discrimination and health: Evidence from the National Latino and Asian American Study (NLAAS). *Journal of Frailty & Aging, 5,* 111–117. doi:10.14283/jfa.2016.90

Spencer, M. S., Chen, J., Gee, G. C., Fabian, C. G., & Takeuchi, D. T. (2010). Discrimination and mental health-related service use in a national study of Asian Americans. *American Journal of Public Health, 100,* 2410–2417.

Stop AAPI Hate. (2023). *2023 data update.* https://stopaapihate.org/

Sue, D. W. (2010). Microaggressions, marginality, and oppression: An introduction. In D. W. Sue (Ed.), *Microaggressions and marginality* (pp. 3–24). Wiley.

Takei, I., & Sakamoto, A. (2011). Poverty among Asian Americans in the 21st century. *Sociological Perspectives, 54*(2), 251–276. doi:10.1525/sop.2011.54.2.251

Takeuchi, D. T., Hong, S., Gile, K., & Alegría, M. (2007). Developmental contexts and mental disorders among Asian Americans. *Research in Human Development, 4*(1–2), 49–69. doi:10.1080/15427600701480998

Takeuchi, D., Zane, N., Hong, S., Chae, D., Gong, F., Gee, G.,Walton, E., Sue, S., & Alegria, M. (2007). Immigrant-related factors and mental disorders among Asian Americans. *American Journal of Public Health, 97*, 84–90.

Tran, T. V., Manalo, V., & Nguyen, V. T. D. (2007). Nonlinear relationship between length of residence and depression in a community-based sample of Vietnamese Americans. *International Journal of Social Psychiatry, 53*(1), 85–94.

US Census Bureau. (2020). Facts for Features: Asian/Pacific American Heritage Month: May 2021. https://www.census.gov/newsroom/releases/archives/facts_for_features_special_editions/cb11-ff06.html

Viruell-Fuentes, E. A., Miranda, P. Y., & Abdulrahim, S. (2012). More than culture: Structural racism, intersectionality theory, and immigrant health. *Social Science & Medicine, 75*, 2099–2106. doi:10.1016/j.socscimed.2011.12.037

Vo, L. T., & Hom, L. D. (2018). Transforming Orange County: Assets and needs of Asian Americans & Native Hawaiians and Pacific Islanders. Asian Americans Advancing Justice – Orange County. https://transformingoc.advancingjustice-oc.org/AAAJ-OC_fullBook1.pdf

Waldman, K., Stickley, A., Araujo Dawson, B., & Oh, H. (2022). Racial discrimination and disability among Asian and Latinx populations in the United States. *Disability and Rehabilitation, 44*(1), 96–105. 10.1080/09638288.2020.1760363

Wen, M., Shi, L., Zhang, D., Li, Y., Chen, Z., Chan, B., Chen, L., Zhang, L., Li, H., Li, J., & Su, D. (2023). Racial-ethnic disparities in psychological distress during the COVID-19 pandemic in the United States: the role of experienced discrimination and perceived racial bias. *BMC Public Health, 23*(957). https://doi.org/10.1186/s12889-023-15912-4

Williams, D. R., & Mohammed, S. A. (2009). Discrimination and racial disparities in health: Evidence and needed research. *Journal of Behavioral Medicine, 32*, 20–47. doi:10.1007/s10865-008-9185-0

Williams, D. R., Yu, Y., Jackson, J. S., & Anderson, N. B. (1997). Racial differences in physical and mental health: Socio-economic status, stress and discrimination. *Journal of Health Psychology, 2*(3), 335–351. https://doi.org/10.1177/135910539700200305

Wu, E. (2014). *The color of success: Asian Americans and the origins of the model minority*. Princeton University Press.

Yip, T. (2018). Ethnic/racial identity: A double-edged sword? Associations with discrimination and psychological outcomes. *Current Directions in Psychological Science, 27*(3), 170–175. https://doi.org/10.1177/0963721417739348

Yip, T., Chung, K., & Chae, D. H. (2024). Vicarious racism, ethnic/racial identity, and sleep among Asian Americans. *Cultural Diversity & Ethnic Minority Psychology, 30*(2), 319–329. https://doi.org/10.1037/cdp0000534

Yip, T., Gee, G. C., & Takeuchi, D. T. (2008). Racial discrimination and psychological distress: The impact of ethnic identity and age among immigrant and United States-born Asian adults. *Developmental Psychology, 44*, 787–800. doi:10.1037/0012-1649.44.3.787

Yu, N., Pan, S., Yang, C. C., & Tsai, J. Y. (2020). Exploring the role of media sources on COVID-19-related discrimination experiences and concerns among Asian people in the United States: Cross-sectional survey study. *Journal of Medical Internet Research, 22*(11), e21684. https://doi.org/10.2196/21684

Zhang, W., & Hong, S. (2013). Perceived discrimination and psychological distress among Asian Americans: Does education matter? *Journal of Immigrant and Minority Health, 15*, 932–943. doi:10.1007/s10903-012-9676-5

Zhang, W., & Ta, V. M. (2009). Social connections, immigration-related factors, and self-rated physical and mental health among Asian Americans. *Social Science & Medicine, 68*, 2104–2112. doi:10.1016/j.socscimed.2009.04.012

Zia, H. (2022). The Vincent Chin Legacy guide: Asian Americans building the movement. https://www.vincentchin.org/legacy-guide

4
The Intersection of Racism and Marginalized Identities Among Asian Americans

Jun Sung Hong, Sofie Hana Aaron, Cindy C. Sangalang, Jane J. Lee, and Joong Won Kim

Diversity of Asian Identities in America

Asian Americans are among the fastest-growing racial/ethnic groups in the United States (Budiman & Ruiz, 2021). The growth of the Asian population in the United States has been driven by sustained immigration and refugee resettlement during the 1970s and 1980s, and has doubled since the 1980s (Asia Society, 2023a). According to the World Population Review (2023), the Asian population in the United States comprised 5.6% of the total population in 2023. The largest Asian groups in the United States are Chinese (>5.0 million), Indian (>4.4 million), and Filipino (>4.0 million) origin. However, the 22 million Asians currently residing in the United States can trace their roots to more than 20 countries in East and Southeast Asia and the Indian subcontinent (Pew Research Center, 2021).

Despite the unique and distinct Asian populations in the United States, data on this population have traditionally been aggregated, which tends to obscure critical within-group differences and information on disparities (Kauh et al., 2021). Furthermore, Asian Americans have tended to be grouped with Pacific Islanders under the Asian American and Pacific Islander umbrella (USA Facts, 2021). Experiences associated with anti-Asian–related xenophobia and discriminatory acts in the wake of the COVID-19 pandemic in 2019 underscored essential differences across the

Jun Sung Hong, Sofie Hana Aaron, Cindy C. Sangalang, Jane J. Lee, and Joong Won Kim, *The Intersection of Racism and Marginalized Identities Among Asian Americans* In: *Addressing Anti-Asian Racism with Social Work, Advocacy, and Action.* Edited by: Meirong Liu and Keith T. Chan, Oxford University Press. © Oxford University Press 2024. DOI: 10.1093/oso/9780197672242.003.0004

Asian American community. Undocumented, low-income, elderly, and limited English-proficient Asians were most adversely affected by COVID-19 and were less likely to seek help due to perceived anti-Asian xenophobia (Le et al., 2020). While aggregated data suggest that Asians are less likely than the overall US population to live in poverty, disaggregated data on Asian American subgroups revealed that Burmese and Bhutanese have a poverty rate that is significantly higher than the average in the United States (Lopez et al., 2017). These findings suggest that Asians in the United States tend to differ in sociodemographic characteristics such as language, educational attainment, socioeconomic status, insurance coverage, and health outcomes (Yom & Lor, 2022). It is also likely that their experiences of racism differ when other aspects of their social identities, such as citizenship/immigration status, socioeconomic status (SES), sex, sexual orientation/gender identity, multiracial identities, and religiosity/spirituality, are considered. This chapter focuses on intersecting identities and how they might foster or inhibit racism experienced by Asians in the United States. We highlight the potential implications of these perspectives for future research and social work practice.

Racism and Intersection of Identities Among Asians in the United States

Crenshaw (1989) proposed that "the intersectional experience is greater than the sum of racism and sexism" and "any analysis that does not take intersectionality into account cannot sufficiently address the particular manner in which Black women are subordinated" (p. 140). Crenshaw (1989) first coined the term "intersectionality," although the root of the concept of intersectionality can be traced back to Sojourner Truth's "Ain't I a Woman" speech in 1851 (Muirhead et al., 2020). Intersectionality was developed by feminists and critical race theorists to consider the meaning and consequences of multiple categories of social identities (Cole, 2009). Intersectionality as a framework facilitates understanding of how two or more aspects of social identities (e.g., race, immigration status, sex, and sexual orientation/gender identity) might intersect to derive privilege and penalties (Evans-Winter, 2021).

Citizenship/Immigrant Status

Xenophobia targeted at Asian immigrants in the United States is nothing new: Asians in the United States have confronted a long history of exclusion and inequity related to immigration policies. Anti-immigration affecting Asians could be traced to the mid-19th century, when thousands of Chinese laborers first migrated to the United States for transcontinental railroad labor. Chinese, Japanese, and South Asians were among the largest Asian ethnic groups who migrated to the Americas from the late 19th to early 20th centuries (Lee, 2007). Retaining ties to their homelands and forming diasporic communities, they were targets of some of the first federal immigration laws that excluded immigrants based on race (Lee, 2007). Chinatowns, where Chinese immigrants settled, were regarded as dangerous places where drugs, gambling, and prostitution were prominent (Sabharwal et al., 2022). The stereotypes of Chinatowns as "foreign" and "uncivilized," combined with fear of Chinese immigration, set the precedent for the passage of anti-immigration policies, such as the Chinese Exclusion Act (CEA) of 1882, which banned all Chinese from entering the United States (Calavita, 2000). However, between 1882 and 1920, approximately 17,300 Chinese entered the United States through Canada and Mexico (Lee, 2003).

In the aftermath of the CEA, a large number of Japanese laborers, along with Koreans and Indians, arrived to replace the Chinese for cheap labor in various sectors (Asia Society, 2023b), which was soon followed by anti-Japanese laws. Later, a series of anti-Asian legislations were passed: the Immigration Act of 1917 (Asiatic Barred Zone Act), which was aimed at preventing "undesirables" from migrating to the United States; the Johnson-Reed Immigration Act of 1924, which curbed Japanese immigration (Wang, 2008); and the Tydings-McDuffie Act of 1935, which placed an annual quota on Filipino migration (Sobredo, 2018). It was not until 1952 when Asian immigrants were granted naturalization rights (Kilty, 2002).

Tangentially came states passing anti-miscegenation laws (barring interracial marriages) with anyone of Asian and White descent, beginning with Japanese and Chinese individuals, and these policies eventually extended to anyone with more than one-eighth of "Mongolian, Malay, or Asiatic" blood (Sohoni, 2007, p. 608). It wasn't until 1967 that these laws were deemed unconstitutional, yet, much like in the aftermath of the granting of naturalization rights in 1952, there was still "the presumption of foreignness as part of the socially constructed racial identity" of being Asian (Saito, 1997). This presumption of foreignness is a sentiment that lingers to this day.

The COVID-19 pandemic in 2020 reinforced anti-immigrant sentiments in the United States, which were heightened by a racist and xenophobic discourse by political leaders and politicians ("kung flu"), polarized views on undocumented immigration, fear of "invasion," competition for jobs and resources, and spreading of inaccurate information (Garcini et al., 2020). In the aftermath of the pandemic, immigrants from Central and Latin American and Asian countries were confronted with a series of attacks, such as raids by Immigration and Customs Enforcement, threats to the Deferred Action for Childhood Arrival program, separation of families, and restrictions on asylum (Page et al., 2020). Asians, regardless of their citizenship, were under attack for China's perceived role in spreading the COVID-19 pandemic. Anti-Asian sentiment also reinforced the "perpetual foreigner" narrative, which has been especially pervasive since the beginning of the COVID-19 pandemic. The perpetual foreign stereotype purports that certain ethnic minorities will continue to be perceived as the "other" despite their citizenship status (e.g., "Where are you really from?") (Huynh et al., 2011) because they are perceived as being unassimilated to American culture. Wang and Santos's (2022) study identified 11 types of racism commonly experienced by Asian Americans, one of which was being told to go back to an Asian country. The perpetual foreigner narrative also reinforced anti-Chinese sentiment, with people being told that Chinese culture is "backward" and that "unsanitary" Chinese dietary habits were the cause of the COVID-19 pandemic (Borja et al., 2020).

Sexism

The shooting rampage at massage spas in an Atlanta community on March 16, 2021, which left eight people dead (of which six were women of Asian descent) outraged many Asian American women who argued that racism and misogyny are inseparable in their experience (Chang, 2021). Despite the salience of racism and sexism, research that examines the intersectional experience of Asian American women is limited (Mukkamala & Suyemoto, 2018). As Mukkamala and Suyemoto (2018) contend, the limited attention to their intersectional experiences led to an oversimplification of their experiences with racism and sexism by assuming their experiences to be similar to Asian American men and White women. However, Mukkamala and Suyemoto's (2018) findings on the intersectional experiences of discrimination against Asian American women concluded that the stereotype of Asian women as quiet and submissive could create unique experiences of pressure and invisibility, which would create experiences that differ from Asian American men. Also, given that Asian women in the United States experience more than one form of prejudice, they are at a higher risk of victimization than their Asian male counterparts. According to the findings by Stop AAPI Hate, approximately 3,795 anti-Asian hate crimes were reported from March 2020 to February 2021 (Jeung et al., 2021). Of the hate crimes, women made up a far higher percentage of hate crime victimization at 68% compared to men at 29% (Jeung et al., 2021).

Intersectional discrimination against Asian women in the United States, particularly racialized sexual objectification, could be traced to the history of US imperialism. For centuries, the intersection of Orientalism and sexism was pervasive in American society (Forbes et al., 2023). The Page Act in 1875 barred Chinese and Japanese women from migrating to the United States because of stereotypes of Asian women as sex workers who would likely undermine the morality of White men (Zhu, 2010). The Page Act was an anti-prostitution law that paved the way for the CEA in 1882 (Zhu, 2010). However, the public shift from demonizing Asian women to perceiving them as comfort to White men was evident in subsequent policies (Forbes et al., 2023). The War Bride Act of 1945 was later enacted to permit the migration of Japanese, Korean, and Filipina women married to US servicemen (Forbes et al., 2023). Since then, the stereotypical portrayals of Asian women as "dragon ladies" (i.e., hypersexual Asian women) and geisha or "China dolls" (i.e., hyperfeminine and sexually subservient Asian women) have been pervasive in the US media (see Lee, 2018). The sexual objectification of Asian women was also evident in the high rate of sexual trafficking of Asian women for prostitution in the United States (Forbes et al., 2023). We see the monolith and binary of Asian men primarily being undersexualized and weak and Asian women as one-dimensional sexual objects (Matsumoto & Zhang, 2020). These stereotypes additionally intersect in unique and varied ways with those who hold multiracial Asian identities. Frequently, those with mixed backgrounds are boxed into feeling "othered"; often, perceived ambiguity in race and culture leads to exoticization, objectification, and fetishization (Gay et al., 2022).

Sexual Orientation/Gender Identity

In 1991, the Broadway play *Miss Saigon*, set in Vietnam and focused on the relationship between an American serviceman and a Vietnamese woman in a brothel, received an overwhelmingly negative response from the Asian American community (McConnell & Holloway, 2018). Activists argued that the musical reinforced sexism and Orientalism due to the protagonist, a Vietnamese woman, being depicted as a "virgin-turned-prostitute" falling in love with a White American serviceman and dying by suicide as a symbol of her undying love for the serviceman. The Lambda Legal Defense and Education Fund, which championed lesbian, gay, bisexual, transgender, and queer (LGBTQ) rights, used *Miss Saigon* as a fundraising event, drawing protests from the members of the Asian Lesbians of the East Coast and Gay Asian and Pacific Islander Men of New York, along with nearly 500 racial minorities, who perceived the Broadway hit as racist and upholding a history of colorism, orientalism, and colonialism (McConnell & Holloway, 2018). Some actors of Asian descent had been cast, but the role of the "Engineer" (written as half-French, half-Vietnamese) was to be reprised by the White British actor Jonathan Pryce. The Lambda Legal Defense and Education Fund refused to cancel the fundraiser, and, despite protests, Pryce performed the role with tinted foundation and eyelid prosthetics (Paulson, 2017).

Asian American LGBTQ individuals, both as individuals and as a group, face considerable discrimination and prejudice. They frequently encounter homophobia and transphobia in the heterosexual community (including their ethnic community). The intensity of heterosexism tends to be stronger in Asian cultures than in mainstream US culture, and same-sex attraction is seen as violating many traditional values which uphold heterosexuality as the only acceptable form of intimate relationships (Kimmel & Yi, 2004; Szymanski & Sung, 2010). Moreover, many Asian American LGBTQ individuals perceive the Asian American ethnic community as being conservative, rejecting same-sex attraction, and feeling unsupported in their LGBTQ identity (Chung & Szymanski, 2006). In addition, Asian American LGBTQ individuals often face racism in the mainstream LGBTQ community (Chae & Yoshikawa, 2008). An interview study found that Asian gay men reported feeling discriminated against primarily in gay settings (Wilson & Yoshikawa, 2004). The *minority stress theory* can provide a useful framework for understanding the experience of racism and sexism of Asian American LGBTQ individuals. LGBTQ individuals in general experience various forms of minority-related stress, which are similar to other oppressed groups (e.g., racial minorities), such as discrimination, rejection, and prejudice-related events (e.g., hate crime) (McConnell et al., 2018). However, according to the minority stress theory, individuals from multiple oppressed social groups are at significant risk of reporting stress and negative life events due to their nondominant statuses, which potentially exacerbate mental health problems (Meyer, 1995, 2003). Despite the increasing body of empirical research on health disparities in minority populations, research on the mental health and health disparities of multiple-minority individuals (e.g., LGBTQ people of color) is limited (Ramirez & Paz Galupo, 2019). However, extant studies found that being a sexual or gender minority along with being a racial/ethnic minority would likely lead to worse health outcomes. A higher level of health and mental health conditions among LGBTQ people of color than among heterosexual people of color or White LGBTQ individuals has been well documented. For instance, Stepanikova et al.'s (2017) study found higher levels of negative biomarkers that are linked to chronic health problems (e.g., hypertension) for individuals with a high amount of perceived discrimination. There is the additional complexity of exploring sexual orientation and gender identity while navigating microaggressions and discrimination as a biracial or multiracial Asian American, with feelings of dysphoria and feeling forced to validate one identity over another (Taketomo, 2012). Mereish and Bradford (2014) also reported that sexual minority women of color in their study had a higher rate of substance abuse than their heterosexual ethnic minority or White sexual minority counterparts.

Religiosity/Spirituality

The diversity of religious beliefs in the United States has risen to a historical high, and one of the increasingly prominent religious groups in the United States is the Sikhs. Sikhs in the United States are estimated at between 250,000 and 500,000 in number (Joshi, 2006; Smith, 2002). Despite the growing presence of Sikh communities in the United States, they are disproportionately affected by religious bigotry, prejudice, and violence (Sikh Coalition, 2021). According to the US Department of Justice (2023), which released the Federal Bureau of Investigation (FBI) Hate Crime Statistics in 2021, a total of 1,590 religious-based hate crimes were reported, and anti-Sikh incidents constituted the second-largest hate crime. In the aftermath of

9/11, the Sikh Coalition reported receiving thousands of reports from the Sikh community about hate crimes, discrimination and bullying in school and the workplace, and racial and religious profiling (Sikh Coalition, n.d.), which mirror the experiences of Muslims after 9/11 (Abu-Ras & Suarez, 2009; Ahluwalia & Pellettiere, 2011). These experiences are not unique to the Sikh communities, whose residents emigrated from Punjab, India, and have been settled in the United States for more than 130 years. Sikhs have been targets of bias, prejudice, and xenophobic violence for generations, which can be traced to an incident in the early 1900s in Bellingham, Washington, where lumberjacks attacked Sikh mill workers and forced them out of the city (Sikh Coalition, 2021). The racist terrorism experienced by Sikh and South Asian American communities never subsided, and the stress of violence continues to plague the Sikh American community (Singh, 2013). One of the worst attacks occurred on August 5, 2012, when Wade Michael Page, a 40-year-old White supremacist in Oakwood, Wisconsin, shot and murdered six Sikhs in the *gurdwara*, a Sikh place of worship (Sikh Coalition, 2021).

According to Joshi (2006), the racialization of religion ascribes certain phenotypical features to a specific group and is attached to race/ethnicity. The long-standing racialization of religion in the United States perpetuates the privilege of the dominant religious groups (e.g., White Christians). The maintenance of White, Anglo-Saxon purity became tremendously important to many religious leaders, politicians, and citizens, resulting in the marginalization of minority religious groups, such as Hindus, Sikhs, and Muslims. Also, the racial/religious othering that comes with the racialization of religion has historically been used to justify dehumanizing non-Christian groups. Interestingly, as Joshi (2006) pointed out, South Asians have become a part of an undifferentiated category of brown-skinned people and have been associated with the US enemy due to their religious beliefs (i.e., Muslims). Consequently, South Asian Americans, including Hindus, Sikhs, Muslims, and even Christians have been targets of Islamophobia-motivated hate crimes and violence because of their brown skin, a proxy for "Muslim" in the eyes of mainstream Americans (Joshi, 2006).

An estimated 8% of Jews in the United States identify as "Jews of color" (Black, Asian, Hispanic, some other race, or multiracial) (Pew Research Center, 2021). Parallel with rising anti-Asian hate in the United States, there has been a rise in anti-Semitism—with conspiracy theories around COVID-19 also targeting Jews and Israel (Shaheed, 2020). Jewish culture and Asian racial identities fall under the transgression of "model minorities" and have experienced paralleled discriminatory experiences (Freedman, 2005, p. 69). For example, as far back as the 1880s in the United States, Jews, and Chinese laborers were compared and stereotyped as greedy and money hungry, and, with the 1924 Immigration Act, the barring of Asian groups and quota settings were discriminatory racial exclusion policies that inspired Adolph Hitler and Nazi sympathizers in Germany (Freedman, 2005, pp. 83–90; Ross, 2018; Young, 2018). Existing within multiple marginalized spaces, Asian Jews experience anti-Asian hate, anti-Semitism, and microaggressions (Kuhn & Robinson, 2021).

Multiracial and Biracial Identities

In 2000, the US Census Bureau made distinct changes to the race and ethnicity categories to allow respondents to self-identify as "some other race" and also gave individuals the option to select multiple racial categories (Sandefur et al., 2004). That year the Census saw 1.8 million Americans self-identify as Asian in combination with another racial group; this number increased to 4.1 million in 2020 and highlighted the highest population concentrations were in Hawai'i, Nevada, and Washington State (Barnes & Bennett, 2002; Jones et al., 2021; Monte & Shin, 2022; PEW Research, 2023). Much research and curricula operate from a "monoracial-only paradigm of race" and often omit the complexities and unique stressors that emerge from having intersecting racial identities (Harris, 2020; Nadal, 2021).

Historically, with the treatment of multiracial Asians in society, a notable pattern of othering and ostracization has emerged. Abroad, in places such as Japan, following the American occupation (1945–1952), biracial Japanese children (*hāfus*) were often the children of military men and Japanese women and were called *konketsuji* and looked down upon by the community, seen as reminders of having lost the war (Jozuka et al., 2020). In the Filipino community, following the colonization of the Spanish, there were distinct hierarchies created based on blood purity, with *mestizos*—children of mixed marriages—in the middle of the hierarchical ladder (Combs & Johnston-Guerrero, 2022, 2361–2362). In Korea, children of Korean women and United States servicemen following the Korean War, often referred to as "Amerasians," were discriminated against, a practice bolstered by Korean political figures regularly speaking about the impurity of mixed-race unions and refusing to put in place anti-discrimination laws and policies (Halloran,

1976). In the United States, as of 2021, more than 40% of marriages in Hawai'i are interracial, and for many Kānaka Maoli (Native Hawai'ians, the Indigenous people of Ka Pae 'Āina or Hawai'i), this multiracial identity has culminated in the term *hapa* (short for *hapalua*) meaning "part" Kānaka Maoli (Kulesza, 2021). *Hapa* has derogatory roots, originating during colonial times in Hawai'ian history when a self-governed Kānaka Maoli population was driven to work on American-run plantations alongside Chinese, Filipino, Korean, and Japanese immigrant laborers in the early 20th century (Krogstad, 2015). The usage of *hapa* was meant to delegitimize the legacies of Kānaka Maoli sovereignty and put a contingency on blood quantum, so that being mixed somehow minimized one's multiracial identity, despite traditional Kānaka Maoli genealogical practices having no such prior precedent (Boyanton, 2023). Despite this, today *hapa* has been reclaimed to serve as a term of empowerment and self-identification for many mixed-race Kānaka Maoli with Asian ancestries and non-Hawai'ians from Hawai'i with mixed ancestries.

Of the limited studies and reports on multiracial Asian Americans, many are framed in the Asian–White binary and seen through "a white racial frame" (Chong & Song, 2022). Based on multiracial health determinant studies done—which are usually Black–White centric—there is a common trend of community disjointedness and a social sense of rejection with those who identify as Asian in combination with other racial groups (Feagin, 2020, p. 11). Mental health screenings addressing Black, Indigenous, and Other People of Color (BIPOC) and LGBTQ+ mental health indicate that those who identify as multiracial were "most likely to screen positive or at-risk for alcohol/substance use disorders, anxiety, depression, eating disorders, and psychosis" (Mental Health America, 2020). These unique stressors all culminate in the unofficial term, "racial imposter syndrome," which describes the intersectionality and complexities of having contrasting perceived versus personal identities (Donnella, 2018).

There is a reported pattern of insecurity with multiracial Asian Americans in "claiming space" with one's own identity and experiences of filtered discrimination unique to each (Cheang, 2020). Microaggressions and dealing with being the target of unsolicited questions or comments are also a large part of being Asian American and especially play a large part in one's day-to-day multiracial experience. As cited by Nadal et al. (2011), one of the most dominant reported microaggressions identified with multiracial individuals is isolation or exclusion from one of the racial groups they partially identify with. Other reported microaggressions experienced by multiracial Asian Americans are (1) others pathologizing one's racial experiences (i.e., "You don't look Asian enough to really understand"; (2) feeling dehumanized by "racial objectification," (i.e., being asked "What are you?"); (3) and having your identities stereotyped against each other. While there are few studies and reports on this, an example of combative identities can be seen with Naomi Osaka, a mixed-race Japanese Haitian woman who is a four-time Grand Slam singles champion (Gay et al., 2022). In 2019, Osaka renounced her American nationality to retain her Japanese nationality, and, as a result, many Americans felt Osaka "forfeited her Black identity" (Wilkinson, 2021). Following Osaka's first grand slam win, her Haitian identity was also erased from announcements, with articles mainly focusing remarks on her being the first female Japanese player to win (Sang, 2019).

Because most health models and hate crime reporting is monoracially centric, they lack the ability to reflect the complexity of being multiracial. Social workers are in unique positions to advocate for and take into account these intersecting identities of multiracial Asian communities—and should be intentional in creating new models and interventions to benefit and uplift the nuanced identities of multiracial populations.

Implications for Research

Despite well-documented experiences of racism and marginalization among Asian populations in the United States, there remain considerable gaps in research focused on these communities. These gaps are attributed not only to the tendency to overlook the vast heterogeneity of Asian American, Native Hawai'ian, and Pacific Islander (AANHPI) populations but also to limitations in federal investments and legislation that offer systems and resources to support such research (Dong, 2019). A recent study highlighted that only 0.17% of clinical research projects funded by the National Institutes of Health (NIH) between 1992 and 2018 went to studies focused on AANHPI participants (Đoàn et al., 2019). There is a clear need for increased funding and research toward understanding the diverse experiences of Asian communities in the United States that acknowledge the significance of the multiple and intersecting identities of this population.

The NIH's special interest in epidemiologic studies in AANHPIs demonstrates that we currently lack adequate information on how environments and contexts interplay with social, cultural, and biological factors pertinent to AANHPI individuals to impact health (National Institutes of Health, 2021). This chapter points to opportunities for research that can inform the development and implementation of policies and programs to understand these intersecting factors and address the effects of racism on health and well-being. Specifically, attention to current and historical US policies and systems that discriminate against Asian subgroups is critical for understanding health disparities. As extant systems influence the social and political rhetoric that often prompts negative attitudes and perspectives toward different communities, research that extricates stereotypes and exclusionary attitudes from the intersectional identities of Asians in the United States may present multilevel strategies for intervention.

Notably, research on intersectionality can present challenges due to the complexity of individual and group identities. Thus, the heterogenous experiences of Asians in the United States warrant community-engaged approaches that can support culturally relevant research and subsequent strategies to address disparities and marginalization. Building representative research teams can foster participant engagement to enable nuanced perspectives and disaggregate data across identities and subgroups (Kanaya et al., 2022). Furthermore, such partnerships can empower communities, give voice to groups that have been historically marginalized, and support the training of a future workforce that can appropriately serve AANHPI populations in the United States (Wallerstein et al., 2018).

Implications for Social Work Practice

Our overview of historical and contemporary experiences of intersectional racism for Asian Americans offers important implications for policy and practice within social work. Fundamentally, adopting intersectionality as a framework is essential for understanding and attending to the needs, challenges, and strengths of diverse communities within the Asian American population. Social work interventions must operate at multiple levels to dismantle racism alongside other forms of marginalization tied to gender and gender identity, sexual orientation, immigrant status and generation, religion, and other markers of social location. As the field of social work continues to advance anti-racism as a key approach in challenging oppressive systems and advocating for social justice (Council on Social Work

Education, 2023; National Association of Social Workers, 2022), understanding the experiences of Asian Americans alongside other communities of color is necessary for carrying out this work. We highlight a few key implications below.

Increase Education and Awareness. A first step toward more inclusive social work practice is to increase education and awareness of Asian American community experiences and histories. Given the omission of knowledge regarding the struggles and contributions of racialized minority groups in the United States, a greater infusion of ethnic studies content across the educational pipeline can enhance cross-cultural learning within communities broadly as well as support professional training for practitioners working within communities of color (Maglalang et al., 2022). Although there is a growing awareness that the Asian American population is comprised of heterogenous groups representing diverse nationalities, ethnicities, languages, and cultures, it is essential to recognize there is also variation in immigration statuses and histories of migration. For example, some Asian American families—including multiracial Asian Americans—have lived in the United States for multiple generations (Chang et al., 2013), whereas more recently settled Asian immigrants may have immigrated with particular visas or held green cards, arrived as refugees, or are undocumented. These contexts help to explain the complex challenges facing Asian Americans, particularly vulnerable groups such as those who are low-income (Lee et al., 2022), elderly, have limited English proficiency (Le et al., 2020), or have experienced war or migration-related traumas (Sangalang et al., 2022). The expansion of Asian American Studies curriculum in the United States presents opportunities to not only learn about these rich histories from an intersectional perspective (Azhar et al., 2021; Venkataramanan, 2023) but also to demystify and discredit the persistent stereotypes associated with Asian Americans that mask the challenges they face.

Strengthen Culturally Responsive Practices and Community Partnerships. Despite documented needs and challenges, Asian Americans overall have low rates of healthcare and social service utilization compared to other racialized groups (Kim & Keefe, 2010; Oh & Jeong, 2017). These patterns reflect cultural and language challenges as well as structural barriers, including a lack of culturally tailored services, discrimination, financial insecurity, limited access to health insurance, and concerns about sanctions and stigma for accessing public benefits among Asian immigrants, sexual minorities, gender minorities, and older adults (Kim & Keefe, 2010;

Ma et al., 2021; Matthews et al., 2022; Touw et al., 2021). Training social workers and other professionals through the lenses of cultural humility and structural competence (Azhar et al., 2021; Fisher-Borne et al., 2015; Shelton et al., 2019) can aid in developing and implementing more culturally responsive practices across intersectional Asian American communities. In addition, existing ethnic- and community-based organizations that serve and mobilize Asian American communities can provide local expertise on Asian American communities but may have limited financial resources or institutional partners that can expand the scope of their work. Efforts to bolster community engagement and collaboration with these organizations offer promising avenues for closing gaps in services for Asian American populations.

Advocate for Inclusive Policies. Given histories of exclusion and violence, the consequences of racism and intersecting forms of oppression for Asian Americans are long-standing, far-reaching, and occur at multiple levels (Man, 2020). Social work practices must be backed by inclusive and equitable policies that account for ways that past and present forms of racism and xenophobia intersect with sexism, heterosexism, transphobia, bigotry toward religious minorities, class-based oppression, and other forms of discrimination in contributing to challenges and disparities affecting Asian American communities. In addition, funding at federal, state, and local levels is needed to expand research and services that attend to the needs of the Asian American population at large. Finally, concurrent efforts to collect population-based data disaggregated by ethnic group are essential to assessing the diverse and complex needs reflected across Asian American communities (Shimkhada et al., 2021).

Conclusion

Along with our implications for practice, it is also critical to increase racial awareness of Asian Americans and focus on the historical context of diversity, equity, and inclusion. As various theorists of race and ethnicity have argued, Asian Americans are triangulated, and the experiences of anti-Asian racism must be parceled out of the analysis (Ferguson, 2012; Kim, 1999). It is also essential to pay attention to the ways that racial stratification is triracial, driving a wedge between two racial minority groups, such as African Americans and Asian Americans (Eng & Han, 2019; Kim, 1999). This is important because research often obfuscates the complex racial biographies and experiences of Asian Americans. For example, the term "Asian American, Pacific Islander, and Desi Americans" (APIDA) does not adequately capture the complexities of the particular ethnic group that passes as Chinese, thus falling into xenophobia-based racial discrimination. Yet knowledge and cultural understanding of race (e.g., ethnoracial) is uncritical of the racial gray area in which Asian Americans are racialized and subjected to particular forms of sexism and racism, even at the level of the academic understanding that obscures rather than clarifies data on Asian Americans, one of the fastest growing racial and ethnic group in the United States. This raises important questions about how to first conceptualize diversity and inclusion of Asian Americans given the compilation of national identities that factor heavily into, for example, the intraethnic divide (Eng & Han, 2019; Kim, 1999). Also, given the current racial climate regarding affirmative action, it is critical not to forget significant historical moments when Asian Americans made alliances with other racial/ethnic minority groups, such as the Black Power movement, which was aimed at uplifting all.

References

Abu-Ras W. M., & Suarez Z. E. (2009). Muslim men and women's perception of discrimination, hate crimes, and PTSD symptoms post 9/11. *Traumatology*, *15*(3), 48–63.

Ahluwalia, M. K., & Pellettiere, L. (2010). Sikh men post-9/11: Misidentification, discrimination, and coping. *Asian American Journal of Psychology*, *1*(4), 303–314.

Asia Society. (2023a). Understanding our perceptions of Asian Americans. https://asiasociety.org/education/understanding-our-perceptions-asian-americans

Asia Society. (2023b). Asian Americans then and now: Linking past to present. https://asiasociety.org/education/asian-americans-then-and-now

Azhar, S., Farina, A., Alvarez, A. R. G., & Klumpner, S. (2021). Asian in the time of COVID-19: Creating a social work agenda for Asian American and Pacific Islander communities. *Social Work*, *67*(1), 58–68.

Barnes, J., & Bennett, C. (2002). The Asian population: 2000. Census 2000 Brief. US Department of Commerce Economics and Statistics. Administration.https://www2.census.gov/library/publications/decennial/2000/briefs/c2kbr01-16.pdf

Borja, M., Jeung, R., Yellow Horse, A., Gibson, J., Gowing, S., Lin, N., Navins, A., & Power, E. (2020). Anti-Chinese rhetoric tied to racism against Asian Americans stop AAPI hate report. Asian Pacific Policy & Planning Council. https://stopaapihate.org/wp-content/uploads/2021/04/Stop-AAPI-Hate-Report-Anti-China-Rhetoric-200617.pdf

Budiman, A., & Ruiz, N. G. (2021, April 9). Key facts about Asian origin groups in the US. Pew Research Center. https://www.pewresearch.org/short-reads/2021/04/09/asian-americans-are-the-fastest-growing-racial-or-ethnic-group-in-the-u-s/

Calavita, K. (2000). The paradoxes of race, class, identity, and "passing": Enforcing the Chinese Exclusion Acts, 1882–1910. *Law & Social Inquiry, 25*(1), 1–40.

Chae, D. H., & Yoshikawa, H. (2008). Perceived group devaluation, depression, and HIV-risk behavior among Asian gay men. *Health Psychology, 27*(2), 140–148.

Chang, A. (2021, March 19). For Asian American women, misogyny and racism are inseparable, sociologist says. NPR. https://www.npr.org/2021/03/19/979336512/for-asian-american-women-misogyny-and-racism-are-inseparable-sociologist-says

Chang, J., Natsuaki, M. N., & Chen, C.-N. (2013). The importance of family factors and generation status: Mental health service use among Latino and Asian Americans. *Cultural Diversity and Ethnic Minority Psychology, 19*(3), 236–247.

Cheang, K. H. (2020). Asian American sociality after the anti-relational turn in queer theory. *Criticism, 62*(1), 157–163.

Chong, K. H., & Song, M. (2022). Interrogating the "White-Leaning" thesis of White–Asian multiracials. *Social Sciences, 11*(3), 118. https://doi.org/10.3390/socsci11030118

Chung, Y. B., & Szymanski, D. M. (2006). Racial and sexual identities of Asian American gay men. *Journal of LGBTQT Issues in Counseling, 1*(2), 67–93.

Cole, E. R. (2009). Intersectionality and research in psychology. *American Psychologist, 64*(3), 170–180. https://doi.org/10.1037/a0014564

Combs, L. D., & Johnston-Guerrero, M. P. (2022). At home or on tour? Mixed race Filipina/o American reflections on identity and visiting the motherland. *The Qualitative Report, 27*(10), 2359–2376.

Council on Social Work Education. (2023, March 20). Social work leadership roundtable joint statement on DEI, anti-racism, and systems change. https://www.cswe.org/news/newsroom/swlr-joint-statement-on-dei-anti-racism-and-systems-change/

Crenshaw, K. (1989). Demarginalizing the intersection of race and sex: A black feminist critique of antidiscrimination doctrine, feminist theory and antiracist politics. *University of Chicago Legal Forum, 140*(1), 139–167.

Donnella, L. (2018, January 17). "Racial imposter syndrome": Here are your stories. NPR. 'Racial Impostor Syndrome': Here Are Your Stories : Code Switch : NPR

Đoàn, L. N., Takata, Y., Sakuma, K.-L. K., & Irvin, V. L. (2019). Trends in clinical research including Asian American, Native Hawaiian, and Pacific Islander participants funded by the US National Institutes of Health, 1992 to 2018. *JAMA Network Open, 2*(7), e197432–e197432.

Dong, X. (2019). Advancing Asian health equity: Multimodal approach to translate research into practice and policy. *Journal of the American Geriatrics Society, 67*(S3), S476–S478.

Eng, D. L., & Han, S. (2019). *Racial melancholia, racial dissociation: On the social and psychic lives of Asian Americans*. Duke University Press.

Evans-Winters, V. E. (2021). Race and gender intersectionality and education. In *Oxford Research Encyclopedia of Education*. Oxford University Press.

Feagin, J. R. (2020). *The white racial frame: Centuries of racial framing and counter-framing*. Routledge.

Ferguson, R. A. (2012). *The reorder of things: The university and its pedagogies of minority difference*. Oxford Academic.

Fisher-Borne, M., Cain, J. M., & Martin, S. L. (2015). From mastery to accountability: Cultural humility as an alternative to cultural competence. *Social Work Education, 34*(2), 165–181.

Forbes, N., Yang, L. C., & Lim, S. (2023). Intersectional discrimination and its impact on Asian American women's mental health: A mixed-methods scoping review. *Frontiers in Public Health*. https://doi.org/10.3389/fpubh.2023.993396

Freedman, J. (2005). Transgressions of a model minority. *Shofar, 23*(4), 69–97. http://www.jstor.org/stable/42944291

Garcini, L. M., Domenech Rodríguez, M. M., Mercado, A., & Paris, M. (2020). A tale of two crises: The compounded effect of COVID-19 and anti-immigration policy in the United States. *Psychological Trauma: Theory, Research, Practice, and Policy, 12*(S1), S230–S232.

Gay, T. M., Farinu, O. T. O., & Issano Jackson, M. (2022). "From all sides": Black-Asian Reddit communities identify and expand experiences of the multiracial microaggression taxonomy. *Social Sciences, 11*(4), 168.

Halloran, R. (1976, June 2). Now-grown children of G. I.'s in Korea are bitter. *The New York Times*. https://www.nytimes.com/1976/06/02/archives/nowgrown-children-of-gis-in-korea-arebitter.html

Harris, J. C. (2020). Multiracial faculty members' experiences with teaching, research, and service. *Journal of Diversity in Higher Education, 13*(3), 228–239.

Huynh, Q. L., Devos, T., & Smalarz, L. (2011). Perpetual foreigner in one's own land: Potential implications for identity and psychological adjustment. *Journal of Social and Clinical Psychology, 30*(2), 133–162.

Jeung, R., Yellow Horse, A., Popovic, T., & Lim, R. (2021). Stop AAPI hate national report. https://stopaapihate.org/wp-content/uploads/2021/05/Stop-AAPI-Hate-Report-National-210316.pdf

Jones, N., Marks, R., Ramirez, R., & Ríos-Vargas, M. (2021). Improved race and ethnicity measures reveal US population is much more multiracial. United States Census Bureau. https://www.census.gov/library/stories/2021/08/improved-race-ethnicity-measures-reveal-united-states-population-much-more-multiracial.html

Joshi, K. Y. (2006). The racialization of Hinduism, Islam, and Sikhism in the United States. *Equity & Excellence in Education, 39*, 211–226.

Jozuka, E. & Jones, V. (2020, September 23). Japan's hafu stars are celebrated. Bus some mixed-race people say they feel like foreigners in their own country. *CNN*. Why some in Japan's hafu community say they feel like foreigners in their own country | CNN

Kanaya, A. M., Hsing, A. W., Panapasa, S. V., Kandula, N. R., Araneta, M. R. G., Shimbo, D., Wang, P., Gomez, S. L., Lee, J., Narayan, K. M. V., Mau, M. K. L. M., Bose, S., Daviglus, M. L., Hu, F. B., Islam, N., Jackson, C. L., Kataoka-Yahiro, M., Kauwe, J. S. K., Liu, S., . . . Hong, Y. (2022). Knowledge gaps, challenges, and opportunities in health and prevention research for Asian Americans, Native Hawaiians, and Pacific Islanders: A report from the 2021 National Institutes of Health Workshop. *Annals of Internal Medicine, 175*(4), 574–589.

Kauh, T. J., Read, J. N. G., & Scheitler, A. J. (2021). The critical role of racial/ethnic data disaggregation for health equity. *Population Research and Policy Review, 40*, 1–7.

Kilty, K. M. (2002). Race, immigration, and public policy: The case of Asian Americans. *Journal of Poverty, 6*(4), 23–41.

Kim, C. J. (1999). The racial triangulation of Asian Americans. *Politics & Society, 27*(1), 105–138.

Kim, W., & Keefe, R. H. (2010). Barriers to healthcare among Asian Americans. *Social Work in Public Health, 25*(3–4), 286–295.

Kimmel, D. C., & Yi, H. (2004). Characteristics of gay, lesbian, and bisexual Asians, Asian Americans, and immigrants from Asia to the USA. *Journal of Homosexuality, 47*, 143–172.

Krogstad, J. M. (2015). Hawaii is home to the nation's largest share of multiracial Americans. *PEW Research Center*. Hawaii is home to the nation's largest share of multiracial Americans | Pew Research Center

Kuhn, G., & Robinson, R. (2021). Why the Atlanta shootings and racism are Jewish issues. Jews of Color Initiative.https://jewsofcolorinitiative.org/newsletter/why-the-atlanta-shootings-and-anti-asian-racism-are-jewish-issues/

Kulesza, P. (2021). The Indigenous World 2021: Hawai'i. *IWGIA*. The Indigenous World 2021: Hawai'i - IWGIA - International Work Group for Indigenous Affairs

Le, T. K., Cha, L., Han, H. R., & Tseng, W. (2020). Anti-Asian xenophobia and Asian American COVID-19 disparities. *American Journal of Public Health, 110*(9), 1371–1373.

Lee, E. (2003). *At America's gates: Chinese immigration during the exclusion era, 1882–1943.* University of North Carolina Press.

Lee, E. (2007). The "yellow peril" and Asian exclusion in the Americas. *Pacific Historical Review, 76*(4), 537–562.

Lee, J. (2018). East Asian "China doll" or "dragon lady"? *Bridges: An Undergraduate Journal of Contemporary Connections*, 3(1), 2. https://scholars.wlu.ca/cgi/viewcontent.cgi?article=1026&context=bridges_contemporary_connections

Lee, M., Yeo, H., & Mowbray, O. (2022). Low-income Asians living in the United States: A scoping review on challenges, factors, strength, and social work implication. *Journal of Ethnic & Cultural Diversity in Social Work*, 33(1), 65–82. https://doi.org/10.1080/15313204.2022.2154880

Lopez, G., Ruiz, N. G., & Patten, E. (2017, September 8). Key facts about Asian Americans, a diverse and growing population. Pew Research Center. https://www.pewresearch.org/factank/2017/09/08/key-facts-about-asianamericans.

Ma, K. P. K., Bacong, A. M., Kwon, S. C., Yi, S. S., & Đoàn, L. N. (2021). The impact of structural inequities on older Asian Americans during COVID-19. *Frontiers in Public Health*, 9. https://www.frontiersin.org/articles/10.3389/fpubh.2021.690014

Maglalang, D. D., Sangalang, C. C., Mitchell, F. M., Lechuga-Peña, S., & Nakaoka, S. J. (2022). The movement for ethnic studies: A tool of resistance and self-determination for social work education. *Journal of Social Work Education*, 58(4), 733–746.

Man, S. (2020). Anti-Asian violence and US imperialism. *Race & Class*, 62(2), 24–33.

Matsumoto, K., & Zhang, Y. (2020). Orientalism and the legacy of racialized sexism: Disparate representational images of Asian and Eurasian women in American culture. *Stanford University*, 17, 114–125.

Matthews, A. K., Li, C.-C., Bernhardt, B., Sohani, S., & Dong, X. Q. (2022). Factors influencing the well-being of Asian American LGBT individuals across the lifespan: Perspectives from leaders of community-based organizations. *BMC Geriatrics*, 22(1), 909.

McConnell, E. A., Janulis, P., Phillips II, G., Truong, R., & Birkett, M. (2018). Multiple minority stress and LGBT community resilience among sexual minority men. *Psychology of Sexual Orientation and Gender Diversity*, 5(1), 1–12.

McConnell, K., & Holloway, K. (2018). Asian, American, and queer. *FAU Undergraduate Research Journal*, 7, 70–79.

Mental Health America. (2020). Why imposter syndrome goes deep for multiracial people. Why Imposter Syndrome Goes Deep for Multiracial People | Mental Health America (mhanational.org)

Mereish, E. H., & Bradford, J. B. (2014). Intersecting identities and substance use problems: Sexual orientation, gender, race, and lifetime substance use problems. *Journal of Studies on Alcohol and Drugs*, 75(1), 179–188.

Meyer, I. H. (1995). Minority stress and mental health in gay men. *Journal of Health and Social Behavior*, 36, 38–56.

Meyer, I. H. (2003). Prejudice, social stress, and mental health in lesbian, gay, and bisexual populations: Conceptual issues and research evidence. *Psychological Bulletin*, 129, 674–697.

Monte, L., & Shin, H. (2022). Broad diversity of Asian, Native Hawaiian, Pacific Islander population. United States Census Bureau. https://www.census.gov/library/stories/2022/05/aanhpi-population-diverse-geographically-dispersed.html#:~:text=Hawaii%2C%20Washington%2C%20and%20Nevada%20are,in%20combination%20with%20another%20race.

Muirhead, V. E., Milner, A., Freeman, R., Doughty, J., & Macdonald, M. E. (2020). What is intersectionality and why is it important in oral health research? *Community Dentistry and Oral Epidemiology*. https://doi.org/10.1111/cdoe.12573

Mukkamala, S., & Suyemoto, K. L. (2018). Racialized sexism/sexualized racism: A multimethod study of intersectional experiences of discrimination for Asian American women. *Asian American Journal of Psychology*, 9(1), 32–46.

Nadal, K. L., Wong, Y., Griffin, K., Sriken, J., Vargas, V., Wideman, M., & Kolawole, A. (2011). Microaggressions and the multiracial experience. *International Journal of Humanities and Social Sciences*, 1(7), 36–44.

Nadal, K. L. (2021). *Filipino American psychology: A handbook of theory, research, and clinical practice* (2nd ed.). Wiley.

National Association of Social Workers. (2022, February 23). NASW anti-racism statement. https://www.socialworkers.org/News/News-Releases/ID/2403/NASW-Anti-Racism-Statement

National Institutes of Health. (2021). Notice of Special Interest (NOSI): Epidemiologic studies in Asian Americans, Native Hawaiians, and Pacific Islanders (Parent R01 Clinical Trial Not Allowed). https://grants.nih.gov/grants/guide/notice-files/NOT-HL-`.html

Oh, H., & Jeong, C. H. (2017). Korean immigrants don't buy health insurance: The influences of culture on self-employed Korean immigrants focusing on structure and functions of social networks. *Social Science & Medicine, 191*, 194–201.

Page, K. R., Venkataramani, M., Beyrer, C., & Polk, S. (2020). Undocumented US immigrants and Covid-19. *New England Journal of Medicine, 382*, e62.

Paulson, M. (2017). The battle of "Miss Saigon": Yellowface, art and opportunity. *The New York Times*. https://www.nytimes.com/2017/03/17/theater/the-battle-of-miss-saigon-yellowface-art-and-opportunity.html

Pew Research Center. (2023). What Census calls us. https://www.pewresearch.org/interactives/what-census-calls-us/

Pew Research Center. (2021, April 29). Key facts about Asian Americans, a diverse and growing population. https://www.pewresearch.org/short-reads/2021/04/29/key-facts-about-asian-americans

Pew Research Center. (2021). 9. Race, ethnicity, heritage and immigration among US Jews. https://www.pewresearch.org/religion/2021/05/11/race-ethnicity-heritage-and-immigration-among-u-s-jews/

Ramirez, J. L., & Paz Galupo, M. (2019). Multiple minority stress: The role of proximal and distal stress on mental health outcomes among lesbian, gay, and bisexual people of color. *Journal of Gay & Lesbian Mental Health, 23*(2), 145–167.

Ross, A. (2018). How American racism influenced Hitler. *The New Yorker.* https://www.newyorker.com/magazine/2018/04/30/how-american-racism-influenced-hitler

Sabharwal, M, Becerra, A., & Oh, S. (2022). From the Chinese Exclusion Act to the COVID-19 pandemic: A historical analysis of "otherness" experienced by Asian Americans in the United States. *Public Integrity.* https://doi.org/10.1080/109999922.2022.2120292

Saito, N. T. (1997). Alien and non-alien alike: Citizenship, "foreignness," and racial hierarchy in American law. *Oregon Law Review, 76*, 261–346.

Sandefur, G., Campbell, M., & Eggerling-Boeck, J. (2004). Critical perspectives on racial and ethnic differences in health in late life: Racial and ethnic identification, official classifications, and health disparities. National Research Council (US) Panel on Race, Ethnicity, and Health in Later Life. https://www.ncbi.nlm.nih.gov/books/NBK25522/

Sang, E. (2019, January 28). Stop erasing Naomi Osaka's Blackness. *Next Shark.* Stop Erasing Naomi Osaka's Blackness (nextshark.com)

Sangalang, C. C., Vang, C., Kim, B. J., & Harachi, T. W. (2022). Effects of trauma and postmigration stress on refugee women's health: A life course perspective. *Social Work, 67*(3), 207–217.

Shaheed, A. (2020). Rise in antisemitic hatred during COVID-19 must be countered with tougher measures, says UN expert. United Nations Human Rights Office of the High Commissioner. https://www.ohchr.org/en/press-releases/2020/04/rise-antisemitic-hatred-during-covid-19-must-be-countered-tougher-measures

Shelton, J., Kroehle, K., & Andia, M. M. (2019). The trans person is not the problem: Brave spaces and structural competence as educative tools for trans justice in social work. *Journal of Sociology & Social Welfare, 46*(4), 97–124.

Shimkhada, R., Scheitler, A. J., & Ponce, N. A. (2021). Capturing racial/ethnic diversity in population-based surveys: Data disaggregation of health data for Asian American, Native Hawaiian, and Pacific Islanders (AANHPIs). *Population Research and Policy Review, 40*(1), 81–102.

Sikh Coalition. (2021). Combating bias, bigotry, and backlash: Sikh American civil rights policy priorities. https://www.sikhcoalition.org/wp-content/uploads/2020/07/2020-Policy-Priorities-v1.0.pdf

Sikh Coalition. (n.d.). Fact sheet on post-911/discrimination and violence against Sikh Americans. https://www.sikhcoalition.org/images/documents/post_9.11_fact_sheet_revised.pdf

Singh, J. (2013). Memory, invisibility, and the Oak Creek Gurdwara massacre. *Sikh Formations, 9*(2), 215–225.

Smith, T. W. (2002). Religious diversity in America: The emergence of Muslims, Buddhists, Hindus and others. *Journal for the Scientific Study of Religion, 41*(3), 577–585.

Sobredo, J. (2018). The 1934 Tydings-McDuffie Act and Filipino Exclusion: Social, political and economic context revisited. In D. O. Flynn, J. Sobredo, & A. Giráldez (eds.), *Studies in Pacific History* (pp. 155–169). Routledge.

Sohoni, D. (2007). Unsuitable suitors: Anti-miscegenation laws, naturalization laws, and the construction of Asian identities. *Law & Society Review, 41*(3), 587–618.

Stepanikova, I., Bateman, L. B., & Oates, G. R. (2017). Systemic inflammation in midlife: Race, socioeconomic status, and perceived discrimination. *American Journal of Preventive Medicine, 52*(Suppl 1), S63–S76.

Szymanski, D. M., & Sung, M. R. (2010). Minority stress and psychological distress among Asian American sexual minority persons. *The Counseling Psychologist, 38*(6), 848–872.

Taketomo, A. (2012). *"The double bind of triple jeopardy: Exploring the impact of multiple minority stress on LGBTQ-identified Asian women in America*. Master's thesis, Smith College. https://scholarworks.smith.edu/theses/881

Touw, S., McCormack, G., Himmelstein, D. U., Woolhandler, S., & Zallman, L. (2021). Immigrant essential workers likely avoided Medicaid and SNAP because of a change to the public charge rule. *Health Affairs, 40*(7), 1090–1098.

US Department of Justice. (2023). FBI releases supplement to the 2021 Hate Crime Statistics. https://www.justice.gov/crs/highlights/2021-hate-crime-statistics

USA Facts. (2021, May 17). AAPI demographics: Data on Asian American ethnicities, geography, income, and education. https://usafacts.org/articles/the-diverse-demographics-of-asian-americans/

Venkataramanan, M. (2023, June 27). The fight for Asian American studies in colleges gains momentum. *The Washington Post*. https://www.washingtonpost.com/nation/2023/06/27/asian-american-studies-colleges-universities/

Wallerstein, N., Duran, B., Oetzel, J. G., & Minkler, M. (2018). *Community-based participatory research for health: Advancing social and health equity* (3rd ed.). Jossey-Bass.

Wang, J. S. (2008). The double burdens of immigrant nationalism: The relationship between Chinese and Japanese in the American West, 1880s-1920s. *Journal of American Ethnic History, 27*(2), 28–58.

Wang, S. C., & Santos, B. M. C. (2022). "Go back to China with your (expletive) virus": A revelatory case study of anti-Asian racism during COVID-19. *Asian American Journal of Psychology, 13*(3), 220–233.

Wilkinson, A. (2021). Yes, Naomi Osaka is Japanese. And American. And Haitian. *The Conversation*. Yes, Naomi Osaka is Japanese. And American. And Haitian (theconversation.com)

Wilson, P. A., & Yoshikawa, H. (2004). Experiences of and responses to social discrimination among Asian and Pacific Islander gay men: Their relationship to HIV risk. *AIDS Education and Prevention, 16*, 68–83.

World Population Review. (2023). Asian population. https://worldpopulationreview.com/state-rankings/asian-population

Yom, S., & Lor, M. (2022). Advancing health disparities research: The need to include Asian American subgroup populations. *Journal of Racial and Ethnic Health Disparities, 9*, 2248–2282.

Young, P. (2018). When America's racist immigration law inspired Hitler. Long Island Wins. https://longislandwins.com/immigration-history/when-americas-racist-immigration-law-inspired-hitler/

Zhu, M. M. (2010). The Page Act of 1875: In the name of morality. *SSRN Electronic Journal.* https://doi.org/10.2139/ssrn.1577213

5
Understanding and Dismantling the "Model Minority" Stereotype

Lalaine Sevillano and Kirin Macagupay

Historical Context of the Model Minority Stereotype

Since the onset of COVID-19 at the beginning of 2020, more than 10,000 incidences of discrimination against people of Asian American, Native Hawai'ian, and Pacific Islander (AANHPI) descent have been documented (Jeung et al., 2021). Nascent literature shows that this spike in visible anti-AANHPI discrimination is associated with increased adverse health outcomes such as anxiety, depression, physical symptoms, and sleep difficulties (Lee & Waters, 2021). Yet this most recent wave of anti-AANHPI discrimination is only part of the racist legacy that AANHPI populations have been subjected to throughout US history. In the late 1800s, Asian immigrants were described as "yellow peril," a term popularized to instill fear of job loss at the hands of Asian immigrants and codified into the 1882 Chinese Exclusion Act. This fear resulted in Congress passing restrictive laws prohibiting entry to the United States for people from Asia between the 1880s and 1920s. These laws stymied immigration from Asia and the success of Asian immigrants. Indeed, fear of Asian immigrants continued during World War II, as demonstrated by the arrest of Japanese immigrants and citizens accused of espionage and disloyalty. The next wave of Asian immigrants arrived via the Immigration and Nationality Act of 1965, and, as Asian populations gained citizenship, "perpetual foreigner" was coined to emphasize that, even as US citizens, AANHPI are not considered by some to be fully American (Armenta et al., 2013). Awareness of the perpetual foreigner stereotype significantly predicts lower hope and life satisfaction for AANHPI students, even after controlling for perceived discrimination (Huynh et al., 2011). With the educational and financial success of some AANHPI, the term "model minority" emerged in the 1960s and reinforced a false stereotype of AANHPI as the exemplar racial minority group (Yoo et al., 2015). Now following COVID-19, the term "kung-flu virus" has been used to place blame on AANHPI peoples for the pandemic. Despite the continued legacy of racial oppression highlighted above, research with AANHPI is limited across the social sciences, including in higher education (Museus & Quaye, 2009) and social work (Corley & Young, 2018).

In more contemporary times, the "model minority" is a term used to (falsely) describe AANHPI as the exemplar racial minority group because of their educational and financial success (Yoo et al., 2015). Similar to other AANHPI scholars (e.g., Suh et al., 2023), we move away from using the term "model minority myth" and explicitly name it the model minority *stereotype* (MMS) because a myth implies that the preconceived notion about a certain group is neutral, whereas a stereotype "represents an oversimplified opinion, prejudiced attitude, or uncritical judgment" (Merriam-Webster, n.d.). Some may argue that the MMS is harmless because it lauds—albeit superficially— values such as a strong work ethic and socioeconomic success. However, the MMS, when internalized by AANHPI individuals, has been shown to have varying detrimental effects (Walton & Truong, 2023).

In 1965, during the height of the Civil Rights Movement, the controversial Moynihan Report was written under the direction of the office of President Lyndon B. Johnson. The report suggested that the disintegration of the Black nuclear family was to blame for the significant poverty within these communities, thereby shifting the focus and blame for racial inequities from systemic racism to Black families (Patterson, 2010). The following year, William Pettersen, a professor of sociology at the University of California Berkeley, penned a *New York Times Magazine* article "Success, Japanese-American Style," which heralded Japanese Americans as a model minority group. The article claimed "by any criterion of good citizenship that we choose, Japanese Americans are better than any other group in our society, including native born Whites" (p. 20). The article attempted to explain that Japanese Americans were most successful because of "pride in their heritage," work ethics, and cultural values, whereas [people with African descent][1] were removed from their country and therefore, their culture (Pettersen, 1966, p. 41). The Pettersen article gave birth to the term "model minority," setting a false narrative that cultural values of hard work lead to wealth and success. However, in contemporary times, Pettersen's assumption is better known as the MMS and as a mechanism of anti-blackness. An analysis of 112 works on the MMS and its impact on AANHPI individuals in higher education mentioned the MMS yet failed to account for its purpose—to maintain anti-Black racism and White supremacy (Poon et al., 2016). There is a growing movement that recognizes the MMS as a tool to "shift negative international attention" (Hartlep, 2017, p. 5), specifically to distract from the Civil Rights Movement. Pettersen's MMS construct helped fortify ideas of meritocracy and the "American Dream" still prevalent.

The MMS and Impact on Health and Well-Being of AANHPI Populations

A scoping review indicates that the MMS is associated with social, educational, and health outcomes among AANHPI individuals (Walton & Truong, 2023). Social impacts were related to identity development, socialization practices, and forms of belonging. Authors note that most studies found that the MMS had negative impacts on social outcomes including the pressure to live up to the MMS and being perceived as "nerdy," socially awkward (Clemons, 2019; Museus & Park, 2015), and as perpetual foreigners and not "true" Americans (Chua & Fujino, 1999). Collectively, these experiences are connected to feelings of invisibility (Vang, 2016) and incapability of holding leadership roles (Adamos, 2019). The MMS was also found to be associated with adverse educational outcomes such as academic self-efficacy and academic achievement (Walton & Truong, 2023). In addition, AANHPI students felt great pressure to achieve due to the expectations generated by the MMS (e.g., Assalone & Fann, 2017). These expectations were not only held by the students themselves, but also by parents/caregivers, peers, and faculty/staff (Wong, 2015). As such, AANHPI students felt increased anxiety and stress due to fear of failure and disappointing others. Students' lack of help-seeking behaviors were compounded by teachers assuming that AANHPI students did not need help, ultimately leading to decreased self-esteem and self-efficacy (Walton & Truong, 2023).

Walter and Truong (2023) also found various studies showing that the MMS has adverse health consequences in areas such as physical health functioning (Benet-Martinez & Haritatos, 2005), alcohol and substance use (Jackson et al., 2015), and overall health (Nicholson & Mei, 2020). The majority of studies included in the scoping review examined mental health outcomes such as depression and psychological distress. Quantitative studies suggested mixed results in that the internalization of the MMS was associated with increased depression and anxiety (e.g., Atkin et al., 2018), but also decreased depression (Cheng et al., 2017) especially when AANHPI individuals believe that they are "naturally intelligent and successful" compared to other minoritized racial groups (Walter & Truong, 2023, p. 405). In summary, scholars (e.g., Yoo et al., 2015) suggest that the internalization of the MMS may result in unrealistic pressures to succeed, potentially leading to poorer academic performance (e.g., Wong & Halgin, 2006) and more mental health challenges, including suicide (Cohen, 2007). As such, extending our understanding of how the MMS operates could improve the ways in which we support minoritized racial/ethnic AANHPI adolescents as they cope with psychosocial, academic, and health challenges (Xie et al., 2021).

Using Critical Race Theory to Dismantle the Model Minority Stereotype

Critical race theory (CRT) is a framework for examining power structures that maintain racial inequities (Kolivoski et al., 2014, p. 269). CRT grounds our analysis of how institutions such as social work perpetuate racism and ultimately negatively impact AANHPI mental health and well-being. In particular, we use CRT to critique how the MMS is harmful for many reasons including (1) masking the diversity of the AANHPI community, (2) believing AANHPI individuals are successful and do not experience challenges, (3) believing AANHPI individuals do not experience mental health disparities, (4) placing the AANHPI community as a wedge between White people and other minoritized racial groups, and (5) assuming that AANHPI individuals do not need resources and support.

First, the MMS ignores the heterogeneity of AANHPI groups. The AANHPI population grew by 81% between 2000 and 2019, outpacing the 70% growth by Hispanics (Budiman & Ruiz, 2021). As the fastest growing racial group, the AANHPI population is estimated to reach 46 million by 2060 (Budiman & Ruiz, 2021). The AANHPI population is composed of people with roots stemming from more than 20 countries. The six largest origin groups are Chinese (23%), South Asian (20%), Pilipinx (18%), Vietnamese (9%), Korean (8%), and Japanese (6%; Budiman & Ruiz, 2021). The smaller origin groups are Mongolian, Malaysian, and Okinawan (Monte & Shin, 2022). About 45% of AANHPI people live in the western part of the United

States, of which 30% (6.7 million) live in California (Budiman & Ruiz, 2021). Other states with large AANHPI populations include New York (1.9 million), Texas (1.6 million), New Jersey (958,000), and Washington (852,000; Budiman & Ruiz, 2021).

A majority of the AANHPI population (57%) are immigrants, including 71% of AANHPI adults, while only 14% of all Americans were born elsewhere (Budiman & Ruiz, 2021). Despite the majority of AANHPI not being native to the United States, 72% of AANHPI individuals are proficient in speaking English (Budiman & Ruiz, 2021). Each AANHPI subgroup has its own unique US immigration history (Trinh-Sevrin et al., 2009). For example, under the American colonization of the Philippines, Pilipinx were considered American "nationals," a status that made them less susceptible to the Immigration Act of 1924, which placed overwhelmingly xenophobic regulations on other racial minorities' immigration to the United States (Buenavista et al., 2009). On the other hand, Hmong were displaced to various refugee camps around Asia before they settled in California (Srinivasan & Guillermo, 2000). Today AANHPI immigrants comprise 14% of undocumented immigrants in the United States (Budiman & Ruiz, 2021).

Second, as a homogenous group, AANHPI individuals appear to be doing well or better than other racial groups (including non-Hispanic White individuals) across health and SES outcomes. Within the context of health, AANHPI individuals are less likely to report fair or poor health status than any other racial groups (National Center for Health Statistics, 2019). In fact, AANHPI populations have lower prevalence rates than most, if not all, racial groups across a multitude of health outcomes such as circulatory, cardiovascular, and respiratory diseases; cancer; and difficulties in functioning (National Center for Health Statistics, 2019). Across behavioral health outcomes (e.g., smoking cigarettes, obesity), AANHPI populations are also faring better than other racial groups (National Center for Health Statistics, 2019). AANHPI individuals also report fewer mental health problems including feeling less depressed than other racial groups (National Center for Health Statistics, 2019).

Aggregated data show that AANHPI individuals have the highest income and are the best educated racial group in the United States. Households headed by AANHPI individuals have higher median annual household incomes ($85,000) compared with all US households ($61,800; Budiman & Ruiz, 2021). In fact, 12 AANHPI subgroups have higher annual median household incomes than that of all US households (Budiman & Ruiz, 2021).

AANHPI groups also have the lowest unemployment rate among all racial groups (US Bureau of Labor Statistics, 2019). Perhaps the most prominent area of success for AANHPI people is within the context of education. Robust literature indicates that AANHPI individuals outperform all racial groups in academic achievement (e.g., Hsin & Xie, 2014), college enrollment (59% vs. 41%; National Center for Education Statistics, 2024), and degree attainment (54% vs. 33%; Budiman & Ruiz, 2021).

However, disaggregated data indicate that AANHPI individuals face socioeconomic disparities. For example, although AANHPI individuals are less likely to live in poverty compared to general US population (10% vs. 13% respectively), 12 out of the 19 largest AANHPI subgroups had similar or higher poverty rates than the US average (Budiman & Ruiz, 2021). Within the context of higher education, 61% of AANHPI individuals have a bachelor's degree (US Census Bureau, 2020), but disaggregated data reveal that not all AANHPI subgroups share this educational success. For example, only 15% of Bhutanese adults have a college degree (Budiman & Ruiz, 2021). Research shows that many subgroups within the AANHPI population face barriers to access (Ramakrishnan & Ahmad, 2014), retention (Kim & Sakamoto, 2014), and attainment (US Census Bureau, 2019). These types of disparities make the AANHPI population the most economically divided racial/ethnic group in the US (Kochhar & Cilluffo, 2018).

Despite the aforementioned success in SES measures, AANHPI individuals are disproportionately underrepresented in leadership positions across various industries in the US (Lu et al., 2020). In fact, AANHPI individuals make up only 2% of CEOs in the S&P 500 companies in the United States, and this percentage has stalled for the past decade (Goldman Sachs, 2022). In the public sector, AANHPI individuals make up almost 7% of the federal professional workforce, yet less than 5% of the highest federal level positions are held by AANHPI (US Department of Health and Human Services, 2023). In academia where AANHPI individuals seem to dominate, only 2.3% of college and university presidents in the United States are AANHPI (American Council on Education, 2016, as cited in Seltzer, 2017). Furthermore, despite leading all other racial minority groups at the tenured-faculty level, AANHPI individuals only comprise 3% of college deans (American Council on Education, 2016, as cited in Seltzer, 2017). Many scholars have used the phrase "bamboo ceiling" to describe the systemic barrier toward management for AANHPI individuals.

Third, contrary to what the MMS would like for everyone to believe, AANHPI individuals do experience racism, and racism adversely impacts AANHPI health and SES outcomes. An integrative review of the empirical literature on discrimination and health indicated that discrimination is indeed a significant factor to poorer mental and physical health for AANHPI individuals (Nadimpalli & Hutchinson, 2012). Moreover, emerging literature indicates that AANHPI individuals are experiencing an increase in adverse health outcomes such as anxiety, depressive symptoms, and sleep difficulties since the onset of COVID-19 (Lee & Waters, 2021). Keeping AANHPI as a homogenous group is the typical practice in scholarly research. In fact, the 2000 Census was the first US Census to recognize the heterogeneity of the AANHPI population. Because of this practice, AANHPI individuals have been invisible in policy debates regarding matters such as healthcare because they are seemingly less likely to be at risk for various health conditions. However, disaggregated data show that subgroups within AANHPI population are at risk for negative health outcomes such as cardiovascular disease (Abesamis et al., 2016) and certain cancers (Chen, 2005).

Fourth, MMS is used as a wedge and tool of anti-blackness. In most recent times, we witnessed this division during the Supreme Court's decision to overturn affirmative action. A 2005 study (Espenshade & Chung) indicated the acceptance rate for AANHPI applicants would increase the most while admissions for Black African American and Latinx students would significantly decrease. Moses et al. (2019, p. 7) explain how AANHPI individuals are exploited as a "model minority" whose admissions credentials are used to uphold a certain definition of "merit" characterized by academic accomplishments only. Yet the narratives of some AANHPI students were used against affirmative action to falsely imply that AANHPI college applicants would be negatively affected by race-based admission policies. (i.e., Affirmative Action; Lee, 2021). The series of litigations against Harvard by AANHPI applicants were analyzed by Patil (2022), who found the amicus briefs by the Asian American Legal Defense and Education Foundation and other groups explicitly distance their position from any alignments with whiteness while highlighting that affirmative action can be advantageous for AANHPI individuals and other minorities. In particular, these organizations state that defeating affirmative action will entrench White privilege and maintain using the AANHPI community as a wedge to punish other marginalized groups and undermine legitimate race-conscious admissions.

Fifth, unfortunately, the invisibility of these disparities perpetuate the MMS. Despite being the fastest growing racial group in the United States (López et al., 2017), the AANHPI population remains the least studied. In fact, between 1992 and 2018, NIH funded only 529 studies centered on AANHPI participants, composing only 0.17% of NIH's budget during that period (Đoàn et al., 2019). As noted above, a content analysis of 1,690 articles published in four prominent social work journals over an 11-year period found that only 123 articles (7.28% of the total content) discussed interventions specific to BIPOC populations and only 14 proposed some form of social work intervention with AANHPI clients (Corley & Young, 2018).

How Social Workers Can Dismantle MMS Across Micro, Meso, and Macro Levels

Historically, social work has not focused on the needs of AANHPI individuals (Corley & Young, 2018; Rao et al., 2021). Additionally, the MMS has been critiqued in various fields such as education (e.g., Poon et al., 2016), psychology (e.g., Niwa et al., 2011), and sociology (e.g., Chou & Feagin, 2015), but social work has minimally participated in that debate. However, at a time when AANHPI individuals are facing dual pandemics, it is imperative for social workers to increase their ability to address the multiple social inequalities that AANHPI individuals are facing if they are to uphold these values. The AANHPI community is experiencing a significant increase in discrimination marked by physical attacks, verbal abuse, and microaggressions (Jeung et al., 2021). Emerging literature shows that this increase in anti-AANHPI discrimination is correlated with a rise in AANHPI mental health concerns (Wu et al., 2021). Compounding these elevated levels of racism and adverse mental health outcomes is that AANHPI individuals in general are least likely to ask for mental health help (Misra et al., 2020). The injurious consequences of racism coupled with lack of research with AANHPI individuals exacerbate the need for social work to collaborate with and support AANHPI individuals. Social workers are principled by the Code of Ethics (National Association of Social Workers [NASW], 2021) to "challenge social injustice" and "pursue social change." To this end, we offer ways that social workers can dismantle the MMS across ecological levels.

Micro Level

Interpersonally, social workers—especially those with dominant identities (e.g., White, cisheterosexual)—should use their privilege to disrupt racism on behalf of minoritized populations, including AANHPI individuals. Compared to other minoritized racial groups, AANHPI individuals are more likely to use avoidance to cope with discrimination (Edwards & Romero, 2008) potentially contributing to adverse mental health outcomes and internalizing self-blame (Wei et al., 2010). Allies can help by disarming the microaggression by forcing perpetrators to reflect on their actions and/or by facilitating a critical dialogue about the offense (Sue et al., 2019).

Research has shown that clinicians who are aware of the harm caused by stereotypes and the ways in which they uphold White supremacy are better equipped to facilitate disrupting the internalization of stereotypes (Haskins & Singh, 2015). However, research has also shown that a majority of mental health professionals are not trained in assessing and addressing race-based trauma (Hemmings & Evans, 2018). As such, social workers should continue to seek learning opportunities on how to become more anti-racist and decolonial practitioners. Additionally, social work clinicians can also dismantle the MMS by incorporating culturally responsive frameworks in their practice with AANHPI individuals. Hwang (2021) recently developed a preventive intervention framework that aims to cultivate critical consciousness and strengthen ethnic identity in AANHPI individuals: the Awareness of Stereotype Internalization on Asian Narratives and Preventing Racism and Identity Distancing through Empowerment (Asian Pride; Hwang, 2021). The Asian Pride framework includes (1) raising individual and collective awareness, (2) deconstructing stereotypes and racist narratives that promote intra- and intergroup othering and inferiorization, (3) increasing emotional connection and rehumanizing interpersonal relationships, (4) fostering a sense of ethnic pride and bicultural competence, and (5) empowering through social justice and individual and collective action (Hwang, 2021, p. 603).

Meso Level

Social Work Education
Social work programs need to engage, recruit, and train more AANHPI social workers. Meta-analytic data show that clients prefer therapists who

share their racial/ethnic background and also view therapists from their own racial/ethnic group more favorably (Cabral & Smith, 2011). This is not to say that non-AANHPI social workers could not facilitate this healing, but studies show that representation matters (Zane et al., 1994). Moreover, research shows that a majority of mental health workers are not trained in assessing and/or addressing race-based trauma (Hemmings & Evans, 2018). This suggests that the number of mental health workers trained in facilitating the healing of AANHPI individuals from race-based trauma is even smaller. As it currently stands, AANHPI individuals are underrepresented across social work programs. In 2021, AANHPI individuals comprise 7.6% of undergraduates in the United States (Fabina et al., 2023), but only 2% of students in bachelor of social work programs and only 3% of students in masters of social work programs (Council on Social Work Education, 2019). This limited pipeline possibly contributes to AANHPI individuals' underrepresentation in the social work field as well, making up only 3.7% of employed social workers in the United States while making up 6% of the nation's labor force (Bureau of Labor Statistics US Department of Labor, 2020a, 2020b). The very limited research on the experiences of AANHPI social work students indicate that AANHPI social work students encounter ethnic discrimination (Kwong, 2018), incongruence between cultural and social work values (Diaz, 2002), and lack of validation from social work faculty and field supervisors (Yan, 2008). These negative experiences could be contributing to the underrepresentation of AANHPI individuals in the social work field.

Community Organizing
A critical response to myths, stereotypes, and hate includes intentional efforts to collaborate and unify causes. For macro practitioners, coalitions and strategic partnerships help capitalize on collective efforts. Several organizations and movements resist the MMS via community organizing and cross-sector advocacy. One example is the Asian Solidarity Collective (ASC), a nonprofit organization based in San Diego, California. With a mission to "activate Asian American social justice consciousness, condemn anti-blackness, and build Asian solidarity intersectionality with Black, Brown and Indigenous folks, people with disabilities, queer and trans people of color, and all oppressed communities" (Asian Solidarity Collective, 2019), the ASC's work includes civic engagement and policy, political education, transformative leadership development, community building, and collective action. Nationally, the People's Collective for Justice and Liberation

(2021) was formed in the wake of COVID, in 2020, by Gregory Cendana and DJ Kuttin Kandi in response to COVID-related scapegoating of the Asian American community.

Macro

Advocating for Asian American, Native Alaskan, and Pacific Islander-Serving Institution Designation

The US Department of the Interior Office of Civil Rights administers the Minority Serving Institution (MSI) program, supporting Historically Black Colleges and Universities (HBCUs), Hispanic-Serving Institutions (HSIs), Tribal Colleges and Universities, and, recently, Asian American and Pacific Islander-Serving Institutions (AAPISIs). The AAPISI designation, edited to AANAPISI to encompass Native American Alaskan and Native Hawai'ians, was created to address systemic racial inequities facing AANHPI individuals and to support institutions that serve large numbers of AANHPI college students (Park & Chang, 2010). Most institutions that qualify for HSI funding also qualify for AANAPISI funding, yet they must choose between which designation to pursue. The HSI funding opportunity is much larger, and although no one wants to see resources limited, the impact is that lower-income AANHPI student groups continuously receive less support, thus increasing the risk of attrition. These contrasting narratives complicate conversations on issues like affirmative action. In recognition of the MMS and exclusion of AANHPI individuals in higher education policy (Park & Chang, 2010), AANHPI communities mobilized to advocate for the federal AANAPISI designation to support institutions that serve large numbers of AANHPI students (Park & Teranishi, 2008). What is critical to the AANIPISI and other MSI designations are possibilities for advancing racial justice and solidarity by explicitly aligning AANHPI interests with other communities of color in MSI legislation (Poon et al., 2016).

In California, advocacy efforts to mitigate the potential dip in AANAPISI funding led to the historic creation of Education Codes affecting the California State University and California Community College systems. These codes created the AANHPI Student Achievement Programs which aim to provide culturally responsive supports to improve the educational experiences and academic achievements of low-income, underserved, first-generation AANHPI students, as well as other historically marginalized student groups (Villavicencio & Macapugay, 2024).

California's Stop the Hate Fund

In California, thanks to the intense advocacy of community members, grassroots organizations, and the Commission on Asian and Pacific Islander American Affairs (CAPIAA), an institutional response to the MMS and COVID-related hate was the formation of California Government Code §8260. This authorized the California Department of Social Services (CDSS), in consultation with the CAPIAA, to administer the Stop the Hate Program, formed in 2021 (Stop the Hate Funding, 2023). The program supports nonprofit organizations in the state to provide support and services to victims, survivors, and family members of hate crimes. Funding also supports activities to prevent hate incidents. More importantly, the program is not limited to AANHPI-serving organizations, giving opportunities for other communities who have experienced or are at greatest risk of experiencing incidents of bias and hate crimes, including Black/African Americans, Indian/Native American and Tribal peoples, Latinx LGBTQ+, Middle Eastern, and North African as well as people with disabilities and minoritized religious groups (e.g., Muslim, Sikh, and Jewish). Funding specifically supports four core areas:

1. *Direct services*, including mental health and complementary health services; wellness and community healing; legal services; and navigation, case management, and referral.
2. *Prevention services*, including cultural work that deepens understanding and empathy; youth development; senior safety and ambassador/escort programs; individual and community safety planning; bystander training, de-escalation techniques; and working across racial groups and other impacted populations to strengthen alliances
3. *Intervention services*, including outreach and training on hate incidents and hate crimes, services for survivors, and the rights of survivors; community-centered alternative approaches to repair harm; coordination and liaising with local government and other institutional partners; and coordinated regional rapid response. In fiscal year 2021–2022, $20 million was allocated to 80 organizations, with $91.4 million in funding for 2023 and 2024 to a total of 173 organizations.

Social workers should advocate for similar initiatives like the Stop the Hate Program in their respective states to help protect minoritized populations from experiences of bias and hate crimes.

Social Work Research with AANHPI Individuals

Another critical action social workers can take is to address the inadequate representation of AANHPI individuals in social work research. As mentioned earlier, between 1992 and 2018, the NIH funded only 529 studies centered on AANHPI participants, composing only 0.17% of NIH's budget during that period (Đoàn et al., 2019). Specific to the field of social work, a content analysis of 1,690 articles published in four prominent social work journals over an 11-year period found that only 14 articles proposed some form of social work intervention with AANHPI clients (Corley & Young, 2018). A recent content analysis of research on the Grand Challenges of Social Work aimed at eliminating racism found that studies about AANHPI individuals and Indigenous Peoples were four to five times less frequent than studies about African American and Latinx American populations (Rao et al., 2021).

Conclusion

In summary, the MMS, created by a White academic to explain the supposed success of a particular community, is rooted in long-standing racism, with its impacts still seen today. It is harmful because (1) it ignores the heterogeneity of AANHPI groups and hides health disparities within AANHPI subgroups, (2) it distorts and minimizes actual experiences of racism faced by AANHPI individuals, (3) it places AANHPI individuals as a wedge between White individuals and other racial minority groups, and (4) it assumes that AANHPI populations do not need resources and support. Social work has historically ignored the mental health needs of AANHPI individuals, but it can no longer afford to do so. In a profession whose core values include diversity, the worth and dignity of a human being, and social justice, social workers must play an active role in disrupting the MMS by recognizing and uplifting the challenges and strengths of AANHPI communities.

Note

1. Authors replaced an outdated term used by Pettersen.

References

Abesamis, C. J., Fruh, S., Hall, H., Lemley, T., & Zlomke, K. R. (2016). Cardiovascular health of Filipinos in the United States: A review of the literature. *Journal of Transcultural Nursing, 27*(5), 518–528. https://doi.org/10.1177/1043659615597040

Adamos, J. L. (2019). *Splinters from the bamboo ceiling: Understanding the experiences of Asian American men in higher education leadership.* Doctoral dissertation, University of San Francisco.

Armenta, B. E., Lee, R. M., Pituc, S. T., Jung, K.-R., Park, I. J. K., Soto, J. A., Kim, S. Y., & Schwartz, S. J. (2013). Where are you from? A validation of the foreigner objectification scale and the psychological correlates of foreigner objectification among Asian Americans and Latinos. *Cultural Diversity & Ethnic Minority Psychology, 19*(2), 131–142. https://doi.org/10.1037/a0031547

Assalone, A. E., & Fann, A. J. (2017). Understanding the Influence of Model Minority Stereotypes on Asian American Community College Students. *Community College Journal of Research and Practice, 41*, 422–435.

Asian Solidarity Collective. (2019). https://www.asiansolidaritycollective.org

Atkin, A. L., Yoo, H. C., Jager, J., & Yeh, C. J. (2018). Internalization of the model minority myth, school racial composition, and psychological distress among Asian American adolescents. *Asian American Journal of Psychology, 9*(2), 108–116. https://doi.org/10.1037/aap0000096

Budiman, A., & Ruiz, N. G. (2024, April 14). Key facts about Asian origin groups in the US. Pew Research Center. https://www.pewresearch.org/short-reads/2021/04/29/key-facts-about-asian-origin-groups-in-the-u-s/

Cabral, R. R., & Smith, T. B. (2011). Racial/ethnic matching of clients and therapists in mental health services: A meta-analytic review of preferences, perceptions, and outcomes. *Journal of Counseling Psychology, 58*(4), 537–554. https://doi.org/10.1037/a0025266

Benet-Martínez, V., & Haritatos, J. (2005). Bicultural identity integration (BII): Components and psychosocial antecedents. *Journal of Personality, 73*(4), 1015–1049. https://doi.org/10.1111/j.1467-6494.2005.00337.x

Budiman, A. (2020). Key findings about US immigrants. Pew Research Center. https://www.pewresearch.org/fact-tank/2020/08/20/key-findings-about-u-s-immigrants/

Bureau of Labor Statistics US Department of Labor. (2020a). 2020 Annual Averages—Employed persons by detailed occupation, sex, race, and Hispanic or Latino ethnicity. https://www.bls.gov/cps/cpsaat11.htm

Bureau of Labor Statistics US Department of Labor. (2020b). Labor force characteristics by race and ethnicity, 2019. https://www.bls.gov/opub/reports/race-and-ethnicity/2019/home.htm

Chen, M. S. (2005). Cancer health disparities among Asian Americans. *Cancer, 104*(S12), 2895–2902. https://doi.org/10.1002/cncr.21501

Cheng, A. W., Chang, J., O'Brien, J., Budgazad, M. S., & Tsai, J. (2017). Model minority stereotype: Influence on perceived mental health needs of Asian Americans. *Journal of Immigrant and Minority health, 19*(3), 572–581. https://doi.org/10.1007/s10903-016-0440-0

Chua, P., & Fujino, D. C. (1999). Negotiating new Asian-American masculinities: Attitudes and gender expectations. *Journal of Men's Studies, 7*(3), 391–413. https://doi.org/10.3149/jms.0703.391

Chou, R. S., & Feagin, J. R. (2015). *Myth of the model minority: Asian Americans facing racism* (2nd ed.). Routledge. https://doi.org/10.4324/9781315636313

Clemons, C. (2019). Model minority expectations: Exploring with young Chinese American college students who seek career counseling. ETD Collection for Fordham University. AAI13885211. https://research.library.fordham.edu/dissertations/AAI13885211

Cohen, E. (2007, May 16). Push to achieve tied to suicide in Asian American women. *CNN.* http://www.cnn.com/2007/HEALTH/05/16/asian.suicides/

Corley, N. A., & Young, S. M. (2018). Is social work still racist? A content analysis of recent literature. *Social Work*, 63(4), 317–326. https://doi.org/10.1093/sw/swy042

Council on Social Work Education. (2019). 2019 Statistics on social work education in the United States: Summary of the CSWE annual survey of social work programs.

Diaz, T. P. (2002). Group work from an Asian Pacific Island perspective: Making connections between group worker ethnicity and practice. *Social Work with Groups*, 25(3), 43–60.

Đoàn, L. N., Takata, Y., Sakuma, K. L. K., & Irvin, V. L. (2019). Trends in clinical research including Asian American, Native Hawaiian, and Pacific Islander participants funded by the US National Institutes of Health, 1992 to 2018. *JAMA Network Open*, 2(7), e197432–e197432.

Edwards, L.M., & Romero, A.J. (2008). Coping with discrimination among Mexican descent adolescents. *Hispanic Journal of Behavioral Sciences*, 30, 24–39.

Espenshade, T. J., & Chung, C. Y. (2005). The opportunity cost of admission preferences at elite universities. *Social Science Quarterly*, 86, 293–305. doi:10.1111/ssqu.2005.86.issue-2

Fabina, J., Hernandez, E. L., & McElrath, K. (2023). *School enrollment in the United States: 2021*. American Community Survey Reports, US Census Bureau.

Goldman Sachs (2022). Asian Americans are racking up successes—Except for getting the top executive jobs. https://www.goldmansachs.com/intelligence/pages/asianomics-in-america-article.html

Hartlep, N. D. (2017). Special issue editor's introduction: 50 Years of model minority stereotype research. *Journal of Southeast Asian American Education and Advancement*, 12(2), 1–8. https://doi.org/10.7771/2153-8999.1160

Haskins, N., & Singh, A. (2015). Critical race theory and counselor education pedagogy: Creating equitable training. *Counselor Education and Supervision*, 54, 288–301. https://doi.org/10.1002/ceas.12027.

Hemmings, C., & Evans, A. (2018). Identifying and treating race-based trauma in counseling. *Journal of Multicultural Counseling and Development*, 46, 20–39. https://doi.org/10.1002/jmcd.12090

Hsin, A., & Xie, Y. (2014). Explaining Asian Americans' academic advantage over whites. *Proceedings of the National Academy of Sciences—PNAS*, 111(23), 8416–8421. https://doi.org/10.1073/pnas.1406402111

Huynh, Q. L., Nguyen, A. M. D., & Benet-Martínez, V. (2011). Bicultural identity integration. In S. Schwartz, K. Luyckx, & V. Vignoles (eds.), *Handbook of identity theory and research* (pp. 827–842). Springer.

Hwang, W.-C. (2021). Demystifying and addressing internalized racism and oppression among Asian Americans. *The American Psychologist*, 76(4), 596–610. https://doi.org/10.1037/amp0000798

Jackson, K. M., Barnett, N. P., Colby, S. M., & Rogers, M. L. (2015). The prospective association between sipping alcohol by the sixth grade and later substance use. *Journal of Studies on Alcohol and Drugs*, 76(2), 212–221. https://doi.org/10.15288/jsad.2015.76.212

Jeung, R. M., Horse, A. J., Popovic, T., & Lim, R. (2021). Stop AAPI Hate National Report. Ethnic Studies Review.

Kim, C., & Sakamoto, A. (2014). The earnings of less educated Asian American men: Educational selectivity and the model minority image. *Social Problems*, 61(2), 283–304.

Kochhar, R., & Cilluffo, A. (2018). Income inequality in the US is rising most rapidly among Asians. Pew Research Center. https://www.pewresearch.org/social-trends/2018/07/12/income-inequality-in-the-u-s-is-rising-most-rapidly-among-asians/

Kolivoski, K. M., Weaver, A., & Constance-Huggins, M. (2014). Critical race theory: Opportunities for application in social work practice and policy. *Families in Society*, 95(4), 269–276. https://doi.org/10.1606/1044-3894.2014.95.36

Lee, J. (2021). Reckoning with Asian America and the new culture war on affirmative action. *Sociological Forum (Randolph, N.J.), 36*(4), 863–888. https://doi.org/10.1111/socf.12751

Lee, S., & Waters, S. F. (2021). Asians and Asian Americans' experiences of racial discrimination during the COVID-19 pandemic: Impacts on health outcomes and the buffering role of social support. *Stigma Health, 6*, 70–78.

López, G., Ruiz, N. G., & Patten, E. (2017). Key facts about Asian Americans, a diverse and growing population. *Pew Research Center, 8*.

Lu, Q., Liu, Y., & Huang, X. (2020). Follower dependence, independence, or interdependence: A multi-foci framework to unpack the mystery of transformational leadership effects. *International Journal of Environmental Research and Public Health, 17*(12), 1–19. https://doi.org/10.3390/ijerph17124534

Misra, S., Le, P. D., Goldmann, E., & Yang, L. H. (2020). Psychological impact of anti-Asian stigma due to the COVID-19 pandemic: A call for research, practice, and policy responses. *Psychological Trauma, 12*(5), 461–464. https://doi.org/10.1037/tra0000821

Merriam-Webster. (n.d.). Stereotype. Merriam-Webster.com dictionary. https://www.merriam-webster.com/dictionary/stereotype

Monte, L. M. & Shin, H. B. (2022, May 25). 20.6 million people in the US identify as Asian, Native Hawaiian or Pacific Islander. https://www.census.gov/library/stories/2022/05/aanhpi-population-diverse-geographically-dispersed.html

Moses, M. S., Maeda, D. J., & Paguyo, C. H. (2019). Racial politics, resentment, and Affirmative Action: Asian Americans as "model" college applicants. *Journal of Higher Education, 90*(1), 1–26. https://doi.org/10.1080/00221546.2018.1441110

Museus, S. D., & Park, J. J. (2015). The continuing significance of racism in the lives of Asian American college students. *Journal of College Student Development, 56*(6), 551–569. https://doi.org/10.1353/csd.2015.0059

Museus, S. D., & Quaye, S. J. (2009). Toward an intercultural perspective of racial and ethnic minority college student persistence. *Review of Higher Education, 33*(1), 67–94. https://doi.org/10.1353/rhe.0.0107

Nadimpalli, S. B., & Hutchinson, M. K. (2012). An integrative review of relationships between discrimination and Asian American health. *Journal of Nursing Scholarship: An Official Publication of Sigma Theta Tau International Honor Society of Nursing, 44*(2), 127–135. https://doi.org/10.1111/j.1547-5069.2012.01448.x

National Association of Social Workers. (2021). NASW code of ethics. https://www.socialworkers.org/About/Ethics/Code-of-Ethics/Code-of-Ethics-English

National Center for Education Statistics. (2024). College enrollment rates. *Condition of Education.* US Department of Education, Institute of Education Sciences. https://nces.ed.gov/programs/coe/indicator/cpb

National Center for Health Statistics. (2019). Percentage of angina for adults aged 18 and over, United States, 2019–2022. *National Health Interview Survey.* https://wwwn-cdc-gov.proxy.lib.pdx.edu/NHISDataQueryTool/SHS_adult/index.html

Nicholson, H. L., & Mei, D. (2020). Racial microaggressions and self-rated health among Asians and Asian Americans. *Race and Social Problems, 12*(3), 209–218. https://doi.org/10.1007/s12552-020-09293-1

Niwa, E. Y., Way, N., Qin, D. B., & Okazaki, S. (2011). Hostile hallways: How the model minority myth shapes peer discrimination and the well-being of Asian Americans in school. *Asian American and Pacific Islander Children and Mental Health, 1*, 193–218.

Park, J. J., & Chang, M. J. (2010). Asian American and Pacific Islanders serving institutions: The motivations and challenges behind seeking a federal designation. *AAPI Nexus, 7*, 107109.

Park, J. J., & Teranishi, R. T. (2008). Asian American Pacific Islander serving institutions: Historical perspectives and future prospects. In M. Gasman, B. Baez, & C. S. Turner (eds.), Understanding minority-serving institutions (pp. 111–126). State University of New York Press.

Patil, M. (2022). Requisite realignment: Affirmative action, Asian Americans, and the Black-White binary. *University of Pennsylvania Law Review, 170*(6), 1625–1660.
Patterson, J. T. (2010). *Freedom is not enough: The Moynihan Report and America's struggle over black family life—From LBJ to Obama.* Basic Books.
The People's Collective for Justice and Liberation (PC4JL). (2021). https://peoplescollective4jl.org/
Pettersen, W. (1966). Success story, Japanese-American Style. *New York Times Magazine*, 41.
Poon, S. D., Kodama, C., Byrd, A., Chan, J., Manzano, L., Furr, S., & Bishundat, D. (2016). A critical review of the model minority myth in selected literature on Asian Americans and Pacific Islanders in higher education. *Review of Educational Research, 86*(2), 469–502. https://doi.org/10.3102/0034654315612205
Ramakrishnan, K., & Ahmad, F. Z. (2014). State of Asian Americans and Pacific Islanders series. (Review of State of Asian Americans and Pacific Islanders Series). www.americanprogress.org
Rao, S., Woo, B., Maglalang, D. D., Bartholomew, M., Cano, M., Harris, A., & Tucker, T. B. (2021). Race and ethnicity in the social work grand challenges. *Social Work, 66*(1), 9–17. https://doi.org/10.1093/sw/swaa053
Seltzer, R. (2017, March 2). Failing to keep. *Inside Higher Ed.* https://www.insidehighered.com/news/2017/03/02/racial-gap-among-senior-administratorswidensswidens
Stop the Hate Funding (STH). Award Announcement Fiscal Years 2022–2023 and 2023–2024. (2023, August 23). California Department of Social Services (CDSS). https://cdss.ca.gov/Portals/9/CivilRights/(STH)_AWARD_ANNOUNCEMENT_FY_2022-2023_AND_2023-2024.pdf?ver=2023-08-21-150032-497
Sue, D. W., Alsaidi, S., Awad, M. N., Glaeser, E., Calle, C. Z., & Mendez, N. (2019). Disarming racial microaggressions: Microintervention strategies for targets, White allies, and bystanders. *American Psychologist, 74*(1), 128–142. https://doi.org/10.1037/amp0000296
Suh, H. N., Rice, K. G., & Osborne, A. (2023). Development and validation of the model minority stereotype-response scale. *Counseling Psychologist*, https://doi.org/10.1177/00110000231197687
US Census Bureau. (2019). 2018 American Community Survey single-year estimates. *United States Census Bureau.* https://www.census.gov/newsroom/press-kits/2019/acs-1year.html
US Census Bureau. (2020). US Census Bureau releases new educational attainment data (No. CB20-TPS.09). *United States Census Bureau.* https://www.census.gov/newsroom/press-releases/2020/educational-attainment.html
US Department of Health and Human Services. (2023, May 30). Biden-Harris Administration hosts historic Asian American, Native Hawaiian, and Pacific Islander Federal employee leadership development conference. *Www.hhs.gov.* https://www.hhs.gov/about/news/2023/05/30/biden-harris-administration-hosts-historic-asian-american-native-hawaiian-pacific-islander-federal-employee-leadership-development-conference.html#:~:text=Of%20federal%20employees%20at%20the
Vang, K. S. (2016). *Educational experience of Southeast Asian students at three California State University of California Campuses.* Doctoral dissertation, California State University, Fresno.
Villavicencio, C. & Macapugay, K. (2024). Community to capitol advocacy framework: State-level advocacy for Asian American, Native Hawaiian, and Pacific Islander students in higher education. *AAPI Nexus: Policy, Practice and Community, 21*(1&2).
Walton, J., & Truong, M. (2023). A review of the model minority myth: Understanding the social, educational and health impacts. *Ethnic and Racial Studies, 46*(3), 391–419. https://doi.org/10.1080/01419870.2022.2121170
Wei, M., Heppner, P. P., Ku, T.-Y., & Liao, K. Y.-H. (2010). Racial discrimination stress, coping, and depressive symptoms among Asian Americans: A moderation analysis. *Asian American Journal of Psychology, 1*(2), 136–150. https://doi.org/10.1037/a0020157

Wong, B. (2015) A blessing with a curse: Model minority ethnic students and the construction of educational success. *Oxford Review of Education, 41*(6), 730–746. https://doi.org/10.1080/03054985.2015.1117970

Wong, F., & Halgin, R. (2006). The "model minority": Bane or blessing for Asian Americans? *Journal of Multicultural Counseling and Development, 34*, 38–49.

Wu, C., Qian, Y., & Wilkes, R. (2021). Anti-Asian discrimination and the Asian-white mental health gap during COVID-19. doi:10.4324/9781003206521-9

Xie, M., Fowle, J., Ip, P. S., Haskin, M., & Yip, T. (2021). Profiles of ethnic-racial identity, socialization, and model minority experiences: Associations with well-being among Asian American adolescents. *Journal of Youth and Adolescence, 50*(6), 1173–1188. https://doi.org/10.1007/s10964-021-01436-w

Yan, M. C. (2008). Exploring cultural tensions in cross-cultural social work practice. *Social Work, 53*(4), 317–328. http://www.jstor.org/stable/23718875

Yoo, H. C., Miller, M. J., & Yip, P. (2015). Validation of the internalization of the model minority myth measure (IM-4) and its link to academic performance and psychological adjustment among Asian American adolescents. *Cultural Diversity & Ethnic Minority Psychology, 21*(2), 237–246. https://doi.org/10.1037/a0037648

Zane, N., Enomoto, K., & Chun, C-A. (1994). Treatment outcomes of Asian- and White-American clients in outpatient therapy. *Journal of Community Psychology, 22*(2), 177–191. https://doi.org/10.1002/1520-6629(199404)22:2<177::AID-JCOP2290220212>3.0.CO;2-7

6
Asian American, Racial Solidarity, and Black Lives Matter

Robert Cosby, Meirong Liu, and Keith T. Chan

Introduction

The history of Asian Americans in interaction and solidarity with other racial minority groups includes many examples of powerful and moving coalitions between Asian and Black communities in the past century. Major leaps forward in promoting racial justice date back to historic abolitionist movements and the Civil Rights movement and more recently to Black Lives Matter (BLM) and activism in addressing anti-Asian racism. Solidarity between African American and Asian American communities throughout US history serves as testament to the power of communities of color uniting to influence major societal changes through legislative protections, advocacy, and greater social consciousness.

Although there are many examples of Asian Americans allying with Black empowerment, the Asian American movement in the 1960s, in collaboration with the Civil Rights movement, is perhaps the most consequential. This movement coalesced "Third World" peoples (a term coined by Kwame Ture and Charles V. Hamilton (1967) in their book *Black Power: The politics of liberation*) and provided a framework for reform, positing that true and lasting change can only be accomplished through unity between African Americans and peoples from nations that were oppressed through a history of colonialism. It was during this period of social change that the term "Asian American" was coined by historian and activist Yuji Ichioka to encompass the multiple Asian ethnic groups who lived in the United States and to emphasize solidarity among Asian Americans and also with African, Latino, and Native Americans and with people around the world impacted by US militarism (Maeda, 2016).

Creating Racial Solidarity

Creating strong group solidarity among various racial minorities to battle racism is a proven method for success (Chong & Rogers, 2005). Empowerment for racial minorities is possible through mutual support and solidarity among different ethnic and racial groups. This unity is crucial in addressing the ongoing issues of racial and ethnic oppression. With the recent rise of xenophobia and White nationalism in the United States, the need for communities of color to stand together against racism has never been more urgent. There have been many examples of powerful and moving coalitions between Asian and Black communities in the past 200 years that have spurred significant progress in racial justice. For example, civil rights pioneer Frederick Douglass advocated for Chinese and Japanese immigrants, urging Americans not to fear Asian languages or cultures. In his immigration lecture in 1867, Douglass highlighted that the United States was not racially, ethnically, or religiously homogeneous.

> It is this great right I assert for the Chinese and Japanese, and for all other varieties of men equally with yourselves, now and forever.... Chinese immigration should be settled upon higher principles than those of a cold and selfish expediency. There are such things in the world as human rights. They rest upon no conventional foundation, but are eternal, universal, and indestructible. Among these, is the right of locomotion; the right of migration; the right which belongs to no particular race, but belongs alike to all and to all alike.... I want a home here not only for the Negro, the mulatto, and the Latin races; but I want the Asiatic to find a home here in the United States, and feel at home here, both for his sake and for ours. (Douglass, 1867)

During the Philippine–American War in 1898, the experiences of the Filipino people resonated with the Black community because of shared histories of centuries of Western colonialism. Both groups have long histories of being oppressed. Examples include imperialism, racism, and economic exploitation (Nadal et al., 2022). The Philippines in the Pacific Ocean include more than 7,640 islands, of which 2,000 are or have been inhabited. For many centuries explorers, survivors, and settlers made homes on the Philippine archipelago. Many of these settlers on the islands did not know of the people living on several other inhabited Philippine islands. This meant that, for centuries and generations, the cultural experiences of settlers from China and India who inhabited or visited the islands did not have a dominating influence on the cultural development of semi-native Philippine island inhabitants. However, for more than 300 years (from 1565 to 1898), Spanish oppression brought European-style colonization to the islands, featuring indebted servitude and slavery. Last, the United States brought its own brand of colonization to these Asian islands by using the Philippines to site strategic military bases (Subic Bay Naval Base and Clark Air Base), as well as using the islands as tourist destinations and on commerce routes; the Philippines finally gained independence from the United States in 1946, and turnover of the military bases occurred in 1991 and 1992.

Many African American/Black soldiers in World War I and World War II who were stationed in the Philippines empathized with peoples of the islands, in part because of the many commonalities of racism and collective oppression they saw in the plight of Pinoy (men) and Pinay (women) and Black men and women. In the early 20th century, prominent African American leaders, including Ida B. Wells and Henry M. Turner, supported the Philippine Islands' demand for independence from the United States.

Later, during the 1960s, many African American individuals and communities protested against US policies concerning the Vietnam War. Malcolm X, the Nation of Islam's second most powerful leader behind Elijah Muhammad, opposed the war as early as 1954, when he compared that war to the Mau Mau rebellion in Kenya. Malcolm X connected the dots, showing an uncomfortable link to the impact of colonization on people of color in both places. The result was that many African Americans were sympathetic to the plight of Vietnamese immigrants being exposed to racism in the United States. In short, both groups, Black Americans and Vietnamese immigrants, were and are subject to White racism and oppression. What is less known is how both groups embrace this collective oppression and their response to it. This may be a larger area for further research and is another example of how historic similarities in oppression have produced the potential for collective solidarity. History has recognized that collective oppression does not often lead to the oppressed embracing colonization and their oppressors in a favorable way.

A History of Colonial Oppression

Over the course of the 19th and early 20th centuries, the period known for modern cartography, explorers, artists, and businesspersons in Great Britain were among the most employed cartographers of record for much of the world. Cartography involves making maps based on "exploring," visiting, establishing trade routes, dividing, conquering, and colonizing a land. In this way, the British have benefited from the spoils across many continents. The motto "The sun never sets on the British Empire" was an example of their oppressive dominance and the almost global sovereignty of Great Britain for almost three centuries. The British Empire encompassed Hongkong, Singapore, Malaysia, India, and arbitrarily divided up lands and territories in Africa and the area known as the Middle East. Maps newly drawn by the colonizing British and their cartographers created countries that defied the populations that lived within them while securing European access to great wealth, such as the diamond mines and gold fields of Africa. The new boundaries effectively divided tribes, families, religious shrines, and the ways of life for fishing groups, trading groups, and nomadic herders; these divisions have created conflicts ever since. This has had a negative impact on Asian and Black populations because British colonizers held deeply seated biases against people of color.

The Vietnam War is a more recent example of shared oppression. Vietnam and its fight for unification presented an opportunity to expand the Cold War between the United States and Western anti-communist powers and China and the Soviet Union, who sought communist influence over Vietnam. These global power groups sought to use their colonial power to mandate leadership in Vietnam. In 1954, the United States agreed to assist its ally, France, who had lost the France–Vietnam War. This effectively broke Vietnam into two countries. North Vietnam was led by Ho Chi Minh, and later by Le Duan and the League for the Independence of Vietnam under communist rule. South Vietnam (Republic of Vietnam) was led by five different noncommunist but autocratic rulers, beginning with Emperor Bao Dai in 1932, who supported Japanese invaders of Vietnam during World War II. Bao Dai was replaced by Ngo Dinh Diem and then Nguyen Van Thieu. The Vietnam War ended with Nguyen Van Thieu surrendering to communist North Vietnam and the United States exiting Saigon, the South Vietnam capital. The unification of North and South Vietnam followed under communist rule.

The reason for this long narrative example is to show similarities of oppression among Black people in the United States and Asians in colonized countries such as Vietnam. Many Black people and Vietnamese refugee immigrants to the United States understand the shared similarities of oppression in both countries. Understanding culture and how it plays into oppression has always been an important and necessary part of understanding the fight for civil rights.

The Civil Rights Movement

The Civil Rights Movement which began in the 1950s was rooted in addressing the lack of fundamental human rights of non-White persons in the United States, as segregation and the brutality of violence directed at oppressed persons became increasingly undeniable and unacceptable. In 1954, the US Supreme Court's landmark decision in *Brown v. Board of Education* said that separate but equal schools and the practice of separating school children by race were not acceptable under federal law. This decision set the stage for the dismantling of *Jim Crow* laws and other Exclusion Acts which enforced segregation and negatively impacted Black and Asian American populations. In 1955, the death of Emmett Till (Tell, 2020) was perhaps the first case that captured national attention regarding whether Black lives mattered in a racist and segregationist society.

For Black men, there is also a bitter irony in having to fight as soldiers for a country that did not deem that their lives mattered. In much of the 20th century, Black men were drafted as soldiers in the US military to flight in conflicts which took place in Asian countries. The mandate to fight for the United States and for their freedom and rights as citizens were consistent expectations for Black men, as they had been asked to do from the Revolutionary War, to the Mexican–Cuban War, to World War I and World War II, to the Korean War, and Vietnam War. In part, there was patriotism, but in part, there was the requirement that Black men enlist, be conscripted and fight, or would not be granted fundamental human rights. Some Black individuals served and were recognized years later as military heroes, some paid with their lives, but most Black service men and women who fought in these wars were denied the same recognition in the United States offered to White service men and women in similar capacities. Similarly, Japanese Americans who served in the 442nd in the Army during World War II enlisted to prove their patriotism, but were also denied recognition until more recently in history (Go for Broke National Education Center, 2024).

Black Veterans of the Vietnam War were in a strange place where they could see the similarities between Asian and Black oppression. Black service men and women were welcomed home to a strangely familiar level of racism that polarized young and old, from those who wanted peace and those who wanted victory, or at least peace with honor. Many Southeast Asians, such as Vietnamese refugees, along with refugees from Cambodia, Laos, and Thailand, immigrated to the United States. These individuals and families, many of whom worked or served in support roles with US GIs, were discriminated against in ways to that of Black individuals. They were taunted and ridiculed as the enemy by White individuals who opposed the Vietnam War. Vocal opponents knew little or couldn't care less about Black sacrifices.

Other examples of support and collaboration include Black leaders in sports who collaborated with Civil Rights leaders like Martin Luther King, Jr. In 1964, Muhammad Ali, who converted to Islam in 1964, said he would go to jail rather than fight against the Vietnamese people. He and Martin Luther King, Jr. and other Civil Rights movement members disagreed with each other in a number of areas but agreed to a strategy of nonviolence for the Civil Rights movement that included the Black population and other racial and ethnic groups. Ali said that the Vietnamese people and Black people were similar in that "we are victims of the same system of oppression." The result of Ali's stance against the Vietnam War and his refusal to be inducted into the US Army was that he was severely punished. He was convicted by an all-White jury in Houston Federal Court of evading the draft. The result was swift punishment: on April 28, 1967, Muhammad Ali was stripped of his heavyweight boxing Championship Title, fined $10,000, and sentenced to five years in prison. Martin Luther King Jr. also took strong stands against the Vietnam War. On April 4, 1967 (exactly one year before he was killed) King opposed the Vietnam War on moral grounds. He said, "my conscience leaves me no other choice." King described the war's deleterious effects on both America's poor and on Vietnamese peasants. During a sermon at Riverside Church in 1967, he insisted that it was morally imperative for the United States to take radical steps to halt the war through nonviolent means (The Martin Luther King Research and Education Institute, 2024).

Asian American activists also include Grace Lee Boggs, who spent much of her life advocating for civil rights and was a noted figure in Detroit's Black Power movement, and Yuri Kochiyama, who consistently raised the need throughout the 1960s and 1970s for Black reparations to mend the long legacy of anti-Black social structures and practices that have harmed Black communities (Ahuja, 2014).

Following the racist murder of Vincent Chin, Black civil rights leaders like Reverend Jesse Jackson and leaders of the National Association for the Advancement of Colored People played a critical role in bringing attention to his case. The multicultural coalition that came together in that fight helped form the basis of the Rainbow Coalition, which later became a prominent political organization that raised public awareness and pursued social justice, civil rights, and political activism. Many Asian American organizations, such as the Asian Pacific Environmental Network and Organizing Asian Communities, have long histories of working in multiracial solidarity with African Americans. During the summer of 2020, many Asian Americans made deep commitments to standing up for Black lives. The emphasis on Black Lives as a movement polarizes some people who fail to see that Black lives are part of all lives. As such, all lives matter, and life for Black individuals should be as important as for people of any color. All are important. However, through systemic racism and bias, many Black lives are ended prematurely, with rancor and malice. George Floyd, an African American man died at the hands of police officers on May 25, 2020. The police officer used a chokehold on Floyd, who was detained for a suspected misdemeanor crime. Asking whether a person's life is worth more than a forgery offense once proved guilty is just one more example of bias and the impact of racism. The Floyd incident was the tipping point for people worldwide. Each person could see for themselves what happened that day.

The United States is recognized as a great nation, one respected for its rule of law, and its fairness across the land, including the rights of all citizens regardless of color. This has meant embracing what the US Constitution stands for: freedom for all, fairness, and democracy. However, the death of George Floyd clearly showed the oppression of Black individuals. Many people, including Asian immigrants and Asian American citizens who have been oppressed, could relate to and empathize with what happened to George Floyd in May 2020. George Floyd's death and the publicity it engendered made people question what had happened in the same way that people questioned what had happened when watching the televised nightly news during March 1965, when Martin Luther King, Jr. and the Southern Christian Leadership Conference (SCLC) staged peaceful marches from Selma to Montgomery, Alabama (Garrow, 2015). The marches were meant to channel moral outrage about an event that occurred on February 18, 1965, while Jimmy Lee Jackson, a civil rights worker and a church deacon, was unarmed and participating in a peaceful voting rights march in his hometown of Selma, Alabama. Selma was predominantly Black yet had no representation on the City Council or in the mayor's office. The SCLC and other group were helping local Selma residents to register to vote. Lee was reported to have come to the aid of his mother and father who were also protesting. His mother had been knocked down and beaten by state troopers. Jackson was subsequently severely beaten, shot, and killed by James Bonard Fowler, an Alabama state trooper. The peaceful March from Selma to Montgomery Alabama was initiated by the SCLC in response to no action taken in response to Jackson's death.

On that March 7, which came to be known as Bloody Sunday, 600 or so nonviolent protesters were subjected to police officers beating men and women with clubs, knocking people down with torrents of water from fire hoses, and police dogs attacking peaceful marchers. It was a consciousness-raising time at the Edmund Pettus Bridge that led to two additional marches with local and national participants that resulted in a successful March over 54 miles from Selma to Montgomery (the state capital) with more than 25,000 persons assembled at the State Capitol Building. The Selma March and its national television visibility helped mobilize federal aid and led to the US Congress passing the Voting Rights Act of 1965. President Lyndon Johnson signed the bill into law on August 6, 1965.

Asians have looked at the processes and policies developed as a result of this hard-fought battle to secure voting Rights for all citizens. One example of the gains of the act is the removal of literacy tests used in many US Southern states to limit the numbers of those that were eligible to vote. Similar actions are now reappearing where states are choosing to challenge mail in ballots, forcing eligible voters to use of drivers licenses to identify residency, place of residence action and scaring would be voters that immigration or other groups may take away their citizenship or residency if they try to vote.

In 2013, Patrisse Cullors, Alicia Garza, and Opal Tometi, three Black women, created the Black Lives Matter Foundation in response to the acquittal of Trayvon Martin's murderer (Black Lives Matter Foundation, 2022). Its mission is to "eradicate White supremacy and build local power to intervene in violence inflicted on Black communities by the state and vigilantes." By actively combating and countering acts of violence, fostering Black imagination and innovation, and celebrating Black joy, the Black Live Matter Foundation aims to achieve progress in the lives of Black people. Some might suggest that the death of George Floyd was the domino that led to a cascade of reactions to the deaths of so many. One might further suggest that this was a time of racial reckoning in the United States, with particular focus on racism perpetrated against Black individuals (Harrelson & Levin, 2022).

This reaction has included marches across the United States, the development of policy, briefs and requests for support. BLM built international support and visibility that gained recognition and polarized protest groups from some traditional law and order groups such as law enforcement in several cities. Individuals and groups supporting protests have also provided multilingual resources to help Asian Americans talk about BLM within their families and communities (Jones, 2023). During the rise of hate crimes during the COVID-19 pandemic, African American leaders stepped up in solidarity with the Asian American community (Jones, 2021).

Asian Americans now comprise about 7% of the total US population, but the real number is higher, given that they also represent 10% of the undocumented population (Curammeng et al., 2017). The Asian community is very heterogeneous, representing peoples from many countries and geographic locations around the world. The Asian community is also actively growing. Asian Americans recorded the fastest population growth rate among racial and ethnic minorities in the United States (Budiman & Ruiz, 2021). Because of this heterogeneity there is also a considerable amount of diversity within the Asian community. Individuals racialized as Asian American come from more than 40 different ethnic groups, each with its own distinct migration history, languages, religious affiliations, and cultural practices (Curammeng et al., 2017).

Histories of Similar Oppression

Asian Americans have been impacted both on the interpersonal and institutional levels since the first Asian immigrants arrived in the United States in the late 1700s. The first major wave of Asian immigration to the United States occurred in the 1850s, when young Chinese men were recruited to provide cheap labor during the country's industrialization period. During this time the Chinese represented as much as 20% of California's labor force (Asia Society, 2024). Chinese laborers worked in the fishing and mining industries, held factory jobs, and made some of the most significant contributions to the construction of the transcontinental railroad in the United States from the East Coast to the West Coast. The falsehoods perpetrated against Asian immigrants built upon the same types of racist hyperbole used with other minorities. One of these falsehoods was "minorities are coming to steal White jobs." This morphed into tropes of minorities taking White women, taking White property, taking White people's money, telling lies about White people, and the like (Chou & Feagin, 2015; Gross, 2008). These Historically, as these lies take hold they serve as major motivating factors for the proliferation of anti-Asian racism and violence in the United States. For example, in 1854, the California Supreme Court provided legal cover and institutional reinforcement for anti-Asian violence in its ruling on *People vs. Hall*, which mirrored earlier anti-Black racist legislation. The 1854 decision prevented people of Asian descent from testifying against a White person in court (Brockell, 2021). This same legal justification had been used against Black individuals in many states, particularly in the South and Midwest. Such language was also used against other minorities, such as Native Americans (Chin, 2013; Gross, 2008).

On October 24, 1871, in Los Angeles' Chinatown neighborhood, a mob of approximately five hundred people attacked Chinese residents and lynched seventeen Chinese men and boys. Both historic and present-day violent racist attacks on Asian Americans have many similarities to attacks on African Americans. As has been often the case, the rationale for the attacks is illegitimate and based on false narratives. The pattern and practice of racism has legitimized the actions of White individuals through legislation enacted at state and federal court levels. This legislation sanctioned such interpersonal violence, legitimizing it and not punishing the perpetrators, even those who committed murder. These codified actions further institutionalized the marginalization of Asian Americans and hardened the actions of White Americans as oppressors. The US Congress passed the Chinese Exclusion Act in 1882, marking the first time in US history that a specific group of immigrants could be barred entry into the country based on their race and nationality (Lee, 2002).

The similarities of oppression endured by Black and Chinese individuals should be noted. Chinese were denied the opportunity to become US citizens by being excluded by law from immigrating to the United States. As well, Chinese in the United States were denied their civil rights as a people for more than 60 years. In 1857, the US Supreme Court Dred Scot decision denied Black people citizenship and relegated all Black individuals who were descendants of slaves from ever being free or being US citizens. This decision ignited the abolitionist fire and led to the US Civil War. In the facts of the Dred Scott case a Dr. John Sandford, a US Army Surgeon and Officer, claimed ownership of a slave, Dred Scott, his wife Harriet and their two children. The Scotts sought legal help in a St. Louis, Missouri, court, stating that their rights as Missouri citizens were violated. Dr. Sandford, over an 11-year period, sought to argue in court to enforce his position, stating that as slave owner, despite living on federal land and in a "free state," the Scotts were purchased in a slave state, and as such Scott could never be free from bondage as an indentured servant. In the Dred Scott case, the US Supreme Court decided with Sandford and against Scott. The decision denied Black people, who were offspring or descendants of slaves from ever being free citizens. In effect, once a slave, always a slave, and their offspring must also always be slaves (Allen, 2010; National Archives, 2022). The Dred Scott decision, long recognized as one of the most egregious decisions of the Supreme Court was largely made moot with the passage of the 13th Amendment abolishing slavery and 14th Amendments, which guaranteed US citizenship and due process for any US citizen. Specifically, the 14th Amendment protects any citizen, regardless of race or ethnicity. Asian Americans and Black Americans have cited this protection. The 14th Amendment mandates that "No State shall make or enforce any law which shall abridge the privileges or immunities of citizens of the United States; nor shall any State deprive any person of life, liberty, or property, without due process of law; nor deny to any person within its jurisdiction the equal protection of the laws of the US Constitution." This constitutional right remained the law of the land until the *Plessy v. Ferguson* Supreme Court decision in 1896, which undermined equal protection for African Americans under Jim Crow laws at the state level. In effect and in law, *Plessy v. Ferguson* established a new form of institutionalized segregation. The history of racism continued into the 20th century.

The Chinese Exclusion Act of 1882 proved to be highly effective in systematically denying entry to Chinese immigrants and excluding Chinese Americans from exercising civil rights for more than 60 years, until it was repealed in 1943. The most egregious example of federally enforced anti-Asian racism came during this same decade, when the US government moved to imprison more than 120,000 Japanese Americans during World War II, many of whom were US citizens. Japanese Americans were rounded up and sent to concentration camps throughout the United States.

The "model minority" stereotype (MMS) (Poon et al., 2016) disrespects Black people as well as Asians. The MMS has since been weaponized to deny the existence of structural racism that oppresses individuals by denying wrong-doing, systematically disenfranchising the oppressed, and categorically, by law and practice, supporting the oppressors. The MMS is another way that those in power mask the economic and cultural oppression used to justify actions that continue to oppress. Leveraging the story of relative financial success of top-earning Asian American individuals and families delegitimizes other minority groups, be they Japanese, Korean, or Filipino. The MMS allows the dominant culture to convince itself that because certain Asian Americans are doing well, other minorities should be able to achieve the same results with no outside help; unfortunately, the MMS is so prevalent that many Asian Americans also ascribe to it, thus refusing to see other groups that share a commonality of struggling to overcome racial oppression (Museus, 2013).

The struggle for acceptance in a White and non-pluralistic society creates continued complexities and commonalities of racism. It is important that Black and Asian Americans seek common ground. Four hundred years of Black people surviving oppression has shown other minorities what they do not want. The remarkable examples of solidarity between African American and Asian American communities throughout US history serve as a testament to the power of communities of color when united. It is essential to continue to educate about our shared histories and experiences. Some concrete steps that communities of color can take to show solidarity and be stronger allies to each other include promoting anti-racist literature, having conversations across races, recognizing their own racial biases, and engaging in community and policy initiatives.

References

Ahuja, N. (2014). Postcolonial critique in a multispecies world. In J. Dublino, Z. Rashidian, & A. Smyth (Eds.), *Representing the modern animal in culture* (pp. 227–237). Palgrave Macmillan.

Allen, A. (2010). *Origins of the Dred Scott Case: Jacksonian jurisprudence and the Supreme Court, 1837–1857*. University of Georgia Press.

Armstrong, J. E. (2010). *From theory to practice: The Powell doctrine*. Doctoral dissertation, US Army Command and General Staff College.

Asia Society. (2024). Asian Americans then and now. https://asiasociety.org/education/asian-americans-then-and-now

Black Lives Matter Foundation. (2022). Black lives matter. https://blacklivesmatter.com/

Brockell, G. (2021, March 18). The long, ugly history of anti-Asian racism and violence in the US. *The Washington Post.* https://www.washingtonpost.com/history/2021/03/18/history-anti-asian-violence-racism/

Budiman, A., & Ruiz, N. (2021). Key facts about Asian Americans, A diverse and growing population. Pew Research Center. https://www.pewresearch.org/fact-tank/2021/04/29/key-facts-about-Asian Americans/

Chin, G. J. (2013). A Chinaman's chance in court: Asian Pacific Americans and racial rules of evidence. *University of California Irvine Law Review, 3*, 965.

Chong, D., & Rogers, R. R. (2005). Racial solidarity and political participation. *Political Behavior, 27*(4), 347–374. https://doi.org/10.1007/s11109-005-5880-5

Chou, R. S., & Feagin, J. R. (2015). *Myth of the model minority: Asian Americans facing racism.* Routledge.

Curammeng, E. R., Buenavist, T. L., & Cariaga, S. (2017). Asian American critical race theory: Origins, directions, and praxis. *Studies at UCLA Research Briefs, 9*, 1–4. https://issuu.com/almaiflores/docs/ec_tlb_sc_asianam_crt

Douglass, F. (1867). *Frederick Douglass describes the "Composite Nation".* https://www.blackpast.org/african-american-history/1867-frederick-douglass-describes-composite-nation/

Garrow, D. J. (2015). *Bearing the cross: Martin Luther King, Jr., and the southern Christian leadership conference.* Open Road Media.

Go for Broke National Education Center. (2024). *442nd Regimental Combat Team.* https://goforbroke.org/history/unit-history/442nd-regimental-combat-team/

Gross, A. J. (2008). *What blood won't tell: A history of race on trial in America.* Harvard University Press.

Harrelson, A., & Levin, M. (2022). *Lift your voice: How my nephew George Floyd's murder changed the world.* Post Hill Press.

Jones, J. M. (2023). Surviving while Black: Systemic racism and psychological resilience. *Annual Review of Psychology, 74*, 1–25.

Lee, E. (2002). The Chinese exclusion example: Race, immigration, and American gatekeeping, 1882–1924. *Journal of American Ethnic History, 21*(3), 36–62. http://www.jstor.org/stable/27502847

Maeda, D. (2016). The Asian American movement. *Oxford Research Encyclopedias.* https://doi.org/10.1093/acrefore/9780199329175.013.21

McNamara, R. (2017). *In retrospect: The tragedy and lessons of Vietnam.* Vintage.

Museus, S. D. (2013). *The misrepresented minority: New insights on Asian Americans and Pacific Islanders, and their implications for higher education.* Routledge. https://doi.org/10.4324/9781003447931

Nadal, K. L. Y., Corpus, G., & Hufana, A. (2022). The forgotten Asian Americans: Filipino Americans' experiences with racial microaggressions and trauma. *Asian American Journal of Psychology, 13*(1), 51.

National Archives. (2022, March 10). Dred Scott, US Supreme Court Decision of 1857. https://www.archives.gov/milestone-documents/dred-scott-v-sandford

Nguyen-Marshall, V. (2014). Impacts and legacies of war on human rights. In S. J. Henders & L. Cho (Eds.), *Human Rights and the Arts: Perspectives on Global Asia.* Rowman & Littlefield.

Poon, O., Squire, D., Kodama, C., Byrd, A., Chan, J., Manzano, L., Furr, S., & Bishundat, D. (2016). A critical review of the model minority myth in selected literature on Asian Americans and Pacific Islanders in higher education. *Review of Educational Research, 86*(2), 469–502.

Tell, D. (2020). *Remembering Emmett Till.* University of Chicago Press.

The Martin Luther King Research and Education Institute. (2024). *"Beyond Vietnam".* https://kinginstitute.stanford.edu/encyclopedia/beyond-vietnam

Ture, K., & Hamilton, C. V. (1967). *Black Power: The politics of liberation.* Vintage Books.

SECTION II
VOICES OF DIVERSE COMMUNITIES: INTERSECTIONALITIES IN THE EXPERIENCE OF ANTI-ASIAN RACISM

7
The Perceptions of Korean Americans on the Rise of Anti-Asian Racial Discrimination and the Negative Impact on Psychological Distress

Shinwoo Choi, Joo Young Hong, Catherine Hawkins, and Hyejoon Park

Introduction

Since the beginning of Korean immigration to the United States in the 1900s, Korean Americans have experienced racial discrimination and reported detrimental mental health outcomes (Choi, Hong, Kim, & Park, 2020; Lee et al., 2015; Park et al., 2022; Seol et al., 2016). This chapter discusses how racial discrimination toward Korean Americans influences their psychological distress. It proceeds as follows: first, it addresses what anti-Asian racism is and how it is addressed, Korean immigrant history in the United States, key concepts of Korean culture, and Korean Americans' risk of mental health problems. Next, it examines Korean Americans' experiences of racial discrimination. Third, it explores coping strategies—resilience and social support—for Korean Americans in relation to racial discrimination. Finally, it provides implications for policy, practice, and research.

Anti-Asian Racism

As noted by Hope et al. (2022), racism occurs when those from majority ethnic or racial groups in a certain region or society discriminate against those in the minority. Additionally, systematic exclusion from power and resources often takes place due to the privilege resulting from a socially constructed categorization of people that suggests dominant groups are superior to other groups (Hope et al., 2022). Korean Americans, like all Asian Americans, are among the many racial/ethnic minorities vulnerable to targeted acts of racial discrimination (Cho et al., 2022). Some US institutions and people have labeled them "perpetual foreigners" (Hwang, 2021) because of their race, regardless of nativity or assimilation. This chapter focuses on "perceived racial discrimination" for a range of reasons. The term "perceived" focuses on an individual's personal assessment and feelings about an incident, in line with the understanding that perception causes harm regardless of intent (Chau et al., 2018). For example, the same treatment may impact people differently if they believe they are targeted based on their foreign status as an immigrant or as a US citizen.

Korean Americans' awareness of systematic oppression, racial discrimination, and coping strategies is relatively lower than that of other minority groups (Choi, Hong, Kim & Park, 2020). Even immigrants who have lived in the United States for a long time may be oblivious to anti-Asian racism, which was especially the case before the COVID-19 pandemic. Yet even after the outbreak of COVID in the United States and the corresponding backlash of anti-Asian racism, victims were more likely to blame China (as the presumed source of the disease) for their mistreatment than the racism of non-Asian Americans (Choi, Hong, Kim, & Park, 2020).

Korean Immigrants in US History and Their Characteristics

Korean Americans are the fifth largest Asian subgroup in the United States (US Census Bureau, 2018). As of 2017, about 2 million Korean Americans resided in the United States, including 1 million born in Korea and 920,000 born elsewhere, largely in the United States (O'Connor & Batalova, 2019). The earliest Korean immigrants came to the United States at the beginning of the 20th century; most were fleeing poverty, political unrest, and war in Korea (Chung, n.d.). The numbers swelled after the 1965 Immigration and Nationality Act, which ended nationally restrictive quotas for US immigration (O'Connor & Batalova, 2019). Recent Korean immigrants tend to come to the United States as college students or White-collar employees (Chung, n.d.; O'Connor & Batalova, 2019). These Korean Americans typically belong to a higher socioeconomic status (SES) and educational attainment group than the average US individual and other immigrant groups (Chung, n.d.; O'Connor & Batalova, 2019). Korean American parents place a high value on education, investing heavily in their children's success at school and expecting them to demonstrate higher educational achievement as compared to other ethnic groups (Ng, 2019).

Research suggests that, in general, Korean Americans—children of Korean immigrants— differ from their parents in key respects. These include the degree of cultural adaptation, perceived racial discrimination, and mental health outcomes. Koreans who immigrate to the United States as adults tend to speak less fluent English than other immigrant groups (O'Connor & Batalova, 2019), remain monolingual as Korean language speakers, and socialize within Korean religious or nonreligious communities (e.g., Korean churches and temples; Yasui et al., 2018). First-generation immigrants have established a stable cultural identity prior to immigration and are unlikely to adapt to American culture (Duong et al., 2016; Marks et al., 2014). Such tendencies often lead to ethnic and cultural isolation (Yasui et al., 2018) and psychological distress (Cho et al., 2018; Guo & Stensland, 2018). By contrast, second-generation Korean Americans are likely to forge multicultural identities and be "Americanized," socializing within the dominant culture (Kim et al., 2019). However, like their parents, they face marginalization and perception as "perpetual foreigners" (Cheng et al., 2020; Park et al., 2021).

Korean Culture: Collectivism and Confucianism

Korean culture is traditionally influenced by two primary values: collectivism and Confucianism. These values provide a cultural context for understanding the Korean immigrant experience. Asian collectivism emphasizes group norms and values and relationships with others (Oh et al., 2014). It also prioritizes group goals over individual ones and requires the members of a society to have a strong group identity. Scholarship indicates that individual life satisfaction is lower in societies where collectivism is a shared value (Krys et al., 2019; Wang & Lou, 2022). An individual's life satisfaction will be high only when the collectivist values and norms in their society are genuinely integrated and internalized with their own (Ryan & Ryan, 2019).

Confucianism is a worldview codified by the ancient philosopher Confucius (Raj & Raval, 2013). It strongly emphasizes a hierarchical structure between individuals, predetermined by sex, class, and societal roles (National Geographic Society, 2022). For instance, husband–wife, parent–child, teacher–student, master–servant, and man–woman relationships are strictly hierarchical. Questioning and challenging the power differential is considered a moral deficit that will cause social disorder and, potentially, chaos. Unfortunately, Confucianism and collectivism may discourage Korean immigrants from voicing their experiences of racism since these traditional worldviews call on individuals to conform, stay away from trouble, and stay quiet in the face of injustice.

The Model Minority Myth and Korean Americans' Risk of Mental Health Problems

As is the case with other Asian groups, Korean Americans are seen as a "model minority" (Walton & Truong, 2023) because of their relatively high SES. The model minority myth leads to an underestimation of the challenges and difficulties that Korean Americans experience. Since they are not seen as a vulnerable population, their experiences of racism or poor mental health may not be accepted as a social justice issue. Yet the literature consistently finds that Korean Americans suffer from the detrimental effects of racism (Choi, Park, et al., 2020; Lee et al., 2018; Park et al., 2021), and discrimination can take place due to their race, ethnicity, culture, and language.

In addition to racism, many Korean Americans are exposed to risk factors related to acculturation and immigration that could impact their psychological well-being negatively (Cho et al., 2018). While the prevalence of depression is lower among Korean Americans than among the US general population (Brody et al., 2018; Koh, 2018), the suicide rate is higher among Asian women than any other US female group (Forte et al., 2018). Furthermore, Korean Americans, along with other Asian American groups, tend to underutilize mental health services, which may increase their risk of negative outcomes (Koh, 2018; Lee et al., 2021). Korean Americans are more likely to report physical symptoms than mental symptoms (Koh, 2018), reflecting cultural beliefs that mental health issues are shameful. Depression may be seen as a signal of personal weakness (Park et al., 2018). Korean

Americans tend to underreport their symptoms on depression screening scales (i.e., Center for Epidemiologic Studies Depression Scale; Lee et al., 2020). Hence there is a need for greater efforts to find out the actual prevalence of mental health problems among Korean Americans as well as their precursors.

Major Events in Anti-Korean Sentiment in the United States: The Los Angeles Riots and the COVID-19 Pandemic

Much like many other US immigrant groups, Korean immigrants on the West Coast in the 20th century established a plethora of beauty supply shops, convenience stores, liquor stores, Korean restaurants, and other small businesses. In 1992, the Korean American owner of a convenience store shot and killed Latasha Harlins, a 15-year-old African American girl; in her defense, the shop owner claimed that Harlins had stolen from her. The light sentence she received and the brutal beating of Rodney King by White police officers were catalysts of one of the most devastating civil uprisings in US history, the 1992 Los Angeles Riots (Lah, 2017). Many Korean Americans' businesses and property were destroyed, shattering their "American dream"; some returned to South Korea or were too traumatized to return to work due to tragic interminority conflicts and discrimination (Park & Campa, 2022). Historically, when a given minority group suffers from oppression, scarcity of resources, and stigmatization, interminority discrimination often occurs (Chan, 2019; Chou, 2020).

The racial wounds from the events of the 1990s never healed fully, and they reopened during the COVID-19 pandemic (Choi, Hong, et al., 2020). The fact that the virus that causes COVID-19 originated in China coupled with the openly anti-China rhetoric of the US president led to a rising incidence of anti-Asian sentiment and violence. According to Stop Asian American/Pacific Islanders Hate (2021), Korean Americans were the victims of 16.1% of the 10,905 hate incidents against Asians and Pacific Islanders reported between March 19, 2020 and December 31, 2021. Such incidents included verbal harassment, physical assault, and civil rights violations, such as workplace discrimination, refusal of transportation, and discrimination related to housing.

Racial Discrimination and Coping Strategies: Resilience and Social Support

Psychological distress due to racial discrimination toward ethnic minority groups is well documented (Chen & Mallory, 2021; Choi, Weng, Park, & Hong, 2020; Choi, Weng, Park, & Kim, 2020). For example, racial discrimination has detrimental impacts on the sense of community or social belonging and self-esteem of minority individuals (Benner et al., 2018; Verkuyten et al., 2019). Racial minorities often experience severe mental health problems, such as anxiety and depressive symptoms (Lewis et al., 2015; Li, 2014). Bernstein and colleagues (2011) conducted research on 304 Korean immigrants in New York City who had experienced mental health crises and found correlations between exposure to racial discrimination and lower English language skills as well as higher depressive symptoms. By contrast, stress caused by acculturation was not a significant predictor of depression in their study.

Resilience—the ability to adapt to and recover from life challenges and adversity (Bernstein et al., 2017)—has been studied as a modifier of psychological distress among various immigrant groups, including Korean Americans (Akinsulure-Smith, 2017; Bernstein et al., 2017; Bosma et al., 2019). Over time, an individual's gender, age, and diverse cultural and experiential backgrounds influence the dynamics of resilience, which can be promoted by education, prevention programs, and helpful policies (Liu et al., 2020). A study of 285 US Korean immigrants found that resilience helped to buffer the depressive symptoms they exhibited related to cultural shock, acculturation stress, and other traumatic experiences (Bernstein et al., 2017). The study emphasized the importance of providing "resilience-focused interventions" to raise a population's psychological well-being in the presence of life difficulties. A similar study found that interventions targeting resilience elements (generating alternatives to angry outbursts and promoting processes for family cohesion) meaningfully reduce depressive symptoms in Korean American adolescents (Park et al., 2010). In a study conducted in the context of the COVID-19 pandemic, Choi, Hong, et al. (2020) found that resilience was a powerful protective factor against the psychological distress of Korean immigrants.

While resilience elements are widely accepted as positive and protective coping strategies, determining specific strategies related to the ethnic and racial identity (ERI) of minority individuals remains controversial (Park et al.,

2013). Minority individuals often perceive and define themselves through the ERI lens in an ethnically and racially diverse society (Choi, Weng, Park, & Hong, 2020). A study of ERI showed that "ethnic identity pride (EI-Pride)" was a strong resilience strategy that moderated the negative effects of certain levels of perceived discrimination on depressive symptoms and the social connectedness of Korean American college students (Lee, 2005). Lee (2005), found, however, that when the perceived discrimination was high, the buffering effect of EI-Pride was diminished, possibly due to greater opposition to discrimination, which resulted in negative psychological well-being in the presence of stronger EI-Pride. Similarly, ethnic identity worsened the relationship between COVID-19–related racial discrimination and anxiety and depression levels. In contrast, engagement and disengagement coping strategies buffered the negative effects of COVID-19 related to racial discrimination on depression, which resulted in increased life satisfaction (Oh et al., 2022). Oh et al. (2022) argued that "a stronger connection and commitment with Korean identity may result in greater awareness of ethnic differences, therefore increasing the distress associated with racial discrimination" (p. 467). Given that ERI is a dynamic concept and changes according to social, contextual, and individual factors (Deaux, 2018), further research is needed to explore the complicated role of ERI in the impact of racial discrimination.

Social support helps racial minorities greatly in responding to emotional experiences and dealing with perceived racial discrimination. In the presence of social support, individuals feel a sense of belonging and security even with negative experiences (Gerrard et al., 2018). Through ethnic social support, individuals from ethnic and racial minority groups understand that racial discrimination is both a shared experience and a source of harm. Studies on the mediating effect of ethnic social support on the relationship between depression and racial discrimination among Korean immigrants found that those with strong connections with their ethnic community benefited from a coping strategy focused on problems (Choi, Hong, et al., 2020; Noh & Kaspar, 2003). Other studies have found that family members and their social support for ethnic minority groups served as an effective resource of coping mechanisms in the presence of racial discrimination stress (Mossakowski & Zhang, 2014) and major depressive disorders caused by racial discrimination (Ai et al., 2022; Koh, 2018). Along with resilience, social support during the COVID-19 pandemic significantly improved the psychological well-being of Korean immigrants who had faced racial discrimination (Choi, Hong, et al., 2020). Taken together, the aforementioned studies suggest that it is vital that these minority individuals build strong ethnic and racial solidarity within different racial/ethnic minority groups to support and empower each other in the context of racial and ethnic communities.

Implications for Practice, Policy, and Research

Practice Implications

The findings from the previous literature on Korean Americans have considerable implications for direct social work practice. First, social workers should be mindful of how perceived racial discrimination may play a role in deteriorated mental health status in Korean Americans because the previous studies identified a negative association. These findings are essential for practitioners to consider as they provide services. Second, a general implication from the previous literature suggests that social support plays a critical role in Korean Americans' lives, which can be further enhanced through social work interventions. Services that promote social support-building for Korean Americans can assist in putting protective factors in place to offset some of the negative effects of perceived racial discrimination (Choi, Park et al., 2020; Gerrard et al., 2018; Koh, 2018). Religious involvement is a common support that may have either a negative or a positive effect on the mental health of Korean Americans (Ai et al., 2013), and online networking and cultural centers may provide additional forms of support. Social workers should be aware of local resources (e.g., translators and interpreters in hospitals or clinics) and provide Korean American clients with options for building and obtaining support. Social workers can also play a key role in implementing support groups specific to this population as a means of creating a sense of safety and community.

Third, future practice should reflect the unexpected findings from the literature with regard to high racial/ethnic identity and worsened outcomes from perceived racial discrimination. This inconsistency may align with debates among scholars on the effects ERI may have on this population (Park et al., 2013). While Phinney (1996) indicated—and many often believe— that a high (or achieved) ERI has a buffering effect against perceived racial discrimination, the literature has actually found the opposite to be true. Although the findings were unforeseen, they may suggest that those who identify more strongly with their ERI experience stronger reactions to experiences of racism and discrimination. This suggests a possible need to reevaluate how to approach the development of ERI and indicates a need for further research on the topic. Regardless, social workers can approach the subject of ERI with greater caution and sensitivity if it arises during direct practice situations. In addition, because cultural competence is a key skill according to the National Association of Social Workers (2016), social workers should reassess how to approach ERI. Research into the topic is a relevant area for further exploration in social work.

Resilience programs have shown positive results with individuals who experienced discrimination and negative mental health (Dray et al., 2017; Health Resources and Services Administration, n.d.; Khanlou & Wray, 2014; Vo et al., 2015). Such programs include A Whole Community Approach on Social Resilience, Mindful Awareness and Resilience Skills, and Universal Resilience-Focused Intervention.

Though COVID-19 brought much suffering, it also brought the potential benefits of telehealth to the forefront of mental health services. These programs promote using technology for "health care delivery, education, and health information services" (Layfield et al., 2020). Originally used primarily for rural populations and patients with mobility issues, telehealth has expanded to the general population, with numerous studies finding that telehealth programs had positive effects during the pandemic (Matheson et al., 2020). Since many advanced technologies (e.g., videoconferencing, online delivery services) have been implemented (Chong & Rogers, 2005), enhancing those services can be further explored and evaluated. Specifically, since the literature has shown that Korean Americans would benefit from social support in combating discrimination, developing telehealth programs to enhance social support could be a timely practice implementation. Another promising area of evidence-based practice pertains to family dynamics. One important finding is that many Korean American parents do not engage in conversations about discrimination at home with their children. A lower awareness of such sensitive topics could lead to disempowerment, a sense of powerlessness, and poorer mental health status. Future research and practice efforts should address this question. For example, practitioners might help Korean Americans to be better prepared to respond to racial discrimination by participating in racial justice training, awareness workshops, or similar interventions.

Research emphasizes the importance of developing group solidarity among various racial minority groups to combat systematic oppression and discrimination (Cheng et al., 2021; Chong & Rogers, 2005; Cortland et al., 2017; Craig et al., 2020; Hoston, 2009). Historically, facing marginalization and scarce resources, minority individuals and groups have resorted to discriminating against each other (Burson & Godfrey, 2018). For instance, after Japan's bombing of Pearl Harbor in 1941, in addition to rising anti-Asian sentiment, America saw increased anti-Japanese sentiment from other Asian groups (Chan, 2019). Research shows that combatting such tendencies through intergroup support increases the empowerment of ethnic minority individuals as well as their awareness of discrimination (Ouch & Moradi, 2022). The solidarity among and within Asian and Latinx groups in the United States is not as strong as that of Black Americans (Cheng et al., 2021). Korean Americans should realize the importance of building intergroup solidarity for empowerment and long-term psychological well-being (Cheng et al., 2021; Craig et al., 2020).

Policy Implications

Although increasing diversity in a given setting does not guarantee that the incidence of racial discrimination will decrease, it can be a first step. When scholars who study the mental health of racial minority individuals discuss how to reduce the incidence of racial discrimination, they often highlight macro- and meso-level policies and practices. Macro-level policies target broader contexts, such as national-level policies. Meso-level policies target more localized contexts, such as organizational and institutional contexts. Affirmative action is a strong example of a macro-level policy that impacts the level of diversity in an educational institution or workplace. This social policy was designed to ensure that public institutions represent the populations they serve (Anderson et al., 2008). It was created based on the belief that increasing diversity will bring social and educational benefits by creating racial minority role models and leaders (Hinrichs, 2012). Affirmative action is related to social work practice since it influences the racial composition of a given educational setting.

In addition, various national policies aim to promote diversity in educational or professional domains by cultivating minority scholars and professionals. For example, the Council of Social Work Education offers the

Minority Fellowship Program for graduate students. The purpose of this program is to increase the number of racial/ethnic minority professionals who are trained to serve traditionally underrepresented populations with mental health and substance abuse problems (Council on Social Work Education, n.d.). Since simply increasing diversity does not automatically guarantee decreased levels of racial discrimination, further social work intervention is needed.

At the meso level in social work, diversity-related interventions (Denson, 2009; Halferty & Clarke, 2009) are designed to enhance diversity in a given environment. The ultimate objective is to reduce racial bias and improve interracial interactions. These kinds of social work practices can be implemented through various forms, such as community education (Simpson & Yinger, 1985) or discrimination prevention programs (Potocky-Tripodi, 2002).

Research Implications

First, there should be more studies conducted on the Korean American population specifically. Until recently, Asian Americans have been studied as one large group, while the subgroup differences in culture and language have not been taken into consideration. In addition, age, gender, and SES should be studied. Second, the measurement of perceived racial discrimination should be achieved through scales that are more precise and comprehensive (Atkins, 2014). For example, researchers might tailor scales that measure racism by the timing of the event(s) perceived as racist and the developmental stage of the individual (Gee et al., 2019). Likewise, tailoring scales to specific ethnic subgroups may enhance their sensitivity to differences that these groups experience (Rubin & Babbie, 2015).

Furthermore, most of the literature that captured the detrimental effects of racial discrimination was in the form of cross-sectional studies. Future research could expand knowledge by studying the effects of perceived racial discrimination and how Korean Americans cope with their experiences longitudinally. This may also assist in providing insight into how "chronological age, relationships, common life transitions, and social change shape people's lives" (Hutchinson, 2010). This is especially relevant when exploring how perceived racial discrimination impacts individuals and their ability to cope over time and at various developmental stages. Research utilizing this approach could likely raise awareness for how perceptions may differ between children, adolescents, and adults and further inform future practice and prevention.

Last, future studies on Korean Americans' experiences of racial discrimination could contribute to theory development. Previous research relied on theories such as the stress and coping model (Lazarus & Folkman, 1984). However, alternative models exist, such as the model of racism-related stress and well-being (MRSW; Harrell, 2000), that can provide insight into some of the limitations of the stress-coping model. MRSW includes five basic domains—antecedent variables, familial and socialization influences, sources of stress, internal and external mediators, and outcomes—each of which influences a person's experiences of racial discrimination. MRSW appears to provide a more tailored framework to explore the individual factors that could potentially exacerbate the effects of racial discrimination or act as a buffer (such as lowering the impact through effective coping strategies).

Conclusion

Korean Americans have been an important part of the Asian American population in the United States since the early 1900s and have been contributing to their communities through entrepreneurship, cultural diversity, and talent in different areas such as medicine, engineering, athletics, and many more (Oakland Asian Cultural Center, n.d.). With increased awareness of systematic oppression and discrimination as a group, Korean Americans will be much more empowered and better prepared to advocate for themselves. Continuously implementing macro-level efforts to battle systematic oppression is the fundamental way to address such racism. Creating an inclusive society where diversity is celebrated will enhance racial justice, which will benefit the Korean American population along with other Asian American groups.

References

Ai, A. L., Appel, H. B., Lee, J., & Fincham, F. (2022). Family factors related to three major mental health issues among Asian-Americans nationwide. *Journal of Behavioral Health Services & Research, 49*(1), 4–21. https://doi.org/10.1007/s11414-021-09760-6

Ai, A. L., Huang, B., Bjorck, J., & Appel, H. B. (2013). Religious attendance and major depression among Asian Americans from a national database: The mediation of social support. *Psychology of Religion and Spirituality, 5*(2), 78–89. https://doi.org/10.1037/a0030625

Akinsulure-Smith. (2017). Resilience in the face of adversity: African immigrants' mental health needs and the American Transition. *Journal of immigrant and Refugee Studies, 15*(4), 428–448. https://doi.org/10.1080/15562948.2016.1238989

Anderson, E. S., Rawls, J., & Thurmau, A. F. (2008, July). Race, gender, and affirmative action. Resource Page for Teaching and Study. University of Michigan. https://web.archive.org/web/20100604211430/http://www-personal.umich.edu/~eandersn/biblio.htm

Atkins, R. (2014). Instruments measuring perceived racism/racial discrimination: Review and critique of factor analytic techniques. *International Journal of Health Services, 44*(4), 711–734. https://doi.org/10.2190/HS.44.4.c

Benner, A. D., Wang, Y., Shen, Y., Boyle, A. E., Polk, R., & Cheng, Y.-P. (2018). Racial/ethnic discrimination and well-being during adolescence: A meta-analytic review. *American Psychologist, 73*(7), 855–883. https://doi.org/10.1037/amp0000204.supp

Bernstein, K., Park, S. Y., & Nokes, K. M. (2017). Resilience and depressive symptoms among Korean Americans with history of traumatic life experience. *Community Mental Health Journal, 53*, 793–801. https://doi.org/10.1007/s10597-017-0142-7

Bernstein, K. S., Park, S. Y., Shin, J., Cho, S., & Park, Y. (2011). Acculturation, discrimination and depressive symptoms among Korean immigrants in New York City. *Community Mental Health Journal, 47*(1), 24–34. https://doi.org/10.1007/s10597-009-9261-0

Bosma, L. M., Orozco, L., Barriga, C. C., M., R.-L., & Sieving, R. E. (2019). Promoting resilience during adolescence: Voices of Latino youth and parents. *Youth & Society, 51*(6), 735–755. https://doi.org/10.1177/0044118X17708961

Brody, D. J., Pratt, L. A., & Hughes, J. P. (2018). Prevalence of depression among adults aged 20 and over: United States, 2013–2016. *NCHS Data Brief, 303*, 1–8. https://www.cdc.gov/nchs/products/databriefs/db303.htm

Burson, E., & Godfrey, E. B. (2018). The state of the union: Contemporary interminority attitudes in the United States. *Basic & Applied Social Psychology, 40*(6), 396–413. https://doi.org/10.1080/01973533.2018.1520106

Chan, J. (2019). Chinese American Responses to the Japanese American Internment and Incarceration. *Hastings Race & Poverty Law Journal, 16*, 207.

Chau, V., Bowie, J. V., & Juon, H.-S. (2018). The association of perceived discrimination and depressive symptoms among Chinese, Korean, and Vietnamese Americans. *Cultural Diversity and Ethnic Minority Psychology, 24*(3), 389–399. https://doi.org/10.1037/cdp0000183

Chen, S., & Mallory, A. B. (2021). The effect of racial discrimination on mental and physical health: A propensity score weighting approach. *Social Science & Medicine, 285*. https://doi.org/10.1016/j.socscimed.2021.114308

Cheng, H.-L., Kim, H. Y., Reynolds, J. D. (Choi, T.), Tsong, Y., & Joel Wong, Y. (2021). COVID-19 anti-Asian racism: A tripartite model of collective psychosocial resilience. *American Psychologist, 76*(4), 627–642. https://doi.org/10.1037/amp0000808

Cheng, H.-L., Zhang, J., Su, J., & Kim, H. Y. (2020). Race-based marginalization and private racial regard in Asian Americans: Self-esteem and nativity as moderators. *Asian American Journal of Psychology, 11*(3), 187–197. https://doi.org/10.1037/aap0000202

Cho, Y. J., Jang, Y., Ko, J. E., Lee, S. H., & Moon, S. K. (2018). Acculturation, acculturative stress, and depressive symptoms in international migrants: A study with Vietnamese women in South Korea. *Journal of Immigrant and Minority Health, 20*(5), 1103–1108. https://doi.org/10.1007/s10903-017-0661-x

Cho, Y. J., Lee, W. J., Oh, H., Lee, J. O., Kim, B.-K. E., & Jang, Y. (2022). Perceived racial discrimination and mental health in diverse groups of Asian Americans: The differing impacts by age, education, and ethnicity. *Journal of Immigrant and Minority Health, 24*, 970–976. https://doi.org/10.1007/s10903-021-01271-y

Choi, S., Hong, J. Y., Kim, Y. J., & Park, H. (2020). Predicting psychological distress amid the COVID-19 pandemic by machine learning: Discrimination and coping mechanism of Korean immigrants in the US. *International Journal of Environmental Research and Public Health*, *17*(17), 6057. https://doi.org/10.3390/ijerph17176057

Choi, S., Weng, S., Park, H., & Hong, J. (2020). Counter-effects of ethnic and racial identity (ERI) as a buffer against perceived racial discrimination among Asian immigrants. *Smith College Studies in Social Work*, 1–17. https://doi.org/10.1080/00377317.2020.1716598

Choi, S., Weng, S., Park, H., & Kim, Y. J. (2020). Effects of Asian immigrants' group membership in the association between perceived racial discrimination and psychological well-being: The interplay of immigrants' generational status, age, and ethnic subgroup. *Journal of Ethnic & Cultural Diversity in Social Work*, *29*(1–3), 114–135. https://doi.org/10.1080/15313204.2020.1712569

Choi, Y., Park, M., Noh, S., Lee, J. P., & Takeuchi, D. (2020). Asian American mental health: Longitudinal trend and explanatory factors among young Filipino-and Korean Americans. *SSM-Population Health*, *10*, 110542. https://doi.org/10.1016/j.ssmph.2020.100542

Chong, D., & Rogers, R. (2005). Racial solidarity and political participation. *Political Behavior*, *27*, 347–374.

Chou, C. (2020). Anti-Asian Racism during the COVID-19 Pandemic (Webinar). MGH Institute of Health Professions. https://www.mghstudentwellness.org/resources-1/webinar-1

Chung, S. (n.d.). History of Korean immigration to America, from 1903 to present. Boston University School of Theology: Boston Korean Diaspora Project. http://sites.bu.edu/koreandiaspora/issues/history-of-korean-immigration-to-america-from-1903-to-present/_ftn9

Cortland, C. I., Craig, M. A., Shapiro, J. R., Richeson, J. A., Neel, R., & Goldstein, N. J. (2017). Solidarity through shared disadvantage: Highlighting shared experiences of discrimination improves relations between stigmatized groups. *Journal of Personality and Social Psychology*, *113*(4), 547–567. https://doi.org/10.1037/pspi0000100

Council on Social Work Education (CSWE). (n.d). About MFP. https://www.cswe.org/centers-initiatives/minority-fellowship-program/about-mfp/#:~:text=CSWE's%20Minority%20Fellowship%20Program%20(MFP,to%20work%20with%20underrepresented%20and

Craig, M. A., Badaan, V., & Brown, R. M. (2020). Acting for whom, against what? Group membership and multiple paths to engagement in social change. *Current Opinion in Psychology*, *35*, 41–48. https://doi.org/10.1016/j.copsyc.2020.03.002

Deaux, K. (2018). Ethnic/racial identity: Fuzzy categories and shifting positions. *Annals of the American Academy of Political and Social Science*, *677*, 39–47. https://www.jstor.org/stable/26582315

Denson, N. (2009). Do curricular and cocurricular diversity activities influence racial bias? A meta-analysis. *Review of Educational Research*, *79*(2), 805–838.

Dray, J., Bowman, J., Campbell, E., Freund, M., Hodder, R., Wolfenden, L., Richards, J., Leane, C., Green, S., Lecathelinais, C., Oldmeadow, C., Attia, J., Gillham, K., & Wiggers, J. (2017). Effectiveness of a pragmatic school-based universal intervention targeting student resilience protective factors in reducing mental health problems in adolescents. *Journal of Adolescence*, *57*(1), 74–89. https://doi.org/10.1016/j.adolescence.2017.03.009

Duong, M. T., Badaly, D., Liu, F. F., Schwartz, D., & McCarty, C. A. (2016). Generational differences in academic achievement among immigrant youths: A meta-analytic review. *Review of Educational Research*, *86*(1), 3–41.

Forte, A., Trobia, F., Gualtieri, F., Lamis, D. A., Cardamone, G., Giallonardo, V., Fiorillo, A., Girardi, P., & Pompili, M. (2018). Suicide risk among immigrants and ethnic minorities: A literature overview. *International Journal of Environmental Research and Public Health*, *15*(7). https://doi.org/10.3390/ijerph15071438

Gee, G. C., Hing, A., Mohammed, S., Tabor, D. C., & Williams, D. R. (2019). Racism and the life course: Taking time seriously. *American Journal of Public Health, 109*, S43–S47. https://doi.org/10.2105/AJPH.2018.304766

Gerrard, M., Gibbons, F. X., Fleischli, M. E., Cutrona, C. E., & Stock, M. L. (2018). Moderation of the effects of discrimination-induced affective responses on health outcomes. *Psychology & Health, 33*(2), 193–212. http://doi.org/10.1080/08870446.2017.1314479

Guo, M., & Stensland, M. (2018). A systematic review of correlates of depression among older Chinese and Korean immigrants: What we know and do not know. *Aging & Mental Health, 22*(12), 1535–1547. https://doi.org/10.1080/13607863.2017.1383971

Halferty, A., & Clarke, A. (2009). Student-led campus climate change initiatives in Canada. *International Journal of Sustainability in Higher Education, 10*(3), 287–300.

Harrell, S. P. (2000). A multidimensional conceptualization of racism-related stress: Implications for the well-being of people of color. *American Journal of Orthopsychiatry, 70*(1), 42–57. https://doi.org/10.1037/h0087722

Health Resources Services Administration. (n.d.). Telehealth Programs. Retrieved from https://www.hrsa.gov/ruralhealth/telehealth

Hinrichs, P. (2012). The effects of affirmative action bans on college enrollment, educational attainment, and the demographic composition of universities. *Review of Economics and Statistics, 94*(3), 712–722. https://doi.org/10.1162/REST_a_00170

Hoston, W. T. (2009). Black solidarity and racial context: An exploration of the role of Black solidarity in US cities. *Journal of Black Studies, 39*(5), 719–731.

Hope, E. C., Volpe, V. V., Briggs, A. S., & Benson, G. P. (2022). Anti-racism activism among Black adolescents and emerging adults: Understanding the roles of racism and anticipatory racism-related stress. *Child Development, 93*(3), 717–731. https://doi.org/10.1111/cdev.13744

Hutchison, E. D. (2010). A life course perspective. In E. D. Hutchison (ed.), *Dimensions of human behavior: The changing life course* (4th ed., pp. 1–38). Sage.

Hwang, W.-C. (2021). Demystifying and addressing internalized racism and oppression among Asian Americans. *American Psychologist, 76*(4), 596–610. https://doi.org/10.1037/amp0000798

Khanlou, N., & Wray, R. (2014). A whole community approach toward child and youth resilience promotion: A review of resilience literature. *International Journal of Mental Health & Addiction, 12*(1), 64–79. https://doi.org/10.1007/s11469-013-9470-1

Kim, L., Knudson_Martin, C., & Tuttle, A. (2019). Transmission of intergenerational migration legacies in Korean American families: Parenting the third generation. *Contemporary Family Therapy, 41*, 180–190. https://doi.org/10.1007/s10591-018-9485-7

Koh, E. (2018). Prevalence and predictors of depression and anxiety among Korean Americans. *Social Work in Public Health, 33*(1), 55–69. https://doi.org/10.1080/19371918.2017.1415178

Krys, K., Uchida, Y., Oishi, S., & Diener, E. (2019). Open society fosters satisfaction: Explanation to why individualism associates with country level measures of satisfaction. *Journal of Positive Psychology, 14*(6), 768–778. https://doi.org/10.1080/17439760.2018.1557243

Lah, K. (2017, April 29). The LA riots were a rude awakening for Korean-Americans. CNN. https://www.cnn.com/2017/04/28/us/la-riots-korean-americans/index.html

Layfield, E., Triantafillou, V., Prasad, A., Deng, J., Shanti, R. M., Newman, J. G., & Rajasekaran, K. (2020). Telemedicine for head and neck ambulatory visits during COVID-19: Evaluating usability and patient satisfaction. *Head & Neck, 42*(7), 1681–1689. https://doi.org/10.1002/hed.26285

Lazarus, R. S., & Folkman, S. (1984). *Stress, appraisal, and coping*. Springer.

Lee, J. P., Lee, R. M., Hu, A. W., & Kim, O. M. (2015). Ethnic identity as a moderator against discrimination for transracially and transnationally adopted Korean American adolescents. *Asian American Journal of Psychology, 6*(2), 154–163. https://doi.org/10.1037/a0038360

Lee, M., Bhimla, A., Lu, W., & Ma, G. X. (2021). Correlates of mental health treatment receipt among Asian Americans with perceived mental health problems. *Journal of Behavioral Health Services & Research, 48*, 199–212. https://doi.org/10.1007/s11414-020-09704-6

Lee, M., Bhimla, A., & Ma, G. X. (2020). Depressive symptom severity and immigration-related characteristics in Asian American immigrants. *Journal of Immigrant & Minority Health, 22*, 935–945. https://doi.org/10.1007/s10903-020-01004-7

Lee, M., Nezu, A. M., & Nezu, C. M. (2018). Acculturative stress, social problem solving, and depressive symptoms among Korean American immigrants. *Transcultural Psychiatry, 55*(5), 710–729. https://doi.org/10.1177/1363461518792734

Lee, R. (2005). Resilience against discrimination: Ethnic identity and other-group orientation as protective factors for Korean Americans. *Journal of Counseling Psychology, 52*(1), 36–44. https://doi.org/10.1037/0022-0167.52.1.36

Lewis, T. T., Cogburn, C. D., & Williams, D. R. (2015). Self-reported experience of discrimination and health: Scientific advances, ongoing controversies, and emerging issues. *Annual Review of Clinical Psychology, 11*, 407–440. https://doi.org/10.1146/annurev-clinpsy-032814-112728

Li, M. (2014). Discrimination and psychiatric disorder among Asian American immigrants: A national analysis by subgroups. *Journal of Immigrant and Minority Health, 16*(6), 1157–1166. https://doi.org/10.1007/s10903-013-9920-7

Liu, S. R., Kia-Keating, M., Nylund-Gibson, K., & Barnett, M. L. (2020). Co-occurring youth profiles of adverse childhood experiences and protective factors: Associations with health, resilience, and racial disparities. *American Journal of Community Psychology, 65*(1–2), 173–186. https://doi.org/10.1002/ajcp.12387

Marks, A. K., Ejesi, K., & García Coll, C. (2014). Understanding the US immigrant paradox in childhood and adolescence. *Child Development Perspectives, 8*(2), 59–64.

Matheson, B. E., Bohon, C., & Lock, J. (2020). Family-based treatment via videoconference: Clinical recommendations for treatment providers during COVID-19 and beyond. *International Journal of Eating Disorders, 53*(7), 1142–1154. https://doi.org/10.1002/eat.23326

Mossakowski, K. N., & Zhang, W. (2014). Does social support buffer the stress of discrimination and reduce psychological distress among Asian Americans? *Social Psychology Quarterly, 77*(3), 273–295. https://doi.org/10.1177/0190272514534271

National Association of Social Workers. (NASW). (2016). Read the Code of Ethics. https://www.socialworkers.org/About/Ethics/Code-of-Ethics/Code-of-Ethics-English

National Geographic Society. (May 20, 2022). Confucianism. Resource Library: Encyclopedic Entry. https://education.nationalgeographic.org/resource/confucianism.

Ng, G. (2019). Exploring how shame affects Asian Americans in the classroom. *Christian Higher Education, 18*(5), 370–381. https://doi.org/10.1080/15363759.2019.1633832

Noh, S., & Kaspar, V. (2003). Perceived discrimination and depression: Moderating effects of coping, acculturation, and ethnic support. *American Journal of Public Health, 93*(2), 232–238. https://doi.org/10.2105/AJPH.93.2.232

Oakland Asian Cultural Center. (n.d.). Part 8: Contributions of Korean Americans. https://oacc.cc/sf-beginnings-part-8/

O'Connor, A., & Batalova, J. (2019, April 10). Korean immigrants in the United States. Migration Policy Institute. https://www.migrationpolicy.org/article/korean-immigrants-united-states-2017

Oh, J. H., Kim, H. S., & Lee, J. H. (2014). Asian cultural collectivism, acculturation, and life satisfaction among ethnic Asian brides in South Korea. *Asian Women, 30*(3), 23–56. http://www.e-asianwomen.org/xml/02622/02622.pdf

Oh, S., Litam, D. A., & Chang, C. Y. (2022). COVID-19 racial discrimination and mental health of Korean Americans: Role of ethnic identity and coping strategy. *American Psychological Association, 7*(4), 461–470. https://doi.org/10.1037/sah0000407

Ouch, S., & Moradi, B. (2022). Asian American people's intragroup and intergroup collective action: Identifying key correlates. *Journal of Counseling Psychology, 69*(4), 430–442. https://doi.org/10.1037/cou0000606

Park, H., Choi, S., Noh, K., & Hong, J. Y. (2022). Racial discrimination as a cumulative risk factor affecting parental stress on the mental health of Korean Americans (both US- and foreign-born) amid COVID-19: Structural equation modeling. *Journal of Racial and Ethnic Health Disparities.*

Park, I. J. K., Kim, P. Y., Cheung, R. Y. M., & Kim, M. (2010). The role of culture, family processes, and anger regulation in Korean American adolescents' adjustment problems. *American Journal of Orthopsychiatry, 80*(2), 258–266. https://doi.org/10.1111/j.1939-0025.2010.01029.x

Park, I. J. K., Schwartz, S. J., Lee, R. M., & Kim, M. (2013). Perceived racial/ethnic discrimination and antisocial behaviors among Asian American college students: Testing the moderating roles of ethnic and American identity. *Cultural Diversity and Ethnic Minority Psychology, 19*(2), 166–176. https://doi.org/10.1037/a0028640

Park, J., & Campa, A. J. (2022, April 29). Thirty years after it burned, Koreatown has transformed. But scars remain. *Los Angeles Times.* https://www.latimes.com/california/story/2022-04-29/thirty-years-after-it-burned-koreatown-has-transformed-but-scars-remain

Park, M., Choi, Y., Yoo, H. C., Yasui, M., & Takeuchi, D. (2021). Racial stereotypes and Asian American youth paradox. *Journal of Youth and Adolescence, 50*(12), 2374–2393. https://doi.org/10.1007/s10964-021-01519-8

Park, N. S., Jang, Y., & Chiriboga, D. A. (2018). Willingness to use mental health counseling and antidepressants in older Korean Americans: The role of beliefs and stigma about depression. *Ethnicity & Health, 23*(1), 97–110. https://doi.org/10.1080/13557858.2016.1246429

Phinney, J. S. (1996). When we talk about American ethnic groups, what do we mean? *American Psychologist, 51*(9), 918–927. https://doi.org/10.1037/0003-066X.51.9.918

Potocky-Tripodi, M. (2002). *Best practices for social work with refugees and immigrants.* Columbia University Press.

Raj, S. P., & Raval, V. V. (2013). Parenting and family socialization within a cultural context. *Journal of Communications Research, 5*(2), 165–186.

Rubin, A., & Babbie, E.R. (2015). *Empower Series: Essential research methods for social work* (4th ed.). Cangage Learning.

Ryan, W. S., & Ryan, R. M. (2019). Toward a social psychology of authenticity: Exploring within-person variation in autonomy, congruence, and genuineness using self-determination theory. *Review of General Psychology, 23*(1), 99–112. https://doi.org/10.1037/gpr0000162

Seol, K. O., Yoo, H. C., Lee, R. M., Park, J. E., & Kyeong, Y. (2016). Racial and ethnic socialization as moderators of racial discrimination and school adjustment of adopted and nonadopted Korean American adolescents. *Journal of Counseling Psychology, 63*(3), 294–306.

Simpson, G. E., & Yinger, J. M. (1985). *Racial and cultural minorities: An analysis of prejudice and discrimination* (5th ed.). Plenum Press.

Smedley, A., & Smedley, B. D. (2005). Race as biology is fiction, racism as a social problem is real: Anthropological and historical perspectives on the social construction of race. *American Psychologist, 60*(1), 16–26. https://doi.org/10.1037/0003-066X.60.1.16

Stop AAPI Hate. (2021). National report (through December 31, 2021). https://stopaapihate.org/national-report-through-december-31-2021/

US Census Bureau. (2018). Asian alone or in any combination by selected groups. https://data.census.gov/cedsci/table?q=pakistani&g=&lastDisplayedRow=18&table=B02018&tid=ACSDT1Y2018.B02018&vintage=2018&mode

Verkuyten, M., Thijs, J., & Gharaei, N. (2019). Discrimination and academic (dis)engagement of ethnic-racial minority students: A social identity threat perspective. *Social Psychology of Education, 22*(2), 267–290. https://doi.org/10.1007/s11218-018-09476-0

Vo, D. X., Locke, J. J., Johnson, A., & Marshall, S. K. (2015). The effectiveness of the Mindful Awareness and Resilience Skills for Adolescents (Mars-A) intervention on adolescent mental health: A pilot clinical trial. *Journal of Adolescent Health, 56*(2), S27. https://doi.org/10.1016/j.jadohealth.2014.10.054

Walton, J., & Truong, M. (2023). A review of the model minority myth: Understanding the social, educational and health impacts. *Ethnic & Racial Studies, 46*(3), 391–419. https://doi.org/10.1080/01419870.2022.2121170

Wang, H., & Lou, X. (2022). The correlation between self-compassion and life satisfaction varies across societal individualism-collectivism: A three-level meta-analysis. *Journal of Cross-Cultural Psychology, 53*(9), 1097–1116. https://doi.org/10.1177/00220221221109547

Yasui, M., Kim, T. Y., & Choi, Y. (2018). Culturally specific parent mental distress, parent-child relations and youth depression among Korean American families. *Journal of Child and Family Studies, 27*, 3371–3384. https://doi.org/10.1007/s10826-018-1151-z

8
Acculturation and Cultural Socialization Practices of Japanese Immigrant and Temporary Resident Families in the United States

Misa Kayama

Introduction

Currently in the United States, Asians comprise the second largest immigrant group and are expected to become the largest by 2055 (Pew Research Center, 2021). Due to cultural differences, Asian immigrants in the United States, relative to those from Western countries, are at a higher risk of facing acculturation challenges (Tian et al., 2019), such as language barriers, social isolation, and psychological distress (e.g., Seto & Woodford, 2007; Suinn, 2010). *Acculturation* is a psychological and social process in which individuals adjust to another culture while maintaining their culture of origin (e.g., Berry, 2001, 2003). Acculturation challenges can be exacerbated when immigrants are considered solely responsible for adjusting to the host culture (Berry, 2001), which particularly increases the vulnerability of Asian immigrants. Asian immigrants who value group harmony—influenced, for example, by Confucianism—express fear of failing to behave in a culturally expected manner in their host cultures (Albrecht & Ko, 2017; Ling et al., 2014). Yet they may not disclose their acculturation challenges and seek formal support that can label them as "failures," and hence they experience

Misa Kayama, *Acculturation and Cultural Socialization Practices of Japanese Immigrant and Temporary Resident Families in the United States* In: *Addressing Anti-Asian Racism with Social Work, Advocacy, and Action*. Edited by: Meirong Liu and Keith T. Chan, Oxford University Press. © Oxford University Press 2024. DOI: 10.1093/oso/9780197672242.003.0008 social isolation (e.g., Sakamoto et al., 2009; Yeh et al., 2003). Furthermore, acculturation challenges experienced by Asian immigrants are frequently undermined due, in part, to the stereotypes of Asians as a "model minority"—quiet, reticent, and studious (Zhou & Bankston, 2020). Anti-Asian racism, which has a long history in the United States (Gover et al., 2020), also exacerbates their acculturation challenges, including at schools. Asian parents, for example, reported racism as an obstacle to their children's acculturation to US public schools (e.g., Cho & Shin, 2008; Endo, 2016; Kayama & Haight, 2022). This chapter focuses on acculturation challenges and anti-Asian racism experienced by Japanese families in the United States and how parents support their children's adjustment to US local schools using illustrative narratives of Japanese immigrant and temporary resident parents in small southern cities.

Japanese Immigrant and Temporary Residents

Among the diverse Asian immigrant groups in the United States (Pew Research Center, 2021), the Japanese population is one of the important subgroups to examine due to its increases in numbers and diversity and their distinct cultural values and practices. First, Japanese permanent and temporary residents in the United States have increased by 45% in the past two decades (Ministry of Foreign Affairs, 2022), which comprises about 6.4% of the Asian population (US Census Bureau, 2020). In addition, as of 2016, Japanese temporary residents in the United States comprised 6.4% of those from Asian countries (US Department of Homeland Security, 2018). Among Japanese temporary residents, 64% were temporary workers and their families (US Department of Homeland Security, 2018), many of whom were employed by Japanese companies and stayed in the United States for 3–5 years (Japan Institute for Labour Policy and Training, 2008). Temporary resident families experience challenges similar to those faced by new immigrant families, for example, in supporting their children's adjustment to US public schools (see Fry, 2007; Kayama & Yamakawa, 2020a, 2020b). Yet relative to other East Asian groups, there are fewer Japanese resources available for new immigrants and temporary residents outside of major US cities (Kurotani, 2005; Ministry of Foreign Affairs, 2022). Smaller midwestern and southern cities, including those that host US branches of Japanese companies, frequently do not have well-organized Japanese communities that support the acculturation of new temporary resident families (see Akiyama, 2016).

Next, similar to other Asian groups, the Japanese population in the United States is diverse in how they understand and navigate anti-Asian racism, including 19th-century exclusionary laws against Asians (Gover et al., 2020), Japanese internment camps during World War II (Nagata & Takeshita, 1998), and hate crimes associated with the COVID-19 pandemic (COVID-19 Hate Crimes Act, 2021). Japanese Americans, for instance, prioritized assimilation into US society during and after World War II to gain the status of "American," which was critical to avoiding racial discrimination against Japanese people (Nagata & Takeshita, 1998). Yet recent Japanese immigrants and temporary residents who have not experienced anti-Japanese racism may not perceive assimilation into US society as necessary for their survival (Endo, 2016). Furthermore, many recent Japanese immigrants and temporary residents arrive in the United States as majority group members of a contemporary Japanese society that is homogeneous relative to the United States. They, thus, may lack familiarity with racism and do not have cultural socialization practices that protect their children from racism (Kayama & Haight, 2022), which increases their vulnerability to acculturation challenges.

Finally, Japanese immigrants' and temporary residents' experiences of acculturation are shaped by Japanese socialization beliefs and practices that are distinct from those in the majority US culture (e.g., Azuma, 1994; Kayama et al., 2020). Socialization practices in the United States, for instance, emphasize children's independence and individual rights. Children, typically, are encouraged by their parents and educators to explicitly express their thoughts and feelings (Rogoff, 2003; Shweder et al., 2006). In contrast, influenced by Confucianism, Japanese socialization practices value group harmony and belonging. Children are socialized to "read" others' feelings and thoughts that tends to be expressed implicitly (e.g., through facial expression and tone of voice) and accommodate them (Azuma, 1994). Japanese people also are sensitive to others' responses to their differences, particularly their failure to meet societal expectations (e.g., Kayama et al., 2020; Kuroishi et al., 2015). Thus, Japanese immigrant and temporary resident families may prioritize maintaining their social status and avoiding feelings of shame and inferiority by hiding their acculturation challenges instead of seeking formal support (Harkins, 2001; Yeh et al., 2003). Consequently, their voices, including distress, may remain unrecognized by members of US local communities, including educators at their children's schools (Kayama & Haight, 2022).

Acculturation Challenges: Japanese Families' Adjustment to the United States

Across diverse immigrant groups, acculturation to a new culture has significant impacts on children's psychosocial and academic functioning. Many immigrant and temporary resident children are not familiar with US culture, language, and school systems (e.g., Akiyama, 2016; Derderian-Aghajanian & Wang, 2012; Ling et al., 2014; Nguyen & Hale, 2017) and experience psychological distress, so-called *acculturative stress* (Berry, 2003). Some also may develop symptoms of depression (Ling et al., 2014; Suinn, 2010). Acculturative stress can disrupt children's development of self and cultural identity (e.g., Tian et al., 2019) and lower their self-esteem, which can lead to social isolation and withdrawal (Akiyama, 2016; Albrecht & Ko, 2017; Suinn, 2010).

Upon their arrival to the United States, similar to children from other immigrant groups, Japanese children's psychosocial and academic functioning can be affected by their limited English proficiency (Akiyama, 2016; Harkins, 2001; Nozaki, 2000; Seto & Woodford, 2007; Yen et al., 2003). Indeed, Japanese people's (both children and adults) awareness of their inability to communicate in English may lower their self-esteem (Kayama & Yamakawa, 2020a). For example, Haruto, a sixth-grade boy who grew up in the United States until preschool age experienced significant challenges at school due to language barriers when he returned to the United States in fourth grade. His father described,

> Haruto developed a sort of "wall" [between him and others] because he was clearly aware that, "I can't speak English." [Being in the United States for two years], he still has not been able to break down the wall [completely].... He knows and has been conscious about what he can and can't do. Instead of making an effort to overcome what he can't do well, he tends to [avoid and] isolate himself [at school]. (Kayama & Yamakawa, 2020a, p. 196)

Such feelings of inferiority in comparison to other students can further limit his social interactions with peers and educators at his US local school.

Differences in communication styles, or expression of self, also can be a barrier to Japanese children's acculturation. In many Asian cultures, children's direct expression of their preferences, particularly to adults who have authority, such as educators, can be considered disrespectful (Arora & Algios, 2019; Rhee et al., 2003). One Japanese mother described her daughter Aki (seventh grade) who was hesitant to express her needs at school after being in the United States for one year.

> In the US, when she wants [others] to do something for her, she needs to ask them. It's different from Japan where others usually notice what she needs, even before she tells them. My child knows that at her local school, she needs to speak up, but she can't say [what she thinks] immediately. I think she is always cautious at school all day. (Kayama & Yamakawa, 2020b, p. 7)

Even after children become fluent in English, they may continue to face acculturation challenges due to differences in cultural values (Schwartz et al., 2010; Tian et al., 2019). Children, for example, may feel a lack of belonging within peer groups at their US local schools when they do not have common interests, such as TV shows and cartoon characters, which they can enjoy talking about with peers (Kayama & Yamakawa, 2020b). Hiroto's (fourth grade) mother, who has been in the United States for two years, describe his failure to understand jokes and lack of sense of belonging at school.

> For him, having Japanese friends means a lot. He now can speak English, but [at his local school], he doesn't understand jokes. When other children are laughing, he can't laugh. The timing of laughter, [or what they perceive as a joke], is different. Such tiny differences can make him feel, "I'm the only one who is different, who doesn't belong here [local school]." (Kayama & Yamakawa, 2020b, p. 7)

Children's acculturation also can be affected by their parents' adjustment to the host culture. For instance, some Japanese temporary resident parents who reported social isolation in their local communities did not have access to the resources necessary to support their children, which left their children struggling alone at school (Seto & Woodford, 2007). Furthermore, many Japanese parents reported lowered confidence in supporting their children in the host culture. For Japanese immigrant and temporary resident parents, similar to those from other East Asian countries, their children's educational success in the United States is particularly important (e.g., Nukaga, 2012). Despite enormous efforts parents exerted in supporting their children, for example, by searching for English tutors and school districts with highly qualified teachers (Cho & Shin, 2008; Endo, 2016), parents' participation in their children's US local schools may be limited due to language barriers, parents' lack of knowledge of US school systems, and educators who lack cultural sensitivity. As a result, parents reported a feeling of inadequacy in raising their children in the United States (Cho & Shin, 2008; Choi et al., 2013; Endo, 2016; Nukaga, 2012; Qin & Han, 2014).

Parents' sense of inferiority, consequently, may affect their relationships with children at home. Particularly older children (e.g., middle to high school-aged youth) reported their preference for seeking support from peers, including those who have experienced similar acculturation challenges, and their reluctance to disclose challenges they experienced at school to their parents (Harkins, 2001; Yeh et al., 2003). For example, Jun's (seventh grade) mother, after living in the United States for three years, described Jun's reluctance to ask her for help and her feeling of inadequacy in supporting him.

> He doesn't tell me anything about [his local] school. He knows I can't understand English, and says, "It doesn't make any difference if I tell you." ... So, I don't know anything [about what he is doing] at school. What I've done, and can do, is to find a tutor who can [help him] with schoolwork once a week. It's been working well, but that makes me feel that I'm not involved in [my child's education enough]. (Kayama & Yamakawa, 2020a, p. 199)

Japanese Families Navigating Anti-Asian Racism in the United States

Across cultures, racial discrimination negatively affects school-aged children's psychosocial functioning, including low self-esteem and depressive symptoms (e.g., Kiang et al., 2016; Lopez et al., 2016). Likewise, anti-Asian racism can increase the vulnerability of Japanese and other Asian children who face acculturation challenges (e.g., Kanno, 2000; Nozaki, 2000; Yeh et al., 2003). Japanese people, for instance, tend to prioritize maintaining their social status. They may avoid standing out from their group and causing others discomfort (Lebra, 1976) by hiding their differences from the majority groups and remaining silent about others' negative attitudes toward their differences. After World War II, indeed, Japanese American parents expressed their preference for not discussing with their children any experiences of anti-Japanese racism (Nagata & Takeshita, 1998). Some also encouraged their children to downplay their Japanese identity to avoid racism (see Endo, 2016).

Recent Japanese immigrant and temporary resident parents also expressed reluctance to report anti-Asian racism, such as educators' biased attitudes at their children's US local schools (Endo, 2016; Nukaga, 2012). Parents' reluctance, however, obscures their children's psychological distress and reinforces the stereotype of Asians as a model minority. The stereotyped labels can motivate Asian children to fulfill expectations as a model minority but may leave them alone to overcome acculturation challenges. Such stereotypes also prevent them from receiving necessary support (Kiang et al., 2016). Furthermore, educators may misunderstand Japanese immigrant and temporary resident children's school struggles (Kayama & Haight, 2022; Nozaki, 2000). Some elementary school teachers in the United States, for instance, considered inattentive behaviors of Japanese temporary resident children due to their language barriers as problematic, not fitting the stereotype of model minorities, and referred them to specialized services (Nozaki, 2000).

Japanese children also may attempt to fit into their classrooms at their US local schools by concealing their acculturation challenges (Kayama & Haight, 2022), which can delay the identification of their challenges and isolate them at school (Kiang et al., 2016; Nozaki, 2000). For example, one mother of two children, Nozomi (seventh grade) and Yuuki (third grade), described her children's strategies to fit into their classrooms after living in the United States for one year.

> [Many Japanese] children can't say easily to teachers that they don't understand unless teachers ask them, "Do you understand this? Did you get it?" They may just let it go. My children can't speak to [teachers] in English well. Thus, they try to be quiet so they don't [bother their teachers]. I tell them "Ask your teachers," but they say, "I'm good." (Kayama & Yamakawa, 2020b, p. 5)

In addition, Yuuki's language and educational challenges were not noticed by educators for over a year. His mother continued,

> Last year, he had another Japanese child who translated [instructions to Japanese] for Yuuki. His family left recently. After one year in the United States, Yuuki has just started learning English and is overwhelmed now.... He didn't even notice there was a big project due in a week. Also, no one recognized that he didn't understand and reminded him. (Kayama & Haight, 2022, p. 347)

Educators' misunderstandings of these children's school struggles at US schools can be characterized as microaggression. Asian parents in the United States, including those from Japan, acknowledged educators' and community members' openness to diversity and their cultural differences. Yet they may lack understanding or interest in culturally based behaviors, such as reasons for Asian children remaining quiet at school, which can leave children's acculturation challenges unnoticed at school (Cho & Shin, 2008; Kayama & Haight, 2022). Similarly, Japanese parents discussed a lack of cultural diversity in teaching materials at their children's US local schools, such as readings that were predominantly on European American characters, which undermines their Japanese cultural heritage (Endo, 2016). One Japanese parent summarized such responses to their cultural differences, "I think people in the United States generally are *tolerant* of people [from other cultures]" (Kayama & Haight, 2022, p. 346). Yet the mere tolerance, without an understanding of the cultural meanings of their experiences—including challenges—does not support children's acculturation.

Japanese families also may experience microaggression in their local communities. Some parents, for example, are cautious about speaking in Japanese in public spaces (Kayama & Haight, 2022; Kayama & Yamakawa, 2020b). An immigrant mother of elementary and preschool-aged children elaborated on her concern.

> [When speaking in Japanese], I don't want to be told, "What did you say? Something bad [about us]?" Also, when talking to my children in public spaces, for example, when I correct my children in Japanese, other people don't understand [what I say]. They may react as if I am abusing [my children]. (Kayama & Yamakawa, 2020b, p. 8)

Such strategies may reduce the risk of microaggression but can make their Japanese identity invisible and leave them isolated within their local communities (Kayama & Haight, 2022).

Parents' Socialization Practices: Access to Japanese Cultural Resources

For new immigrants and temporary residents across cultures, access to cultural resources of origin appears to be critical to their adjustment to US local communities and schools. Involvement in cultural communities of origin, for instance, can reduce psychological distress (e.g., Akiyama, 2016; Kanno, 2000; Koga, 2009); motivate them to overcome acculturation challenges, including language barriers (Zhang et al., 2018); and help them navigate racism (Dimitrova et al., 2015). Japanese temporary resident and immigrant families in the United States also described mutual social and emotional support they received in their Japanese communities (Nukaga, 2012; Sakamoto, 2006). Yet Japanese families in small cities face significant challenges in accessing Japanese cultural resources (Akiyama, 2016; Kurotani, 2005).

Japanese supplementary schools provide new immigrant and temporary resident children from Japan, including those in some small cities in the United States, with an important context for their acculturation (Akiyama, 2016; Endo, 2013; Kayama & Yamakawa, 2020b). Similar to many supplementary schools for children from other Asian countries (e.g., China, Taiwan, and South Korea; e.g., Lee & Shin, 2008; Liao, 2017; Paik et al., 2017; Uttal & Han, 2011), a central goal of Japanese supplementary schools is to teach children Japanese language and culture as well as academic skills (Ministry of Education, Culture, Sports, Science, and Technology, 2021, 2022). Currently, across the United States, there are 82 Japanese supplementary schools, including in smaller Midwestern and Southern cities (Ministry of Education, Culture, Sports, Science, and Technology, 2022) due, in part, to the relocation of Japanese companies to the United States and the following influx of Japanese temporary residents (Ministry of Internal Affairs and Communication, 2015). Typically, Japanese supplementary schools are established and operated by local Japanese communities and organizations with support from the Japanese government (Ministry of Education, Culture, Sports, Science, and Technology, 2021). At supplementary schools, children receive weekly academic instruction in Japanese, following the Japanese curriculum standard, and participate in seasonal events typically implemented at schools in Japan, such as entrance and graduation ceremonies and a sport festival.

In small communities with limited Japanese cultural resources, Japanese supplementary schools are one of the few contexts in which children and their parents can immerse themselves in Japanese culture and language and experience social and emotional acceptance (Akiyama, 2016; Kayama & Yamakawa, 2020a, 2020b). For example, one mother of elementary and middle school-aged children described her children's supplementary school as a place "like vitamin supplements that give them energy to keep up at their local schools" (Kayama & Yamakawa, 2020a, p. 201). For these children, playing and talking with other Japanese children help them relieve accumulated stress in the English environment and regain a positive understanding of self. Such interactions also motivate children to engage at their local schools. In other words, Japanese supplementary schools provide children with weekly "breaks," or respites, that help them recover from emotional exhaustion (Kayama & Yamakawa, 2020b). Supplementary schools also serve as a safe place where children can develop supportive relationships with other children who have similar acculturation challenges at US local schools (Harkins, 2001; Yeh et al., 2005). Weekly meetings at their supplementary schools, for example, may encourage them to work together to overcome challenges.

Japanese supplementary schools also support children's development of Japanese cultural identity, which can cultivate children's sense of belonging and self-worth as members of their own cultural community (Kayama & Yamakawa, 2020b). Similar to other minority groups across the United States (Haight, 2002; Hughes et al., 2006), such cultural identity can provide some protection (Hughes et al., 2006) and help overcome challenges, including racism, in US local communities and schools (e.g., Kayama & Haight, 2022). Yet children, especially those who have acculturated to the US culture, may become confused with their cultural identity (Kwon, 2018), such as Taich, a fourth-grade boy who has been in the United States for two and half years. His mother reported that Taich informed her,

> I'm here [in the United States] for a long time. I'm not Japanese anymore.... [Some children at the supplementary school] were born in the US and he heard that they are American. He, then, thought that he is in the United States long enough to be considered an American. So, I told him, "You speak Japanese, and you are Japanese no matter where you are living.... We are going back to Japan. So, don't forget what Japanese people have to know about." He said, "That's what [I don't like about] Japanese people." So, I told him, "You're Japanese, too." (Kayama & Haight, 2022, pp. 345–346)

Thus, to support children's development of Japanese identity, parents emphasize the importance of creating opportunities in which their children are exposed to Japanese socialization practices outside of their homes, including at their Japanese supplementary school. Another mother described her son, Kenji (second grade), after living in the United States for 2 years, "He doesn't remember a lot about Japan. [Participation at the supplementary school is] an opportunity where he can remember something he did when he was in Japan, such as seasonal events" (Kayama & Haight, 2023, p. 1003).

Finally, Japanese supplementary schools provide important cultural resources for parents, as well as children. For example, weekly meetings with other Japanese parents at their children's supplementary school allow them to enjoy talking in Japanese and relieve stress. Parents also help each other to adjust to US culture, for instance, by exchanging information about their children's US local schools and other Japanese resources available in the community (Kayama & Yamakawa, 2020a, 2020b). Furthermore, their common experiences of navigating acculturation challenges strengthen their relationships (see Sakamoto, 2006). One Japanese mother described her weekly visits to her child's Japanese supplementary school.

> For us, something we can understand each other as Japanese is important. If we don't come to the supplementary school, there are not many chances we see [Japanese people]. . . . This is a very precious place [for parents] to get together, exchange information about what is happening in Japan, and at times, support each other and [relieve stress] by expressing frustration. It's not easy to find such a person [in my local community]. (Kayama & Yamakawa, 2020b, p. 8)

Note that the experiences of Japanese immigrant and temporary resident families in larger cities with extensive Japanese resources may be somewhat different from the illustrative narratives of parents in small Southern cities presented in this chapter. Although Japanese immigrant and temporary resident families in large urban areas acknowledged Japanese communities as sources of support (e.g., Endo, 2013), they raised concerns about strong ties within the Japanese communities. Such ties can restrict their engagement in activities that are not familiar to other Japanese families, particularly their participation in US local communities. As a result, some may limit their interaction with the Japanese communities (Nukaga, 2012; Sakamoto, 2006).

In smaller, rural areas, however, Japanese families may not have Japanese communities large enough to choose with whom they prefer to interact.

Implications for Supporting Immigrant and Temporary Resident Families

The experiences of Japanese immigrant and temporary resident families in the United States have some implications for diversity, inclusion, and equity.

Diversity

Acculturation is, by definition (Berry, 2001), a process in which both immigrants and members of the host culture adjust to each other. In practice, however, immigrants may be considered solely responsible for adjusting to the new culture, including policies, schools, and other systems. Yet exposure to new cultures is an excellent opportunity for local community members to broaden their perspectives (Sakamoto et al., 2008). For instance, collaboration with supplementary schools provides US public schools with resources for diversity education. Such collaboration allows immigrant and temporary resident children to serve as liaisons between their two cultures, which can motivate them to overcome acculturation challenges, adjust to their new cultures, and contribute to eliminating myths of Asians as model minorities.

Inclusion

A lack of cultural sensitivity among members of the host culture can lead to misunderstandings about the acculturation challenges experienced by new immigrant and temporary resident families. Tolerance and openness to cultural differences do not necessarily lead to acceptance of new cultures brought in by immigrant families. For example, the government implemented the COVID-19 Hate Crimes Act (2021) in response to the heightened anti-Asian hatred during the COVID-19 pandemic. This law may contribute to raising the awareness of anti-Asian racism, but it does not address microaggression that may evolve into hate crimes.

Avoiding microaggressions requires mutual efforts by both immigrants and local community members. Without immigrant children and parents indicating incidents of microaggression, it is likely that they will continue to experience similar incidents. They may benefit from social workers and other professionals who can educate and advocate for them. Increased cultural sensitivity of local community members also is necessary to eliminate microaggression. At school, for instance, educators' understanding of the reasons for Japanese immigrant and temporary resident children's passive attitudes (e.g., remaining quiet) can sensitize them to these children's psychological distress and social isolation. Instead of assuming that children who remain quiet have adjusted well to the local communities and schools, engaging with them (e.g., by individually asking them if they face any challenges) can lead to the identification of children who experience acculturation challenges and the formulation of culturally sensitive intervention programs.

Equity

Japanese and other Asian immigrant and temporary resident families can also benefit from programs that support their acculturation, for example, educational workshops on US cultures, such as their individual rights and the historical contexts of racism in the United States. New immigrants and temporary residents who have not experienced racism in their countries of origin may not recognize structural biases in US local schools and communities (e.g., Uttal & Han, 2011) and may blame themselves for not being capable of supporting their children in overcoming challenges (Choi et al., 2013; Nukaga, 2012; Qin & Han, 2014). The knowledge of US sociocultural contexts, including racism, can help them shift their interpretations of acculturation challenges from their own failure to structural biases and encourage them to seek formal support rather than conceal problems.

Conclusion

Just like other immigrant groups, Japanese immigrant and temporary resident families experience a range of acculturation challenges, from psychological distress, feelings of inferiority and shame, and social exclusion to anti-Asian racism. Consistent with Confucian values of maintaining harmony, Japanese immigrant and temporary resident families may become reluctant to seek formal services for their acculturation challenges. They also may prioritize avoiding conflicts with their local US community members and assume that they are solely responsible for fitting into US society. These Japanese families' responses, however, can reinforce the stereotypes of Asians as a model minority and exacerbate their acculturation challenges.

Yet access to Japanese cultural resources, including supplementary schools, provides a safe place that supports the acculturation of Japanese immigrant and temporary resident families. Mutual support and the respite they receive from other Japanese families help them not only recover from psychological distress, but also motivates them to adjust to their local communities and schools. Japanese supplementary schools also cultivate their sense of belonging and acceptance as members of the Japanese cultural community (Kayama & Yamakawa, 2020b). Unlike the organizations of other minority groups within the United States, such as African American Sunday Schools (Haight, 2002), however, Japanese supplementary schools may not provide direct support for navigating acculturation challenges, including racism (see Ministry of Education, 2021). Yet cultivation of cultural identity likely provides them with the social and emotional support necessary for their adjustment to the United States (Hughes et al., 2006).

Social workers can be involved in supporting Japanese and other Asian families in the United States by advocating for them to initiate conversations with local community members, including on incidents of anti-Asian racism. Educating local community members also increases cultural sensitivity among them. Mediating relationships between immigrant families and local community members can be the first step toward eliminating anti-Asian racism.

References

Akiyama, R. (2016). *Language, culture, and identity negotiation: Perspectives of adolescent Japanese sojourner students in the Midwest, USA* (Publication No. 10242624). Doctoral dissertation, Purdue University. ProQuest Dissertations and Theses Global.

Albrecht, S., & Ko, G. (2017). How do immigrant students develop social confidence and make friends in secondary school? A retrospective study. *Qualitative Report, 22*(9), 2385–2403.

Arora, P. G., & Algios, A. (2019). School-based mental health for Asian American immigrant youth: Perceptions and recommendations. *Asian American Journal of Psychology, 10*(2), 166–181.

Azuma, H. (1994). *Nihon jin no shitsuke to kyo-iku: Hattatsu no nichi bei hikaku ni motozuite* [Discipline and education for Japanese people: Comparison of child development between the US and Japan]. Tokyo Daigaku Shuppan-kai.

Berry, J. W. (2001). A psychology of immigration. *Journal of Social Issues, 57*(3), 615–631.

Berry, J. W. (2003). Conceptual approaches to acculturation. In K. M. Chun, P. Balls Organista, & G. Marin (eds.), *Acculturation: Advances in theory, measurement, and applied research* (pp. 17–37). American Psychological Association.

Cho, E. K., & Shin, S. (2008). Survival, adjustment, and acculturation of newly immigrated families with school-aged children: Cases of four Korean families. *Diaspora, Indigenous, and Minority Education, 2*, 4–24.

Choi, Y., Dancy, B. L, & Lee, J. (2013). Raising children in America: Korean parents' experiences. *Journal of Psychiatric and Mental Health Nursing, 20*(6), 508–513.

COVID-19 Hate Crimes Act, Pub. L. No. 117-13 (2021). https://www.congress.gov/bill/117th-congress/senate-bill/937/text

Derderian-Aghajanian, A., & Wang, C. C. (2012). How culture affects on English language learners's outcomes. *International Journal of Business and Social Science, 3*(5), 172–180.

Endo, R. (2013). Realities, rewards, and risks of heritage-language education: Perspectives from Japanese immigrant parents in a Midwestern community. *Bilingual Research Journal, 36*(3), 278–294.

Endo, R. (2016). The educational aspirations and expectations of Japanese immigrant mothers: Narratives of raising bicultural Nikkei children in the post-1965 diaspora. *Diaspora, Indigenous, and Minority Education, 10*(3), 156–168.

Fry, R. (2007). Perspective shifts and a theoretical model relating to kaigaishijo and kikokushijo, or third culture kids in a Japanese context. *Journal of Research in International Education, 6*(2), 131–150.

Gover, A. R., Harper, S. B, & Langton, L. (2020). Anti-Asian hate crime during the COVID-19 pandemic: Exploring the reproduction of inequality. *American Journal of Criminal Justice, 45*, 647–667.

Haight, W. (2002). *African-American children at church: A sociocultural perspective.* Cambridge University Press.

Harkins, L. F. (2001). Understanding the acculturation process for Kaigaishijo. *Educational Forum, 65*(4), 335–343.

Hughes, D., Rodriguez, J., Smith, P. E., Johnson, D. J., Stevenson, H. C., & Spicer, P. (2006). Parents' ethnic-racial socialization practices: A review of research and directions for future study. *Developmental Psychology, 42*, 747–770.

Japan Institute for Labour Policy and Training. (2008). Dai 7-kai kaigai haken kinmu-sha no shokugyou to seikatsu-ni kansuru chousa kekka [Research report: The 7th study on the work and life of employees sent to abroad]. https://www.jil.go.jp/institute/research/2008/040.html

Kanno, Y. (2000). Bilingualism and identity: The stories of Japanese returnees. *International Journal of Bilingual Education and Bilingualism, 3*(1), 1–18.

Kayama, M., Haight, W., Ku, M., Cho, M. H., & Lee, H. Y. (2020). *Disability, stigmatization, and children's developing selves: Insights from educators in Japan, South Korea, Taiwan, and the US.* Oxford University Press.

Kayama, M., & Haight, W. (2022). Anti-Asian hatred and Japanese parents' support of their children's acculturation to the US. *Social Work, 67*(4), 341–350.

Kayama, M., & Haight, W. (2023) Japanese parents' experiences supporting their school-aged children's acculturation to the US. *Qualitative Social Work, 22*(5), 992–1009.

Kayama, M., & Yamakawa, N. (2020a). Acculturation and a sense of belonging of children in US schools and communities: The case of Japanese families. *Children and Youth Services Review, 119*, 105612.

Kayama, M., & Yamakawa, N. (2020b). Acculturation, cultural self, and identity of Japanese children in US schools: Insights from Japanese temporary resident and immigrant parents. *Identity, 20*(3), 188–207.

Kiang, L., Witkow, M. R., & Thompson, T. L. (2016). Model minority stereotyping, perceived discrimination, and adjustment among adolescents from Asian American backgrounds. *Journal of Youth and Adolescence, 45*(7), 1366–1379.

Koga, N. (2009). *Growing student identities and school competences in sojourning: Japanese children's lived experiences across Japan and the US* (Dissertation No. 3365914). Doctoral dissertation, Boston College. ProQuest Dissertations and Theses Global.

Kuroishi, N., Ikui, Y., & Sano, Y. (2015). What is "normality" among elementary school students? Affective reactions to relative performance. *International Christian University Educational Studies, 57*, 57–67.

Kurotani, S. (2005). *Home away from home: Japanese corporate wives in the United States*. Duke University Press.

Kwon, J. (2018). Third culture kids: Growing up with mobility and cross-cultural transitions. *Diaspora, Indigenous, and Minority Education, 13*, 113–122.

Lebra, T. S. (1976). *Japanese patterns of behavior*. University of Hawai'i Press.

Lee, J. S., & Shin, S. J. (2008). Korean heritage language education in the United States: The current state, opportunities, and possibilities. *Heritage Language Journal, 6*(2), 153–172.

Liao, L. Y. J. (2017). Bridging two worlds: Experiences of Chinese and Taiwanese Americans attending Chinese Heritage Schools in Houston. *Heritage Language Journal, 14*(2), 171–187.

Ling, A., Okazaki, S., Tu, M.-C., & Kim, J. J. (2014). Challenges in meeting the mental health needs of urban Asian American adolescents: Service providers' perspectives. *Race and Social Problems, 6*(1), 25–37.

Lopez, W. D., LeBrón, M. W., Graham, L. F., & Grogan-Kaylor, A. (2016). Discrimination and depressive symptoms among Latina/o adolescents of immigrant parents. *International Quarterly of Community Health Education, 36*(2), 131–140.

Ministry of Education, Culture, Sports, Science, and Technology. (2021). Zaigai kyouiku shisetsu no gaiyou [Overview of educational facilities abroad]. http://www.mext.go.jp/a_menu/shotou/clarinet/002/002.htm.

Ministry of Education, Culture, Sports, Science, and Technology. (2022). Kaigai shijyo kyouiku no gaiyou [Overview: Education of children living abroad]. http://www.mext.go.jp/a_menu/shotou/clarinet/002/001.htm

Ministry of Foreign Affairs. (2022). Kaigai zairyu houjin ninzu chousa toukei [Statistics of Japanese in foreign countries]. https://www.mofa.go.jp/mofaj/toko/page22_003338.html

Ministry of Internal Affairs and Communication. (2015). Guro-baru jinzai ikusei ni kansuru kaigai-shijyo, kikoku-shijyo tou kyouiku ni kansuru jittai chousa [Research on the current status of education for children living abroad and those who have returned from abroad, concerning the global human resource development]. https://www.soumu.go.jp/menu_news/s-news/97809.html#kekkahoukoku.

Nagata, D. K., & Takeshita, Y. J. (1998). Coping and resilience across generations: Japanese Americans and the World War II internment. *Psychoanalytic Review, 85*, 587–613.

Nguyen, E. T., & Hale, J. M. (2017). "You just don't understand me!" Determinants of second generation Asian and Latino youth self-esteem. *International Migration, 55*(5), 44–61.

Nozaki, Y. (2000). Essentializing dilemma and multiculturalist pedagogy: An ethnographic study of Japanese children in a US school. *Anthropology & Education Quarterly, 31*(3), 355–380.

Nukaga, M. (2012). Planning for a successful return home: Transnational habitus and education strategies among Japanese expatriate mothers in Los Angeles. *International Sociology, 28*, 66–83.

Paik, S. J., Rahman, Z., Kula, S. M., Saito, L. E., & Witenstein, M. A. (2017). Ethnic afterschool programs and language schools in diverse Asian American communities: Varying resources, opportunities, and educational experiences (Part 2: How they differ). *School Community Journal, 27*(2), 67–97.

Pew Research Center. (2021). Key facts about Asian Americans, a diverse and growing population. https://www.pewresearch.org/fact-tank/2021/04/29/key-facts-about-asian-americans/

Qin, D. B., & Han, E. J. (2014). Tiger parents or sheep parents? Struggles of parental involvement in working-class Chinese immigrant families. *Teachers College Record*, *116*, 1–32.

Rhee, S., Chang, J., & Rhee, J. (2003). Acculturation, communication patterns, and self-esteem among Asian and Caucasian American adolescents. *Adolescence*, *38*(152), 750–768.

Rogoff, B. (2003). *The cultural nature of human development*. Oxford University Press.

Sakamoto, I. (2006). When family enters the picture: The model of cultural negotiation and gendered experiences of Japanese academic sojourners in the United States. *Cultural Diversity and Ethnic Minority Psychology*, *12*(3), 558–577.

Sakamoto, I., Ku, J., & Wei, Y. (2009). The deep plunge: Luocha and the experiences of earlier skilled immigrants from Mainland China in Toronto. *Qualitative Social Work*, *8*(4), 427–447.

Sakamoto, I., Wei, Y., & Truong, L. (2008). How do organization and social policies "acculturate" to immigrants? Accommodating skilled immigrants in Canada. *American Journal of Community Psychology*, *42*, 343–354.

Schwartz, S. J., Unger, J. B., Zamboanga, B. L., & Szapocznik, J. (2010). Rethinking the concept of acculturation: Implications for theory and research. *American Psychologist*, *65*(4), 237–251.

Seto, A., & Woodford, M. S. (2007). Helping a Japanese immigrant family cope with acculturation issues: A case study. *Family Journal: Counseling and Therapy for Couples and Families*, *15*(2), 167–173.

Shweder, R. A., Goodnow, J. G., Hatano, G., LeVine, R. A., Markus, H. R., & Miller, P. J. (2006). The cultural psychology of development: One mind, many mentalities. In W. Damon & R. Lerner (eds.), *Handbook of child development: Vol. 1 Theoretical models of human development* (6th ed., pp. 716–792). Wiley.

Suinn, R. M. (2010). Reviewing acculturation and Asian Americans: How acculturation affects health, adjustment, school adjustment, and counseling. *Asian American Journal of Psychology*, *1*(1), 5–17.

Tian, L., McClain, S., Moore, M. M., & Lloyd, H. (2019). An examination of ethnic identity, self-compassion, and acculturative stress in Asian international students. *Journal of International Students*, *9*(2), 635–660.

US Census Bureau. (2020). American Community Survey 2019: Table B02018 Asian alone or in any combination by selected groups. https://data.census.gov/cedsci/table?t=Asian&g=0100000US&d=ACS 1-Year Estimates Detailed Tables&tid=ACSDT1Y2019.B02018

US Department of Homeland Security. (2018). Nonimmigrants residing in the United States: Fiscal Year 2016. https://www.dhs.gov/sites/default/files/publications/Nonimmigrant_Population%20Estimates_2016_0.pdf

Uttal, L., & Han, C. Y. (2011). Taiwanese immigrant mothers' childcare preferences: Socialization for bicultural competency. *Cultural Diversity and Ethnic Minority Psychology*, *17*, 437–443.

Yeh, C. J., Arora, A. K., Inose, M., Okubo, Y., Li, R. H., & Greene, P. (2003). The cultural adjustment and mental health of Japanese immigrant youth. *Adolescence*, *38*(151), 481–500.

Zhang, J., Dennis, J. M., & Houseman, C. (2018). The role of family and community bicultural socialization in the bilingual proficiency of immigrant young adults. *International Journal of Intercultural Relations*, *67*, 44–57.

Zhou, M., & Bankston III, C. L. (2020). The model minority stereotype and the national identity question: The challenges facing Asian immigrants and their children. *Ethnic and Racial Studies*, *43*(1), 233–253.

9

Bahaghari

Visibilizing the Experiences and Resistance of LGBTQ+ Filipinx Americans in the Diaspora

Dale Dagar Maglalang and Hillary Nicole Peregrina

Introduction

There are more than 4 million Filipinx[1,2] Americans in the United States, comprising the third largest Asian American subgroup in the country (Budiman, 2021). Filipinx Americans have a long history with the United States: the Treaty of Paris of 1898 initially sold the Philippines to the United States from Spain, which Filipinos resisted, and this eventually led to the Philippine American War of 1898–1902 (Bonus, 2000). Losing the war, the Philippines became a US territory and Filipinos became US nationals. They were able to immigrate to the US to fill jobs in agriculture and the cannery industries. Gaining independence from the United States in 1946, and then having immigration quotas placed on Filipinos, it was not until the Immigration Act of 1965 that Filipinos began to immigrate again to the United States in large numbers through family reunification and job opportunities, specifically as nurses (Bonus, 2000; Choy, 2003). Hence, it is unsurprising that there's a sizeable population of Filipinx Americans in the country. While research has been conducted on Filipinx Americans, more needs to be implemented, and there is a dearth of studies on lesbian, gay, bisexual, transgender, queer plus (LGBTQ+) Filipinx Americans. Given the history and cultural background of Filipinos and how it intersects with the LGBTQ+ culture and recent increase of affronts toward the LGBTQ+ population in the United States (American Civil Liberties Union, 2023), it is imperative to examine the experiences of Filipinx American LGBTQ+ individuals and how the field of social work can work to serve this population.

The purpose of this chapter is to discuss the identity formation of Filipinx American LGBTQ+ individuals and how their intersecting identities shaped their experiences within the Filipinx American diaspora and society at large. We also provide implications for social work research and practice when engaging and working with this population.

History of LGBTQ+ Filipinos

Precolonial History: Gender, Sexuality, and the *Babaylan*

The Indigenous population of the Philippine archipelago was gender-neutral and egalitarian in that women, feminine, and queer people were honored and revered (Francia, 2014; Mananzan, 2003). In comparison to Christian accounts of the creation story of Adam and Eve, Indigenous creation stories passed down through oral traditions depicted a man and a woman emerging from a bamboo together simultaneously (Strobel, 2013). Furthermore, early accounts from Spanish friars depicted egalitarian family systems, where men and women shared equal power, household and parenting roles, and decision-making (Francia, 2014). Gender neutrality continues to persist across Philippine languages that hold gender-neutral pronouns, like *siya* in Filipino, which translates to "he," "she," or "them." Regarding sexuality, little is known about sexuality and sexual behavior prior to Spanish colonization (Nadal, 2021). Accounts from Spanish friars indicated that same-sex sexual and romantic love may have been common among Indigenous Filipinos (Garcia, 2008).

Gender neutrality in the precolonial Philippines is personified in the figure of the *babaylans*, Indigenous spiritual healers and leaders (Francia, 2014; Strobel, 2013). *Babaylans* took on significant roles in providing health and wellness including procuring herbs and potions for physical illnesses, childbirth, and spiritual healing. *Babaylans* also assumed significant roles in tribal government structures and were involved in decision-making in collaboration with the *datus* (tribal chiefs), *baganis* (warriors), and *pandays* (craftspeople) (Francia, 2014; Strobel, 2013). Though a majority of *babaylans* were women, these roles were performed by different genders. Male *babaylans* were known for cross-dressing, and in modern day times could be identified as transgender or queer (Garcia, 2008; Manalansan, 2003).

Spanish Colonization and the Introduction of the Gender Binary

Spain colonized the Philippines from 1521 to 1898 (Francia, 2014; Strobel, 2013). Spanish colonization continues to have a significant influence on Philippine society, including religion through the introduction of Roman Catholicism, Spanish cultural values, and gender role expectations between men and women. Indigenous Filipinos were brutally forced to adapt to Spanish cultural values and religion, shifting from a gender-neutral society to a patriarchal one (Nadal, 2021). Observing the political and cultural influences of the *babaylan* in precolonial Philippine society, Spanish friars introduced *machismo* to subvert the *babaylan*'s role in Indigenous communities (Francia, 2014; Mananzan, 2003). Filipinos were forced to adopt Spanish gender norms of *machismo* (male dominance) and *marianismo* (female submissiveness). Through *machismo*, men were expected to be strong, provide for their families, and assume power over women. Rooted in the image of Jesus's mother, Mary, through *marianismo*, women were expected to be religious, pure, and morally superior to and spiritually stronger than men (Francia, 2014; Mananzan, 2003). With this shift in gender norms, women were objectified and disrespected, leading to gender inequities (Mananzan, 2003). Furthermore, although precolonial society was gender-neutral, because of Catholicism, homosexuality and romantic love between similar genders became unwarranted, leading to LGBTQ+ individuals being viewed as immoral.

Contemporary LGBTQ+ Filipinos

Compared to Western perspectives, sexual orientation in the Philippines is subsumed under the social constructs of gender (Ceperiano et al., 2016; Tan, 1995). The terms predominantly used to describe queer individuals are *bakla* for gay men and *tomboy* for lesbian women. However, in Philippine society, the expected manifestations initially reflected feminine gender expressions for *baklas* and masculine expressions for *tomboys* (Ceperiano et al., 2016). Certainly people who identify within the spectrum of sexuality (e.g., bisexual, asexual, queer, etc.) and beyond gender binaries (e.g., transgender, gender non-conforming, etc.) have always been present, even in the precolonial Philippines. The modern LGBTQ+ population has seen more visibility and discursivity in Philippine society, with continued organizing among LGBTQ+ Filipinos to reconstruct and redefine their identities, create spaces, and establish their own narratives (Ceperiano et al., 2016; Garcia, 2013). The concept of *kabaklaan*, imprecisely translated as "gayness," helps Filipino LGBTQ+ individuals embody different types of queerness across genders, sexual orientation, and socioeconomic status (Garcia, 2013). It's also seen as a performance comprised of postures and gestures that are often seen as "over the top," enacted to deride and find humor in a heteronormative society that marginalizes those who are LGBTQ+ (Diaz, 2018). Through *kabaklaan* Filipino LGBTQ+ individuals continue to survive and thrive by raising the visibility of the Filipino LGBTQ+ population. However, Diaz (2015) argued that the Global South's conceptualization and manifestation of *kabaklaan* challenges gay globality or the Western conceptualization of the LGBTQ+ identity and then complicates how the Filipino diaspora, as in the United States, contends with what it means to be *bakla*. Thus, multigenerational Filipinx Americans may have differing understanding and notions of Filipino *baklas* that may cause tensions, schisms, or, perhaps, even acceptance and healing.

Presently, the state of the LGBTQ+ community in the Philippines continue to progress and challenge heteronormative governmental spaces with more LGBTQ+ identified Filipinos serving in local (village, city) and national positions (Gamboa et al., 2021) and the creation of a national LGBTQ+ political organization, Ladlad Partylist (Benedicto, 2022). Filipino LGBTQ+ artists work to expand the narratives of Filipino LGBTQ+ individuals, especially the stories of transgender women, through film (Diaz, 2018). However, achieving full equity for Filipino LGBTQ+ persons in the Philippines still has a long way to go. For instance, it has been a two-decade struggle to pass the Sexual Orientation and Gender Identity or Expression Equality (SOGIE) Bill in the Philippine House and Senate, which would provide federal protections from discrimination for individuals based on their gender, sexual orientation, and expression (Ladia, 2022). LGBTQ+ organizations and their allies have been able to advocate to pass 31 anti-discrimination ordinances (ADO) in different cities and municipalities in the country as of 2021 (Ladia, 2022).

Filipinx American LGBTQ+ Identity Formation

Limited studies focus on LGBTQ+ identity among diasporic Filipinx Americans living in the United States (Manalansan, 2003; Nadal, 2021; Nadal & Corpus, 2013; Ocampo, 2022). While most of these studies concentrate on the experiences of gay men, studies on the experiences of lesbian, bisexual, and transgender Filipinx Americans remain limited. In comparison to Filipino LGBTQ+ in the Philippines, Filipinx American identity in the United States is constructed not only by gender and sexuality, but also through the intersections of religiosity, familism, culture, race, ethnicity, class, immigration status, and education (Chiongbian et al., 2023; Manalansan, 2003; Nadal & Corpus, 2013; Ocampo, 2022).

Religion

A study on Filipinx American LGB individuals found that, in navigating Filipinx American spaces, they often contended with the assumed negative stance on LGBTQ+ identity espoused by the Roman Catholic religion, which many Filipinx Americans practice due to the enduring residue of Spanish colonization (Nadal & Corpus, 2013). Filipinx American LGB individuals felt that religion was a barrier to coming out and that their competing identities related to their ethnic identity, sexual orientation, and religion could not coexist. In fact, religious family members have used religion to induce feelings of shame and guilt and even performed interventions to dispel or "cure" their homosexuality (Nadal & Corpus, 2013). As a result, Filipinx American LGB individuals rectify these feelings by turning away from religion and maintaining silence about their sexual orientation to not only protect themselves but also to protect their family's reputation—saving face. Similarly, Filipinx American gay college men described contradictory messages they received from Filipino culture, which openly represented gender fluidity in the media while their Catholic backgrounds held strict gender role and heteronormative expectations (Chan, 2017). Being raised Catholic reinforced traditional definitions of masculinity. To manage their parents' expectations and cultural contradictions, participants described the need to monitor their behaviors and perform masculinity in order to conform to others' perceptions of their gender expression (Chan, 2017).

Familism

Coming from a collectivist culture and under the influence of Catholicism, the cultural value of Filipino familism guides how Filipinx American LGBTQ+ individuals negotiate their sexual orientation (Ocampo, 2014, 2022). A study of Filipinx American gay men showed that they viewed their sexual identity as incongruent with the morals (conservative, *machismo*, and Catholic) and gender role expectations of Filipino culture (Ocampo, 2014). To navigate these incongruencies, manage intergenerational conflict, and maintain a sense of social support within their families, Filipinx American gay men learned to compartmentalize parts of their lives by strategically displaying their sexual identities in front of their families through monitoring their gender presentation, mannerisms, tone of voice, clothing, activities they engaged in, and friends that met their family (Ocampo, 2014). Filipinx American gay men who decided to come out to their families made efforts to expand their parents' perceptions of sexual identity by showing different representations of gay men. They also engaged in moral convergence that drew parallels between their lived experiences as gay men and their parents' experiences as new immigrants trying to acculturate to new cultures and lifestyles (Ocampo, 2014).

Race and Ethnicity

Filipinx American LGBTQ+ individuals must negotiate their race and ethnicity and the intersections of their multiple identities. Filipinx American LGBs have felt stronger identification with their Filipino ethnic identity as opposed to their racial identity as Asian American because Filipinos were often left out in discussions within Asian America populations (Nadal & Corpus, 2013). Filipinx American gay men have at times been feminized or assumed to take submissive gender roles (i.e., "bottoms"). In navigating non-Filipinx American LGB spaces, Filipinx American LGB individuals felt that they were either exoticized because of their race and ethnicity or that they had to strip themselves of their racial and ethnic identity to fit into LGBT+ spaces, thus showing how White supremacy manifests even within spaces for marginalized communities (Nadal & Corpus, 2013).

Across the fields of LGBT studies, psychology, and social work, more work need to be done in conceptualizing the sexual identity development in queer people of color. Past research on sexual identity development assumed a universal experience for LGBTQ+ individuals, ignoring the roles of race, ethnicity, religion, and social class (Nadal & Corpus, 2013; Ocampo, 2014). K. L. Nadal (2021) presents the only model for sexual identity development specific to LGBTQ+ Filipinx Americans. According to this model, race, ethnicity, and sexual identity intersect to form 20 different identity statuses ranging from *sensitization/assimilation*, categorized as low sexual identity development, low racial identity, and low ethnic identity to *commitment/integration*, categorized as integrated sexual identity development, integrated racial identity, and integrated ethnic identity (Nadal, 2021).

Im/migration

Immigration and migration also impacted the identity formation of Filipinx American LGBTQ+ individuals. There are differing understanding of gender expressions between *baklas* and tomboys growing up as either US-born or immigrant Filipinx American LGBs, where the former deemed that there's more flexibility in gender expressions, while the latter grew up witnessing *baklas* who conformed to more feminine presentations (e.g., wore feminine clothes and make-up) and tomboys to more masculine presentations (e.g., shorter hair, wore loose-fitting masculine clothes) (Nadal & Corpus, 2013). Filipinx American gay college men defined masculinity as an encompassing expectation to be physically and emotionally strong, independent, and engage in male-dominated activities (i.e., sports) (Chan, 2017). They attributed their initial conceptualization of masculinity to the perspectives of their immigrant parents and their expectations to fulfill traditional gender roles (i.e., *machismo*) for their families (Chan, 2017).

As a reprieve from the watchful eyes of their families back home in the Philippines, immigration granted Filipinx American gay men opportunities to have experiences, redefine their identities, and engage in new lifestyles (Manalansan, 2003). Such opportunities were same-sex romantic partnerships and changing their religious beliefs away from Catholicism and toward atheism or agnosticism as they became more acculturated to life in the United States and lived more secular lifestyles. However, for others, religion became a source of comfort in navigating their experiences and anxieties as they faced hardships adjusting to life in the United States and dealing with financial problems and the uncertainties associated with the AIDS crisis (Manalansan, 2003). For some undocumented immigrant Filipino gay men, their undocumented status impacted their ability to outwardly express their gender and sexual identities because it can potentially attract the attention of the Filipinx American community's "gossip mill" and put their safety at risk (Manalansan, 1997, 2003). Nevertheless, despite their newfound freedom in the United States, participants maintained transnational relationships with their families in the Philippines by sending money remittances and *balikbayan* (repatriate) boxes.

Education

Education also helped influence sexual identity formation among Filipinx American gay men (Ocampo, 2022). Pursuing higher education became an opportunity for Filipinx American gay men to shape their identities and create a positive representation of themselves to their immigrant families who may hold traditional conservative views of sexuality and gender. Attending college exposed Filipinx American gay men to a concepts, theories, and representations of a wider range of gender roles and expressions that served as a developmental catalyst (Chan, 2017). But some Filipinx American gay men had to negotiate their identities alongside their family's expectations, and experiences of anxieties endured because being gay would violate their parents' immigrant dreams for them—have a good career, earn money, and start a family (Ocampo, 2022). To manage tensions concerning their sexual orientation, Filipinx American gay men used academic excellence (e.g., getting good grades, entering prestigious universities, high-paying careers) as a survival tool to ensure that their parents could still be proud of them despite their being gay.

Filipino and Filipinx American LGBTQ+ Issues and Outcomes

Deaths of Filipino and Filipinx American LGBTQ+

Among some of the issues facing Filipino and Filipinx American LGBTQ+ individuals are crimes being committed toward them because of their identities. In 2014, Jennifer Laude, a Filipina trans woman, was murdered by asphyxiation in a motel by US Marine Joseph Scott Pemberton in Olongapo City, Philippines (Velasco, 2020). While Pemberton was convicted of homicide in 2015 and faced 10 years of imprisonment in the Philippines, former Philippine President Rodrigo Duterte pardoned Pemberton in 2020 (Abeleda et al., 2019; Velasco, 2020). Pemberton's defense legal strategy employed the Gay/Trans Panic Defense, which placed the blame on Laude's gender identity as a trans woman as a reason for Pemberton's actions and lowered Pemberton's charges from murder to homicide (Abeleda et al., 2019). Laude's death was not an isolated incident: it is one effect of US neocolonization of the Philippines through US foreign policies like the Visiting Forces Agreement (VFA) that increased US military presence in the country (Abeleda et al., 2019).

In 2020, 20-year-old Filipinx and Korean American Jaxon Sales, was found dead from overdose in an apartment in San Francisco owned by a 41-year-old White man (Ferrannini, 2023). The autopsy report found a mix of drugs in Sales's body, including gamma-hydroxybutyric acid (GHB). To date, no one has been held responsible for Sales's death and supporters of Sales have been demanding further investigation despite an official from the medical examiner's office deeming that further investigation is not needed because GHB is perceived as a common drug used by the gay community (Ferrannini, 2023). Akin to Laude's murder, Sales's death is another reminder of how White supremacy, transphobia, heterosexism, and racism devalues the lives of Filipino and Filipinx American LGBTQ+ individuals.

Mental Health of Sexual Minorities in the Philippines

Research on LGBTQ+ persons in the Philippines may be applicable to understand risk factors associated with suicidality and mental health among sexual minority Filipinx Americans. National, population-based studies of adolescents (ages 15–24) have been conducted to examine relationships between sexual orientation and suicide risk among young gay, lesbian, and bisexual Filipinos (Manalastas, 2013, 2016). In comparison to heterosexual participants, gay and bisexual Filipino youth were twice as likely to experience suicide ideation but not attempt suicide (16% vs. 8%). Stressors associated with elevated suicide risk among gay and bisexual Filipino youth included depression in the past three months, recent suicide of a friend, and experiences of threat and victimization. Among lesbian and bisexual

Filipinas, sexual minority status was associated with increased risk for both suicide ideation and attempt (Manalastas, 2016). In comparison to heterosexual youth, lesbian and bisexual participants were more likely to experience suicide ideation (27% vs. 18%) and suicide attempt (6.6% vs. 3.9%). Stressors associated with elevated suicide risk included peer suicide attempt, experiences of being threatened, victimization, and depression in the past three months (Manalastas, 2016).

Research on LGBTQ+ populations in the Philippines has also sought to examine the relationship between self-stigma and mental health status (Reyes et al., 2015, 2017). These studies found that high self-stigma was associated with poor mental health (psychological distress and global mental health) among LGBT individuals living in the Philippines (Reyes et al., 2015). Another study on gay and lesbian Filipinos indicated that suicidal behavior increased with both internalized and self-stigma (Reyes et al., 2017). These studies underscore the impact of internalized heterosexism and transphobia on mental health outcomes in Filipino LGBT individuals.

Microaggressions and Mental Health Outcomes

Limited studies have been conducted to specifically examine the prevalence of mental health issues among LGBTQ+ Filipina/o Americans (Nadal & Corpus, 2013). While few epidemiological studies are available, research on Filipinx American experiences with racial microaggressions may be useful in understanding the relationship between racial discrimination and mental health outcomes (Nadal et al., 2012, 2022; Nadal & Corpus, 2013). Racial microaggressions have been defined as subtle forms of verbal and behavioral discrimination against people of color (Nadal et al., 2012). In expanding previous understandings of microaggressions, Sue et al. (2007) defined racial microaggressions as "brief, commonplace, daily verbal, behavioral, or environmental indignities, whether intentional or unintentional, that communicate hostile, derogatory, or negative racial slights and insults towards people of color" (p. 271).

A study examined the specific racial microaggressions that Filipinx Americans could experience over their lifetime; 13 microaggressions specific to Filipinx Americans were identified (Nadal et al., 2012). Some of these racial microaggressions are being "alien in one's own land," which is the assumption that Filipinx Americans are foreigners or foreign-born;

"exoticization and sexualization of women and demasculinization of men," where Filipinx American women are viewed as sexual objects while Filipinx American men are desexualized and emasculated; and "pathologizing of cultural values and behaviors," which are messages that idealizes values and communication styles of the dominant/White culture (Nadal et al., 2012). For Filipino Americans, experiences with microaggressions occur on the basis of race, ethnicity, class, gender, and sexuality, suggesting that they may experience a wider range of discrimination and multiple oppressions. Experiences of racial microaggressions were associated with general mental health problems including anxiety, depression, behavioral control, and positive affect (Nadal et al., 2015). Other studies also found a relationship between racial microaggressions, traumatic stress, and culturally related trauma (Nadal et al., 2022). Specifically, the study found that increased experiences with racial microaggressions were associated with greater traumatic stress symptoms, and culturally related trauma was associated with more traumatic stress symptoms (Nadal et al., 2022).

Access to Mental Health Services Among Filipinx Americans

Disparities in access to mental health services in the Filipinx American population persist (Nadal, 2021; Sanchez & Gaw, 2007). One study found that, within their sample, only 2.2% of their participants sought formal mental health services (Nguyen, 2011). Filipinx Americans have low rates of treatment for mental illnesses and do not seek services until they have more severe disorders (Sanchez & Gaw, 2007). Internal barriers within Filipinx Americans to seeking mental health services are navigating the family hierarchy, fatalistic attitudes, religious fanaticism, cultural mistrust of Western medicine, lack of belief in one's ability to change, communication barriers, and lack of culturally competent services (David, 2010a; Sanchez & Gaw, 2007). Due to the role of cultural stigma and concerns for loss of face, individuals may avoid seeking mental health services that could bring *hiya* (shame) to their families or cause them to be a target for gossip (David, 2010a; Nadal, 2021). In addition to internal barriers, systemic barriers to mental health services experienced by Filipinx Americans are their immigration status, specifically undocumented immigrants who may not be able to afford health insurance, and experiences of discrimination in healthcare settings (Martinez et al., 2020). Because of these barriers, Filipinx Americans are more likely to seek support from lay persons in their informal network, such as entrusted friends, family members, and religious leaders in addressing and maintaining their mental health (Alviar & del Prado, 2022; Gong et al., 2003; Nadal & Monzones, 2010; Nicdao et al., 2015). Hesitation to seek mental health services can be more difficult for Filipinx American LGBTQ+ individuals who are negotiating their racial and ethnic, gender, and sexual orientation identities in accessing mental health services and not finding gender-affirming and LGBTQ+ friendly mental health services.

Resistance of LGBTQ+ Filipinx Americans

Despite experiences of discrimination, LGBTQ+ Filipinx Americans in the United States also found ways to resist, survive, and thrive. To understand the resistance of LGBTQ+ Filipinx American communities, Bailey (2009) described forms of *intraventions* or prevention strategies that are implemented by at-risk communities themselves to not only defend themselves from infection but also as a form of resistance and survival. Through ethnographic research of Black and Latino ballroom culture in Detroit, Bailey offered three forms of intravention: creation of a social epistemology, kinship and social support, and HIV/AIDS Prevention Balls (Bailey, 2009). Creation of a social epistemology embraces the shared social knowledge of a kinship system, values, and norms established by community members as opposed to those imposed from outside. Kinship and social support are social relations that redefine prevention work while providing love, care, and service that is comprised of informal consultation with chosen family on issues including intimate relationships, sex, gender, sexual identity, health, hormonal therapy, and body presentation. HIV/AIDS Prevention Balls are partnerships between community-based organizations and ballroom houses to engage in HIV/AIDS prevention activities and to promote messages about HIV risk prevention and reduction (Bailey, 2009). We used Bailey's concept of intravention to examine methods of resistance of LGBTQ+ Filipinx Americans.

Fictive Kinship: It's Not Always Blood Ties That Bind

Research on the experiences of Filipinx American gay men in New York City (Manalansan, 2003) and Filipino and Latino gay men in Los Angeles (Ocampo, 2022) depicted forms of kinship used to ensure social support and community survival. Among Filipinx American gay men, kinship relationships with both Filipinx American and non-Filipinx American gay men were complex processes (Manalansan, 2003). *Barkadas* or group of friends were seen as both a source of support and conflict. *Barkadas* provided support through a variety of transitions with immigrating, adjusting to life in the United States, or coming out as gay (Manalansan, 2003). In addition to support, *barkadas* can also be a site of gossip, which intensified a sense of conflict and competition among Filipinx American gay men (Manalansan, 2003).

Filipinx American gay men have also supported each other through the HIV/AIDS epidemic and offered one another various forms of interventions (Manalansan, 2003). For these men, *fictive kinship* or chosen families became important caretakers of people when they became ill (Manalansan, 2003). Due to the nature of immigrant life, physical distance from family, and the stigma associated with AIDS, not all individuals had access to family members when they were ill and dying. AIDS forced gay Filipinx Americans to create new practices in end-of-life care and death (Manalansan, 2003). They reconfigured practices around wakes and burials for their comrades who could not rely on their family members. Gay Filipinx Americans used fashion shows and drag parties as opportunities to raise money to cover medical expenses and burial costs for their gay Filipinx American friends who passed away (Manalansan, 2003). Performance was also used to institutionalize HIV/AIDS prevention efforts within the Filipinx American LGBTQ+ community. Using the Filipinx American community's idiom for AIDS, "Tita Aida" or "Aunt Aida," members of the community performed in gay bars to promote safe sex practices and distributed health promotion pamphlets and brochures targeting LGBTQ+ Filipinx Americans (Manalansan, 2003). For these performers, performing as Tita Aida was used to address the Filipinx American community's taboo over sex and HIV/AIDS while using a familiar figure that members could relate to (Manalansan, 2003).

Fictive kinship through Filipinx American college organizations also allowed for Filipinx American gay college students to find support (Ocampo, 2022). Within these social networks, they were able to discuss their feelings about race, ethnicity, gender, and sexual identities (Ocampo, 2022). Cultivating spaces for queer people of color (POC) representation allowed them to find role models who taught them to embrace their sexual identity and reject ideas that they had to choose between their ethnic and sexual identities (Ocampo, 2022). In fact, eight campuses of the University of California (UC) system have been holding the annual Queer Pin@y Conference (QPC) for more than a decade, which was established at the University of California Los Angeles (UCLA) in 1999 for Filipinx American LGBTQ+ college students from different UC campuses to congregate, meet other LGBTQ+ Filipinx Americans, and discuss issues affecting the LGBTQ+ Filipinx American community (Queer Pin@y Conference 2009, 2009).

Social Support and Advocacy in Contemporary Filipina/o American Organizations

Currently, various Filipinx American LGBTQ+ organizations in the United States exist to provide social support and advocate for issues affecting not only Filipinx American LGBTQ+ communities but also other marginalized groups, acknowledging each other's intersecting struggle toward liberation. Leadership, Education, Activism, and Dialogue (LEAD) Filipino is a nonprofit organization in San Jose, California, that provides Filipina/o/x Americans with education and opportunities to engage civically in their communities (Francisco, 2020). As a nonprofit organization, LEAD Filipino's focus areas are civic engagement, culturally responsive education, community health initiatives, grassroots campaigns and leadership, and local activism (LEAD Filipino, n.d.). Within LEAD, the Queermittee and Education holds the Queer Lakbay Summit, whose goals are to elevate collective consciousness around the experiences, stories, and innovation of queer Filipinx American leaders nationally (LEAD Filipino, n.d.). Another organization, Sacramento Filipinx LGBTQIA+ (Sac-Fil), founded in 2017 in California by Nikki Abeleda and Daniel Domaguin (Hernandez, 2023), aims to create a space for Filipinx American LGBTQ+ individuals in the region and holds events and advocacy efforts toward raising concerns about human rights issues in the Philippines and intersolidarity movements with other Black, Indigenous, and People of Color (BIPOC) organizations such as Black and Asian solidarity events (Hernandez, 2023). These are just some of the current Filipinx American LGBTQ+ organizations that are working toward establishing spaces, raising visibility, and advocating for policies and issues affecting Filipinx American LGBTQ+ and other marginalized groups.

Implications for Social Work

Conducting Research With LGBTQ+ Filipinx American

As this chapter previously discussed, research on LGBTQ+ Filipinx Americans is sparse. The little research that has been published primarily focuses on gay men. Thus, it is imperative that more research needs to be done that acknowledges different gender identities and sexual orientations within the Filipinx American LGBTQ+ population. In conducting research within this population, several factors must be considered. First, before conducting research and in the attempt to decolonize research, Tuck and Yang (2014) posit researchers to ask themselves whether the academy deserves to have access to such knowledge, who benefits from conducting the proposed research, and whether research is the best method to attain these goals. Researchers should consider using theoretical frameworks that are relevant to the Filipinx American populations, such as the Pilipino American Identity Development Model (Nadal, 2004) and the sexual identity development framework (Nadal, 2021), to make sense of the Filipinx American LGBTQ+ identity. Other factors to consider are the pertinency of familial relationships and reputation, influence of Catholic religion, immigration experience (US-born vs. Philippines-born), duality of the racialization of LGBTQ+ Filipinx American in White LGBT+ spaces and the construction of LGBTQ+ identities within Filipinx American spaces, and gender roles and expressions (e.g., *machismo*) as shaped by culture, religion, immigration, and intergenerational effects of colonization. In conducting research, critical scholars have argued that studies involving marginalized populations often focus on stories related to pain and oppression—perceiving the individual from a deficit perspective (Tuck & Yang, 2014). While at times this is important to underscore the need for changes in practices and policies, researchers should also consider approaching studies from a strength-based perspective, such as employing the *minority strengths model* that acknowledges the importance of social support, community consciousness, and identity pride as sources of positive mental health and well-being for people of marginalized backgrounds (Perrin et al., 2020). Finally, it is important for researchers to build genuine relationships and commitments to Filipinx American LGBTQ+ communities through partnering with leaders, community members, and organizations that are a part of and/or serve this population and involve them in all aspects of the study to ensure that the work being conducted is relevant to, respectful of, and accurate of the lived experiences of Filipinx American LGBTQ+ individuals.

Providing Inclusive Clinical Services to LGBTQ+ Filipina/o Americans

Past research has identified disparities in mental healthcare within the broad Filipinx American community which may be especially exacerbated for LGBTQ+ individuals (Nadal, 2021; Sanchez & Gaw, 2007). Some barriers to mental healthcare within the broad Filipinx American community are family dynamics, cultural stigma, concerns for loss of face, communication barriers, externalization of complaints, cultural mistrust of White institutions, and lack of culturally competent services (David, 2010b; Gong et al., 2003; Sanchez & Gaw, 2007). Furthermore, limited psychosocial interventions specifically target the Filipinx American community, let alone Filipinx American LGBTQ+ individuals (David, 2013). While Filipino American LGBTQ+ individuals navigate these cultural and systemic barriers to mental health services, there may be additional factors specific to their gender and sexual identities that discourage disclosure of symptoms and seeking services.

Peer-Based Mental Health Support

Peer support mental health interventions may offer an additional outlet for LGBTQ+ Filipinx Americans to receive support to address and cope with their experiences. Peer support services (PSSs) are wellness support services provided by a lay individual with a lived experience of recovering from a mental health condition (Fortuna et al., 2020; Shalaby & Agyapong, 2020). Peer support may be delivered in a variety of settings including community-based, inpatient and outpatient services, and through digital technology. Systematic reviews demonstrate an internationally growing trend of including PSSs in mental health and addiction services and show support for the feasibility of both in-person and digital PPSs for diverse populations.

Filipinx American LGBTQ+ individuals may benefit from the use of PSSs to augment their mental health support. Studies on the experiences of LGBTQ+ Filipinx Americans highlight the important role of fictive kinship and peer support in promoting mental health and overall well-being (Manalansan, 2003; Ocampo, 2022). Filipinx American LGBTQ+ individuals in these studies highlighted the importance of social support, seeing positive examples of queer identity among people of color and peer dialogue on issues of race, gender, sexuality, and wellness. In discussing the expansion of the Filipinx American mental health workforce, Chan and Litam (2021) offered suggestions for mental health providers to train Filipinx American community members to provide peer support by teaching coping strategies (i.e., mindfulness and yoga) and establishing wellness groups that discuss stress, health, and wellness. These studies highlight the possibilities of using PSSs, community strengths, and increasing representation and expanding the workforce of Filipinx American mental health providers to improve mental health outcomes in Filipinx American LGBTQ+ communities.

PSSs may also offer some Filipinx American LGBTQ+ individuals with opportunities to receive mental health services through salient religious communities to help them negotiate the multiplicity of their identities. Studies have identified that, rather than seeking formal support from mental health providers, Filipinx Americans are more likely to ask for help from family members, friends, and faith communities as a first line of defense when they experience psychological distress (Abe-Kim et al., 2004; Alviar & del Prado, 2022). Mental health providers must collaborate with churches to overcome cultural and religious stigma toward mental health, particularly among Filipino American families with adolescents (Javier et al., 2014). Integrating PSS into salient community-based spaces including churches and mutual aid organizations may be an effective strategy to increase opportunities for LGBTQ+ Filipinx Americans to receive support for their mental health. When collaborating with religious institutions, PSSs and formal mental health providers must be cognizant of individuals' experiences with Catholicism, specifically previous experiences with religious homophobia/transphobia, religious conversion interventions, and internalized shame and guilt (Alviar & del Prado, 2022; Nadal & Corpus, 2013).

Culturally Responsive and Queer Affirming Mental Health Interventions
Broadly, there have been limited efforts to create culturally responsive mental health interventions for the broad Filipinx American community (David, 2013; Nadal, 2021) and a paucity of queer-affirming interventions

specific to LGBTQ+ Filipinx Americans. In discussing clinical interventions for Filipinos, psychologist Virgilio Enriquez (1994) warns practitioners of *indigenization from without*, or practices that adapt psychosocial interventions and assessments without acknowledging the sociopolitical realities of the group. David (2013) presents the only mental health intervention for Filipino Americans that centers on the decolonization experience. Integrating principles of cognitive behavioral therapy (CBT) (Beck, 1995) and decolonization, the Filipino American Decolonization Experience (FADE) is a 20-session intervention designed to foster within participants empowering views of their personal and social selves, society, and possibilities for creating social change (David, 2013). Components of FADE include didactic lectures and discussions on Filipino/Filipino American history and participants' family histories, psychoeducation on the psychological consequences of colonialism and multiple oppressions, and CBT methods (i.e., journaling, tracking cognitive distortions, emotional and cognitive reactions).

In conceptualizing culturally competent care, K. L. Nadal (2021) discussed that, when working with Filipinx American clients, using nontraditional, Indigenous, and spiritual methods may be important. Nadal described Indigenous counseling as recognizing the cultural values, beliefs, and practices of a group and integrating these into mental health treatment. Indigenous practices may be particularly effective for Filipinx American clients whose own practices include talking to friends, family, and community members to receive informal support regarding their mental health. Integrating culturally appropriate Western therapeutic modalities with Indigenous counseling methods may be effective. For example, psychodynamic methods of free association can be likened to indirect methods of questioning, *pagtatanong-tanong*, used in Filipino psychology (Nadal, 2021). Methods in CBT, including identifying cognitive distortions, can also be useful to discuss the impact of multiple oppressions on an individual's mental health. Due to the cultural emphasis on family harmony and collectivism, family systems therapies may also be useful for Filipinx American clients to gain perspectives on the impact of family dynamics on their mental health. While there have been efforts to tailor psychosocial interventions to Filipinos and Filipinx Americans broadly, more clinical research is needed to create both culturally responsive and queer-affirming psychosocial interventions that recognize the impact of multiple oppressions on LGBTQ+ Filipinx American's mental health outcomes.

Conclusion

The increased attacks on the safety and rights of LGBTQ+ communities not only in the United States but also in the Philippines emphasize the need to continue to do research and provide services to the Filipinx American LGBTQ+ population. The enduring history of survival and resistance of Filipino and Filipinx American LGBTQ+ individuals is a reminder of their resilience and strength that calls for the acknowledgment and celebration of their stories and community. The field of social work has an important role in realizing the fulfillment of these goals to ensure the right to self-determination and liberation of LGBTQ+ Filipinx Americans.

Notes

1. *Bahaghari* translates to "rainbow" in Filipino.
2. We use the letter "x" in Filipinx to honor and acknowledge Filipinx American trans, non-binary, and gender non-conforming individuals who use the term to identify and assert themselves under their own conditions that do not fit within the gender binaries (Barrett et al., 2021).

References

Abe-Kim, J., Gong, F., & Takeuchi, D. (2004). Religiosity, spirituality, and help-seeking among Filipino Americans: Religious clergy or mental health professionals? *Journal of Community Psychology, 32*(6), 675–689. https://doi.org/10.1002/jcop.20026

Abeleda, N., Konefal, M., & Nasol, K. (2019). Gender justice and transgender rights in the Philipinx community. *Asian American Policy Review, 29,* 24–96.

Alviar, S., & del Prado, A. (2022). "You should pray about it": Exploring mental health and help-seeking in Filipino American Catholics. *Asian American Journal of Psychology, 13*(1), 97–111. https://doi.org/10.1037/aap0000266

American Civil Liberties Union. (2023). Mapping attacks on LGBTQ rights in US state legislatures. https://www.aclu.org/legislative-attacks-on-lgbtq-rights

Bailey, M. M. (2009). Performance as intravention: Ballroom culture and the politics of HIV/AIDS in Detroit. *Souls, 11*(3), 253–274. https://doi.org/10.1080/10999940903088226

Barrett, K. U., Hanna, K. B., & Palomar, A. (2021). In Defense of the X: Centering queer, trans, and non-binary Pilipina/x/os, queer vernacular, and the politics of naming. *Alon: Journal for Filipinx American and Diasporic Studies, 1*(2), 125–148. https://doi.org/10.5070/LN41253177

Beck, J. S. (1995). *Cognitive therapy: Basics and beyond.* Guilford.

Benedicto, B. (2022). Finding the rainbow, not the pot of gold: A transpinay's experience in the Philippine electoral system. *Alon: Journal for Filipinx American and Diasporic Studies, 2*(1). https://doi.org/10.5070/LN42156448

Bonus, R. (2000). *Locating Filipino Americans: Ethnicity and the cultural politics of space.* Temple University Press.

Budiman, A. (2021). Filipinos in the US fact sheet. Pew Research Center. https://www.pewresearch.org/social-trends/fact-sheet/asian-americans-filipinos-in-the-u-s/

Ceperiano, A. M., Santos Jr., E. C., Alonzo, D. C. P., & Ofreneo, M. A. P. (2016). "Girl, bi, bakla, tomboy": The intersectionality of sexuality, gender, and class in urban poor contexts. *Philippine Journal of Psychology, 49*(2), 5–34.

Chan, C. D., & Litam, S. D. A. (2021). Mental health equity of Filipino communities in COVID-19: A framework for practice and advocacy. *Professional Counselor, 11*(1), 73–85. https://doi.org/10.15241/cdc.11.1.73

Chan, J. (2017). "Am I masculine enough?": Queer Filipino college men and masculinity. *Journal of Student Affairs Research and Practice, 54*(1), 82–94. https://doi.org/10.1080/19496591.2016.1206021

Chiongbian, S. F., Ilac, E. J. D., Emata, R. R., & Magno, A. R. C. L. (2023). Finding God alongside trials: Catholicism and resilience among queer Filipino emerging adults. *Psychology of Sexual Orientation and Gender Diversity, 10*(2), 246–256. https://doi.org/10.1037/sgd0000508

Choy, C. C. (2003). *Empire of care: Nursing and migration in Filipino American history*. Duke University Press.

David, E. J. R. (2010a). Cultural mistrust and mental health help-seeking attitudes among Filipino Americans. *Asian American Journal of Psychology, 1*(1), 57–66. https://doi.org/10.1037/a0018814

David, E. J. R. (2010b). Cultural mistrust and mental health help-seeking attitudes among Filipino Americans. *Asian American Journal of Psychology, 1*(1), 57–66. https://doi.org/10.1037/a0018814

David, E. J. R. (2013). *Brown skin, White minds: Filipino-/American postcolonial psychology*. IAP Information Age.

Diaz, R. (2015). The limits of bakla and gay: Feminist readings of My Husband's Lover, Vice Ganda, and Charice Pempengco. *Signs: Journal of Women in Culture and Society, 40*(3), 721–745. https://doi.org/10.1086/679526

Diaz, R. (2018). Biyuti from below. *TSQ: Transgender Studies Quarterly, 5*(3), 404–424. https://doi.org/10.1215/23289252-6900781

Enriquez, V. G. (1994). *From colonial to liberation psychology: The Philippine experience*. De La Salle University Press.

Ferrannini, J. (2023). Family of gay son demands formal inquest into his death. *The Bay Area Reporter*. https://www.ebar.com/story.php?ch=news&sc=latest_news&id=322648

Fortuna, K. L., Naslund, J. A., LaCroix, J. M., Bianco, C. L., Brooks, J. M., Zisman-Ilani, Y., Muralidharan, A., & Deegan, P. (2020). Digital peer support mental health interventions for people with a lived experience of a serious mental illness: Systematic review. *JMIR Mental Health, 7*(4), e16460. https://doi.org/10.2196/16460

Francia, L. H. (2014). *A history of the Philippines: From Indios Bravos to Filipinos*. Overlook Press.

Francisco, C. B. (2020). *LEAD: Formation of Filipina/o/x American Leaders*. Masters thesis, San Francisco State University. https://scholarworks.calstate.edu/downloads/r781wn48s

Gamboa, L. C. L., Ilac, E. J. D., Carangan, A. M. J. M., & Agida, J. I. S. (2021). Queering public leadership: The case of lesbian, gay, bisexual and transgender leaders in the Philippines. *Leadership, 17*(2), 191–211. https://doi.org/10.1177/1742715020953273

Garcia, J. N. C. (2008). *Philippine gay culture: Binabae to bakla, silahis to MSM*. University of the Philippines Press.

Garcia, J. N. C. (2013). Nativism or universalism: Situating LGBT discourse in the Philippines. *Kritika Kultura, 20*, 48–68.

Gong, F., Gage, S.-J. L., & Tacata, L. A. (2003). Helpseeking behavior among Filipino Americans: A cultural analysis of face and language. *Journal of Community Psychology, 31*(5), 469–488. https://doi.org/10.1002/jcop.10063

Hernandez, R. (2023). LGBTQIA+ Filipinx find collective healing in identity and a sense of belonging. Mahalaya. https://www.mahalayasf.org/post/lgbtqia-filipinx-find-collective-healing-in-identity-and-a-sense-of-belonging

Javier, J. R., Supan, J., Lansang, A., Beyer, W., Kubicek, K., & Palinkas, L. A. (2014). Preventing Filipino mental health disparities: Perspectives from adolescents, caregivers, providers, and advocates. *Asian American Journal of Psychology*, 5(4), 316–324. https://doi.org/10.1037/a0036479

Ladia, C. E. P. (2022). Queering local governments: LGBTIQ+ movement organizations as strategic brokers for sexual citizenship in Philippine local governments. *Review of Women's Studies*, 32(1), 113–148.

LEAD Filipino. (n.d.). Queer Labkay summit. L.E.A.D Filipino. https://leadfilipino.org/queer-lakbay-summit/

Manalansan, M. F. (1997). Filipino Americans: Transformation and identity. In M. P. P. Root (ed.), *Filipino Americans: Transformation and identity* (pp. 247–256). Sage. https://doi.org/10.4135/9781452243177

Manalansan, M. F. (2003). *Global divas: Filipino gay men in the diaspora*. Duke University Press.

Manalastas, E. J. (2013). Sexual orientation and suicide risk in the Philippines: Evidence from a nationally representative sample of young Filipino men. *Philippine Journal of Psychology*, 46(1), 1–13.

Manalastas, E. J. (2016). Suicide ideation and suicide attempt among young lesbian and bisexual Filipina women: Evidence for disparities in the Philippines. *Asian Women*, 32(3), 101–120.

Mananzan, M. J. (2003). The Filipino women: Before and after the Spanish conquest of the Philippines. In M. J. Mananzan (ed.), *Challenges to the inner room: Selected essays and speeches on women* (pp. 147–174). Institute of Women's Studies, St. Scholastica's College.

Martinez, A. B., Co, M., Lau, J., & Brown, J. S. L. (2020). Filipino help-seeking for mental health problems and associated barriers and facilitators: A systematic review. *Social Psychiatry and Psychiatric Epidemiology*, 55(11), 1397–1413. https://doi.org/10.1007/s00127-020-01937-2

Nadal, K. L. (2004). Pilipino American identity development model. *Journal of Multicultural Counseling and Development*, 32(1), 45–62. https://doi.org/10.1002/j.2161-1912.2004.tb00360.x

Nadal, K. L. (2021). *Filipino American psychology: A handbook of theory, research, and clinical practice*. Wiley. https://doi.org/10.1002/9781118094747

Nadal, K. L., Corpus, G., & Hufana, A. (2022). The forgotten Asian Americans: Filipino Americans' experiences with racial microaggressions and trauma. *Asian American Journal of Psychology*, 13(1), 51–61. https://doi.org/10.1037/aap0000261

Nadal, K. L., & Corpus, M. J. H. (2013). "Tomboys" and "baklas": Experiences of lesbian and gay Filipino Americans. *Asian American Journal of Psychology*, 4(3), 166–175. https://doi.org/10.1037/a0030168

Nadal, K. L., & Monzones, J. (2010). Neuropsychological assessments and Filipino Americans: Cultural implications for practice. In D. E. M. Fuji (ed.), *The neuropsychology of Asian Americans* (pp. 47–70). Psychology Press.

Nadal, K. L., Vigilia Escobar, K. M., Prado, G. T., David, E. J. R., & Haynes, K. (2012). Racial microaggressions and the Filipino American experience: Recommendations for counseling and development. *Journal of Multicultural Counseling and Development*, 40(3), 156–173. https://doi.org/10.1002/j.2161-1912.2012.00015.x

Nadal, K. L., Wong, Y., Sriken, J., Griffin, K., & Fujii-Doe, W. (2015). Racial microaggressions and Asian Americans: An exploratory study on within-group differences and mental health. *Asian American Journal of Psychology*, 6(2), 136–144. https://doi.org/10.1037/a0038058

Nguyen, D. (2011). Acculturation and perceived mental health need among older Asian immigrants. *Journal of Behavioral Health Services & Research*, 38(4), 526–533. https://doi.org/10.1007/s11414-011-9245-z

Nicdao, E. G., Duldulao, A. A., & Takeuchi, D. T. (2015). Psychological distress, nativity, and help-seeking among Filipino Americans. 107–120. https://doi.org/10.1108/S0275-495920150000033005

Ocampo, A. C. (2014). The gay second generation: Sexual identity and family relations of Filipino and Latino gay men. *Journal of Ethnic and Migration Studies, 40*(1), 155–173. https://doi.org/10.1080/1369183X.2013.849567

Ocampo, A. C. (2022). *Brown and gay in LA: The lives of immigrant sons.* New York University Press. https://doi.org/10.18574/nyu/9781479806614.001.0001

Perrin, P. B., Sutter, M. E., Trujillo, M. A., Henry, R. S., & Pugh Jr., M. (2020). The minority strengths model: Development and initial path analytic validation in racially/ethnically diverse LGBTQ individuals. *Journal of Clinical Psychology, 76*(1), 118–136. https://doi.org/https://doi.org/10.1002/jclp.22850

Queer Pin@y Conference 2009. (2009). About Queer Pin@y Conference. QPC 2009 at UCLA. https://qpc2009.wordpress.com/about-2/

Reyes, M. E. S., Davis, R. D., David, A. J. A., Del Rosario, C. J. C., Dizon, A. P. S., Fernandez, J. L. M., & Viquiera, M. A. (2017). Stigma burden as a predictor of suicidal behavior among lesbians and gays in the Philippines. *Suicidology Online, 8*(26), 1–10.

Reyes, M. E. S., Lanic, P. J. P., Lavadia, E. N. T., Tactay, E. F. J. L., Tiongson, E. R., & Tuazon, P. J. G. (2015). Self-stigma, self-concept clarity, and mental health status of Filipino LGBT individuals. *North American Journal of Psychology, 17*(2), 343–350.

Sanchez, F., & Gaw, A. (2007). Mental health care of Filipino Americans. *Psychiatric Services, 58*(6), 810–815. https://doi.org/10.1176/ps.2007.58.6.810

Shalaby, R. A. H., & Agyapong, V. I. O. (2020). Peer support in mental health: Literature review. *JMIR Mental Health, 7*(6), e15572. https://doi.org/10.2196/15572

Strobel, L. M. (2013). *Babaylan: Filipinos and the call of the indigenous.* CreateSpace Independent Publishing.

Sue, D. W., Capodilupo, C. M., Torino, G. C., Bucceri, J. M., Holder, A. M. B., Nadal, K. L., & Esquilin, M. (2007). Racial microaggressions in everyday life: Implications for clinical practice. *American Psychologist, 62*(4), 271–286. https://doi.org/10.1037/0003-066X.62.4.271

Tan, M. L. (1995). From bakla to gay: Shifting gender identities and sexual behaviors in the Philippines. In R. G. Parker & J. H. Gagnon (eds.), *Conceiving sexuality: Approaches to sex research in a postmodern world* (pp. 85–96). Routledge.

Tuck, E., & Yang, K. W. (2014). R-words: Refusing research. In J. Paris & M. Winn (Eds.), *Humanizing research: Decolonizing qualitative inquiry with youth and communities* (pp. 223–258). Sage.

Velasco, G. K. (2020). Queer and trans necropolitics in the afterlife of US empire. *Amerasia Journal, 46*(2), 238–252. https://doi.org/10.1080/00447471.2020.1865049

10
Religion and Spirituality as Buffers Against Islamophobia in the Lives of Asian American Youth

Altaf Husain, Hannan Hijazi, and Sarah Carlis

Introduction

The Muslim community in the United States has experienced anti-Islamic bigotry, also commonly referred to as "Islamophobia," in the decades following the September 11, 2001 (9/11) terrorist attacks (Husain, 2015). Islamophobic attacks intensified during the Trump presidency, against Muslims and other Americans of color. The nature of these attacks ranged from microaggressions between neighbors to verbal harassment from co-workers to retaliatory actions by supervisors and employers to acts of physical violence against Muslims or anyone mistakenly identified as a Muslim. The population of Muslims in the United States, according to estimates by the Pew Research Center, is projected to grow steadily, with numbers large enough to be counted as the second-largest religious group in the United States by 2040 (Mohamed, 2018). Hence, there is a professional imperative for educators, researchers, and practitioners within social work to anticipate this growing population's needs and train current and future generations of social workers to better serve this community.

This chapter is focused on the impact that Islamophobia has on the lives of Muslim youth, specifically those of Asian American ancestry. The latest research shows the need to focus especially on the impact of Islamophobia on Muslim youth. A range of acculturative stressors place a tremendous burden especially on Asian American Muslim youth. They are challenged further due to experiences with bullying, discrimination, and prejudice at school, during extracurricular activities, and in their neighborhoods (Council

Altaf Husain, Hannan Hijazi, and Sarah Carlis, *Religion and Spirituality as Buffers Against Islamophobia in the Lives of Asian American Youth* In: *Addressing Anti-Asian Racism with Social Work, Advocacy, and Action*. Edited by: Meirong Liu and Keith T. Chan, Oxford University Press. © Oxford University Press 2024.
DOI: 10.1093/oso/9780197672242.003.0010

on American Islamic Relations [CAIR], 2023). How are Asian American Muslim youth managing during this period of intensified anti-Islamic bigotry? What role has religion and spirituality played in buffering the impact of intense anti-Islamic bigotry in their lives? The chapter is divided into several sections, starting with an overview of the Muslim population in the United States. Next, we explore the role of religion and spirituality in the lives of Asian American Muslims. The chapter focus shifts to a discussion of anti-Islamic bigotry in the United States, with a subsequent section on the impact of anti-Islamic bigotry on youth. The next section explores how religion and spirituality serve as buffers from the impact of anti-Islamic bigotry. The chapter concludes with recommendations for social work advocacy on behalf of Asian American Muslim Youth.

Muslims in the United States

The Muslim American community is incredibly diverse, drawn from various ethnicities, cultures, and languages (Read, 2008). The Muslim presence in the United States can be traced back more than seven centuries, starting with the arrival of enslaved Africans, mostly from West Africa. Diouf (1998) traced the roots of some of the enslaved Africans and confirmed that they were in fact Muslims. Indeed, contrary to the common misconception associating Arabs predominantly with Islam, most American Muslims are not Arab, and many Americans of Arab descent follow Christianity. Among Muslim Americans, it is common to meet individuals from Africa, including East, North, sub-Saharan, and West regions; African Americans; Arabs spanning the Middle East and North Africa; Asians from Central, East, South, and Southeast regions; and Europeans (Read, 2008). Increasingly, individuals from Central and South America are also joining the Muslim community as converts (Cuartas, 2020). According to US Census data, these communities comprise more than 80 countries across Africa, Asia, and Europe. The majority of Muslim Americans reside in states with substantial immigrant populations like California, Florida, Illinois, Michigan, New York, and Texas. There are dense populations of Muslims in cities like Chicago, Detroit, Houston, Los Angeles, Orlando, and New York. The neighborhood *masjid* serves as a gathering place, displaying the rich cultural tapestry of Muslim Americans.

The unique Islamic culture becomes a blend of shared religious beliefs, traditions, and cultures from their nations of origin, and their integration into mainstream American society. The *masjid* serves as a gathering place for all Muslims, irrespective of their racial or ethnic backgrounds. Flexibility within Islamic teachings allows latitude for Muslims to adopt select American customs, valuing the preservation of their cultural practices if they align with Islamic principles. Linguistic diversity is also seen among Muslims, although all of them can at least recite Arabic, the language of the Qur'an.

Migration of Asian American Muslims to the United States

There is evidence to support the presence of Muslims of Asian background living in the United States since the mid to late 1800s (Leonard, 1994; Takaki, 1998). Many of them, mostly men from northern India (Punjab), arrived through Pacific ports of entry, seeking opportunities for employment in factories and on farms and as miners and railroad workers. They ended up working in northwestern states such as Oregon, Washington, and northern California. Among these men were some Christians, but mostly followers of Hinduism and Islam. While there were minimal barriers to entering the United States, there was no legal pathway for these men to acquire residency or citizenship. There were strict laws prohibiting these "foreign" men from marrying White women, owning or leasing land, or engaging in any activity or transaction that would help them to settle in the United States. Those who intended to stay in the United States had to secure a benefactor, which at that time meant a White property owner, someone who would essentially vouch for them and possibly facilitate their purchases of land by signing as a co-owner. Some of the Indian men married Mexican women, who were ardent Catholics and remained Catholic even after marriage. There are descendants presently in northern California who trace their ancestry to these Indian-Mexican families (Leonard, 1997). Due to heightened racism and discrimination against Asians of any background, a very restrictive immigration apparatus was set up in 1924, which ultimately barred the immigration of Asians and central and southern Europeans (Leonard, 1994). After World War II, some of these measures were relaxed to allow exceptional students from some parts of Asia and North Africa to study at colleges and universities in the United States (Haddad, 2002).

The 1965 immigration reforms, along with the historic civil rights legislation of the 1960s, reopened migration from Asia. Asian Muslims were among those sought after for migration to the United States to meet labor demands in sectors such as medicine and engineering. Asian Muslims have also migrated to the United States on their own, in search of religious freedom and better education and employment opportunities for themselves and their children (Haddad, 2002). The Asian American Muslim population has been increasing steadily in the United States. Typically, three factors are cited to explain this increase in their population: (1) natural birth rates among Asian American Muslims, (2) entry of immigrants and refugees of Asian backgrounds, and (3) conversion to Islam (Husain, 2019). In this chapter, information is provided about the growing population of Asian American Muslim youth. These are youth who self-identify as Asian American and Muslim, and they may trace their ancestry to countries such as Afghanistan, Bangladesh, India, Pakistan, and Sri Lanka; potentially from countries in Southeast Asia such as Cambodia, Indonesia, Malaysia, Philippines, and Thailand; and also from various other parts of Central Asia (Ross-Sheriff & Husain, 2001).

Cultural Background of Asian American Muslims

As noted above, there is tremendous racial, ethnic, and cultural diversity among Asian American Muslims. In addition to their unique national cultures, there is some similarity due to the emergence and persistence of an Islamic culture in the United States. These cultural traditions revolve around the observance of religious obligations such as fasting during the month of Ramadan, attending Friday prayer services, and celebrating the two holidays known as Eid ul Fitr (observed at the end of Ramadan) and Eid al Adha, commemorating the life and family of the Prophet Abraham, *peace be upon him* (Barreto et al., 2008). Unlike in other Western countries, Asian American Muslims typically belong to the local *masjid*, the Arabic term for house of worship, and rarely have an Indian *masjid*, Pakistani *masjid*, or a specific nationality-based congregation. Depending on the size of the local Muslim population, Asian American youth are, therefore, typically growing up among Muslim youth from diverse racial, ethnic, and cultural backgrounds.

The experiences and challenges faced by Asian American Muslim youth are like those faced by other youth of immigrant backgrounds but unique because, in addition to navigating their ethnic/cultural traditions, they are also forming and navigating a religious identity within the context of a multicultural society (Husain et al., 2022). Various acculturative stressors place a tremendous burden on these youth, and they are challenged further due to experiences with bullying, discrimination, and prejudice at school; during extracurricular activities; and in their neighborhoods (CAIR, 2023). Asian American Muslim youth are targeted due to hatred of their non-White, non-European racial/ethnic background, their non-White skin color, and their non-Christian religion, at a time in their lives when they are attempting to develop an identity of their own (see section below on "Impact of Anti-Islamic Bigotry on Youth"). As important as culture is in the lives of Asian American Muslim youth, at times, ironically, adherence to cultural practices such as the types of food they eat, dress they wear, and language(s) they speak other than English may be the provocation for people intent on being bigoted or prejudiced.

Role of Religion and Spirituality in the Lives of Asian American Muslims

Religion and spirituality are critically important in the lives of Asian American Muslims. There is diversity in the levels of knowledge of and adherence to religious teachings and spirituality among Asian Americans. Within the American context, individuals who were already observant Muslims in their country of origin may seek out communities in which to settle depending on the availability of an existing Muslim community, a *masjid*, or an Islamic school (private religious school) for their children (Haddad, 2002). Individuals who were nominally practicing Islam in their countries of origin may continue to remain loosely connected to an organized religious community but maintain some level of spirituality in their personal lives. Research has shown that sometimes the stresses of adjusting to their adopted homeland in the United States may result in these individuals seeking out more opportunities to connect with either others from their own national origin or, in the absence of their fellow country people, they may find at least other Muslims (Haddad & Lummis, 1987; Portes & Zhou, 1993).

Parents play an integral role in socializing their mostly American-born children into the faith community, particularly if there are smaller numbers of Muslims in their immediate community. Weekly gatherings span invitations to homes where friends gather to potlucks at the local *masjid* or Islamic or cultural center, to larger, more ethnic-based gatherings where there is a combination of emphasis on religious learning and fellowship. But being Muslim is not without challenges, and, in that vein, Husain et al. (2022) note that "Muslim youth who self-identify publicly as a hyphenated American (i.e., Muslim American) do so at the risk of bullying and being the target of hate crimes" (p. 49). The next two sections expand further first on anti-Islamic bigotry generally in the United States, then on the impact of that bigotry on Muslim youth.

Anti-Islamic Bigotry in the United States

Within a largely White, Judeo-Christian landscape, Asian American Muslims have been the target of various forms of bigotry, at once rooted in religious intolerance, xenophobia, and racism against those with skin colors ranging between black and brown (Husain, 2015). Due to the dissemination of a false narrative that Islamic teachings promote terrorism and that Muslims are inherently violent, most Muslims end up shouldering the double burden of having to condemn acts of terrorism perpetrated by individuals identifying as Muslims while also attempting to protect themselves from accusations of guilt by association (Husain, 2015). This latter point is especially noteworthy due to the very real threat of Muslims becoming victims of hate crimes and of experiencing discrimination and bullying in schools and on college and university campuses, in neighborhoods, and in places of employment.

Following the attacks of 9/11, the United States has witnessed a surge in violence against people who are Muslims or who were mistaken as being Muslim and who originated from South Asia, West Asia, North Africa, and other communities of color (Bajaj et al., 2016). An estimated 4–7 million Muslim Americans routinely encounter daily discrimination (Aroian, 2012). The micro-level experiences of Muslims directly correlate with larger social (media) and political forces that perpetuate one-sided narratives about Muslims as fanatical, violent, backward, terrorists, or enemies of the state, and "other," thus fostering a suspicious and unassimilable perception (Azeez & Jimoh, 2023; Bajaj et al., 2016; Farooqui & Kaushik, 2022; Lebowitz, 2016; Suleiman, 2017; Tahseen et al., 2019). Notably, according to CAIR, Islam is the most mentioned religion in news coverage, with a significant portion of these mentions being negative (Azeez & Jimoh, 2023; Elkassem et al., 2018). These suspicions cause a sense of conflict among young Muslims regarding their national identity (Farooqui & Kaushik, 2022), while media assaults exacerbate interpersonal discrimination experienced by these youth, creating a heightened sense of unease whenever they are in public (Aroian, 2012; Elkassem et al., 2018; Lebowitz, 2016; Tahseen et al., 2019).

Impact of Anti-Islamic Bigotry on Youth

The way young individuals define themselves and the reactions they receive significantly influence their development, mental health, and overall well-being. Muslim youth face two distinct types of threats: daily experiences of prejudice and discrimination and symbolic threats challenging their Muslim identity and seeking to denigrate it (Farooqui & Kaushik, 2022). Discrimination is a prevalent occurrence during adolescence, a critical phase when individuals explore their self-identity and ascribe meaning to it (Ryan, 2014; Tahseen et al., 2019). By sixth grade, minority children comprehend discrimination, becoming attuned to subtle expressions of prejudice that negatively characterize them (Aroian, 2012).

In educational settings, the identity development of Muslim youth undergoes a process of racialization, often manifested through social exclusion (Tahseen et al., 2019). Consequently, Muslim adolescents report encountering perceived religious, academic, and cultural hostility, resulting in a pervasive sense of being unwelcome and unseen at school (Bajaj et al., 2016). The surge in Islamophobia within schools is fueled by deficient curricula and misinformed teachers, creating a distressing environment for Muslim youth (Lebowitz, 2016). Instances of verbal abuse, such as "Go back to your country" or being labeled "terrorists," escalate to physical assaults, including the persistent removal of *hijabs* for Muslim girls and women (Bajaj et al., 2016; Guo et al., 2019; Sadia, 2022; Suleiman, 2017). The array of distressing experiences for Muslim American youth encompasses incidents like having eggs thrown at their cars, vandalism of local mosques (Sarwar & Raj, 2016), death threats (Aroian, 2012), and pervasive feelings of unwelcomeness in educational institutions (Azeez & Jimoh, 2023; Bajaj et al., 2016; Elsheikh & Sisemore, 2021). The propagation of misinformation, particularly within discussions on national security, significantly contributes to the development of biased perspectives among both peers and school staff (Bajaj et al., 2016). This bias, in turn, leads to the dismissal or oversight of bullying incidents targeting Muslim youth, rendering them either invisible or perceived as unworthy of intervention. Bullying is not confined to supervised areas; it extends to various locations such as cafeterias, fields, hallways, bathrooms, and even buses (Tahseen et al., 2019). Moreover, Muslim youth face discrimination from random strangers (Elkassem et al., 2018; Tahseen et al., 2019), thus intensifying their anxiety and rendering them more susceptible to physical and mental disorders due to compromised immunity (Aroian, 2012; Samari et al., 2018).

The impact of internalized racism is particularly pronounced among young children, fostering the development of dual or even intersectional identities in Muslim youth (Suleiman, 2017). This coping mechanism enables them to assimilate into society, but it demands constant efforts to prove their Americanness, leading to feelings of isolation and a lack of belonging (Tahseen et al., 2019). These youth often find themselves torn between their American and Muslim identities, pressured to choose based on their surroundings (Lebowitz, 2016; Suleiman, 2017). Many Muslim children feel exhausted as they continually strive to affirm their Americanness (Suleiman, 2017).

According to a California survey, 53% of Muslim youth reported religious-based bullying in school, twice the national average (Tahseen et al., 2019). The experience of bullying for Muslim youth is complex, encompassing both direct and indirect forms of aggression in various contexts and by different perpetrators (Tahseen et al., 2019). Muslim American children and youth face discrimination based on ethnicity and religion, with a prevailing belief that they pose a threat to the American way of life (Samari et al., 2018). Many schools convey the incompatible nature of being Muslim and American, fostering perceptions of foreignness, danger, and lack of adherence to American values (Bajaj et al., 2016). Discrimination leaves youth feeling marginalized, disempowered, and hopeless, leading to the internalization of negative stereotypes associated with Islam (Elkassem et al., 2018).

Discrimination is intricately linked to poor mental health outcomes, including low self-esteem, life satisfaction, control, and overall well-being (Elsheikh & Sisemore, 2021; Samari et al., 2018; Tahseen et al., 2019; Williams et al., 2019). Exposure to discrimination influences personality characteristics, increases the risk of chronic disorders, and contributes to externalizing and internalizing behavior problems (Williams et al., 2019). Daily discrimination is also positively associated with an increased risk of any chronic disorder cataloged in the *Diagnostic and Statistical Manual of Mental Disorders* (DSM-IV) (Williams et al., 2019). Furthermore, Muslim youth experience higher levels of posttraumatic stress disorder compared to their peers and higher rates of feelings of alienation, hopelessness, and decreased social support (Lebowitz, 2016; Williams et al., 2019).

Other negative consequences include poor self-concept (Guo et al., 2019) and poor academic performance (Aroian, 2012; Elkassem et al., 2018; Tahseen et al., 2019; Williams et al., 2019). Discrimination is associated with poor health practices such as alcohol and drug use (Williams et al., 2019). Over time, youth can develop a wide variety of psychological and physical stress-related diseases, including depression, anxiety (Lebowitz, 2016), suicidal ideation, anger, paranoia, fear, and hypertension (Ahmed & Hashem, 2016; Aroian, 2012; Elsheikh & Sisemore, 2021; Samari et al., 2018; Tahseen et al., 2019; Williams et al., 2019). Research indicates a concerning prevalence of discrimination incidents within school settings. In one study, 38% of reported incidents involved a teacher or school official (Tahseen et al., 2019). Name-calling and discriminatory behavior in the presence of teachers, staff, and administrators are distressingly common occurrences (Aroian, 2012; Bajaj et al., 2016; Lebowitz, 2016).

Bullying manifests in various forms, encompassing verbal taunts, physical aggression, and attacks on families or communities (Bajaj et al., 2016). The rise of cyberbullying is evident (Azeez & Jimoh, 2023), with Muslim students reporting an increase from 19% to 26% between 2014 and 2017 (Tahseen et al., 2019). Offensive online posts about Islam and Muslims are observed by 57% of respondents (Tahseen et al., 2019). Physical harassment and assaults reported by Muslim adolescents increased from 9% to 19% between 2014 and 2017 (Tahseen et al., 2019). Exposure to discrimination negatively affects mental and physical health, contributing to reduced physical activity, increased body mass index, chronic diseases, and a heightened risk for psychological disorders (Samari et al., 2018; Williams et al., 2019). Having a safe school environment is also needed for social and emotional well-being (Elsheikh & Sisemore, 2021).

A study involving 14 Muslim American adolescents highlighted schools as the primary setting for discrimination (Aroian, 2012). Seven out of nine incidents reported occurred within school settings, with teachers perpetrating half of these class-related incidents (Aroian, 2012). Another study, involving 79 Muslim students aged 12–17, revealed that 50% of participants experienced name-calling in the presence of school staff, while 80% had been subjected to discrimination (Lebowitz, 2016). Additionally, 75% of participants reported that the bullying occurred more than once (Lebowitz, 2016). Regrettably, many Muslim students facing discrimination at school seldom find justice or receive compensation for the mistreatment they endure (Lebowitz, 2016).

Youth have a developmental human need to belong and be connected to society (Suleiman, 2017; Tahseen et al., 2019). Microaggressions in schools create additional challenges, hindering Muslim youth from practicing their religious obligations, such as not providing space or time to allow students to pray, not allowing students to make up assignments, exams that are scheduled on Muslim holidays, or a lack of support for Muslim student organizations. Female students, easily identifiable by their *hijabs*, experience more microaggressions (Elkassem et al., 2018; Tahseen et al., 2019). In one study, all 15 Muslim girls who wore the scarf said that they often considered taking their scarf off due to fear of being attacked (Suleiman, 2017). Muslim boys often feel powerless when unable to defend family members in public spaces, contributing to a constant state of vigilance about their behavior, especially in public (Elkassem et al., 2018).

False perceptions among teachers and school staff regarding the educational values of Muslim students result in misplaced encouragement for enrollment in general-level classes, particularly impacting high-achieving Muslim women (Lebowitz, 2016). Placement in English as a second language (ESL) classes and the minimization of Muslim accomplishments further compound the issue (Lebowitz, 2016). Muslim students report lower levels of feeling respected in school and have a difficult time reconciling their self-image with the negative portrayal of Islam in classroom materials, which in turn lowers their grade point average (GPA) (Tahseen et al., 2019; Williams et al., 2019). Discrimination adversely affects school engagement, attendance, and academic motivation, resulting in reduced academic efficacy among Muslim youth (Williams et al., 2019). Fear of worsening situations often leads to unreported incidents (Elsheikh & Sisemore, 2021; Tahseen et al., 2019).

Muslim youth experience discrimination not only within schools but also through public discourses, including political speeches, laws, and private conversations projecting Islam as a violent religion (Azeez & Jimoh, 2023; Farooqui & Kaushik, 2022; Sadia, 2022). Islamophobia prevents Muslims from building social connections and a sense of community (Elsheikh & Sisemore, 2021). Muslim women face gendered Islamophobia, characterized by perceptions of oppression, and this causes barriers to educational, employment, and social opportunities (Elsheikh & Sisemore, 2021; Farooqui & Kaushik, 2022; Sarwar & Raj, 2016). Muslim girls report that they feel that teachers do not challenge them as they do their peers and that advisers do not provide them with the necessary information regarding postsecondary education because of the misbelief that Islam discourages women working outside the home and getting an education (Tahseen et al., 2019). Challenging these stereotypes becomes crucial for girls striving to redefine the narrative around their identity (Farooqui & Kaushik, 2022; Tahseen et al., 2019).

Religion and Spirituality as Buffers From the Impact of Anti-Islamic Bigotry

Discrimination has been a long-standing issue in America, particularly regarding Black and Brown communities. Anti-Islamic bigotry spiked following 9/11 and continued to be fueled by media portrayals and the tension that accompanies conflicts between America and the Middle East (Bajaj et al., 2016). Therefore the intersectionality of facing discrimination for both racial identity and being a follower of Islam in a post 9/11 America must be taken into consideration when regarding the mental health and well-being of Muslim youth (Samari et al., 2018). Discrimination has been shown to have negative impacts on mental health, affecting areas such as one's self-esteem and life satisfaction and resulting in depression, anxiety symptoms, and psychological distress (Ahmed & Hashem, 2016; Samari et al., 2018; Williams et al., 2019). Discrimination is shown to be linked to multiple indicators of adverse cardiovascular disease outcomes and a decreased likelihood of trust in one's healthcare providers, possibly impacting the follow-through of treatment regimens (Williams et al., 2019). A recent example of this relationship can be seen in the fear and mistrust expressed by communities of color during the COVID-19 pandemic due to contributing factors such as America's history of racist practices embedded in healthcare systems. With the intersection of discriminated-against identities, such as being a person of color and Muslim, having spiritual and religious practices with a built-in coping mechanism is beneficial. These are tools that are not new but instead have a long history of utilization within Black and Brown communities in America. Spirituality may serve as a protective factor for Muslims against negatively impacted well-being caused by discrimination (Hodge et al., 2016). In clinical practice, mindfulness and deep breathing techniques are encouraged as coping skills, and shifting thoughts from negative and hopeless, to positive and hopeful is often a therapy goal. Yet many religious and spiritual practices have had these components embodied within them throughout their entire existence. There is an extensive amount of documentation emphasizing the role major religions have played in contributions that have resulted in advancements in therapeutic efficacy (Sayeed & Prakash, 2013).

Historical intimidation and violence make communities, as well as Muslim youth, reluctant to seek professional help due to skepticism about its efficacy and a preference for confiding in friends or religious figures (Ahmed & Hashem, 2016). Addressing mental health stigma becomes essential in breaking these barriers (Ahmed & Hashem, 2016). Youth employ various coping mechanisms, such as humor, education, and confrontation, in response to discrimination. Increased religiosity emerges as a powerful buffer against anxiety and depression, fostering social support and a sense of belonging (Ahmed & Hashem, 2016). Religious identity serves as a vital protective factor, positively correlating with well-being and happiness (Tahseen et al., 2019). Some Muslim youth reported turning toward prayer or listening to the Quran to deal with discrimination stress (Tahseen et al., 2019). Furthermore, the religious minority status and sociopolitical cultural context were identified as potential factors resulting in higher levels of religiosity among Muslim college students (Tahseen et al., 2019). Support from family, peers, and role models outside the school environment enhances educational resilience and builds a positive self-image (Ahmed & Hashem, 2016; Farooqui & Kaushik, 2022).

Religion and spirituality have always had a hand in healing, as yoga, mindfulness meditation, and reiki practices can be seen reflected in alternative treatment modalities (Sayeed & Prakash, 2013). The steps of the 12-step program design found in groups such as Alcoholics Anonymous, Codependency Anonymous, and Overeaters Anonymous are also guiding principles inspired by spirituality and faith. Therefore, turning to a religious or spiritual belief system to help mitigate the effects of stressors such as discrimination is a cost-effective response that yields many benefits. Within the Islamic belief system, there are five pillars of practice: Proclamation of faith (Shahada), prayer (Salat), almsgiving (Zakat), fasting (Sawm), and pilgrimage to Mecca (Hajj). Each of these pillars holds the potential to be mentally, physically, and emotionally beneficial. Being charitable can be rewarding and make one feel as though they serve a purpose greater than themselves. A study, "Prosocial Spending and Well-Being: Cross-Cultural Evidence for a Psychological Universal," finds that emotional benefits are associated with sharing financial resources with others (Aknin et al., 2013).

Almsgiving is not only emotionally beneficial in countries where resources are plentiful, as one may expect, but is also beneficial in countries where resources are limited and charity may not go as far (Aknin et al., 2013). Many religions and spiritual practices entail some form of charity, whether it be *zakat*, tithes, volunteering time and resources, or engaging in acts of kindness. Asian American Muslim youth experiencing anti-Islamic bigotry can lean on this tenet of almsgiving (*zakat*) to reap its emotional benefits.

Intermittent fasting has been a trending term used by many seeking physical health benefits and mental clarity. Fasting in Islam is practiced during the month of Ramadan and is encouraged on particular days of the week year-round. Benefits associated with fasting patterns like that found in Islamic practice include obesity reduction due to weight loss, reduced insulin resistance, decreased blood pressure and blood glucose, and improved prevention of cancer, cardiovascular diseases, and neurodegeneration (Pakkir et al., 2018). Therefore, fasting can be implemented to decrease the physical impacts associated with discrimination. Discrimination is found to be a risk factor for higher levels of depression (Ahmed & Hashem, 2016; Williams et al., 2019). However, engaging in daily prayer, as Muslims do, has been shown to result in a lower likelihood of reporting clinically significant levels of depression (Hodge et al., 2016). Several studies have emphasized the positive effects of prayers in psychotherapy, particularly among individuals experiencing symptoms of anxiety, tension, depression, and anti-social tendencies (Sayeed & Prakash, 2013). Due to the physical procedure associated with *salat*, there are benefits associated with physical health as well (Sayeed & Prakash, 2013). Components of health and well-being encapsulate physical, spiritual, mental, and emotional health. All factors are characteristics associated with the five pillars of Islam.

Religious and spiritual spaces also give believers a sense of community and belongingness to those with shared beliefs and interests. This community can be a safe space for members to depend on in times of need. Minority communities usually do not resort to relying on external resources for issues faced and instead utilize religious leaders, family members, or community resources as a first line of defense. It is important to remember that with wide-scale discrimination often comes a distrust toward members who share similarities with those who are on the perpetrating end of that discrimination. Shared faith-based spaces may then serve as a way for individuals to let down their defense mechanisms and allow the vulnerability needed to heal. Islam encourages care for one's spiritual, mental, and physical self.

Therefore, to practice Islam means to be engaged in productive behaviors of holistic well-being daily. An example of the benefits of religion and spiritual practices in mental health is reflected in the statistic that more than 84% of scientific studies speak to the power of faith as a protective factor during addiction prevention and recovery (Grim & Grim, 2019). When facing the stressors associated with discrimination, leaning on the strengths of one's faith is a beneficial coping skill.

Being Asian and Muslim means having two characteristics of your identity potentially facing discrimination and therefore needing to rely on stronger systems of support. A study conducted by LeConté Dill among African American youth reflected the young individuals' reliance on God through prayer and the giving over of issues and worries out of their control to a higher spiritual being to handle (2017). Many of the therapeutic approaches that exist today to serve the variety of races and ethnicities living in America are theories rooted in Eurocentric Westernized beliefs. Spirituality serves as a healthy internal coping mechanism, particularly among youth of color, and should be a skill that is more relied upon in mental health treatments (Dill, 2017). Asian American youth who live within a home and community environment that reflects a more Eastern mindset may value things of a more collective nature and more rooted in spiritual and faith-based systems. To aid these youth with facilitating healthy and productive coping skills against discrimination, the therapeutic approach taken must be culturally intelligent. Often religious and spiritual belief systems also have a cultural factor that makes them an inherently culturally intelligent tool. It is not common for Asian American youth to practice a religion that differs from that of their parents or caregivers, therefore the religious and spiritual practices may also serve as a bonding mechanism for families. With communal Islamic observations such as Ramadan, Eid al-adha, Eid al-Fitr, and congregational Friday prayers (*salat al-Jumah*), Asian American Muslim youth can also utilize these gatherings as means to combat social isolation, which poses the threat of intensifying symptoms of depression.

It is recognized that Asian Americans are not a monolith. However, shared cultural and religious factors can shape behaviors and thought processes and cause similarities. With this connectedness, as Asian American youth rely on their belief system to mitigate the effects of discrimination, they would be choosing a culturally sound, affordable, and readily available protective factor to utilize. When discriminatory systems prevent youth of color from having reliable external sources to depend on, religion and spirituality are effective internal tools to employ. In a modern world that relies heavily on outward resources to meet the needs of humans, the tools intrinsically embedded within the species are often overlooked. Religion has had a long-standing relationship with psychiatry and human mental resilience. The separation of religion and psychiatry, particularly psychotherapy, was birthed in modern times due to narratives from Sigmund Freud (Koenig, 2012). For many of the referred-to fathers of psychology and psychoanalysis, the focus of that time was not to be culturally sound. People of color, particularly those who practice religions apart from Christianity, are overwhelmingly a minority in studies that have shaped the field of psychology and other related fields. Therefore, it is of vital importance to pair seeking available information to gain insight with a plan for the creation of future studies within Black, Brown, and Indigenous communities to further knowledge.

Recommendations for Social Work Advocacy on Behalf of Asian American Muslim Youth

It is urgent to address the challenges Muslim youth face especially within school settings due to the discernible data indicating that they feel inadequately supported. To address this, fostering increased opportunities for cross-group interaction and implementing a buddy system could prove beneficial (Guo et al., 2019). Additionally, recommended changes to the curriculum should encompass the inclusion of courses dedicated to religious and cultural education (Aroian, 2012; Lebowitz, 2016). These educational initiatives should be meticulously crafted not only to enhance awareness and appreciation for Muslims but also to dispel prevalent misconceptions perpetuated by mainstream sources. A key facet of the revised curriculum should involve highlighting the positive contributions of Muslims to American society, thus fostering a more inclusive narrative (Tahseen et al., 2019).

Moreover, the establishment of prayer rooms for Muslim students is essential to accommodate their spiritual needs (Guo et al., 2019). Creating designated spaces within schools where Muslim youth can openly and safely discuss their experiences is paramount (Elkassem et al., 2018). Such areas provide a platform for sharing perspectives and fostering community among Muslim students. Recognizing the vital role of educators and school staff, comprehensive training programs should be implemented to equip them with the necessary skills to support children facing microaggressions and discrimination (Elkassem et al., 2018). This training is pivotal in fostering a more inclusive and understanding school environment (Elkassem et al., 2018). Schools should actively encourage greater involvement of Muslim families in school activities and decision-making processes (Tahseen et al., 2019). This collaborative approach ensures that the unique needs and perspectives of Muslim students are taken into consideration in shaping the school environment (Tahseen et al., 2019).

On a broader community level, social workers must initiate public discussions about the pervasive impact of Islamophobia on youth. Engaging the public in these conversations helps raise awareness and underscores the importance of community support in addressing the challenges Muslim youth face (Sadia, 2022). This collective effort is instrumental in fostering an environment of understanding, tolerance, and inclusivity.

References

Ahmed, S., & Hashem, H. (2016). A decade of Muslim youth: Global trends in research. *Journal of Muslim Mental Health*, *10*(1), 1.

Aknin, L. B., Barrington-Leigh, C. P., Dunn, E. W., Helliwell, J. F., Burns, J., Biswas-Diener, R., Kemeza, I., Nyende, P., Ashton-James, C. E., & Norton, M. I. (2013). Prosocial spending and well-being: Cross-cultural evidence for a psychological universal. *Journal of Personality and Social Psychology*, *104*(4), 635–652. https://doi.org/10.1037/a0031578

Aroian K. J. (2012). Discrimination against Muslim American adolescents. *The Journal of School Nursing: The Official Publication of the National Association of School Nurses*, *28*(3), 206–213. https://doi.org/10.1177/1059840511432316

Azeez, I. A. A., & Jimoh, A. A. (2023). The impact of Islamophobia on society, attitudes, policies and the youths. *Eduvest: Journal of Universal Studies*, *3*(7), 1322–1339. https://doi.org/10.59188/eduvest.v3i7.873

Bajaj, M., Ghaffar-Kucher, A., & Desai, K. (2016). Brown bodies and xenophobic bullying in US schools: Critical analysis and strategies for action. *Harvard Educational Review*, *86*(4), 481–505. https://doi.org/10.17763/1943-5045-86.4.481

Barreto, M., Masuoka, N., & Sanchez, G. (2008, March). *Religiosity, discrimination and group identity among Muslim Americans*. Western Political Science Association Annual Conference.

Council on American Islamic Relations. (2023). 2023 bullying report. https://ca.cair.com/losangeles/wp-content/uploads/sites/6/2023/11/CAIR-CA-2023-Bullying-Report_Digital-2-min.pdf

Cuartas, V. H. (2020). *Hispanic Muslims in the United States: Agency, identity, and religious commitment*. Wipf and Stock.

Dill, L. J. (2017). Wearing my spiritual jacket: The role of spirituality as a coping mechanism among African American youth. *Health Education & Behavior*, *44*(5), 696–704. https://doi.org/10.1177/1090198117729398

Diouf, S. A. (1998). *Servants of Allah: African Muslims enslaved in the Americas*. New York University Press.

Elkassem, S., Csiernik, R., Mantulak, A., Kayssi, G., Hussain, Y., Lambert, K., Bailey, P., & Choudhary, A. (2018). Growing up Muslim: The impact of Islamophobia on children in a Canadian community. *Journal of Muslim Mental Health*, 12(1), 3-18. https://doi.org/10.3998/jmmh.10381607.0012.101

Elsheikh, E., & Sisemore, B. (2021). Islamophobia through the eyes of Muslims: Assessing perceptions, experiences, and impacts. *UC Berkley: Othering & Belonging Institute*. https://escholarship.org/uc/item/68t6456f

Farooqui, J. F., & Kaushik, A. (2022). Growing up as a Muslim youth in an age of Islamophobia: A systematic review of literature. *Contemporary Islam*, 16(1), 65-88. https://doi.org/10.1007/s11562-022-00482-w

Grim, B. J., & Grim, M. E. (2019). Belief, behavior, and belonging: How faith is indispensable in preventing and recovering from substance abuse. *Journal of Religion and Health*, 58(5), 1713-1752. https://doi.org/10.1007/s10943-019-00876-w

Guo, Y., Maitra, S., & Guo, S. (2019). "I belong to nowhere": Syrian refugee children's perspectives on school integration. *Journal of Contemporary Issues in Education*, 14(1), 89-105. https://doi.org/10.20355/jcie29362

Haddad, Y. Y. (ed.). (2002). *Muslims in the West: From sojourners to citizens*. Oxford University Press.

Haddad, Y. Y., & Lummis, A. T. (1987). *Islamic values in the United States: A comparative study*. Oxford University Press.

Hodge, D. R., Zidan, T., & Husain, A. (2016). Depression among Muslims in the United States: Examining the role of discrimination and spirituality as risk and protective factors. *Social Work (New York)*, 61(1), 45-52. https://doi.org/10.1093/sw/swv055

Husain, A. (2015). Islamophobia: Anti-Islamic bigotry. In C. Franklin (ed.), *Encyclopedia of social work online*. National Association of Social Workers/Oxford University Press. https://doi.org/10.1093/acrefore/9780199975839.013.964

Husain, A. (2019, February 25). Islam and social work. *Encyclopedia of Social Work*. https://oxfordre.com/socialwork/view/10.1093/acrefore/9780199975839.001.0001/acrefore-9780199975839-e-963.

Husain, A., Mirza, F. Y., & Tirmazi, T. (2022). Muslim youth in the United States. In L. Robinson & M. R. Gardee (eds.), *Radicalisation, extremism and social work practice: Minority Muslim youth in the West* (pp. 48-69). Taylor & Francis.

Koenig, H. G. (2012). Religion, spirituality, and health: The research and clinical implications. *ISRN Psychiatry*, 2012. https://doi.org/10.5402/2012/278730

Lebowitz, J. (2016). Muslim American youth in the post 9/11 public education system. *American Cultural Studies Capstone Research Papers*, 6. https://cedar.wwu.edu/fairhaven_acscapstone/6

Leonard, K. (1994). *Making ethnic choices: California's Punjabi Mexican Americans* (vol. 231). Temple University Press.

Leonard, K. (1997). Changing South Asian identities in the United States. In M. S. Seller & L. Weiss (eds.). *Beyond black and white: New faces and voices in US schools* (pp. 165-179). SUNY Press.

Mohamed, B. (2018). New estimates show U.S. Muslim population continues to grow. Pew Research Center. https://www.pewresearch.org/short-reads/2018/01/03/new-estimates-show-u-s-muslim-population-continues-to-grow/

Pakkir M., Naina, M., Jumale, A., Alatrash, J., & Sukkur, A. (2018). Health benefits of Islamic intermittent fasting. 5. 10.22038/jnfh.2018.30667.1111.

Portes, A., & Zhou. M. (1993). The new second generation: Segmented assimilation and its variants. *Annals of the American Academy of Political and Social Sciences*, 530(1), 74-96.

Read, J. N. G. (2008). Muslims in America. *Contexts*, 7(4), 39-43.

Ross-Sheriff, F., & Husain, A. (2001). Values and ethics in social work practice with Asian Americans: A South Asian Muslim case example. In R. Fong & S. Furuto (eds.), *Culturally competent practice: Skills, interventions, and evaluations* (pp. 75–88). Allyn & Bacon.

Ryan, L. (2014). "Islam does not change": Young people narrating negotiations of religion and identity. *Journal of Youth Studies*, *17*(4), 446–460. https://doi.org/10.1080/13676 261.2013.834315

Sadia, D. S. (2022). The impact of Islamophobia on society, attitude, policies and the youth. *Epistemology*, *10*(11), 112–136.

Samari, G., Alcalá, H. E., & Sharif, M. Z. (2018). Islamophobia, health, and public health: A systematic literature review. *American Journal of Public Health*, *108*(6), e1–e9. https://doi.org/10.2105/AJPH.2018.304402

Sarwar, D., & Raj, D. R. (2016). Islamophobia, racism and critical race theory. *International Journal of Safety and Security in Tourism and Hospitality*, *15*(2), 1–13.

Sayeed, S. A., & Prakash, A. (2013). The Islamic prayer (Salah/Namaaz) and yoga togetherness in mental health. *Indian Journal of Psychiatry*, *55*(Suppl 2), S224. https://doi.org/10.4103/0019-5545.105537

Suleiman, I. O. (2017). Internalized Islamophobia: Exploring the faith and identity crisis of American Muslim youth. *Islamophobia Studies Journal*, *4*(1), 1–12. https://yaqeeninstitute.org/wp-content/uploads/2017/03/InternalizedIslamophobia_ShOmar_Dec2016.pdf

Tahseen, M., Ahmed, S. R., & Ahmed, S. (2019). Muslim Youth in the face of Islamophobia: Risk and resilience. In H. S. Moffic, J. Peteet, A. Z. Hankir, & R. Awaad (eds.), *Islamophobia and psychiatry* (pp. 307–319). Springer International. https://doi.org/10.1007/978-3-030-00512-2_26

Takaki, R. T. (1998). *Strangers from a different shore: A history of Asian Americans*. Little, Brown.

Williams, D. R., Lawrence, J. A., Davis, B. A., & Vu, C. (2019). Understanding how discrimination can affect health. *Health Services Research*, *54*(6), 1374–1388. https://doi.org/10.1111/1475-6773.13222

11

Coping at the Margins

Managing Loneliness for Hmong Older Adults

Cindy Vang, Michael Sieng, and Austin Thao

Introduction

Older adults are at risk for loneliness, particularly as they encounter various age-related losses, including declining health and decreasing social networks (Kemperman et al., 2019; O'Rourke et al., 2018). Although loneliness can be a widespread challenge for older adults, immigrant older adults commonly report higher prevalence of loneliness in comparison to native-born older adults (De Jong Gierveld et al., 2015; Victor et al., 2012; Wu & Penning, 2015). Among immigrants, approximately 37.6 million are registered as refugees worldwide (United Nations High Commissioner for Refugees, 2024). The migration of refugees from their home countries to host countries is typically characterized by traumatic exodus and violence (Bemak & Chung, 2017; Lee & Chang, 2012), which further complicates the process of aging with a range of adversities and losses in host countries including increased dependency, marginalized cultural norms, family conflict, decreasing social networks, loss of social status, isolation, instability, language barriers, declining health, and lack of purpose (Johnson et al., 2019; Vang, Thor, et al., 2021). While these compounding issues influence older refugees' experiences of loneliness, immigrant and refugee older adults have demonstrated a number of coping mechanisms to manage their loneliness.

With the increasing number of refugees, the need to understand how older refugees cope with loneliness remains as urgent as ever. In the United States, an understudied immigrant group with a refugee background are Hmong older adults. Loneliness among refugee Hmong older adults has been conceptualized as "as a complex experience influenced by the trauma and context present in the premigration, displacement, and postmigration

---

Cindy Vang, Michael Sieng, and Austin Thao, *Coping at the Margins* In: *Addressing Anti-Asian Racism with Social Work, Advocacy, and Action*. Edited by: Meirong Liu and Keith T. Chan, Oxford University Press.
© Oxford University Press 2024. DOI: 10.1093/oso/9780197672242.003.0011

phases" (Vang et al., 2023, p. 9). Furthermore, Hmong older adults discussed their loneliness as influenced by a number of challenges, such as decreasing social networks following the deaths of family members, loss of social status and prestige, isolation from their ethnic and cultural community, enduring conflict with younger family members, and feeling uncertain of their future long-term care (Vang, Thor, et al., 2021).

Prior to resettlement in the United States, the Hmong's involvement in the Secret War and their forced migration out of Laos following its end in 1975 involved traumatic experiences of war violence, death of family members, and starvation (Vang, Thor, et al., 2021; Xiong, 2022). A scattered and small body of research has provided some insight into the persistent and poor mental health symptoms (e.g., depressive, posttraumatic stress) that have followed this group since their early resettlement (Westermeyer et al., 1983, 1984). For instance, a recent study found a high prevalence of depressive symptoms among Hmong adults aged 55 and older, indicating that depressive symptoms remain similar to that of when they first resettled in the 1980s (Yang & Mutchler, 2020). While mental health challenges and low access to formal mental health care in the Hmong community has typically been attributed to cultural factors, structural factors related to discrimination and limited cultural sensitivity require greater attention (Vang, Sun, et al., 2021).

Many Hmong older adults residing in the United States today were admitted into the country as parolees, political refugees, or refugees for family reunification (Xiong, 2022). The first wave of Hmong refugees arrived in the United States by the spring of 1976, with the second waves arriving between 1980 and 1995 (Xiong, 2022). While the first wave tended to be educated and spoke some English, the second wave arrived with limited financial and social capital and skills that were devalued in the United States (Xiong, 2022). Therefore, long-standing economic difficulties including unemployment and underemployment have disadvantaged the Hmong community since their arrival. Today, socioeconomic challenges persist for Hmong older adults and their families, including high rates of poverty, where 58% of Hmong Americans are low-income and more than one in four live in poverty (Southeast Asian Resource Action Center & Asian Americans Advancing Justice, 2020). As an older adult group with risk factors (e.g., low socioeconomic status, high depressive symptoms) associated with loneliness, how they cope with loneliness remains relatively unknown. Thus, the purpose of this chapter is to examine how community-dwelling Hmong older adults cope with loneliness.

Coping

Coping is defined as the process of cognitive and behavioral efforts to manage or resolve distress caused by internal and/or external stressors, evolving over time and varying based on context (Lazarus & Folkman, 1984). In response to the distress of loneliness and psychological distress associated with loneliness (e.g., symptoms of depression, posttraumatic stress disorder [PTSD], and anxiety), older immigrants and refugees draw on a combination of coping mechanisms, such as cognitive reframing, religious beliefs and practices, self-distraction, and interpersonal support (Frounfelker et al., 2020; Johnson et al., 2019; Mölsä et al., 2017; Strug et al., 2009). However, migration from their home countries can limit their resources and diminish the social support needed for coping (Im, 2021).

Coping strategies arise from nuanced cultural values, beliefs, and norms given to trauma, loss, religious and spiritual beliefs, and proximity to cultural communities (Ciobanu & Fokkema, 2017; Frounfelker et al., 2020; Mölsä et al., 2017). Coping mechanisms, such as cognitive strategies, can help an individual cope with stressful life situations by reframing, accepting, and thinking positively of a situation (Lou & Ng, 2012; Posselt et al., 2019). For Chinese older adults in Hongkong, cognitive reframing was identified as adjusting expectations of family members, comparing their experiences with other older adults they perceived to be more unhappy, and recognizing the benefits to their family (Lou & Ng, 2012). Religious and spiritual faith and practices were another source of coping (Ciobanu & Fokkema, 2017; Mölsä et al., 2017; Posselt et al., 2019). Romanian migrants ages 57 and older drew on their religion for protection from difficulties, including loneliness (Ciobanu & Fokkema, 2017). Attending church also played a role in social network building and establishing a feeling of belonging (Ciobanu & Fokkema, 2017).

Behavioral strategies and strengthening kin and non-kin social relationships were additional mechanisms for coping with loneliness (Lou & Ng, 2012; Morlett Paredes et al., 2021; Patzelt, 2017; Posselt et al., 2019; Strug et al., 2009). Specifically, behavioral strategies involved activities to keep the mind occupied and distracted from loneliness and psychological distress (Posselt et al., 2019; Strug et al., 2009). For instance, Bhutanese refugees explained the helpful distraction of engaging in games or sports against distress (Chase & Sapkota, 2017). Meanwhile, numerous studies have found complex supportive social relationships among immigrant older adults. Chinese older adults reported more loss in social support networks and relational conflicts with children related to declining power and status in their families (Da & Garcia, 2015). To find supportive social networks outside of their families, Chinese older adults participated in religious activities and English-language classes to socialize with other older immigrants (Da & Garcia, 2015). These experiences of older immigrants and refugees reveal a strong desire to find and build community.

Intersectionality Framework

Intersectionality is increasingly recognized in gerontology as a critical framework to emphasize "how power and inequalities differentially impact historically marginalized groups based on their intersecting identities—identifying as an older adult and minoritized group" (Ma et al., 2021, p. 5). Rooted in Black feminist scholarship, intersectionality was first coined by Kimberle Williams Crenshaw to examine how the intersections of race and gender shaped Black women's experiences with employment (Collins, 1998; Crenshaw, 1991). Instead of analyzing systems individually and separately or as additive factors, intersectionality examines how these systems mutually construct each other (Collins, 1998). In essence, intersectionality views power and privilege through the complexity and intersections of systems to understand how they create specific experiences for marginalized individuals and groups (Bunjun, 2010). These systems emerge from social, cultural, and political contexts, in which macro- and meso-level factors along with individual factors influence experiences (Alvi & Zaidi, 2017).

Intersectional frameworks have been useful to exposing the systems of power, privilege, and oppression. A study of the quality of life among South Asian elderly immigrant women in Canada highlighted the multiple intersections of their challenges and stressors, including cultural isolation and lack of commitment from children and community (Alvi & Zaidi, 2017). In addition, the loss of specific resources (e.g., social networks) hindered the ability to cope in their host country and amplified their loneliness. For older adults holding multiple marginalized social identities, an intersectional analysis of coping can reveal how various social identities shape access to coping mechanisms. Therefore, to deepen our understanding of coping with loneliness, we drew on an intersectionality framework to assist with our examination of the nuanced and intersecting dimensions of social positions that can privilege, minimize, and deny access to coping mechanisms for Hmong older adults.

Methods

Recruitment and Participants

Participants were recruited from May 2018 to December 2018 in Sacramento and Fresno, California, for a constructivist grounded theory study exploring the experiences of loneliness among community-dwelling Hmong older adults. For this chapter, we report on findings related to the coping of participants. Drawing on purposive and snowball sampling, participants were recruited virtually through a social media platform and face-to-face from local Hmong and Southeast Asian nonprofit organizations and clinics, Hmong supermarkets, and a Hmong senior group. Inclusion criteria for the study required participants to identify as Hmong; be 65 years or older; reside in Sacramento or Fresno, California; and have no cognitive impairment. Seventeen participants were included in the final data analysis (Table 11.1). They ranged in age from 65 to 84. Majority of the participants were female (64.7%) and widowed (58.8%).

Data Collection and Analysis

Data collection and analysis occurred iteratively. The first author conducted all semi-structured individual interviews in the Hmong language in the homes of participants, a community center, and a community garden. She identifies as Hmong American, is proficient in the Hmong language, and has prior direct practice experience supporting Hmong older adults living with Type 2 diabetes and hypertension. The interviews focused on eliciting coping mechanisms by asking questions to explore what participants did individually to manage their loneliness, which individuals helped them with their loneliness, and what these individuals did to help them. Other questions inquiring about their conceptualization and experiences of loneliness also prompted responses of coping mechanisms. All interviews were audio-recorded with the permission of participants and transcribed from Hmong to English. The transcribed interviews were uploaded to Atlas.ti to manage the coding process between the first and second authors.

Analysis was conducted following a grounded theory analytic process (Charmaz, 2006). Our analysis process included (a) initial coding, (b) focused coding, (c) theoretical coding, and (d) diagramming. We employed

Table 11.1 Sample sociodemographic characteristics of participants ($n = 17$)

Pseudonym	Age	Gender	Years in US	Marital status	English language proficiency (ELP)	Formal education	Religious/Spiritual beliefs
Pa	69	Female	42	Widowed	No ELP	No formal education	Animism
Mai	66	Female	30	Divorced	No ELP	No formal education	Animism
Chia	66	Female	42	Widowed	Poor	No formal education	Christianity
Meng	67	Male	38	Widowed	Poor	No formal education	Christianity
Tou	78	Male	29	Widowed	No ELP	Some adult school	Animism
Pao	65	Male	38	Divorced	Poor	Some adult school	Animism
Nou	67	Female	29	Widowed	No ELP	Some adult school	Animism
Lee	74	Female	16	Widowed	No ELP	No formal education	Christianity
Chou	80	Male	39	Widowed	Poor	No formal education	Animism
Yer	76	Female	32	Widowed	No ELP	No formal education	Animism
Ka	65	Female	45	Widowed	No ELP	No formal education	Animism
See	70	Female	29	Widowed	No ELP	No formal education	None
Mee	67	Female	39	Married	No ELP	No formal education	Animism
Xiong	68	Male	39	Married	Good	Some college	Animism
Chong	70	Female	23	Married	No ELP	No formal education	Animism
Teng	84	Male	31	Married	No ELP	No formal education	Animism
Sia	70	Female	30	Married	No ELP	No formal education	Animism

constant comparison, memoing, and theoretical sampling to assist with elaborating on the variation of codes, concepts, and categories. The Arizona State University Institutional Review Board approved the study. Additional information on data collection and analysis procedures are detailed elsewhere (Vang, Thor, et al., 2021).

Results

Participants articulated several mechanisms to manage their loneliness. Interspersed in their narratives were access to and exclusion from resources and social networks. Exclusion from mainstream American society was prominent in the social relationships they described as supportive and desired. Participants further drew on beliefs, practices, and skills developed in Laos to strategically cope with their loneliness. These coping mechanisms were organized into themes of seeking support and community, greater power, escaping through activity, and control and avoidance.

Seeking Social Support and Community

Collective and familial values were evident in the ways social support and community were discussed as a prominent mechanism for coping with loneliness. Social support and community were described as meaningful relationships that provided participants with emotional, physical, mental, spiritual, and/or financial support to minimize their experiences of loneliness. Access to and exclusion from social support and community varied on social identities in the Hmong and greater American community including gender, marital status, language abilities, and living arrangements.

Spouse. Spouses were identified as a key support among participants. Some participants referred to their spouses as a "partner" who "talked" with them, problem-solved, eased their concerns, and provided solace. Chou, an 80-year-old Hmong man, explained he was not depressed when he arrived in the United States as a young man "because my wife and children were still alive." Following her death, he reported experiencing depression and suffering. Among widowed participants, their experiences of loneliness were associated with the death of their spouses and the loss of a person to fulfill emotionally supportive roles. Lee recalled, "When I had a husband by my side and had health issues, he would tell me, and I would tell him. When

I was sick, he helped me ... and I was happy." For female participants, their widowhood involved increasing isolation from their extended family and the Hmong community. For instance, Chia, a 66-year-old woman, talked about her decreasing social group following the death of her husband.

> My friends are slowly not coming over as much. His [her husband] phone is silent now. No one calls it anymore. There is only mine. I am not an important person, so they call and ask how I am doing only. When it comes to friends, joking, and laughing, it is just women now. I am so lonely.

Children. Although many participants discussed having communication issues with their children, they also described their children as sources of vital caregivers, interpreters, and emotional support. In these roles, their children assisted as a liaison when language barriers occurred and transported them to stores and appointments. Participants also spoke of their children as crucial sources of emotional support when they were depressed and lonely. A participant discussed her daughters and their support when she felt lonely and depressed.

> Whenever I begin to have depression, I call my daughters to talk with me. I have three daughters. If I am depressed and lonely, I call my daughters that I did this and that and I do not have this and that. They say this and that back and I am happy again. For me, that's it. (Mai, Female, 66)

Relatives. Relatives were prominent social support for coping with loneliness. Some participants were able to relocate close to their relatives upon resettlement in the United States. They discussed feeling happiness when they were able to "follow" their relatives in the United States again, especially those who were initially resettled in different parts of the country. Chou talked about his loneliness while he was separated from his relatives. He explained "some resettled in the south and some resettled in the north. I was lonely and missed my relatives. . . .That was what my depression was about." However, relatives in the same city could not always see one another, as described by Yer.

> There are still some brothers, sisters-in-law, sons, and daughters-in-law who live here and love me too, but like I said I do not know how to drive. If I want to see them, they have to come pick me up. If they do not come pick me up, it could be years before I get to them.

Hmong Community. Participants who engaged in socialization with Hmong community members reported how these social relationships alleviated their experiences of loneliness. Two participants explained their preference to socialize with Hmong older adults because their physical abilities and talking styles were more compatible. Participants were able to socialize in various settings including Hmong stores, churches, and Hmong senior groups. For instance, Mai discussed going to Hmong stores and meeting Hmong people. She said they talked, and she would forget the time and her loneliness.

Five participants were recruited from a Hmong senior group that met twice a week. Chou, a member of this group, talked about enjoying the socialization he received from attending the group. However, Meng, a 76-year-old man, discussed that while Hmong women talked with him, Hmong men were not as open to talking with him. Lee discussed the benefits of the social support she found with other Hmong women in the Hmong senior group. Additionally, Lee found companionship with older Hmong women residing in her apartment complex. She discussed bringing food to them and providing massages when they were ill. The companionship of other Hmong women provided Lee with a sense of purpose to support others and helped to alleviate her loneliness.

Romantic Companion. A romantic companion was desired and sought among widowed and divorced male participants to cope with their loneliness. Without a wife, male participants talked about lacking a female "friend" who they could "joke" with and who could "speak nicely" to them. Pao, a 65-year-old man, was seeking relationships with Hmong "girls" in Laos after his divorce. He discussed that his happiness was tied to talking and seeing Hmong girls from Laos to "forget" his depression. However, his ex-wife, children, and relatives were "blocking" him from sending money overseas to them. On the other hand, Chou was in search of an older Hmong woman to marry in the United States. He shared, "The way to release it [loneliness] is if there is an older woman to joke with and is willing to be my friend. I am unable to release my depression and loneliness."

Greater Power

Participants discussed religious and spiritual beliefs as mechanisms that helped them cope with their loneliness. They described experiences of connections to a power greater than themselves or through spiritual rituals by drawing on their religious and spiritual beliefs for healing and clarity.

In Search of Healing. Participants found their religious and spiritual beliefs helped heal them when their health was poor and they were feeling lonely. Healing was discussed as recovering from physical ailments through prayers and spiritual treatments. Lee, a 74-year-old Hmong woman, explained how prayers to Jesus helped her recover from illnesses, including colds. Chong, a 70-year-old woman, talked about seeking shamans to help with her health issues. She described her complexion as pale, a sign that she was not well. Her health issues had worsened in the United States, and she was skeptical about the diagnosis of depression she had received from doctors. She held onto the belief that her physical health could recover if her spiritual well-being was better.

They said I have depression. But I do not think it is just depression. I have a lot of other

> health issues. When they [spiritually] looked into it, they said my spirit fell there [in Laos] and has not returned since when we were fleeing [through the jungles of Laos]. It's been many years since my spirit fell. I do not have my spirit because it lives in the ground now. It is in the ground and will not rise....Whoever [spiritually] looks into it, says that.

In Search of Clarity. Participants sought clarity for their physical and emotional state through religious and spiritual beliefs. Among participants who practiced Shamanism, the answers they found through spiritual beliefs helped them make sense of their lonely state as a condition outside of their physical and emotional control. Yer, a 76-year-old woman, explained that her loneliness when her husband's health declined was related to her spiritual well-being. She believed her spirit had begun to mourn her husband's passing long before he died and manifested in her years of loneliness preceding and following his death.

Escaping Through Activity

Participants discussed engaging in activities as a distraction to cope with their loneliness. Activities included walking, exercising, gardening, and raising animals. Participants engaged in the activities daily or often. Only Lee discussed exercising for the purpose of health and wellness. She talked about running in the morning to exercise and maintain her health. She found that running along with prayers helped her manage her loneliness. More than half of participants could no longer drive; therefore, the opportunity to walk around and see new things helped participants cope with loneliness. Participants explained that walking helped to calm the restlessness they would feel build up when they stayed home all day. They further discussed their preference to wander outside their homes to see their neighborhoods, supermarkets, or gardens.

Among participants, gardening was the preferred activity they engaged in when they felt lonely. Participants gardened in their backyards and in community gardens. Gardening was described as an "escape" from their long days at home, as described by Mai.

> I plant things at the garden.... I wander here and there. Look here and there. Dig, dig, dig. Suddenly, when I look, when I look at my watch, it's already noon. Go home. When I do that, the day and time seems short for me.... If I stay here [home] all day and all night, it feels long all the time.

Along with gardening, raising animals was a practice carried over from Laos. Participants discussed mainly raising chickens in their homes. Similar to gardening, spending time with animals helped participants cope with their loneliness during days that felt long. Mee, a 67-year-old woman, recalled that raising chickens had another benefit as it provided her with the means to help others by giving them away for free to older community members who "wanted to eat some chicken." On the other hand, Teng felt confined by laws that regulated how many animals one could raise and how to raise animals. While he continued to raise chickens in his backyard, he worried that neighbors would report him.

Control and Avoidance

Participants discussed the practice of learning to control and avoid feeling lonely to manage their loneliness. Although they acknowledged their feelings of loneliness, participants felt it was best to push their feelings aside. They explained the need to control and avoid was an approach to prevent from becoming "disabled and crazy," suffering even more, and developing chronic illnesses. Chia recalled seeking the advice of a doctor when she was feeling lonely and depressed. The doctor advised her to "get a hold of" herself. To prevent further decline, Chia practiced controlling and avoiding her feelings of loneliness and depression. She said she "got better a few times." Mai described controlling herself when she felt lonely and depressed about her financial situation.

> Sometimes like I said, if I am lonely and depressed, not thinking about it is best. If I keep thinking about it, I will think about this and that, about expenses, and this and that, then I will feel depressed and lonely. If I just keep to myself and do not think about those things and forget it, then I will be fine too.

Participants shared that they also informed other Hmong older adults to control themselves when they were feeling lonely.

Discussion

This study examined coping mechanisms among Hmong older adults when they experienced loneliness, using the framework of intersectionality. Rather than only seeing their coping mechanisms as individual cognitive and behavioral efforts to manage their loneliness, we were also interested in understanding how multiple social identities shaped their coping. Along with gender and ethnicity, age, immigrant status, marital status, language abilities, and physical abilities intersected to produce unique experiences for participants. While their resources and social networks were evidently limited, Hmong older adults strategically drew on existing cultural practices and beliefs and social relationships to cope with loneliness. Coping mechanisms were constructed as a reliance on a higher power, seeking support and community, escaping through activity, and controlling and avoiding. These findings contribute to the growing literature that suggests the need for culturally sensitive and nuanced approaches to support Hmong older adults cope with loneliness (Vang, Sun, et al., 2021).

The results are consistent with empirical studies that established the significance of maintaining and rebuilding social relationships and social support (Chen & Feeley, 2014; Wu et al., 2010). Among the majority of participants, relationships with their families, clan, and the Hmong community helped with the management of loneliness. The narratives of participants highlighted the limitations and opportunities (e.g., proximity to family and community, availability of land) to strengthen existing relationships and build new relationships. Identities, such as gender and marital status, intersected to create complex social relationships that further isolated specific groups of Hmong older adults. Notably, the majority of participants expressed interest in maintaining relationships and receiving support from their family and relatives, while several participants indicated interest in relationships with Hmong individuals not related to them, specifically those who were seeking romantic relationships. These existing and desired social relationships highlight the complex ways in which Hmong older adults have maintained and shifted their perception and understanding of family and community.

Findings of religious and spiritual practices and beliefs as coping mechanisms align with previous research (Ciobanu & Fokkema, 2017; Kirkpatrick et al., 1999; Reis & Menezes, 2017). Participants discussed feeling lonely during moments of hopelessness and loss and turning to their religious and spiritual beliefs to manage their emotions. They used prayers to seek divine intervention in difficult situations attributed to their loneliness and spiritual rituals to seek guidance that linked their physical and spiritual well-being. While some of the spiritual rituals did not provide relief from loneliness, the spiritual explanations of loneliness helped participants make sense of their experiences.

Participants also coped by controlling and avoiding emotions of loneliness on their own or through escaping in activities. These findings support an earlier study of lonely older adults who coped with loneliness through avoidance and participating in solitary activities (McInnis & White, 2001). With their diminished resources and abilities, many participants felt compelled to control their emotional distress to avoid becoming lonelier. A few participants reported that the practice of emotion-focused control was effective. Furthermore, through gardening, raising animals, and exercising, participants were able to relieve their loneliness or manage it temporarily. These nonsocial diversions and active practices underline the mental resilience and resourcefulness of participants.

Limitations and Implications

We acknowledge some limitations of our study. As a qualitative study, we aimed to illuminate deep and rich interpretations of participant experiences. Therefore, the historical, social, and political context in which Hmong older adults became refugees and resettled in the United States may not be applicable to other older adults with a refugee background. We speak to additional power, linguistic, and cultural limitations in another paper (Vang, Thor, et al., 2021).

Results of our study provide implications for practice, policy, and research to consider individual- and community-level changes to improve the lives of Hmong older adults. For practitioners who work directly with Hmong older adults, understanding how this population copes with loneliness can aid in the provision and advocacy of culturally responsive programs and services. These cultural implications are often neglected by practitioners trained to work in a system rooted in Western values and practices, which in turn can result in oppressive spaces for older adults who do not subscribe to these values and practices. For example, the religious and spiritual beliefs and social systems of Hmong older adults must be understood, respected, and prioritized beyond individual psychotherapy. Therefore, future research should include Hmong older adults to investigate religious and spiritual beliefs and practices as interventions to address loneliness.

Community-based programs informed by Hmong older adults and operated by members of the Hmong community are also essential to the long-term well-being of Hmong older adults. The intersectional analysis of Hmong older adults revealed their experiences of marginalization from the larger American community and the Hmong community. For instance, the absence of social relationships with non-Hmong people in their narratives highlights their ongoing alienation from American society. The experiences of widowed Hmong women provide additional complexity to the exclusionary social practices in the Hmong community upon the death of a male spouse. Programs and services should center these particular groups to better understand how to support their needs against these marital and gender-based marginalizations. Culturally responsive programs should also consider that a significant portion of Hmong older adults only speak the Hmong language and desire support and community from Hmong individuals who are aware of and sensitive to their cultural preferences and experiences. Future research should explore the cultural efficacy of programs (e.g., adult day programs) employing such strategies as social locations to reduce loneliness.

Findings highlight the need for community-level interventions to focus on strengthening those mechanisms Hmong older adults draw upon to cope. Participants of this study coped with loneliness through engaging in various activities (e.g., gardening, exercising, and raising animals) and social support networks. Practitioners and stakeholders should advocate for more community gardens embedded within Hmong communities, along with land to raise animals as a means to reduce loneliness and minimize economic challenges. Providing land for Hmong older adults to engage in gardening can be an intervention to not only address loneliness and increase social relationships, but also improve their physical well-being and sustain their traditional lifestyle of growing their own food. These gardening and farming practices may also bring in affordable and diverse food options to the communities they are situated in.

Conclusion

Our study of the coping mechanisms employed by Hmong older adults broadens the understanding of loneliness among aging immigrants, particularly those who faced a traumatic exodus from their home countries and endured long-standing social, cultural, and economic marginalization in their host countries. Although Hmong older adults reported familiar coping strategies, the use of an intersectionality framework helped to emphasize the nuanced experiences of how these coping strategies functioned. For Hmong older adults, the strengths and maintenance of cultural values and practices have helped manage loneliness. However, some of these same cultural values and practices also harm specific groups in the community, such as Hmong women. Moving forward, we hope that our study sheds light on the necessity for intersectional and culturally sensitive work to improve the lives of all older adults.

References

Alvi, S., & Zaidi, A. U. (2017). Invisible voices: An intersectional exploration of quality of life for elderly South Asian immigrant women in a Canadian sample. *Journal of Cross-Cultural Gerontology*, 32(2), 147–170.

Bemak, F., & Chung, R. C. Y. (2017). Refugee trauma: Culturally responsive counseling interventions. *Journal of Counseling & Development, 95*(3), 299–308.

Bunjun, B. (2010). Feminist organizations and intersectionality: Contesting hegemonic feminism. *Atlantis: Critical Studies in Gender, Culture & Social Justice, 34*(2), 115–126.

Charmaz, K. (2006). *Constructing grounded theory: A practical guide through qualitative analysis.* Sage.

Chase, L., & Sapkota, R. P. (2017). "In our community, a friend is a psychologist": An ethnographic study of informal care in two Bhutanese refugee communities. *Transcultural Psychiatry, 54*(3), 400–422.

Chen, Y., & Feeley, T. H. (2014). Social support, social strain, loneliness, and well-being among older adults: An analysis of the Health and Retirement Study. *Journal of Social and Personal Relationships, 31*(2), 141–161.

Ciobanu, R. O., & Fokkema, T. (2017). The role of religion in protecting older Romanian migrants from loneliness. *Journal of Ethnic and Migration Studies, 43*(2), 199–217.

Collins, P. H. (1998). The tie that binds: Race, gender and US violence. *Ethnic and Racial Studies, 21*(5), 917–938.

Crenshaw, K. (1991). Mapping the margins: Intersectionality, identity politics, and violence against women of color. *Stanford Law Review, 43*(6), 1241–1299.

Da, W. W., & Garcia, A. (2015). Later life migration: Sociocultural adaptation and changes in quality of life at settlement among recent older Chinese immigrants in Canada. *Activities, Adaptation & Aging, 39*(3), 214–242.

De Jong Gierveld, J. D. J., Van der Pas, S., & Keating, N. (2015). Loneliness of older immigrant groups in Canada: Effects of ethnic-cultural background. *Journal of Cross-Cultural Gerontology, 30*(3), 251–268.

Frounfelker, R. L., Mishra, T., Dhesi, S., Gautam, B., Adhikari, N., & Betancourt, T. S. (2020). "We are all under the same roof": Coping and meaning-making among older Bhutanese with a refugee life experience. *Social Science & Medicine, 264*, 113311.

Im, H. (2021). Falling through the cracks: Stress and coping in migration and resettlement among marginalized Hmong refugee families in the United States. *Families in Society, 102*(1), 50–66.

Johnson, S., Bacsu, J., McIntosh, T., Jeffery, B., & Novik, N. (2019). Social isolation and loneliness among immigrant and refugee seniors in Canada: A scoping review. *International Journal of Migration, Health and Social Care, 15*(3), 177–190.

Kemperman, A., van den Berg, P., Weijs-Perrée, M., & Uijtdewilligen, K. (2019). Loneliness of older adults: Social network and the living environment. *International Journal of Environmental Research and Public Health, 16*(3), 406.

Kirkpatrick, L. A., Shillito, D. J., & Kellas, S. L. (1999). Loneliness, social support, and perceived relationships with God. *Journal of Social and Personal Relationships, 16*(4), 513–522.

Lazarus, R. S., & Folkman, S. (1984). *Stress, appraisal, and coping.* Springer.

Lee, S., & Chang, J. (2012). Mental health status of the Hmong Americans in 2011: Three decades revisited. *Journal of Social Work in Disability & Rehabilitation, 11*(1), 55–70.

Lou, V. W., & Ng, J. W. (2012). Chinese older adults' resilience to the loneliness of living alone: A qualitative study. *Aging & Mental Health, 16*(8), 1039–1046.

Ma, K. P. K., Bacong, A. M., Kwon, S. C., Yi, S. S., & Đoàn, L. N. (2021). The impact of structural inequities on older Asian Americans during COVID-19. *Frontiers in Public Health, 9*, 1–8.

McInnis, G. J., & White, J. H. (2001). A phenomenological exploration of loneliness in the older adult. *Archives of Psychiatric Nursing, 15*(3), 128–139.

Mölsä, M., Kuittinen, S., Tiilikainen, M., Honkasalo, M. L., & Punamäki, R. L. (2017). Mental health among older refugees: The role of trauma, discrimination, and religiousness. *Aging & Mental Health, 21*(8), 829–837.

Morlett Paredes, A., Lee, E. E., Chik, L., Gupta, S., Palmer, B. W., Palinkas, L. A., Kim, H., & Jeste, D. V. (2021). Qualitative study of loneliness in a senior housing community: The importance of wisdom and other coping strategies. *Aging & Mental Health, 25*(3), 559–566.

O'Rourke, H. M., Collins, L., & Sidani, S. (2018). Interventions to address social connectedness and loneliness for older adults: A scoping review. *BMC Geriatrics, 18*(1), 1–13.

Patzelt, A. (2017). "A totally new world has been opening up for me": Experiences of older German migrants who are actively involved in the German-speaking community in Ottawa, Canada. *Journal of Ethnic and Migration Studies, 43*(2), 218–234.

Posselt, M., Eaton, H., Ferguson, M., Keegan, D., & Procter, N. (2019). Enablers of psychological well-being for refugees and asylum seekers living in transitional countries: A systematic review. *Health & Social Care in the Community, 27*(4), 808–823.

Reis, L. A. D., & Menezes, T. M. D. O. (2017). Religiosity and spirituality as resilience strategies among long-living older adults in their daily lives. *Revista brasileira de enfermagem, 70*, 761–766.

Southeast Asia Resource Action Center & Asian Americans Advancing Justice. (2020). Southeast Asian American Journeys. https://www.searac.org/wp-content/uploads/2020/02/SEARAC_NationalSnapshot_PrinterFriendly.pdf

Strug, D. L., Mason, S. E., & Auerbach, C. (2009). How older Hispanic immigrants in New York City cope with current traumatic stressors: Practice implications. *Journal of Gerontological Social Work, 52*(5), 503–516.

United Nations High Commissioner for Refugees. (2024). Refugee data finder. https://www.unhcr.org/refugee-statistics/

Vang, C., Sieng, M., & Zheng, M. (2023). Conceptualizing loneliness among a Hmong older adult group: Using an intersectionality framework. *Asian American Journal of Psychology, 14*(4), 340–349.

Vang, C., Sun, F., & Sangalang, C. C. (2021). Mental health among the Hmong population in the US: A systematic review of the influence of cultural and social factors. *Journal of Social Work, 21*(4), 811–830.

Vang, C., Thor, P., & Sieng, M. (2021). Influencing factors of loneliness among Hmong older adults in the premigration, displacement, and postmigration phases. *Journal of Refugee Studies, 34*(3), 3464–3485.

Victor, C. R., Burholt, V., & Martin, W. (2012). Loneliness and ethnic minority elders in Great Britain: An exploratory study. *Journal of Cross-Cultural Gerontology, 27*(1), 65–78.

Westermeyer, J., Neider, J., & Vang, T. F. (1984). Acculturation and mental health: A study of Hmong refugees at 1.5 and 3.5 years postmigration. *Social Science & Medicine, 18*(1), 87–93.

Westermeyer, J., Vang, T. F., & Neider, J. (1983). Migration and mental health among Hmong refugees: Association of pre- and postmigration with self-rating scales. *Journal of Nervous and Mental Disease, 171*(2), 92–96.

Wu, Z., & Penning, M. (2015). Immigration and loneliness in later life. *Ageing & Society, 35*(1), 64–95.

Wu, Z. Q., Sun, L., Sun, Y. H., Zhang, X. J., Tao, F. B., & Cui, G. H. (2010). Correlation between loneliness and social relationship among empty nest elderly in Anhui rural area, China. *Aging and Mental Health, 14*(1), 108–112.

Xiong, Y. S. (2022). *Immigrant agency: Hmong American movements and the politics of racialized incorporation*. Rutgers University Press.

Yang, M. S., & Mutchler, J. E. (2020). The high prevalence of depressive symptoms and its correlates with older Hmong refugees in the United States. *Journal of Aging and Health, 32*(7–8), 660–669.

12
The Impact of Anti-Asian Racism on the Psychosocial Well-Being of Older Asian Americans

A Systematic Review

Fei Sun, Siyu Gao, Ethan Liu, and Yali Feng

Introduction

The older Asian American population is experiencing rapid growth. In 2020, there were approximately 3.9 million Asian Americans aged 65 and older, constituting around 5% of the total aging population in the United States. This number is projected to double, reaching 7.8 million by 2060 (Administration on Community Living [ACL], 2020). The ongoing expansion of the older Asian American demographic can be ascribed to several key factors, including the overall increase in the Asian American population and rising life expectancy in the United States. Additionally, immigration patterns, birth rates, and aging of the existing population have all played roles in shaping the distinct growth patterns of various Asian ethnic groups.

In 2010, the five largest ethnic groups among older Asians were Chinese, Filipino, Japanese, Indian, and Korean (National Asian Pacific Center on Aging, 2013). However, by 2020, the leading five groups have changed to Chinese, Indian, Filipino, Vietnamese, and Korean (US Census Bureau, 2020). This evolving demographic landscape underscores the importance of understanding the distinctive life experiences of older Asian Americans from different ethnic and cultural backgrounds.

Older Asian Americans face some common challenges, including language barriers, cultural adjustment, and health disparities. For example, many may have limited access to culturally competent healthcare and social services and experience social isolation due to language and transportation barriers (Wu & Qi, 2022). However, older Asian Americans are a diverse group in terms of country of origin, acculturation, pre-immigrant experience and other social demographic characteristics. Asian Americans' personal experiences and cultural heritage, with a particular focus on familial values and intergenerational support, serve as a foundation from which they might derive resilience and adaptability in navigating adversities such as inequitable treatment and racial discrimination.

Racism is the inherent belief in the superiority or inferiority of individuals or groups based on their perceived racial characteristics. It can manifest in various forms, such as discrimination, prejudice, or bias, and can lead to unequal treatment, opportunities, or access to resources for people of different races (Reskin, 2012). Racism can be observed in both individual and systemic dimensions, whereby "individual racism" refers to personal beliefs and actions, while "systemic racism" refers to the broader, institutionalized patterns of discrimination and inequality that persist in society.

The social, economic, and political inequalities due to racism affect the well-being of marginalized racial/ethnic groups disproportionally (Chatters et al., 2021; Paradies et al., 2015). Asian Americans are found to suffer psychological distress, anxiety, depression, or depressive symptoms due to chronic experiences of discrimination (Gee et al., 2009; Nadimpalli & Hutchinson, 2012). Moreover, older Asian Americans may experience the intersectionality of racism and agism (Steward et al., 2023) that affects their well-being. Racism and agism can create a double-jeopardy scenario, hindering access to food, transportation, housing, quality healthcare, social services, and long-term care—essential resources that are especially vital for the well-being of older adults.

Understanding Healthy Aging Within the Context of Racism

Healthy aging theorists are drawn to what defines "successful aging," a term originally coined by Rowe and Kahn (1987) to describe an older age with preserved health, physical functionality, and social engagement (Rowe & Kahn, 1998). The maintenance of health, social being, and independence serve as key indicators for healthy aging (Berkman et al., 1993), but it raised the questions of whether this prescribed definition aligns with the perspectives of older adults (Phelan et al., 2004) and whether individuals with physical and cognitive impairment or those from disadvantaged backgrounds can also experience successful aging. It is not uncommon to live with an age-related functioning decline in later life. Given that, a revised definition of successful aging focused on how less healthy people maintain "successful" aging. Baltes and Baltes (1990) were among the first to propose that coping strategies are critical to sustaining optimal function in age-related decline. While acknowledging age-related deterioration, the impact of such decline depends on a coping process consisting of selection, optimization, and compensation to deal with pain, loss, and grief (Baltes & Baltes, 1990). Many older adults with chronic diseases and diminishing functions continued to report high well-being and perceive themselves as successful agers (Strawbridge et al., 2002). These positive coping strategies included accepting personal limitations, adapting to age-associated loss, and applying previous valuable life experiences (Phelan & Larson, 2002).

Coping strategies for healthy aging have evolved from above-described individual efforts to deal with life stressors to community action and policy advocacy used to combat social inequalities such as racism and discrimination. This is due to the growing recognition of systematic factors affecting the well-being of older adults (Rowe & Kahn, 2015). Structural factors such as chronic poverty, hazard exposure, and inadequate access to medical care and other resources and supports disproportionally affect ethnic minority groups (Bach et al., 2004). Older Asian Americans, for example, tend to have limited access to healthcare and social services due to language and cultural barriers (Wu & Qi, 2022). Built on current healthy aging theories that provide a comprehensive list of individual, family, community, and environmental factors that affect the well-being of older adults, this chapter addresses an urgent need to investigate racism as a factor affecting the well-being of older Asian Americans and multilevel coping strategies to combat racism.

Research Aims

Recent research has predominantly centered on racism as a social driver of health disparities (Chatters et al., 2021; Gee et al., 2009), with limited attention given to its impact on psychosocial well-being among old Asians. Psychosocial well-being broadly encompasses one's overall mental health, psychological, and social well-being. It includes a person's psychological and emotional stability as well as their ability to form and maintain positive relationships and engage in productive and fulfilling activities. In light of recent advancements in healthy aging theories (Phelan et al. 2004; Rowe & Kahn, 2015) and the cumulative inequality theory (Dannefer, 2003), this chapter endeavors to achieve three aims: (1) to provide a comprehensive overview of the experiences of racism or discrimination experienced by older Asian Americans, (2) to elucidate the intricate interplay between racism and the psychosocial well-being of older Asian Americans, and (3) to summarize strategies, encompassing policies and practices, employed to mitigate racism among older Asian Americans. The goal is to gain a deeper understanding of the experiences of racism among older Asian Americans, the multifaceted relationship between racism and psychosocial well-being, and the response strategies used.

Methods

This study uses a systematic review approach following the Preferred Reporting Items for Systematic Reviews and Meta-Analyses (PRISMA) guidelines (Page et al., 2021).

Search Method

Initial search was conducted on April 19, 2023, using six databases: PsycINFO, Medline, CINAHL, the Cochrane Library (the Cochrane Central Register of Controlled Trials), Web of Science, and Scopus. Additionally on May 2, 2023, we performed cross-search through ProQuest and EBSCO that combined to include 10 additional databases: Sociological Abstracts, Social Services Abstracts, International Bibliography of the Social Sciences (IBSS), Publicly Available Content Database, APA PsycArticles, Coronavirus Research Database, Academic Search Ultimate, AgeLine, Family & Society Studies Worldwide, and Health Source: Nursing/Academic Edition.

Four groups of keywords encompassed older adults, Asian Americans, racism, and psychology well-being. They were searched in titles and abstracts of articles published between January 1, 2000 and April 1, 2023, using the following search string ("aged" OR "older" OR "elder" OR "senior" OR "geriatric") AND ("Asian American*" OR "Japanese American*" OR "Chinese American*" OR "Vietnamese American*" OR "Asian Indian American*" OR "Cambodian American*" OR "Hmong American*" OR "Korean American*" OR "Filipino American*") AND ("racial trauma" OR "racial prejudice" OR "racial prejudices" OR "racial bias" OR "everyday racism" OR "racial discrimination" OR "covert racism" OR "racism" OR "microaggression*" OR "hate crime*" OR "discriminate*" OR "bias*" OR "prejudice*" OR "Anti-Asian") AND ("psychological consequences" OR "psychological well-being" OR "psychosocial impact" OR "quality of life" OR "mental health" OR "depressive symptoms" OR "anxiety" OR "sleep disorder" OR "suicide ideation" OR "distress").

Figure 12.1 depicts the search process. The original search yielded 689 search results. After removing 256 duplicates, 433 records were included in the title and abstract screening. Subsequently, 26 studies were included for full-test screening, which led to 14 studies included in final review. These articles met the following criteria: being published in peer-reviewed journals between January 1, 2000 and April 1, 2023; being an empirical study that examines racism, stereotype, prejudice, discrimination, or microaggression and focuses on older Asians including specific older Asian groups in the sample; and includes measures psychological well-being.

Data Collection and Extraction

Two reviewers screened titles and abstracts for eligible studies independently, with decisions blind to one another. If any disagreement existed, a third reviewer resolved the conflict and made a final decision. The three-person team adopted the same process in a later full-article review. Interscreener reliability was 90%, and interrater reliability of full articles was 92%. Basic information extracted from studies consisted of demographic characteristics (i.e., age and ethnicity), geographic areas of the study (i.e., nationwide, regional), study aims, and study design (qualitative or quantitative). Additionally, major findings were summarized revolving around the experience of racism among older Asian Americans; the relationships among age, racism, and psychosocial well-being; and policy and practice proposed to address racism.

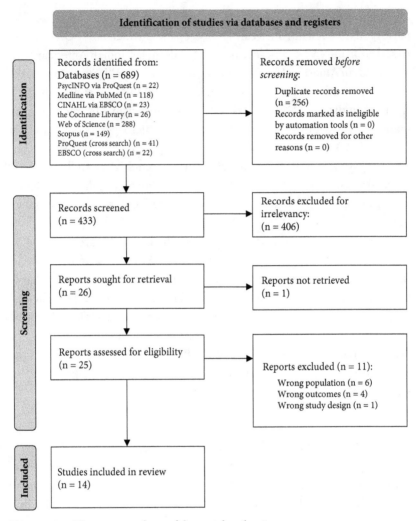

Figure 12.1 The consort chart of the article selection process.

Results

Characteristics of Included Studies

Characteristics of the included studies are presented in Table 12.1. The sample sizes of the 14 articles ranged from 175 to 1,360,487. Eleven studies, accounting for 78.6%, used secondary data sources, including the National Latino and Asian American (NLASS) study, the Population Study of Chinese

Table 12.1 Study characteristics of 14 included studies

Id	Authors	Year	Research aim	Methods (primary or secondary)	Sample size	Geography	Ethnicity	Focus on older adults only (y/n)	Age mean (SD)	Psychosocial well-being
1	Cho, Hai & Jang	2023	Mental distress in relation to life stressors and social capital.	Secondary Asian American Quality of Life (AAQoL)	533	Austin, Texas	Chinese, Asian Indian, Korean, Vietnamese, Filipino, Other Asian	Yes	69.4 (6.88)	Kessler Psychological Distress Scale 6 (K6)
2	Cho et al.	2022	Perceived racial discrimination, mental distress, and other moderators	Secondary (AAQoL)	2,609	Austin, Texas, US	Chinese, Asian Indian, Korean, Vietnamese, Filipino, Other Asian	No	69 (6.88)	Kessler Psychological Distress Scale 6 (K6)
3	Dong, Chen, & Simon	2014	Discrimination, unfair treatment, and responses to unfair treatment.	Primary (In-person interviews)	3,159	Chicago, United States only	Chinese American	Yes	72.8 (8.30)	Self-rated health
4	Han et al	2023	Racism, discrimination associated with the pandemic on negative mental health symptoms	Primary (Survey)	175	Baltimore-Washington and the New York Metropolitan area, US	Korean American	Yes	71 (8.00)	Adapted General Anxiety Disorder-7, CESD Scale, and the Impact to Event Scale-Revised.
5	Jang et al	2010	Depression symptoms and perceptions of discrimination.	Primary (Survey)	472	Tampa and Orlando, Florida, US	Korean American	Yes	69.9 (7.04)	A 10-item CES-D

(*continued*)

Table 12.1 Continued

Id	Authors	Year	Research aim	Methods (primary or secondary)	Sample size	Geography	Ethnicity	Focus on older adults only (y/n)	Age mean (SD)	Psychosocial well-being
6	Jang et al	2023	Perceived racial discrimination, ethnic resources, and mental distress	Secondary (Data from SOKA)	2,150	California, New York, Texas, Hawai'i, and Florida, US	Korean American	Yes	73.4 (7.97)	Kessler Psychological Distress Scale 6 (K6)
7	Li et al	2022	Discrimination in healthcare setting and psychological distress	Secondary (CHIS Survey)	1,360,487	California, US	Chinese, Japanese, Korean, Filipino, Vietnamese, South/Southeast Asian, or Other Asian.	Yes	64.35 (0.61)	Kessler Psychological Distress Scale (K6)
8	Li & Dong	2017	Self-reported discrimination and depressive symptoms and identifies subgroups that are more likely to report experiencing discrimination.	Secondary (PINE study)	3,004	Chicago, United States	Chinese American	Yes	72.6 (8.20)	Patient Health Questionnaire (PHQ-9)
9	Li, Gee & Dong	2018	Racial discrimination and suicidal ideation	Secondary (PINE study)	3,157	Chicago, United States	Chinese American	Yes	72.3 (8.30)	Suicide ideation in the past month

10	Li, McLaughlin, & Zhang	2020	Acculturation, discrimination, and healthy aging, within the context of age and gender	Secondary (PINE study)	3,056	Chicago, United States	Chinese American	Yes	72.2 (8.40)	No cognitive impairment (C-MMSE) & high physical functioning
11	Misra & Hunte	2016	Discrimination and self-rated health.	Secondary (Survey data from Diabetes Indian American study)	1,824	Houston, TX; Phoenix, AZ; Washington, DC; Boston, MA; San Diego, CA; Edison, NJ and Parsippany, NJ	Asian Indians	No	45.7 (12.80)	Self-rated health
12	Rollock & Lui	2016	Discrimination and intimate social (spousal and more distal) relationships on psychological distress	National Latino and Asian American Study (NLAAS)	1,142	United States	Vietnamese, Filipino, Chinese, Other	No	45.07 (13)	Kessler Psychological Distress Scale (K10)
13	Yip, Gee & Takeuchi	2008	Ethnic identity, discrimination and mental health	NLAAS	2,047	United States	Vietnamese, Filipino, Chinese, Other	No	40.11 (0.73)	Kessler Psychological Distress Scale (K10)
14	Siordia & Covington-Ward	2016	Perceived ethnic discrimination and self-rated mental health/health	NLAAS	4,559	United States	Chinese, Non-Chinese Asians, Mexican, Non-Mexican Latinos	No	40.7 (15.2)	Self-rated health and mental health

Elderly (PINE) Study, the Study of Older Korean Americans (SOKA), the City of Austin Asian American Quality of Life (AAQoL) survey study, the California Health Interview Survey (CHIS), and the Diabetes Among Indian Americans (DIA) study. The other three studies utilized primary data collection methods. The participants' average age ranged from 40.11 (standard deviation [SD] = 0.73) to 73.4 (SD = 7.97). All studies reported occurrences of unfair treatment, perceived discrimination, and racism among participants. The prevalence rate of racism or discrimination experienced ranged from 7.2% to 30% across studies. Examples of perceived discrimination included daily unfair treatment assessed using questions like "Whether they had ever been discriminated against or treated unfairly due to their race or ethnicity" (Jang et al., 2023), and perceived discrimination in healthcare settings, where questions such as "Over your entire lifetime, how often have you been treated unfairly when getting medical care?" (Li et al., 2022) were used.

Relationship Between Age and Experience of Discrimination/Racism

Studies have identified an inverse relationship between age and experience of discrimination and racism among older Asian Americans. Two studies compared older Americans to their younger counterparts (Misra & Hunte, 2016; Rollock & Lui, 2016), revealing that older adults were less likely to report or perceive racial discrimination. Most studies focused on variations within the older Asian group, indicating a general low rate of discrimination perceived by older Asians and a declined likelihood of reporting instances of discrimination associated with advanced age (Dong et al., 2014; Jang et al., 2023; Li et al., 2022; Li & Dong, 2017). One specific study among Chinese Americans aged 60 or older in Chicago (Dong et al., 2014) found younger age was associated with a greater tendency to report discrimination and adopt response behaviors. This finding aligned well with two other studies indicating a negative association ($r = -.06$ to $-.13$) between perceived discrimination and age among a diverse group of older Asian adults (Cho et al., 2023; Jang et al., 2023; Rollock & Lui, 2016). Additionally, a subgroup difference was noted in one study (Cho et al., 2023), which reported the Asian Indian group had a comparatively lower rate of perceived discrimination in comparison to the Chinese group.

These collective findings suggested that older Asian adults were less likely to encounter discrimination, possibly due to social isolation, or discern instances of discrimination due to lack of awareness and thereby were notably less inclined to report such events to authorities or others. One possible explanation could stem from the difficulties of distinguishing racial discrimination from other types of discrimination. For example, one study (Li et al., 2018) emphasized that Chinese older adults may be more desensitized or may not be able to distinguish the sources of discriminative acts, whether stemming from age, ethnicity/race, culture, or other factors. Alternative more encouraging explanations might be that, when adults grow older, they may develop more resilience and adaptation, a shift in priorities from negative external experiences to more intrinsic values such as personal contentment and emotional well-being, a broader perspective due to richer life experience, and more selective social interaction.

Relationship Between Racism/Discrimination and Psychosocial Well-Being

Studies consistently indicate a negative relationship between discrimination/racism and psychosocial well-being among older Asian Americans (Cho et al., 2022, 2023; Jang et al., 2023; Li et al., 2022; Rollock & Lui, 2016; Siordia & Covington-Ward, 2016; Yip et al., 2018). Li, Gee, and Dong (2018) found a significant association (r = 0.4) between experiences of discrimination and the presence of suicidal ideation among older Chinese Americans. More specifically, those with experience of discrimination had a 1.9 times increased risk of suicidal ideation over a 30-day period. Perceived racial discrimination including unfair treatment was also strongly correlated with psychological distress (Jang et al., 2023, Li et al., 2022; Rollock & Lui, 2016; Yip et al., 2018), depression symptoms (Li & Dong, 2017), poorer health and mental health status (Cho et al., 2022, Dong et al., 2014; Misra & Hunte, 2016), and poor physical and psychosocial functioning (Li et al., 2020), and even changes in routine activities out of fear (Han et al., 2023).

Studies have underscored the impact of various contextual factors on moderating the relationship between racism and psychosocial well-being. In their investigation, Cho et al. (2022) focused on the moderation effects of age, education, and ethnicity. They found that influence of perceived racial discrimination on mental distress was more pronounced for those aged 60 or older (odds ratio [OR] = 3.29) than the younger group (OR = 1.63). Additionally, the relationship between mental distress and perceived racial discrimination was more salient among Vietnamese individuals and the less-educated groups compared to other Asian groups and highly educated groups (Cho et al., 2022). In another study, Cho et al. (2023) did not find a moderating effect of social network, family solidarity, or community cohesion among a sample of 533 older Asians. But the moderating effect of a sense of community was significant among a sample of 2,150 older Korean Americans (Jang et al., 2023), suggesting the diverse experiences of specific Asian groups. Other contextual factors examined in these studies included nativity (Rollock & Lui, 2016), ethnic identity (Yip et al., 2008), and spousal support (Rollock & Lui, 2016). To effectively mitigate the detrimental consequences of racism and discrimination, it is also imperative to prioritize the needs of older Asian Americans deemed most vulnerable to racism and psychosocial distress.

Few articles have explored the mediators between racism and psychological well-being, leading to non-definitive conclusions. Only one study conducted by Jang et al. (2010) among a sample of 472 older Korean Americans in Florida found the sense of control as a significant mediator between perceived discrimination and depressive symptoms.

Diverse Practice and Policy Strategies to Address Racism/Discrimination

More than half of these studies (n = 8) provided practice implications for their findings to address racism or discrimination. The consistent findings underscored the need to integrate an anti-racism component in the healthcare and social service systems to effectively address psychosocial distress among older Asian Americans. Particularly in the healthcare settings, service professionals must recognize and confront implicit biases and discriminatory behaviors toward specific groups (Li & Dong, 2017; Li et al., 2018; Jang et al., 2023; Misra & Hunte, 2016) and improve communication with older patients (Li et al., 2022). Other strategies included improving the locus of control and coping mechanisms among older Asian populations (Jang, 2010; Misra & Hunte, 2016), promoting intergenerational support (Cho et al., 2023), relying on ethnic community support (Jang, 2023), and engaging in interdisciplinary efforts to directly address racism to achieve equality (Cho et al., 2022).

Five articles have offered some policy recommendations to tackle issues of racism. Three emphasized that policies need to address barriers and stressors within the healthcare and social care systems, specifically by integrating the cultural and linguistic needs of older Asians (Cho et al., 2023; Jang et al., 2023; Misra & Hunte, 2016). Effective policy measures should involve adapting established mental health and wellness programs, such as chronic illness management and fall prevention, in a culturally sensitive manner for older Asians. This adaptation should include providing cultural competency training to healthcare employees and fostering partnerships through community engagement with associations and organizations that serve older Asian Americans.

Additionally, two articles specifically put forth policy recommendations tailored for distinct Asian groups. One article highlighted the importance of directing policy attention to older Vietnamese Americans, recognizing their unique traumatic experiences during the immigration journey (Cho et al., 2022). Another article underscored the necessity of addressing barriers for Asian Indians within the healthcare system due to their low use of healthcare services (Misra & Hunte, 2016). The final article by Han et al. (2023) took a preventive approach by offering policy recommendations to address hate crimes against older Asians. It advocated for the integration of Asian history and studies into the education system, aiming to confront historical and structural challenges related to anti-Asian racism. Overall, these policy recommendations collectively formed a multifaceted strategy to combat racism and its various manifestations.

Discussion

This systematic review provides a comprehensive overview of the documented experiences of racism among older Asians, revealing a significant prevalence (ranging from 7.2% to 30%) of racism and discrimination within the older Asian American population. It is important to acknowledge that a majority of these studies concentrated on three states with the highest Asian populations—California, New York, and Texas (ACL, 2020). However, the inclusion of additional areas such as Chicago and Hawai'i broadens the scope and context of the findings. Due to underreporting tendency among older Asians, the reported frequency rate of racism incidents among older Ascians may not necessarily reflect the true level of prevalence. Instead, it may suggest an increased vulnerability for this demographic, possibly stemming from limited awareness of this issue or insufficient access to resources for mitigation.

Remarkably, older Asian American's recognition and reporting of racism appear to be less sensitive when compared to younger age groups. Yet the negative impact on their psychosocial well-being may be more substantial (Cho et al., 2023). This finding contrasts with research on African American women (Greer & Spalding, 2017), where age served as a buffer for psychological outcomes associated with exposure to racism. Greer and Spalding (2017) found that young African American women experienced higher levels of anxiety due to racism than their older counterparts. The inconsistency underscores the necessity for further studies to explore how older Asian Americans navigate and cope with racism-related experiences.

The cumulative findings contribute to the development of a conceptual model (see Figure 12.2) that elucidates the intricate relationship between racism and psychosocial well-being. Racism has a direct negative effect on psychosocial well-being, and, furthermore, it may exert indirect effects via possible mediators such as health, sense of control, and coping strategies on psychosocial well-being. Underneath the direct effect line, the figure also highlights individual, family, community and societal contextual factors that may moderate the relationship between racism and psychosocial well-being.

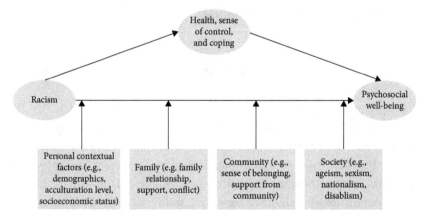

Figure 12.2 A conceptual model of the relationship between racism and psychosocial well-being.

Contextual factors such as age, ethnicity, acculturation, education, duration of residence, informal support, and sense of community may contribute to the variations of individual experiences of racism among older Asians (Jang et al., 2023; Li & Dong, 2017; Rollock & Lui, 2016). When applied to older Asian Americans, racism may intersect with systematic inequalities such as ageism, nationalism, and immigration discrimination to affect psychosocial well-being. But the intersectionality between racism and other societal inequalities did not receive much attention in the included articles.

The framework includes a more comprehensive list of mediators or moderators implied but not necessarily empirically tested in the 14 studies. For example, acculturation level, especially citizenship status, was found to affect older Asian Americans' experience of racism (Chan, 2020), but it has not been empirically examined in moderating the relationship between racism and psychosocial distress. A holistic approach is necessary to address the multifaceted challenges faced by older Asian Americans in the context of racism and discrimination.

Implications for Research

The findings of this systematic review have highlighted several urgent areas for future research. First, the limited number ($n = 14$) of included studies, all employing a cross-sectional design, indicates a need for more research on older Asians in different regions and employing longitudinal approaches. Extending study sites to other than urban areas in states such as California, New York, Texas, Hawai'i, and Florida, where Asians are a high proportion of the population, to include the experience of challenges older Asians face in rural areas or cities where traditionally no congregation of older Asians exists, warrants more attention (Sun et al., 2015). Additionally, there is a pressing need for more research to explore the longitudinal effects of racism on psychosocial well-being in later life. In alignment with the cumulative disadvantage theory (Dannefer, 2003), it is essential to recognize that early racism experience affects personal and professional development via access to financial resources, health, and social capital.

Second, more research is needed to examine the contextual factors that moderate the relationship between racism/discrimination and psychosocial well-being. At the individual level, those with poor health literacy and English language deficiency (Gee & Ponze, 2010) may experience amplified perceptions of discrimination, particularly in healthcare settings. At family and community levels, conflicts, support, and a sense of belonging within these environments can also affect the impact of racism. Subgroup differences in racism experiences among Chinese, Indians, Koreans, and Vietnamese (Cho et al., 2022) suggest that more research is needed for specific Asian groups. At the societal level, there is a need to delve into the multiple and interconnected dimensions of social inequalities experienced by older Asians over their lifetime, such as sexism, nationalism, and ableism (Zubair & Norris, 2015). This exploration is vital for unveiling the role of multiple social inequalities, as opposed to racial identity alone, in shaping the psychosocial well-being of older Asian Americans. This line of research needs to move beyond a potentially pathologizing approach because strengths in individuals, family, community, and cultures can buffer racism observed in these Asian groups.

Last, more research is required to uncover the underlying mechanisms through which racism affects the psychosocial well-being of older Asians, not limited to the pathways such as health behaviors and coping strategies proposed in Figure 12.2. It is possible that racism largely affects psychosocial well-being directly, but more empirical research is needed to affirm the existence or nonexistence of indirect effects via intermediate pathways. This comprehensive exploration will contribute to a more holistic understanding of the impact of racism on the psychosocial well-being of aging ethnic minority individuals.

Implications for Practice and Policy

Recognizing the contextual factors and mediators in Figure 12.2 shed light on the nuanced relationship between racism and psychosocial well-being among older Asians, which also yielded practice and policy implications. Practice and policy recommendations centered on the integration of antiracist components within healthcare and social service systems to mitigate psychosocial distress among this demographic.

Specifically, practice should be tailored to address the specific needs of older Asian groups, with a focus on the most vulnerable subgroups, including women, those with low socioeconomic status, advanced age, and experiences of social isolation. Simultaneously, building on older Asians' individual strength and resilience to respond to racism (Kwong et al., 2015) is crucial. Recognizing the positive aspects drawn from their ethnic and cultural background is equally essential, illustrating that ethnicity support and cultural elements can serve as valuable resources for older Asian Americans. These practices will help create a more supportive and understanding environment for older Asians, acknowledging the challenges due to racism and discrimination as well as their distinctive individual and cultural strengths.

Practice should also target potential perpetrators who exert racism, particularly within the health and social care sectors, public services, and governmental domains; this is paramount. Encouraging healthcare professionals to recognize and address implicit biases and discriminatory behaviors (Li & Dong, 2017; Li et al., 2018; Jang et al., 2023; Misra & Hunte, 2016) is crucial for improving communication and fostering a more inclusive environment for older Asian patients.

In terms of policy implications, combating racism against older Asians is aligned with federal laws, such as the Title VII of Civil Rights Act (1964), that explicitly prohibit discrimination in employment and receipt of governmental financial assistance based on race, birthplace, ancestry, culture, or language. Evidence from this systematic review suggests concrete measures to be implemented in state or local anti-racism policy initiatives such as integrating Asian cultural and linguistic considerations into existing mental health and wellness programs, providing culturally sensitive delivery, and implementing cultural competency training for healthcare employees. For example, aiming at advancing civil rights and mitigating discriminatory practice can potentially serve as a main preventive measure against suicide among older Chinese Americans (Li et al., 2018). Additionally, fostering partnerships through community engagement with organizations dedicated to serving older Asian Americans aligns with the broader goal of promoting inclusivity and addressing the unique challenges faced by this demographic. While these suggestions are promising, we must acknowledge existing deficiencies in current policies addressing racism among older Asians. There is a pressing need to champion additional policy initiatives across various levels to embrace a multifaceted strategy to effectively combat racism and its diverse manifestations among older Asian Americans.

Several limitations of this systematic review need to be noted. First, we included discrimination in our search; although it is highly possible that discrimination against older Asians was due to racism, it cannot be ruled out that discrimination was due to other characteristics of the person (e.g., ethnicity, age, disabilities, gender). Second, we focused on a broadly defined psychosocial well-being that encompassed subjective self-rated health and suicidal thoughts. As older Asian Americans tend to show somatic symptoms of psychological distress (Jiang et al., 2019), future reviews need to include all somatization symptoms due to mental health concerns.

Conclusion

This systematic review provides a comprehensive overview of empirical evidence concerning the influence of racism and discrimination on the psychosocial well-being of older Asian Americans. The findings consistently highlight the significant adverse effects of racism/discrimination on older Asians, despite the fact that they are less likely to recognize or report racism compared to their young counterparts. Notably, the negative effects are not homogeneously shared among older Asian Americans given various moderating factors such as individual factors (e.g., socioeconomic status), family dynamics (e.g., spousal support), community attributes (e.g., sense of community belonging), and societal factors (e.g., nationalism).

Moreover, the review identifies potential mechanisms—such as acculturation stress, health-related factors, and coping strategies—through which racism/discrimination may impact psychosocial well-being. However, we emphasize that further evidence is needed to fully elucidate these mechanisms. The review underscores the complexity of the relationship between racism/discrimination and psychosocial well-being among older Asian Americans, urging continued research to enhance our understanding of these dynamics. More importantly, given the surge in hate crimes targeting individuals of Asian descent during the COVID-19 pandemic (Takamura et al., 2022), the enduring prevalence of the "model minority" stereotype, and the tendency to underreport incidents among older Asians, it is imperative to call for innovative policy and practice efforts to address racism and discrimination and promote optimal psychosocial well-being of older Asians.

References

References marked with an asterisk indicate studies included in the systematic review.
Administration on Community Living (ACL). (2020). 2020 Profile of Asian Americans age 65 and older. https://acl.gov/sites/default/files/Profile%20of%20OA/AsianProfileReport2021.pdf

Bach, P. B., Pham, H. H., Schrag, D., Tate, R. C., & Hargraves, J. L. (2004). Primary care physicians who treat blacks and whites. *New England Journal of Medicine, 351*(6), 575–584.

Baltes, P. B., & Baltes, M. M. (1990). Psychological perspectives on successful aging: The model of selective optimization with compensation. In P. B. Baltes & M. M. Baltes (eds.), *Successful aging: Perspectives from the behavioral sciences* (pp. 1–34). Cambridge University Press.

Berkman, F., Seeman, T. E., Albert, M., Blazer, D., Kahn, R., Mohs, R., Finch, C., Schneider, E., Cotman, C., McClearn, G., Nesselroade, J. (1993). High, usual and impaired functioning in community-dwelling older men and women: Findings from the MacArthur Foundation research network on successful aging. *Journal of Clinical Epidemiology, 46*, 1129–1140.

Chan, K. (2020). The association of acculturation with overt and covert perceived discrimination for older Asian Americans. *Social Work Research, 44*(1), 59–71.

Chatters, L. M., Taylor, H. O., & Taylor, R. J. (2021). Racism and the life course: Social and health equity for Black American older adults. *Public Policy & Aging Report, 31*(4), 113–118.

*Cho, Y. J., Hai, A. H., & Jang, Y. (2023). Life stressors, social capital, and mental distress in older Asian Americans. *Journal of Ethnic & Cultural Diversity in Social Work, 32*(6), 316–327.

*Cho, Y. J., Lee, W. J., Oh, H., Lee, J. O., Kim, B. E., & Jang, Y. (2022). Perceived racial discrimination and mental health in diverse groups of Asian Americans: The differing impacts by age, education, and ethnicity. *Journal of Immigrant and Minority Health, 24*(4), 970–976. https://doi.org/10.1007/s10903-021-01271-y

Civil Rights Act of 1964. (1964, July 2). Enrolled Acts and Resolutions of Congress, 1789 - 2011; General Records of the United States Government, Record Group 11; National Archives Building, Washington, DC. https://www.archives.gov/milestone-documents/civil-rights-act

Dannefer, D. (2003). Cumulative advantage/disadvantage and the life course: Cross-fertilizing age and social science theory. *Journals of Gerontology Series B: Psychological Sciences and Social Sciences, 58*(6), S327–S337.

*Dong, X., Chen, R., & Simon, M. A. (2014). Experience of discrimination among US Chinese older adults. *Journals of Gerontology Series A: Biological Sciences and Medical Sciences, 69*(Suppl 2), S76–S81. https://doi.org/10.1093/gerona/glu150

Gee, G. C., Hing, A., Mohammed, S., Tabor, D. C., & Williams, D. R. (2019). Racism and the life course: Taking time seriously. *American Journal of Public Health, 109*(S1), S43–S47. doi:10.2105/AJPH.2018.304766

Gee, G. C., & Ponce, N. (2010). Associations between racial discrimination, limited English proficiency, and health-related quality of life among 6 Asian ethnic groups in California. *American Journal of Public Health, 100*(5), 888–895.

Greer, T. M., & Spalding, A. (2017). The role of age in understanding the psychological effects of racism for African Americans. *Cultural Diversity and Ethnic Minority Psychology, 23*(4), 588.

*Han, H. R., Min, D., Yun, J. Y., Joo, J. H., Lee, H. B., & Kwon, S. (2023). The impact of anti-Asian racism on routine activities and mental health among Korean American older adults and their caregivers. *Frontiers in Public Health, 11*, 958657. https://doi.org/10.3389/fpubh.2023.958657

*Jang, Y., Chiriboga, D. A., Kim, G., & Rhew, S. (2010). Perceived discrimination, sense of control, and depressive symptoms among Korean American older adults. *Asian American Journal of Psychology, 1*(2), 129–135. https://doi.org/10.1037/a0019767

*Jang, Y., Cho, Y. J., Park, N. S., Chiriboga, D. A., Hong, S., & Kim, M. T. (2023). Perceived racial discrimination and mental distress in older Korean Americans: The moderating role of ethnic resources. *Ethnicity & Health, 28*(1), 1–11. https://doi.org/10.1080/13557858.2021.2022105

Jiang, L., Sun, F., Zhang, W., Wu, B., & Dong, X. (2019). Health service use among Chinese American older adults: Is there a somatization effect? *Journal of the American Geriatrics Society, 67*(S3), S584–S589.

Kwong, K., Du, Y., & Xu, Q. (2015). Healthy aging of minority and immigrant populations: Resilience in late life. *Traumatology*, 21(3), 136.

*Li, C. C., Matthews, A. K., Yen, P. S., Chen, Y. F., & Dong, X. (2022). The influence of perceived discrimination in healthcare settings on psychological distress among a diverse sample of older Asian Americans. *Aging & Mental Health*, 26(9), 1874–1881. https://doi.org/10.1080/13607863.2021.1958146

*Li, L. W., & Dong, X. (2017). Self-reported discrimination and depressive symptoms among older Chinese adults in Chicago. *Journals of Gerontology Series A: Biological Sciences and Medical Sciences*, 72(Suppl 1), S119–S124. https://doi.org/10.1093/gerona/glw174

*Li, L. W., Gee, G. C., & Dong, X. (2018). Association of self-reported discrimination and suicide ideation in older Chinese Americans. *American Journal of Geriatric Psychiatry*, 26(1), 42–51. https://doi.org/10.1016/j.jagp.2017.08.006

*Li, L. W., McLaughlin, S. J., & Zhang, J. (2020). Healthy aging in older Chinese Americans: Associations with immigrant experiences. *Journal of Aging and Health*, 32(9), 1098–1108. https://doi.org/10.1177/0898264319889122

*Misra, R., & Hunte, H. (2016). Perceived discrimination and health outcomes among Asian Indians in the United States. *BMC Health Services Research*, 16(1), 567. https://doi.org/10.1186/s12913-016-1821-8

Nadimpalli, S. B., & Hutchinson, M. K. (2012). An integrative review of relationships between discrimination and Asian American health. *Journal of Nursing Scholarship*, 44(2), 127–135.

National Asian Pacific Center on Aging (NAPCA). (2013). Asian Americans and Pacific Islanders in the United States aged 65 years and older: Population, nativity, and language. https://www.napca.org/wp-content/uploads/2017/10/65-population-report-FINAL.pdf

Page, M. J., McKenzie, J. E., Bossuyt, P. M., Boutron, I., Hoffmann, T. C., Mulrow, C. D., Shamseer, L., Tetzlaff, J. M., Akl, E. A., Brennan, S. E., Chou, E., Glanville, J., Grimshaw, J. M., Hróbjartsson, A., Lalu, M. M., Li, T., Loder, E. W., Mayo-Wilson, E., McDonald, S., ... Moher, D. (2021). The PRISMA 2020 statement: An updated guideline for reporting systematic reviews. *BMJ*, 372, 71. https://doi.org/10.1136/bmj.n71

Paradies, Y., Ben, J., Denson, N., Elias, A., Priest, N., Pieterse, A., Gupta, A., Kelaher, M., & Gee, G. (2015). Racism as a determinant of health: A systematic review and meta-analysis. *PloS One*, 10(9), e0138511. https://doi.org/10.1371/journal.pone.0138511

Phelan, E. A., Anderson, L. A., Lacroix, A. Z., & Larson, E. B. (2004). Older adults' views of "successful aging": How do they compare with researchers' definitions? *Journal of the American Geriatrics Society*, 52(2), 211–216.

Phelan, E. A., & Larson, E. B. (2002). "Successful aging": Where next? *Journal of the American Geriatrics Society*, 50(7), 1306–1308.

Reskin, B. (2012). The race discrimination system. *Annual Review of Sociology*, 38, 17–35. doi:10.1146/annurev-soc-071811-145508.

*Rollock, D., & Lui, P. P. (2016). Do spouses matter? Discrimination, social support, and psychological distress among Asian Americans. *Cultural Diversity & Ethnic Minority Psychology*, 22(1), 47–57. https://doi.org/10.1037/cdp0000045

Rowe, J. W., & Kahn, R. L. (1987). Human aging: Usual and successful. *Science*, 237, 143–149.

Rowe, J. W., & Kahn, R. L. (1998). *Successful aging*. Pantheon.

Rowe, J. W., & Kahn, R. L. (2015). Successful aging 2.0: Conceptual expansions for the 21st century. *Journals of Gerontology Series B: Psychological Sciences and Social Sciences*, 70(4), 593–596.

*Siordia, C., & Covington-Ward, Y. D. (2016). Association between perceived ethnic discrimination and health: Evidence from the National Latino and Asian American Study (NLAAS). *Journal of Frailty & Aging*, 5(2), 111–117.

Steward, A. T., De Fries, C. M., Dunbar, A. Z., Trujillo, M., Zhu, Y., Nicotera, N., & Hasche, L. (2023). A phenomenological understanding of the intersectionality of ageism and racism among older adults: Individual-Level Experiences. *Journals of Gerontology Series B*, 78(5), 880–890.

Strawbridge, W. J., Wallhagen, M. I., & Cohen, R. D. (2002). Successful aging and well-being: Self-rated compared with Rowe and Kahn. *The Gerontologist, 42*(6), 727–733.

Sun, F., Gao, X., & Coon, D. W. (2015). Perceived threat of Alzheimer's disease among Chinese American older adults: The role of Alzheimer's disease literacy. *Journals of Gerontology Series B: Psychological Sciences and Social Sciences,* 70(2), 245–255.

Takamura, J. C., Browne, C., Jeung, R., Yellow Horse, A. J., Kwok, D., & Howard, D. (2022). Asian American elders: Caught in the crosshairs of a syndemic of racism, misogyny, and ageism during coronavirus disease 2019. *Public Policy & Aging Report,* 32(3), 87–93.

US Census Bureau. (2020). https://data.census.gov/table?q=aging+chinese+american

Wu, B., & Qi, X. (2022). Addressing health disparities among older Asian American populations: Research, data, and policy. *Public Policy Aging Report,* 32(3), 105–111. https://doi.org/10.1093/ppar/prac015

*Yip, T., Gee, G. C., & Takeuchi, D. T. (2008). Racial discrimination and psychological distress: The impact of ethnic identity and age among immigrant and United States-born Asian adults. *Developmental Psychology,* 44(3), 787–800. https://doi.org/10.1037/0012-1649.44.3.787

Zubair, M., & Norris, M. (2015). Perspectives on ageing, later life and ethnicity: Ageing research in ethnic minority contexts. *Ageing & Society,* 35(5), 897–916.

SECTION III
DISMANTLING ANTI-ASIAN RACISM: MICRO, MEZZO, AND MACRO-LEVEL STRATEGIES

13

The Role of Social Work and Storytelling in Eliminating Anti-Asian Racism and Hate Crimes

Sofie Hana Aaron, Juliann Li Verdugo, Jane J. Lee, Hye-Kyung Kang, Tam Q. Dinh, and Michael S. Spencer

The Essential Role of Social Work in Addressing Hate

Social work plays an important role in eliminating racism and addressing anti-Asian hate crimes because of its commitment to equity, inclusion, and social justice as well as its focus on understanding complex systems from micro, meso, and macro perspectives. As professionals, social workers wield the tools to empower diverse individuals and communities, to advocate on social and political issues, and to engage in coalition building (National Association of Social Workers, 2015). A 2017 analysis by the Council on Social Work Education demonstrated a paucity of Asian American representation in the social work field, with Asian Americans comprising only 3% of graduates with a master of social work degree, and 1.9% of graduates with a bachelor's degree in social work that year (Council on Social Work Education, 2017). Such disproportionate minority representation remains prominent within the field today—in 2023, only 3.3% of licensed social workers nationwide identified as Asian, compared to the majority (58.5%) identifying as non-Hispanic White (Zippia, 2023). Despite a lower number of Asian American social workers, Asian diaspora professionals involved in community activism and clinical social work have been instrumental in building community resilience and leading culturally informed healthcare efforts. These initiatives have led to various culturally competent and diverse

Sofie Hana Aaron, Juliann Li Verdugo, Jane J. Lee, Hye-Kyung Kang, Tam Q. Dinh, and Michael S. Spencer, *The Role of Social Work and Storytelling in Eliminating Anti-Asian Racism and Hate Crimes* In: *Addressing Anti-Asian Racism with Social Work, Advocacy, and Action*. Edited by: Meirong Liu and Keith T. Chan, Oxford University Press. © Oxford University Press 2024. DOI: 10.1093/oso/9780197672242.003.0013 solutions resulting in transformative changes bettering the lives of Black, Indigenous, and People of Color (BIPOC) and Asian American, Native Hawaiian, and Pacific Islander (AANHPI) communities to date (Cho, 2023).

Hate and discrimination impact a myriad of issues extending beyond physical and verbal attacks. Systemic issues—some examples include stigmatization of help-seeking, mental health stigma, and Westernized healthcare policies—often prevent Asian Americans from receiving culturally relevant care and prohibit conversations around mental health. Indeed, AANHPI individuals are known to access healthcare services at significantly lower rates compared to their non-Hispanic White counterparts. Microaggressions and racial discrimination act as deterrents for those with language barriers and a mistrust of the medical system (Bai, 2022). The homogenization of racial and ethnic groupings within AANHPI communities, both in research and in education, further lends to an incomplete picture of existing health disparities and unique community needs. Consistently, we see that Western policies act as barriers, perpetuating anti-Asian racism, discrimination, and hate. Given and in spite of these persisting challenges, through education, curriculum, and research, as well as through uplifting and centering the stories of AANHPI communities, social workers can play a vital and invaluable role in mitigating these effects and incidences.

The Role of Storytelling in Combating Hate

While AANHPI voices matter, their stories often go untold for a variety of cultural and systemic reasons. Storytelling is traditionally important within Asian diasporas, given that sharing narratives can serve as a meaningful way for the community to break from the reductive monolith of being merely "Asian American," allow them to challenge racial stereotypes and caricatures, and give space for an individual to reclaim and narrate their truthful experiences of identifying as AANHPI (CAAM, 2023). Storytelling is additionally a tool used extensively by social workers, community activists, and clinicians, and it is a framework that can "incorporate in everything from violence prevention and trauma reduction programs to medical care and psychotherapy" (Janssen, 2023). For example, *narrative therapy* is an evidence-based psychotherapy intervention focused on the empowerment of a client to "reauthor" their own lived experiences and share openly about their stories (Seo et al., 2015). Storytelling and narrative reclamation can thus be a space for healing, combating hate, and pushing back on prevailing misconceptions and for disseminating shared learning, development, and culturally relevant information (Drumm, 2013). Testimonials and stories can additionally help "chip away at institutional and individual biases and prejudices," challenging systemic racism (Wang, 2019). For instance, storytelling can push back against the "model minority" myth that has often silenced AANHPI voices and pitted minority groups against one another instead of creating space for solidarity, collaboration, and mutual aid or support within these communities.

Within this chapter, our authors reclaim and share personal narratives about varying facets of identifying as AANHPI, each presenting their individual stories and the impact of social work on their personal and professional lives. The authors additionally speak to their own engagement with experiencing discrimination and anti-Asian hate from the individual to the institutional level. We present these stories in hopes of amplifying and uplifting AANHPI voices, as well as to illuminate the notable variation in unique lived experiences and counter the misleading homogeneity of the broad "Asian American" label. Following the presentation of our narratives, we discuss implications for practice, policy, and research, and we conclude with a call to action for social workers to counter anti-Asian racism and hate. Of note, while our narratives are far from representative of all AANHPI voices, we each speak to different areas and topics relevant to the social work field and hope to pave the way for further storytelling from others in the AANHPI community.

Land Acknowledgment

Our authors in this chapter all presently reside on or near the stolen ancestral homelands of the Coast Salish people in Washington State, specifically in the traditional territory of the Suquamish, Stillaguamish, and Muckleshoot People, and the People of the Inside, the Duwamish. We have a responsibility to acknowledge and learn the histories of cultural genocide, Indigenous land dispossession, and colonialism. We give deep respect to the people of the land that we find ourselves on today. While our stories may not originate from this land, we give value to the stories of those before us and resist terminal narratives and the erasure of Indigenous histories (Duwamish Tribe, 2023).

How I Became Asian

Michael S. Spencer

My ethnicity is Native Hawaiian, Japanese, Chinese, English, and Irish. People in Hawai'i refer to people of my background in many ways: *hapa*, chop suey, mixed, poi dog, or mutt. Growing up, I never felt these terms to be derogatory, and, in fact, I've described myself in these ways. This phenomenon is not really uncommon in Hawai'i as nearly a quarter of its population identify with more than one race. However, this distinction of being multiracial did trigger a variety of feelings. In particular, it reflected that you were not "pure," in contrast to those who never married outside of their race, ethnicity, or nationality. Not necessarily bad, but different. Different enough that feelings of acceptance in those communities were a challenge. As I grew into my teen years, I felt very separated from my Asian heritage and, with that, some resentment. My experiences changed once again when I left Hawai'i to pursue higher education on the US continent.

Like night and day, people's perception of me suddenly changed. No longer was I mixed, but rather I became read by others as "Asian." I never really understood this word, "Asian," particularly growing up in Hawai'i where "Asian" is a rather meaningless construct. Not even Japanese or Chinese or Korean, just Asian. How can a group of people who are so different and in fact, have a long history of hating one another all be lumped into one group? How could I become Asian when I could never fit in with the purebreds among my peers? As I pondered the reasons for this change, my first thoughts were lack of exposure or knowledge of the immigration history and diversity of Asian Americans, including multiracial Asians. In fact, few schools in the United States teach this history. However, as I explore this through a critical race lens, I begin to question why this history is not taught and what purpose lumping all Asian groups together might have within a White supremacist society.

Aggregating groups of people together serves many purposes. First, this phenomenon supports the notion of race as a social construct with rather clearly defined boundaries. These boundaries identify ingroups and outgroups around which societal processes, such as policies and practices, are shaped. Second, aggregating people en masse makes it difficult to understand the distinctions that make people unique, including immigration history and status, language, and culture. For example, without these subtle understandings, it becomes increasingly difficult to distinguish the specific needs of these groups and how to best reach and access them for services. Within the scope of research, this leads to the inability to disaggregate and look at specific groups of Asian Americans because of the small sample sizes that result from not taking this group's diversity into consideration. In fact, in many cases, the data are just useless. Third, the lumping of Asian Americans allows stereotypes of people to continue. There are images of Asian American women as submissive and/or temptresses who serve the desire of men, and images of Asian American men as either emasculated or perhaps a martial artist. Other stereotypes that support the notion of the model minority myth also stem from this aggregated status—that all Asians are highly educated and do well in school and are therefore slightly higher on the race hierarchy compared to other racial groups that do poorly. Asians then act as a point of reference between the dominant White culture and other racial minorities and serve as the model minority that all other races should aspire to. This adds to the complexity of race relations because it pits minorities against minorities as well. At the same time, this point of reference further dictates how much Asian Americans can also succeed in the United States, serving as a glass ceiling.

Finally, the aggregation of Asian American allows us to target groups of people by removing the things that make Asian Americans distinct and human. In warfare, the grouping and stereotyping of people allows the dominant group to dehumanize and kill their enemy. This can play out similarly in a White supremacist society, where we all look alike, sound alike, and therefore share both the desirable and undesirable characteristics of the group. The uniqueness and struggles across and within Asian ethnicities are equally ignored. The murder of Vincent Chin, a Chinese man in Detroit who was killed because of the backlash against Japanese cars, is an excellent case example. With the rising tide of hate in the United States and the growing reality of White nationalism in this country, this continues to be a problem.

So how does this impact social work? As a social worker who studies the role of racism and discrimination on the health and well-being of racial and ethnic minorities, our ability to track economic and social disadvantage across and within groups is important. There are comparatively far fewer studies that have looked at specific Asian American ethnic groups and therefore very little is known at the population level. Social workers working with diverse Asian American populations should take it upon themselves to learn about the history of these groups, how policies and practices in the United

States have impacted their immigration stories, as well as the strengths and challenges that they encounter in their communities. Social workers can recognize and see their clients as distinct by learning about cultural values and norms and maybe even a little bit of their languages. For example, I have found it useful to minimally learn three words from as many ethnicities as possible, such as "hello," "thank you," and "please." And last, social workers must live their commitment to anti-racism by not only actively serving these populations but also by working with other groups to understand the impact of racism and hate against Asian Americans in the United States and to advocate and take action against such hate.

As I return to my own identity, I realize that my trigger being called "Asian" by continental US Americans has less to do with how I was treated as a multiracial child and more to do with lumping nearly half the world's population and myself into this somewhat meaningless category. I understand this is rooted in White supremacy. I am committed to anti-racism as a member of this group and as a multiracial ally to other ethnic groups to which I do not belong. Hate has no place at all in our beloved community, and I will continue to work daily to reverse the impact of racism and hate until my last breath.

Jeong: Connectedness Through Immigration, Health, and Social Change

Jane J. Lee

In 1983, my mother emigrated from South Korea to the United States, joining my father whom she had married the year before. They were among the many Korean immigrants who flocked to Los Angeles in search of better economic opportunities and refuge from political instability. They settled into a modest apartment near Koreatown and began their life together with intense optimism. My father initially worked as a reporter for a Korean newspaper and later transitioned into real estate. As their financial situation improved, they diligently saved until they could purchase their own home—an accomplishment my mom still recounts with pride. By that time, my older sister was four and my twin sister and I had just turned one. Despite our positive outlook, we would face a series of challenges during the decade that followed. Key events that unfolded during these formative years were instrumental in steering me toward a career in social work.

The Headaches

When I was four years old, my father fell ill with relentless headaches. He turned to a Korean doctor referred by friends who told him it was stress and that he should go back to Korea alone to rest. He did as he was told, and, within a week, he had a stroke and was admitted to the hospital. My mother, frantic and overwhelmed, left me and my sisters in the care of her brother. She sorted out her expired passport and flew to Korea as soon as she could—she had not expected to be returning to the country she had left behind so soon. After landing at the airport, she went straight to the hospital with the subtle realization that she had nowhere else to go. She found my father in a wheelchair and was told that he had a tumor growing in his brain.

She spent the next two weeks caring for him as nurses administered medications. She slept and ate alongside other patients, which led to creeping thoughts that she, herself, was unwell. While the days felt long, my father's condition seemed to be improving. Once my mother received enough reassurance from the doctor that my father would be okay, she flew back to the United States to relieve our uncle from her three toddlers.

When my father returned a couple months later, he came back an entirely different person. Excess weight adorned his frame due to the side effects of his medications, and his personality had undergone a complete shift. He was erratic and irritable and spoke about things my mother did not understand. Not long after his return, he collapsed and was rushed to the hospital. The doctors immediately advised that he undergo surgery to remove the persistent tumor. The subsequent months were an agonizing haze that involved painful procedures, chemotherapy, and radiation therapy. After carting me and my sisters to school, my mother would drive long hours to accompany my father to appointments. While my father slowly lost all his hair, the financial strains of his illness continued to build, and our home fell subject to foreclosure.

I remember the drive to our new rental apartment; I felt an unsettling mix of emotions as a child who was unaware of the reasons that we were moving but was enthralled by the aura of novelty that surrounded us. My sisters and I attended a new school and tried our best to fit in. While we were hoping for consistency and stability in our new environment, my father's illness and temperament were mercurial. Some weeks, he seemed like his usual self, while other days he could barely walk. One evening, my father fell off his bed and lost the use of his legs. He was, once again, taken to the hospital where only a couple weeks later, he passed away.

The Silence

I wish the broken healthcare system was not the main setting of the early years of my parents' life in America. While the events related to my father's passing can be told in multiple ways with greater or fewer details, my mother often considers the *could haves* or *should haves*: he *could have* gotten surgery sooner if we had taken him to the proper doctor. We *should have* known something was wrong. She is always assuming responsibility in these alternative scenarios. But then, she concludes that, regardless, the story would have the same ending, unintentionally acknowledging the inherent unfairness of her situation in which the system was not built for her or her family.

What remains striking, though, is the rarity with which the stories surrounding my father's illness have been shared. Perhaps this stems from our family's disinterest in receiving any form of sympathy, or maybe it is our collective attempt to protect one another from the burden of our experiences. By speaking of our pain, we are afraid of inflicting pain on those around us. So it is better to just stay silent.

This silence becomes unbearable when you learn that it is systemic. Cathy Park Hong writes in *Minor Feelings*, "In [immigrants'] efforts to belong in America, we act grateful, as if we've been given a second chance at life. But our shared root is not the opportunity this nation has given us but how the capitalist accumulation of White supremacy has enriched itself off the blood of our countries. We cannot forget this" (Hong, 2020, p. 90).

The sense that my mother could not complain or garner any sympathy was tied to this expectation that she was to stay quiet and be grateful. As Koreans and immigrants in America, we were constantly told that this was not our country. The language barriers, our lack of health insurance, and the feeling that we were always misunderstood were just some of the reminders that we were outsiders. Yet, to avoid being labeled as complainers or difficult to deal with, we were not to cause a scene or speak up; we were not to take up space.

April 29, 1992

The 1992 Los Angeles riots had occurred amid my father's illness when I was five years old. The unrest that followed the acquittal of the officers involved in the beating of Rodney King was a cumulative reaction to a long history of racial injustice, economic disparities, and social inequality. It was a warranted outrage. In *Twilight: Los Angeles, 1992*, a play by Anna Deavere Smith (1994) about the riots, she notes that the verdict could be understood as its cause, but "beneath this surface explanation is a sea of associated causes."

In Korean, the riots are referred to as *sa-i-gu*, which translates to "April 29"—the date the officers were acquitted. The experiences and perspectives of the riots were varied across the Korean community—many were angry, some were fearful, and others were in disbelief. I came across Smith's play during the summer after my freshman year in college, when I was an intern at the K. W. Lee Center for Leadership in Koreatown—a nonprofit organization designed to foster the growth of future Korean American leaders. The program had been developed in response to *sa-i-gu* and the apparent lack of leadership in the Korean community. I was immediately reminded of our community's invisibility and the lack of space we held, realizing how our insignificance was the result of oppressive systems and generations of trauma.

In Smith's introduction to the play, she explains how "few people speak a language about race that is not their own." Yet many Asian Americans often struggle to even discuss their own race. While there are multiple reasons behind this struggle, silence leads to more confusion and pain. If we do not address them, they will only grow and overflow.

Only a couple weeks prior to the Rodney King incident, Latasha Harlins, a 15-year-old African American girl, was shot in South Central Los Angeles by Soon Ja Du, a Korean American woman. Latasha was at a convenience store owned by Soon Ja and a dispute over a bottle of orange juice culminated in Soon Ja shooting and killing Latasha as she was leaving the store. While Soon Ja was charged with murder, she was convicted of voluntary manslaughter and received a relatively light sentence. The African American community felt disrespected and misunderstood by Korean American store owners, while Korean Americans felt unfairly targeted. Anger and tensions mounted alongside the Rodney King verdict, underscoring the multiple ways in which racism leads to hate and division.

My aunt and uncle owned a liquor store in Koreatown during this time. I remember visiting the store with my sisters after church on Sundays. We would drink Snapples behind the register while my uncle would speculate about the next winning lottery numbers with customers. He seemed to know everyone who came in by name. My aunt and uncle had made a conscious effort to accommodate Black patrons and to create a space where everyone would feel welcome. When the riots happened, their Black customers stood in front of their store to protect it. They told the rioters, "Not Lee's store," and deterred anyone from entering. Their store was unscathed from any vandalization. It was proof that hate was not insurmountable and that there were paths toward compassion and community building. These paths would bring me to social work as I sought ways to advocate for a more inclusive society where there was greater understanding and support for racial and ethnic minority communities.

Hate

Hate, just like love, is a complicated word because it can mean so many different things depending on the context and the people involved. While hate can lead to violence, it can also manifest as exclusion, mistrust, and even self-doubt.

As a child, my acute awareness of hate began with my mother refusing to recognize it. Whether it was a racist comment from the cashier at the grocery store or a remark from my elementary school teachers, my mom would maintain her smile as I felt growing confusion and shame about their interactions. Perhaps she did notice and just ignored these slights so she did not have to deal with them. She was raising three daughters on her own in a new country, and there were seemingly more important issues to handle.

Ultimately, my experiences with hate point to the structures that perpetuate prejudice and exacerbate inequities. Underlying my mother's challenges in dealing with my father's illness are forms of hate that infiltrate the systems that Asian Americans navigate in the United States. Social work became part of my commitment toward changing these systems and working toward a more equitable and just society.

During the COVID-19 pandemic, when we saw a spike in anti-Asian crimes across the country, the hate was palpable. I was worried about my mother, who lived alone, and I would call her daily to check in. "Be mindful of your surroundings," I would tell her. Instead of brushing off my guidance as she usually would, she shared her own concerns and those of her friends.

The fear, however, somehow felt like an overreaction. As I avoided leaving the house alone, there were few people who checked in. Nobody outside of the Asian community seemed to acknowledge what was going on, and I would keep these thoughts to myself. This is what hate does—it silences, it divides, it gaslights.

Jeong

It is not unusual to me that my thoughts turn to my mother and her experiences when I think about my own commitments to social justice. In Korean culture, there is the concept of *jeong* that refers to a deep bond and connection between individuals built through shared experiences. It is imbued with a sense of loyalty, affection, and empathy—to call this relationship special is an understatement.

My mother's unspoken sacrifices and suppressed pain led me to social work. They created my purpose and shaped my desire to address the social and structural barriers that prevent communities from receiving the care and compassion they deserve. I knew that this work had to be done in partnership with communities and by building relationships—the deep relationships where there is an abundance of mutual respect and love that brought me here in the first place.

My initial pursuit of social work as an attempt to empower marginalized communities brought to light my own disempowerment as an Asian American woman in this country. It sparked the "minor feelings" that Hong writes about in her book that "occur when American optimism is enforced upon you, which contradicts your own racialized reality, thereby creating a static of cognitive dissonance" (Hong, 2020, p. 56).

In my first year as a tenure-track social work professor, a colleague I had recently met visited my office to welcome me. She admired the tidiness of my workspace and exclaimed how I was always so put together. It was a sincere compliment, which I graciously received. Yet I had not felt put together at all and had been struggling to figure out my role in academia. Regardless, this interaction was a reminder that I had to be composed and keep a smile on my face—the same smile that my mother maintained after my father's passing. I felt compelled to uphold the model minority stereotype that I had unconsciously internalized, and this pressure had created a widening rift between who I truly was and how I was perceived.

Healing

Today, more than 30 years after the Los Angeles riots, Smith's point that we must reach across ethnic boundaries still rings true.

> The boundaries of ethnicity do yield brilliant work ... [though] the price we pay is that few of us can really look at the story of race in its complexity and its scope. If we were able to move more frequently beyond these boundaries, we would develop multifaceted identities and we would develop a more complex language. (Smith, 1994, p. xxv)

Rather than repress my family's struggles and ignore the hate that has shaped the history of Asian Americans in this country, I have learned to break this silence. My work with communities, guidance from generous mentors, and experiences with adversity have demonstrated the power of sharing our knowledge and resources. Sharing leads to abundance.

Through social work, I hope to foster this complex language for the growth and healing of our communities. I know that there is no singular story of Asian Americans in the United States—our histories are complicated, and our experiences are vast. As a daughter of immigrants, as a social worker, and as a teacher, I want to know and share these stories.

So, we must use our voice and take up space.

Finding Myself in a Time of Disconnect: My Jewish and Korean Identity

Sofie Hana Aaron

I've always looked ethnically ambiguous. Growing up, I was regularly asked questions like, "But where are you *really* from?" and "What are you?" Despite these skeptical and invasive questions from others, I managed to maintain some internal sense of belonging. My Oma, my dad's mother, helped me with this because she made sure to connect me to my Jewish-German ancestry and heritage. After escaping persecution in Germany in 1939, she and her family became refugees in New York City. After arriving, while mainly left to assimilate alone, they connected with the Hebrew Immigrant Aid Society (HIAS). HIAS had social workers and support systems that helped my Oma's father find employment in Worcester, Massachusetts, as a cantor, a member of the clergy in synagogues who led congregations in song (Heller, 2023). In a letter written to her six grandchildren, my Oma recalled,

When I think back of our experiences during those first months in the US, so filled with wonder. We had never seen traffic lights before. We had never been exposed to people of color or Asians. The skyscrapers of New York were awe- inspiring to us. The freedom that we felt that we could go anywhere, eat in restaurants, go to movies and no store had signs that Jews were unwelcome, were all incredible experiences. Not that there was no antisemitism here as well, but it wasn't sanctioned by the government. (Aaron, 2016)

The antisemitic hate that my family endured is still fueled in American society today. Jews comprise approximately 2% of the US population but experience the majority of "religious-based hate crimes," with the Anti-Defamation League reporting a recent spike in the use of antisemitic slurs, hate speech, and attacks (ADL, 2023; Lee, 2023). In 2018, 11 congregants were murdered by a neo-Nazi at Tree of Life Synagogue in Pittsburgh; in 2022, a terrorist held a Texas synagogue and its congregants hostage on Shabbat, the Jewish Sabbath; throughout the pandemic, right-wing conspiracy theorists and politicians spread misinformation, claiming things such as wildfires started by "Jewish space lasers" and that the Holocaust was a hoax (Chait, 2021; Deliso, 2022; Department of Justice, 2023; Levitt, 2022). The rise in antisemitic attacks, although not new, ran in parallel with a rise in anti-Asian hate during the pandemic and a spread of White supremacist misinformation. With the ever-increasing reach of social media, misinformation has become a pervasive way to target and spread antisemitic and anti-Asian rhetoric. I've felt a sustained sense of pain and sadness that these facets of my identity—being both Jewish and Korean American—are such prominent targets of hate and discrimination in this country.

Feeling this sadness at the state of the world and unsure of my place within it, my studies in music as an undergraduate introduced me to community advocacy work after I joined a prison creative arts project bringing music and theater into Michigan penitentiaries. Through the program, I learned that social work could act as a conduit of my love for music and the arts and my interest in social justice and activism. In my subsequent studies as a master of social work student, I was given more than simply the tools to find a purpose and to engage in activism: I was able to recontextualize my Asian identity and felt pushed to investigate and learn more about my Korean heritage. At this time, I felt ready to ask my mom to share her narrative.

My mom's story began under martial law because she was born into a military dictatorship in Seoul, South Korea. A photo she showed me, archived from her childhood, has her standing beside her older sister, my *imo*. Forbidding metal army barracks loom behind them as they pose in the Hangang neighborhood in Yongsan-gu, the base used by the US Army where my *halmeoni* (grandmother) worked as a waitress. She raised my mom and *imo* as a single mom, which was extremely unusual for a Korean woman in the 1960s. She is fierce, hardworking, and extremely resilient, despite growing up in poverty during the Japanese colonization and occupation of Korea. As a child, not only did she lose her family, but she also had war fully halt her formal education at nine years old. In the 1970s, my *halmeoni* met my grandfather, an active army serviceman stationed in Korea. Despite the American military and South Korea heavily discouraging intermingling, my grandparents fell in love and decided to marry—a decision met with prejudice, discrimination, and legal hurdles—which resulted in my mom and *imo* being legally adopted and immigrating to Missouri a year later, in June 1980.

After arriving in the United States and only a few months into learning English, my mom withdrew from language courses and decided to sink or swim. Self-conscious of what she perceived to be a thick accent, she stopped speaking around others. In high school, she intentionally took closing shifts at fast food chains to avoid speaking to the customers. Language, accent discrimination, and specifically "pathologizing of communication styles" are major points of discrimination against Asian American immigrant communities still today (Sue et al., 2007). As an immigrant she felt as though she was another one of thousands who were left to suffer in silence alone, without any knowledge of or access to social services and a fundamental lack of resources. Schools are places where youth can build resilience, and can act as social safety nets. It is necessary and vital for schooling systems to be cognizant of the diverse socioeconomic, linguistic, and cultural needs of communities, families, and the youth they serve in order to provide culturally responsive care. My mom sought out opportunities for herself and persisted in spite of a lack of social or emotional support. Using Pell Grants and loans, she pursued a degree in architecture and eventually found her footing in Seattle, Washington. She met my dad a few years later.

Today, I sit in the country my Oma fled to in 1939, and in the same city in which my mom reinvented herself when she was my age in 1989. I reflect on how hate and discrimination has been interwoven into our identities, and I am inspired by my Oma and my mom's resilience in the face of hardships they have endured and the challenges and obstacles that were in their way. I can see how stigmatization and acculturation has brought me to where I am today, informing my personal and professional growth. When thinking of my Korean identity, I'm grateful that social work provided me with the space to explore my intersecting identities.

And yet, with this said, there still lingers a disconnect in my own identity and a feeling of misplacement. I hold sadness for the pieces I know are missing and lost from my own cultural experiences: when I visited my family in Seoul, I could only silently smile and nod at the dinner table, not understanding a single word of the conversation. I hold sadness and a feeling of loss from the times my peers told me that I didn't "count as Asian" because I didn't speak Korean or look "Asian enough." But how could I not look "Asian enough" when I didn't look "White enough" either? Or "Jewish enough"? I feel another layer of alienation in these moments and, with time, have subconsciously internalized these questions.

Being Asian American is a unique experience for each of us, and no one is any "one thing." I'm not just Jewish, nor am I just White, nor am I just Korean. I exist at an intersection of identities where I am frequently an unexpected member of my communities, and I experience prejudices and stereotypical questions due to how others may perceive me to be. As social workers, it is our responsibility to look beyond one's singular identity and consider the person holistically, also taking note of internalized prejudices and biases before engaging in culturally competent communication. In a way I believe art and music act as beautiful supplements to overcoming this because they cut to emotion in a way that may transcend language. And while I have learned these skills in a professional context, I can't help but think that I built this skill long before my studies, from my *halmeoni*. I think of the times when she tries to tell me she loves me in broken English, and instead, we embrace each other, bridging the invisible divide and finding a shared comfort beyond words.

Triple Jeopardy: Racism, Coloniality, and Misogyny

Hye-Kyung Kang

On March 16, 2021, a news alert flashed on my phone: "Eight killed in shootings at Asian massage parlors." Following the terrifying updates with bits and pieces of information, "happening now," from various news outlets, my heart sank: a mass murder of Asian women at their workplaces in Atlanta, by an unknown gunman. Staring at the wording, *Asian massage parlors*, I felt sickened. I knew where this was going. It was revealed that six of the eight victims murdered were women of Asian descent, later identified as Soon Chung Park, Hyun Jung Grant, Suncha Kim, Yong Ae Yue, Xiaojie Tan, and Daoyou Feng. As the reports repeated the phrase, *Asian massage parlors*, these Asian women victims were rendered only as sex workers, or even immoral temptresses, devoid of humanity.[1]

That sickening feeling was confirmed when I saw the next day's headlines, where the suspect, a White gunman named Robert Aaron Long, was portrayed as a "sex addict" who "patronized the same parlors" and "lashed out at what he saw as sources of temptation" (Associated Press, 2021). The victims were depicted as the cause of their own murder based solely on the killer's narrative to negate the accusations of racial motives. There was no verification that Long ever patronized the same spas or that the spas he targeted were places of sex work. Even if they were, sex work does not deserve a mass murder. Soon Chung Park, Hyun Jung Grant, Suncha Kim, Yong Ae Yue, Xiaojie Tan, and Daoyou Feng were human beings with families and friends who loved them. Instead, Asian women's lives are rendered cheap, like the low-wage, toil-filled jobs that we often occupy: domestic workers, nail salon or spa employees, nursing home aids, and cleaners.

Reading those headlines, my mind flashed back to the March 1995 murder of Susana Blackwell, her unborn child, and her friends and advocates Phoebe Dizon and Veronica Laureta, at the King County Courthouse. In the morning when the story broke, news outlets reported the murders as a domestic violence killing. When I heard the news, a chill went down my spine; I was working at Seattle Rape Relief at that time and had accompanied gender-based violence survivors as an advocate to the same courthouse in the past. *That could have been me*, I thought.

By that afternoon, the narrative about the murders made an ugly turn; it was no longer a story about an abusive husband killing his estranged wife and her friends but rather about an Asian "mail order bride" and her "duped husband." The headlines read: "Mail-order wife killed by spouse at courthouse" (*The Washington Post*, 1995); "Mail order bride shot dead outside divorce courtroom" (*Tampa Bay Times*, 1995); and, finally, "Murder suspect said wife duped him from the start" (*The Spokesman Review*, 1995). The Asian women victims were no longer humans who deserved life; instead, the

White male perpetrator was humanized as a victim of a "scam." The notion was that since the White man married an Asian "mail order bride," she *owed* him her life in domesticity even though he was abusive to her. These stories robbed Susana Blackwell of humanity; she was treated as a purchased object that the buyer could use for whatever he wanted, including abuse.

The triple jeopardy of anti-Asian racism, colonialism, and misogyny produces a dehumanizing narrative about Asian American women that conspires to erase them (and even obliterates their lives, as in the cases above). And this dehumanizing narrative has deep historical roots. The Page Act of 1875, which prohibited the immigration of unfree laborers and women brought for "immoral purposes," specifically named Asian women ("Mongolian prostitutes"). The law required *all* Chinese women to be interrogated upon entry to prove they were *not* a prostitute (Ngai, 2021). Such racist practices of the Act effectively stemmed the growth of the Asian population in the United States while proliferating a stereotype of Asian women as an immoral and corrupting influence. In the 1900s, Chinese women were accused of being prostitutes spreading the "unique, Chinese strain" of syphilis that infused "a poison in the Anglo-Saxon blood" (Chang, 2003).

In both the Atlanta and Seattle mass murders, there is a disturbing parallel between the narrative of Asian women from a former US colony and a White American man and the history of Western colonizing nations taking, using, and debasing everything that belongs to their colonies, including human beings. US military occupation—often a legacy of colonialism—in Asia reproduces a narrative about Asian women as expendable spoils of war. Ngai (2003) states that the US military presence in Asia, during both wartime and postwar occupation, created sex trade markets to serve American military men. These markets exist often with the (formally or informally) occupied government's participation or selective regulation (i.e., punishing Asian sex workers instead of American customers) as part of the bargain to secure US military and economic cooperation (Choe, 2009). Such history inculcates the racist narrative about Asian women as exotic, subservient, and immoral sex objects. As Korean American author Marie Myong-Ok Lee (2021) writes, the "cultural attitudes and stereotypes about Asian women don't end when a soldier returns home. They become incorporated into American culture."

Indeed, in US popular culture, Asian women are portrayed as colonial sex objects who literally sacrifice their lives to serve White men who refuse to see them (e.g., *Miss Saigon, Madama Butterfly*). Until recently, nearly all Hollywood films that had Asian roles featured Asian women as wordless rape victims of a war or would-be rape victims only to be rescued by a White "hero." These stereotypes have a lasting impact on the contemporary imagining of Asian women and put them in jeopardy of sexual assault and harassment.

As early as in high school, much older White men approached me in public places—grocery stores, parks, malls—to tell me how I reminded them of "girlfriends" they had in Korea while in the military or what a good time they had with "all those pretty little girls" at a military base in Thailand. I was frozen with fear of these men, yet I was too ashamed and confused to call them out; after all, I never saw an Asian woman speak in American movies. Nor had I been taught about racism, coloniality, and misogyny at school. Deep inside, it felt wrong and creepy. But I had no language for it. For the most part, we didn't even exist—on screen, in textbooks, or in the national consciousness. How can you speak when your history is erased and your voice is perpetually silenced?

But this is exactly why we must speak out and generate our own narratives. In 1993, two years before the murder of Susanna Blackwell, Phoebe Dizon, and Veronica Laureta, a group of nearly 20 mostly Asian American women in Seattle who were involved in gender-based violence, human services, and community organizing—including Alice Ito, Judy Chen, Diane Narasaki, Emma Catague, Maria Batayola, Denise Tung Sharify, June Myers, and myself—started coalescing around the issue of gender-based violence, sexism, misogyny, and racism against Asian American and Pacific Islander communities. We worked together for the next two years to create an organization with a vision to resist this pernicious triple jeopardy and produce counter-narratives to reclaim our space and safety through community outreach, education, and organizing. Asian and Pacific Islander Women and Family Safety Center (APIWFSC), founded in 1995, filled the lacuna in our communities: a community-based and grassroots organization that specifically articulated intersectionality (racism, sexism, patriarchy, classism, ableism, coloniality, heterosexism, and immigration status-based oppression) in gender-based violence. APIWFSC later merged with Chaya, an organization that served domestic violence survivors in the South Asian community, to form API Chaya in 2011. API Chaya continues the innovative and radical work.

APIWFSC was built on a long tradition of community organizing and mobilization in AANHPI communities (many examples are discussed in this volume). In fact, APIWFSC had three major organizing lineages that were pertinent to the local Seattle/King County Asian American communities: the Japanese American Redress Movement, the Philippines cross-national democracy movement/anti-Marcos organizing, and the Cannery Workers Union organizing. Many co-founders of APIWFSC had been involved in those movements and brought their history to our organizing. We were continuing the movement of resisting dehumanizing narratives through our voices and actions.

The most potent weapon of anti-Asian racism is erasure—of our voice, our presence, and our humanity. What can social workers do? We as AANHPI social workers must remember that activism and organizing is our heritage. Connect the intersecting forces of oppression and create multiple counter-narratives that put our experiences and lives at the center. Our narratives matter.

From the Street to the Boardroom: The Manifestation of Anti-Asian Sentiment and Racism

Tam Dinh

A few months into the COVID-19 pandemic, I started to lose control of my body. At first it was a twitch in my right eye, one that lasted for the next several months. Then came the racing heartbeat, followed by cold sweats. Finally, it was the dizziness and nausea that made it difficult to fully engage in everyday activities.

Initially, I attributed these symptoms to growing old and the result of feeling the stress of the world being turned upside down by COVID-19. It wasn't until I read the first page of *Minor Feelings*, by Cathy Park Hong (2020)—"My depression began with an imaginary tic"—that I was reminded of how traumatic stress, also known as psychological trauma, impacts the body. For the past 11 years, I have taught social work students how trauma affects the body and how this could be passed down from one generation to another (i.e., intergenerational trauma), yet it took me so long to finally realize it within myself.

While physical attacks and hate crimes on Asians were increasing and getting more attention during the pandemic, the increased acts of microaggressions in professional settings were not as apparent. Yet, suddenly, in board rooms, in leadership meetings, and in conversation with colleagues, I noticed a palpable increase in acts of microaggression toward myself and toward my colleagues of color. Strategic moves on my part were labeled sneaky. I was asked if I thought my role was just to listen or to actually give an opinion. I was tone policed. Fingers were pointed in my face. I was reprimanded for talking too much, or too long, and was informed that these were code of conduct violations. When I asked my predecessors, who were mainly White and male, if they experienced the same thing, they expressed shock and vehemently said no.

Asian females are often expected to be docile, quiet, and submissive, so even when I showed up in a more muted and measured version of myself, often, it was still too much for others. The impossible no-win dichotomizing stereotypes means that the minute I expressed disagreement or just an opinion, I suddenly became the scheming, controlling dragon lady.

I had thought that growing up in Idaho as a seven-year-old boat refugee child had made me immune to microaggressions. Juvenile comments like "Where are you from?," "Hey, ching-chong," "Me love you long time," and the like only garnered an internal eye roll. Yet the microaggressions from those who claimed to be equity-focused and social justice-minded were hard to process. When it was from peers who were supposed to know better or from colleagues who were supposed to be my friends and allies, it hit deeper and more painfully.

Most people who read this will probably think that I am writing about them. The reality is that, most likely, they are right. Most of us are complicit in perpetuating racial injustices in one way or another. Have we witnessed bad behaviors, inappropriate comments, and scapegoating toward Asians and kept silent? Worse, have we tried to minimize a harmful situation and explained away racist behaviors? Have we maintained the status quo while saying, "It's complicated. It's not in our policy. We shouldn't compromise our standards...."

A bitter pill to swallow is that these things happen in our social work profession as well. There are so many things that our profession has given me that are priceless, such as an in-depth understanding of human nature and a broader understanding of the history, systems, and environments that impact one's actions and experience. It has given me values and a Code of Ethics to help maintain my accountability to my clients, colleagues, and community. The social work profession has given me a wide range of tools and skills to be of service to those in need in a way that they need it.

However, the demographic of social workers, our curriculum, the way we teach, and the standards we use have not changed that much from our White, middle-class, charity model history despite what we think. The world needs social workers more than ever, yet we are likely guilty of inadvertently gatekeeping the very students who are needed for an increasingly diverse and complex racialized world.

As we teach our students and serve our clients and communities, it is imperative that we do not recreate or further exacerbate White supremacy values and norms. To do this, we need to engage in deeply intensive and honest discernment of our own power, privilege, and positionality. We need to radically rethink how our perspectives and values, actions and inactions, maintain and perpetuate systems of oppression and White supremacy. Most importantly, we need to sincerely and courageously hold ourselves, each other, and our systems accountable to make these changes, to urgently work toward anti-racist efforts to eliminate Asian prejudice, discrimination, and hate crimes.

Discussions

It is impossible to reflect on Asian identity without acknowledging the roles of racism, xenophobia, discrimination, and violence in shaping each unique experience. From blatant forms of objectification and "perpetual foreigner othering" to gender-based violence and misogyny, anti-Asian racism is insidious and can contribute to how we internalize our own sense of self (Liu, 2022). Each of our authors speaks to their individual encounters of inherent bias and implicit hate, the marginalization of their identities, and the historical shortcomings in the healthcare and political systems that have caused emotional and physical tolls on themselves, their families, and their communities.

Often, we may think of physical harm when referring to hate crimes, and less of the implicit, emotional, and micro-aggressive forms of racism that also exist. Extending beyond physical forms of hate, many of our narratives center around the dearth of research findings encompassing the nuances of different Asian identities and related health outcomes, coupled with the harm that is caused when anti-Asian racism is not examined through a critical race lens. When research and studies homogenize Asian communities, as seen in our collective narratives, this results in stigmatization in healthcare, in the preservation of shame when experiencing cultural differences and prevention from seeking help, in macro systems maintaining structures built on White supremacist ideals, and in the continued silencing of minoritized and multifaceted identities (Li Verdugo et al., 2023; Liu, 2022; Smith, 1994).

Between 2021 and 2023, more than 44 states have introduced bills or taken other steps that would prohibit educators from discussing topics such as racism, sexism, and critical race theory (AARI, 2022; Lambert, 2023; Schwartz, 2021). One example is from May 2023, when the governor of Florida mandated the teaching of "Asian American and Pacific Islander history in K-12 public schools" while simultaneously signing bills to no longer allow public universities to teach diversity, equity, and inclusion and limiting the teaching of gender studies and intersectionality, which, in itself, is weaponizing and pitting one minority against others (Nittle, 2023; Yam, 2023). Beyond advocating for equitable policy change and promoting community and collaboration among ethnic minority groups, it is essential to consider the intersectionality and multifaceted nature of the Asian American experience when looking at one's identity, especially when engaging with different AANHPI communities through social work practice.

"Asian American" is a historically complex concept. On the one hand, it is rooted in the "scientific" racism that classified humans by "race" (Omi & Winant, 2014). The Asiatic Barred Zone Act (the Immigration Act of 1917) was one of the first official policies that assigned all Asians to one group to prohibit them from immigrating to the United States. Asians never asked for this erasure of differences and homogenizing of vast populations, and deleterious consequences of such erasure are discussed extensively in this volume.

On the other hand, "Asian American" is a political term coined by Asian American activists (such as the Asian American Political Alliance) in the 1960s to mobilize people of Asian descent and to increase visibility and effectiveness of their political organizing (Le Espiritu, 1992). Influenced by the Civil Rights movement and the Black Power movement, these Asian American activists reclaimed the term "Asian" to politicize their identity and build a progressive pan-ethnic coalition. Thus, Asian American identity today was born of Asian political activism and critical race consciousness.

Additionally, Asian American history has operated with a collectivist perspective in partnership with other historically marginalized communities and minoritized groups, features robust interracial and intergroup coalition building, and has strongly influenced political activist movements. It is impossible to fully understand the Asian American experience without examining the larger context of racism and colonialism in the United States through an intersectional lens. To omit the narratives and histories of Asian Americans from social work education and curriculum is to engage in a form of oppression and an erasure of voices.

Conclusion

A common thread weaving our narratives together is a call to action for our peers, colleagues, and future social workers. As advocates, practitioners, activists, and community members, we must each independently and collectively engage in continuous learning, educating ourselves and others in current policy issues and contributing to interventions and solutions to better future interactions with prevailing oppressive systems in our society. Social workers must be intentional in recognizing shortcomings in their present practices when engaging with Asian diaspora communities. We have the capacity to serve as strong advocates for AANHPI clients and the larger community, embracing social justice principles, practicing culturally relevant care, and taking steps to destigmatize mental health and pursuing culturally informed mental health services. Our call to action also relates to advocacy and research implications since social workers must be involved with community-based partnerships and intersectional coalition building. The combination of and advocacy for all these collaborative efforts will contribute to long-lasting systemic changes to eliminate anti-Asian racism, discrimination, and hate.

Note

1. An abbreviated version of this piece was published as an op-ed in *The Seattle Times*, March 17, 2021.

References

AARI: Asian American Research Initiative. (2022). *Organizing for Ethnic Studies Toolkit*. San Francisco State. Stop AAPI Hate Reports and Resources. https://asianamericanresearchinitiative.org/project/organizing-for-aas-cpios-toolkit/

Aaron, M. (2016). *Letters to my grandchildren* (1st ed.). Exilic Press.

Associated Press. (2021). Police investigate suspect's motive in Atlanta-Area killings. WTTW News Crime & Law. https://news.wttw.com/2021/03/17/police-investigate-suspect-s-motive-atlanta-area-killings

ADL. (2023). Press release: US antisemitic incidents hit highest level ever recorded, ADL audit finds. Anti-Defamation League. https://www.adl.org/resources/press-release/us-antisemitic-incidents-hit-highest-level-ever-recorded-adl-audit-finds

Bai, N. (2022). *Addressing Asian and Pacific Islander mental health in the US*. Stanford Medicine News Center.

CAAM. (2023). *Asian American storytellers*. Center for Asian American Media. https://artsandculture.google.com/story/asian-american-storytellers-center-for-asian-american-media-caam/SwWRiDBzRu8yIg?hl=en

Chait, J. (2021). Marjorie Taylor Greene blamed wildfires on secret Jewish space laser. *New York Magazine: The Intelligencer*. https://nymag.com/intelligencer/article/marjorie-taylor-greene-qanon-wildfires-space-laser-rothschild-execute.html

Chang, I. (2003, May 21). Fear of SARS, fear of strangers. *The New York Times*. https://www.nytimes.com/2003/05/21/opinion/fear-of-sars-fear-of-strangers.html

Cho, S. (2023). *Asian discrimination: In the field of social work*. Electronic Theses, Projects, and Dissertations. 1731. https://scholarworks.lib.csusb.edu/etd/1731

Choe, S.-H. (2009). Ex-prostitutes say South Korea and US enabled sex trade near bases. *The New York Times*. https://www.nytimes.com/2009/01/08/world/asia/08korea.html

Council on Social Work Education. (2017). 2016 Statistics on social work education in the United States. https://www.cswe.org/CMSPages/GetFile.aspx?guid=6e8bc9e7-ebd6-4288-bc7a-d2d427d68480

Deavere, A. (1994). *Twilight: Los Angeles, 1992 on the road: A search for American character* (1st ed.). Anchor Books.

Deliso, M. (2022). Hostage incident at Texas synagogue a terrorist act and hate crime: FBI. ABC News. https://abcnews.go.com/US/hostage-incident-texas-synagogue-terrorist-act-hate-crime/story?id=82404960

Department of Justice. (2023). Jury recommends sentence of death for Pennsylvania man convicted for Tree of Life Synagogue shooting. Office of Public Affairs Press Release. https://www.justice.gov/opa/pr/jury-recommends-sentence-death-pennsylvania-man-convicted-tree-life-synagogue-shooting

Drumm, M. (2013). The role of personal storytelling in practice. The Institute for Research and Innovation in Social Services. https://www.iriss.org.uk/resources/insights/role-personal-storytelling-practice

Duwamish Tribe. (2023). Duwamish land acknowledgement. https://www.duwamishtribe.org/

Heller, W. (2023). Cantors. The YIVO Encyclopedia of Jews in Eastern Europe. https://yivoencyclopedia.org/article.aspx/Cantors

Hong, C. P. (2020). *Minor feelings: An Asian American reckoning* (1st ed.). One World.

Janssen, S. (2023). Stories we tell, stories we hear—Valuable therapeutic tools. Social Work Today. https://www.socialworktoday.com/archive/exc_0519_4.shtml

Kang, H. (2021). Racist, colonialist, and misogynist narrative abets violence against Asian Women. Opinion: *The Seattle Times*. https://www.seattletimes.com/opinion/racist-colonialist-and-misogynist-narrative-abets-violence-against-asian-women/

Lambert, D. (2023). National wave of anti-CRT measures trickles into California schools. EdSource. https://edsource.org/2023/national-wave-of-anti-crt-measures-trickle-into-california-schools/688862

Le Espiritu, Y. (1992). *Asian American panethnicity: Bridging institutions and identities* (vol. 231). Temple University Press.

Lee, L. (2023). Why is there a rise in antisemitism? KCRA3. https://www.kcra.com/article/antisemitism-rise/44042243

Lee, M. (2021). The U.S. military's long history of Anti-Asian dehumanization. *Korean Quarterly, Spring Issue.* https://www.koreanquarterly.org/stop-asian-hate/embedded-stereotypes/

Levitt, M. (2022). Synagogue hostage crisis reminds us that neo-Nazis aren't the only ones targeting Jews. The Washington Institute for Near East Policy. https://www.washingtoninstitute.org/policy-analysis/synagogue-hostage-crisis-reminds-us-neo-nazis-arent-only-ones-targeting-jews

Li Verdugo, J., Oh, H. Y., & Jang, Y. (2023). Mental health of Asian American caregivers of family members with severe mental illness. *Psychiatric Services, 74*(10), 1100–1103.

Liu, S. (2022). *We were dreamers: An immigrant superhero origin story.* Harper Collins.

National Association of Social Workers (NASW). (2015). Developing a social work response to racism, hate crimes, and police use of force. NASW: Michigan Chapter. https://www.nasw-michigan.org/page/Racism/A-Social-Work-Response-to-Racism-Hate-Crimes-and-Police-Use-of-Force.html

Ngai, M. (2021). Racism has always been part of the Asian American experience. *The Atlantic.* https://www.theatlantic.com/ideas/archive/2021/04/we-are-constantly-reproducing-anti-asian-racism/618647/

Nittle, N. (2023). Florida bill would bring bans on gender studies and critical race theory to colleges and university. The 19th News(letter): Education. https://19thnews.org/2023/04/florida-house-bill-999-higher-education-race-gender/

Omi, M., & Winant, H. (2014). *Racial formation in the United States* (3rd ed.). Routledge.

Schwartz, Sarah. (2021). Map: Where critical race theory is under attack. Education Week. http://www.edweek.org/leadership/map-where-critical-race-theory-is-under-attack/2021/06

Seo, M., Kang, HS, Lee, Y. J., & Chae, S. M. (2015). Narrative therapy with an emotional approach for people with depression: Improved symptoms and cognitive-emotional outcomes. *Journal of Psychiatric and Mental Health Nursing, 22*(6), 379–389. https://pubmed.ncbi.nlm.nih.gov/25753316/

Smith, A. D. (1994). *Twilight—Los Angeles, 1992 on the road: A search for American character* (1st ed.). Anchor Books.

Sue, D. W., Bucceri, J., Lin A. I., Nadal, K. L., & Torino, G. C. (2007). Racial micro-aggressions and the Asian American experience. *Cultural Diversity and Ethnic Minority Psychology, 13*, 72–81.

Tampa Bay Times. (1995, rev. 2005). Mail-order bride shot dead outside divorce courtroom. *Tampa Bay Times Archive.* https://www.tampabay.com/archive/1995/03/03/mail-order-bride-shot-dead-outside-divorce-courtroom/

The Spokesman Review. (1995). Murder suspect said wife duped him from the start: Blackwell testified at annulment hearing days before shootings.

Wang, E. W. (2019). *The collected schizophrenias: Essays.* Graywolf Press.

The Washington Post. (1995). Mail-order wife killed by spouse at courthouse. *The Washington Post Archive: Politics.* https://www.washingtonpost.com/archive/politics/1995/03/03/mail-order-wife-killed-by-spouse-at-courthouse/25ea0461-3a78-447c-a069-b4eeca9a0840/

Yam, K. (2023). DeSantis criticized for mandating Asian American history while banning courses on 'systemic racism'. *NBC News Asian America.* https://www.nbcnews.com/news/asian-america/desantis-criticized-mandating-asian-american-history-banning-courses-s-rcna84972

Zippia. (2023). Licensed social worker demographics and statistics in the US. https://www.zippia.com/licensed-social-worker-jobs/demographics/

14
Reflecting on Racism Within the Social Work Profession and Developing an Anti-Racist Workforce

Kenny Kwong

Background

There has been a rising tide of Anti-Asian racism, hate, and violence against Asian Americans during the outbreak of COVID-19. During social, economic, and political crises, Asian Americans as a group are often scapegoated for pandemic outcomes. Though acts of discrimination and violence against Asian Americans have increased since the beginning of COVID-19, the long history of xenophobic and racist attitudes toward Asian American communities is often ignored in the present-day discourse on racial tensions in the United States (Nakayama, 2021). Studies show that anti-Asian xenophobia, racism, and discrimination negatively impact Asian Americans' mental health, sense of self and identity, and self-esteem, particularly among adolescents and young adults (Benner et al., 2018; Schmitt et al., 2014).

The Grand Challenge to Eliminate Racism (GCER) calls for the social work profession to strengthen evidence-based practice and practice-based research to improve the conditions of daily life for those impacted by racism and White supremacy and facilitate dialogues and change at the individual, community, organizational, professional, and societal levels (Teasley et al., 2021). This chapter addresses the call from the GCER in the context of growing anti-Asian racism and violence in the United States and reflects on the role of social workers in response to this Grand Challenge. It then discusses how the social work profession can eradicate racism and xenophobia through developing an anti-racist workforce and expanding both the number and ranks of multilingual and multicultural social workers trained in anti-racist and anti-oppressive practice. Several critical challenges impacting the development of an anti-racist social work workforce will be reviewed. Recommendations for building collaborative efforts to develop an anti-racist workforce are discussed.

Social Work Grand Challenge to Eliminate Racism

Social work is rooted in its social justice value and committed to enhancing an individual's well-being and help meet the basic human needs of all people, with particular attention to the needs and empowerment of people who are vulnerable and living in poverty (National Association of Social Workers, 2021). The Educational Policy and Accreditation Standards (EPAS) asserts that the purpose of social work is fulfilled through its quest for "social, racial, economic, and environmental justice by reducing inequalities and ensuring dignity and respect for all" (Council on Social Work Education [CSWE], 2022, p. 9). The central idea of social work's commitment to human rights, social justice, anti-racism, diversity, equity, and inclusion is emphasized in Competency 2, Advance Human Rights and Social, Racial, Economic and Environmental Justice; and in Competency 3, Engage Anti-Racism, Diversity, Equity, and Inclusion (ADEI) in Practice, demonstrating the profession's commitment to enhance anti-oppressive and anti-racist social work practice. Increased attention to social justice, structural inequality, and strategies to promote anti-oppressive practice have guided both practice and teaching in social worker's responses to marginalized and vulnerable populations (Miller & Garran, 2017).

There is an urgent need for the social work profession to address systemic racism and White supremacy, both within the profession and within society. Social workers have a moral duty to dismantle racism and speak out against discrimination and institutional systems that perpetuate hierarchies and injustice against marginalized racial minorities. Despite social work's articulated stance on racism, the profession has not adequately addressed racism and White supremacy (Teasley et al., 2021). There are many examples of how the social work profession has supported practices and policies that harmed oppressed and marginalized people. Park (2008) has documented the role of social workers in the removal, incarceration, and resettlement of Japanese Americans during World War II. From February of 1942 through March 1946, approximately 120,000 Japanese Americans were incarcerated in American internment camps. Park describes social workers' complicity in the disruption of an established culture, including many who were native-born citizens, and argues that while social workers eased the difficulties faced by the incarcerated, more could have been done to protest the activities of a nation that was enacting racist practice and polices targeting a marginalized yet highly established subpopulation group. Torpy (2000) traced social workers' roles in the involuntary sterilization of 3,406 Native American women during the 1970s, often forcing them to comply with these procedures by threatening to remove their children or welfare benefits. Under the Trump administration, social workers also faced numerous ethical dilemmas about the treatment of oppressed and marginalized people. For example, social workers are tasked with providing mental health care for undocumented youths separated from parents or guardians in detention facilities (Byers & Shapiro, 2019). For undocumented youths, separation from their parents can constitute a traumatic experience (Zucker & Greene, 2018), especially when they have followed a difficult journey from their country of origin, and these experiences may have long-lasting and negative impacts on their mental health. All these examples of complicity illustrate that social workers have not always found ways to navigate and transcend the moral failures of government and at times have been integral to the implementation of unjust policies (Byers & Shapiro, 2019).

The GCER acknowledges that the United States was built on the long history of racism and White supremacy that continues to affect significantly the daily lives of all residents. Racist policies, bias, and discriminatory practices continue to promote racial inequality in a myriad of ways. It is important for practitioners, educators, and researchers to collaborate, innovate, and apply research evidence to tackle those important issues facing our society. To address the impacts of racism and xenophobia against Asian Americans, two specific priorities suggested by the GCER are relevant: (1) develop an anti-racist social work workforce that creates opportunities for transdisciplinary collaboration and promotes access to resources to advance civic engagement to build racial equity and (2) examine the social work profession to combat racist policies and practices and revise social work education to address structural inequalities and White privilege and their impact on individual and group outcomes (Teasley et al., 2021). To meet these two priorities, the following important topics to respond to priorities suggested by the Grand Challenge will be explored: (1) pipeline issues in developing an anti-racist social work workforce; (2) reasons and challenges in pursuing a career in social work among minority students; (3) career-related stress and concerns among minority social work students and practitioners; (4) the "model minority" myth and unmet service needs of Asian Americans; and (5) inclusion of race and ethnicity in social work research.

Pipeline Issues in Developing an Anti-Racist Social Work Workforce

Creating pipelines within social work educational programs that recruit and train more members of minority racial-ethnic groups is critical for developing an anti-racist social work workforce. According to the Council of Social Work Education (2021), 3.3% of master's degree (MSW) and 2.7% of bachelor's degree in social work (BSW) graduates in 2020 were Asians. These rates were much lower when compared with the percentage of Asians (7%) in the total US population (Budiman & Ruiz, 2021). The Asian population grew by 88% between 2000 and 2019 and had the fastest growth rate of any major racial or ethnic groups in the United States (Budiman & Ruiz, 2021). The study by Kwong (2018a) confirmed the trend of a tremendous gap in recruiting and training adequate number of Asian American social workers to serve the needs of Asian American populations. The study found that only 15.8% of Asian American social work respondents thought about a social work career prior to entering college. Fifty-six percent indicated that social work was their first or primary career choice, while 44% made a career change to pursue social work.

Similarly, there was also a significant gap in recruiting and training adequate number of Hispanic/Latino social workers. Although Hispanics/Latinos constitute 17.6% of the US population, 13.5% of MSW and 15.6% of BSW graduates were Hispanic/Latinos in 2017, and represented only 9.5% of active social workers with a master's degree or higher in the United States (Salsberg et al., 2017). While Black individuals or African Americans represented 19.1% of active social workers, a rate comparable to their population percentage in the United States, their pass rate in social work licensing exams was substantially lower than for White individuals. The Association of Social Work Boards (ASWB) recently published a Final Report on the 2022 ASWB Exam Pass Rate Analysis (Association of Social Work Boards [ASWB], 2022). The national sample included 44,041 White, 13,884 Black, and 8,416 Hispanic/Latino MSW graduates who took the licensing exam between 2018 and 2021. Differences were observed in first-time pass rates among racial/ethnic subgroups, the largest occurring between White test-takers (with a pass rate of 85.8%) and Black test-takers (with a pass rate of only 44.5%). The pass rates for Hispanic/Latinos and Asians were 63% and 71%, respectively. Such disparity is grossly disproportionate and may reflect deep bias in the design of standardized test. The pass rate disparities highlight possible challenges, constraints, and restrictions affecting test-takers from marginalized communities and have received both national and local scrutiny.

The low pass rates among historically marginalized communities (as defined in the report among those identified as Black, Hispanic/Latino, Asian, or Native American/Indigenous peoples) were a major concern affecting career options and advancement among them, resulting in a lack of Black, Hispanic/Latino, and indigenous licensed social workers to serve diverse populations. Census data have shown consistently that historically marginalized groups disproportionately experience socioeconomic hardship related to higher poverty rates, lower household income, and disparities in obtaining access in educational resources (Shrider et al., 2021). The ASWB (2022) suggests that test-takers from marginalized communities may be more likely to experience challenges in accessing comprehensive and effective exam preparation resources, not have sufficient time to prepare for the test, and lack adequate financial resources to pay for the exam.

Reasons and Challenges in Pursuing a Career in Social Work Among Minority Students

Several studies explored the role of family psychosocial history, mental health, and violence on career choices and found that a family history of trauma, violence, mental illness, and substance abuse might influence a person's decision to pursue a career in social work (Daniel, 2011; Sellers & Hunter, 2005; Wilson & McCrystal, 2007). Students coming from a disturbed and chaotic family background with a significant history of violence and family psychopathology were likely to pursue a career in social work and choose mental health or health as their practice concentration (Sellers & Hunter, 2005). Unresolved psychosocial trauma may also affect the retention of social workers because unresolved issues are likely to reoccur in direct practice when they experience tremendous work-related stress with little support (Wilson & McCrystal, 2007). Daniel (2011) studied factors that influenced minority students' interest in and decision to pursue a career in social work and found that many ethnic and racial minority students were discouraged by family and friends who believed social work was a poor career choice because of its lack of professional status in their specific racial and ethnic communities, its lack of financial return, and a high level of commitment and career-related demands. Minority students are motivated to become social workers because of their desire to serve poor and vulnerable populations and their belief in the profession as the most effective way to support their communities (Daniel, 2011). However, low salaries and compensation and low occupational status have negatively affected many entering into the field (Daniel, 2011; Moriarty & Murray, 2007).

Shen (2013) explored the relationship between internalized stereotyping, parental pressure, and parental support on career choices among 315 Asian American undergraduate and graduate students and found that parental influence and pressure on career choices significantly predicted internalized academic and career-related stereotypes. The study found that those who internalized Asian American stereotypes were more likely to choose culturally valued majors (such as science and technology) than non–culturally valued majors (such as social work, mental health counseling, and human services). Ghosh and Fouad (2016) found that acculturation and endorsement of cultural values, differences in major and career-related values, and intergenerational conflicts regarding major- and career-related values predicted major differences in family expectations on career choices. The same study found that Asian parents and their children might not communicate clearly and adequately about their expectations regarding career choices and majors. Poon (2014) argued that for some Asian American students, choosing a career might be influenced by their personal interests or family expectations. Their immigrant experiences living in a racialized society also shaped the social environments within which they made career choices. Kwong (2018a) explored career choice, barriers, and prospects of Asian American social workers and found that social work was a dream career for them because of their idealism of the profession, strong altruistic vision of social work, and their desire to serve their populations.

Career-Related Stress and Concerns Among Minority Students and Practitioners

Daniel (2011) summarized several career-related concerns raised by minority students, such as a lack of ability to effect change due to agency bureaucracy and "the negative and stereotypic perceptions of poor and minority clients" (p. 904). Students from marginalized minorities believed that they would be targets of prejudice and discrimination within the social work profession. Among Asian American social workers, their perceptions of discrimination and a glass ceiling due to their perceived organizational fairness may affect their perceived career prospects and their decisions to stay in the job (Kwong, 2018a). Work-related stress is common for social work practitioners in today's workforce. Over time, work-related stress could result in burnout, workplace injury, impaired performance, impaired cognitive functioning, decreased concentration, and poor health and mental health (Arrington, 2008; Kwong, 2016).

Given the profession's client-centered focus and the complexity of client situations and needs, stress is a major concern for social workers who provide direct services. Kwong (2018b) explored work-related stress and career experiences of Asian American social workers and found that many experienced high levels of work-related stress and encountered numerous job challenges including heavy workload, being unable to balance professional and personal life, difficult/challenging clients, receiving few resources to adequately accomplish work tasks, inadequate compensation, and limited opportunities for career advancement. Under less-than-optimal work conditions (such as limited resources and getting minimal support from co-workers and/or supervisors), social workers are often pushed to the limit when trying to complete their work. The study by Kwong (2018b) showed that higher perceived stress was associated with higher secondary trauma, burnout, and job-related health problems. Having an occupational stressor was a factor predicting secondary trauma and compassion satisfaction among Asian American social workers. Because of these constraints and difficulties, Asian Americans might consider a career change, resulting in increasing challenges in the retention of Asian American social workers and causing more service gaps for Asian American populations.

Model Minority Myth and Unmet Service Needs of Asian Americans

The internalized model minority myth is the belief that Asian Americans in the United States have more educational and financial success compared with other racial groups (Kwong, 2022). The model minority myth has influenced the social work profession in its relative disregard for the real service needs of Asian Americans and can have enduring negative consequences for Asian American children, families, and communities (Shih et al., 2019). The myth presumes that Asian Americans are free from experiences of racism, discrimination, and oppression and that Asian American students are problem-free and can succeed with little institutional support and services. Such assumptions prevent society from recognizing the educational needs as well as emotional concerns of Asian American students (Yoo et al., 2015).

The model minority myth glorifies the successful experiences of a select few Asian immigrants and renders invisible problems such as high rates of poverty among specific subgroups of Asian Americans, wealth and income disparities, and health and mental health issues (Shih et el., 2019). Consequently Asian American communities are often excluded from public policy debates regarding affirmative action, civil rights, and access to health and mental health services (Chao et al., 2010) and are left out of social service provisions. This masks the needs of the most vulnerable Asian American communities and disregards their needs for assistance and services. Consistent with how stereotypes, privilege, and oppression operate in our society, the model minority myth draws on the experiences of a select few (the model) and generalizes those successful stories to the entire Asian American population (Shih et al., 2019). It is important for social workers to be aware that Asian Americans continue to face discrimination and oppression as obstacles to career advancement and be conscious of how structural and systemic racism and stereotypes, such as the model minority myth, create barriers for Asian Americans to access mental and physical health services. To work toward social justice for Asian American families, social work scholars and practitioners need to be aware of our own bias, assumptions, and values, as well as power dynamics and hierarchies in our interactions with whom we work, whether it is in our research, education, or direct practice (Shih et al., 2019).

Lack of Inclusion of Race and Ethnicity in Social Work Research

To address racism, anti-Asian violence, and xenophobia, social work researchers play an important role in accumulating evidence and research data disaggregated by race and ethnicity. This can enrich our knowledge of culturally and ethically appropriate interventions that address structural racism and its detrimental effects (Teasley et al., 2021). More social work research needs to center race, racism, and White supremacy as core study constructs and explicitly discusses racial and ethnic disparities (Corley & Young, 2018; McMahon & Allen-Meares, 1992; Woo et al., 2018). A content analysis study by McMahon and Allen-Meares (1992) found that social work research typically refrained from centering race in its inquiry, with less than 6% of published literature focusing on racial and ethnic minorities. Much of social work research on race focused on Black and Brown communities and excluded many other ethnic groups who also experience racism and oppression. Asian Americans, one of the fastest growing minority populations and having diverse cultures (Budiman & Ruiz, 2021), remain one of the most underresearched racial/ethnic groups. McMahon and Allen-Meares (1992) argue that most of the literature on social work practice with minorities is naïve and superficial and fails to address their social contexts. Such lack of knowledge poses significant constraints on the effectiveness of social work with minority populations. A recent study by Corley and Young (2018) showed very limited progress in the inclusion of race and ethnicity in social work research since the 1990s, and found only 7% of articles published between 2005 and 2015 in four major social work journals included content related to racial and ethnic minorities.

Another recent content analysis of articles published between 2006 and 2015 in three social work journals showed that although race and ethnicity were referenced in many journal articles, there was a tendency among researchers to treat race and ethnicity as control variables rather than key constructs in their inquiry (Woo et al., 2018). Most studies that engaged race and ethnicity focused on a single racial or ethnic group and about one-fourth of studies made comparisons between different racial/ethnic groups. Although there may be variations within a large racial/ethnic group, only a few studies investigated subgroups within a major racial/ethnic group. Approximately one-third of the studies' participants were from specific regions of the United States, whereas most studies used a national sample (Woo et al., 2018). The study found that participants of those studies that considered race and ethnicity seriously were typically African Americans or Latina/o Americans. The number of studies that included these groups was four to five times greater than the number of studies that included Asian Americans and/or Native Americans. These findings suggest the tremendous need to integrate racial/ethnic groups and subgroups who historically have received little attention in social work research. Given that race and ethnicity are socially constructed, explaining how race and racism are conceptualized in these studies will be an important step toward initiating more dialogues on race in social work research (Woo et al., 2018). When conducting social work research, it is important for both researchers and partitioners to understand any inherent bias and knowledge gap in the research given its lack of inclusion of race and ethnicity and to evaluate the design, data collection, analysis, and interpretation of results using an anti-racist and anti-oppressive perspective (CSWE, 2022).

Revisioning Social Work Education to Eradicate Racism and Anti-Asian Violence

To eradicate racism and anti-Asian violence, schools of social work need to periodically assess the extent to which their curricula and educational content are related to racism, oppression, and racial equity (Teasley et al., 2021). Whereas schools of social work have largely promoted diversity and difference in their curricula, their efforts to facilitate racial equity can be strengthened by placing greater attention on disparities and inclusion and promoting explicit dialogues on racism and White supremacy (Woo et al., 2022). Attention to disparities and inclusion is critical in clinical social work courses embracing a person-in-the-environment approach and in macro social work courses. This approach helps train more social workers to make broad changes that promote equity and justice in society and institutions. Addressing disparities and inclusion in social work curricular will help promote students' active engagement in difficult dialogues about injustice, inequity, and oppression. It is important for social work instructors to consider ways in which they can teach culture and diversity without reinforcing privileged statuses or norms while also facilitating critical discussions of power, inequity, oppression, and injustice in the classroom. Dialogues on race, racism, oppression, and power are often difficult because students and faculty have diverse backgrounds, share different racial perspectives, and are at different levels of the racial hierarchy. When heated emotional exchanges around these topics occur, there is a strong fear of self-disclosure (Sue et al., 2011). Those who recognize their role consciously or subconsciously and make a commitment to eliminate racism and foster racial equity are made aware that this is a process of life-long learning and growth in their social work career (Teasley et al., 2021). Promoting racial equity begins with more accurate information and includes self-reflection and an examination of internalized superiority/inferiority and power/oppression.

Raising Critical Reflection and Self-Awareness Using Cultural Humility Framework

Tervalon and Murray-Garcia (1998) define cultural humility as "a lifelong commitment to self-evaluation and self-critique, to redressing the power imbalances in the patient–physician dynamic, and to developing mutually beneficial and non-paternalistic clinical and advocacy partnerships" (p. 123). They reiterate that a cultural humility framework becomes imperative when acknowledging the intersections of multiple identities. It helps providers listen to their patients' stories and admit that "they do not know when they truly do not know" (p. 119). According to Gottlieb (2021), the concept of cultural humility encompasses three major principles: (1) committing oneself to an ongoing process of compassionate self-awareness and inquiry; (2) being open and teachable and striving to see culture as clients see them, rather than as workers define them; and (3) considering social systems and attending to the power and privilege that have shaped reality as both workers and clients experience it. Practitioners need to be aware of their own considerable power—both real and perceived—within the worker–client relationship and commit to equalizing that imbalance to the greatest extent possible. Cultural humility acknowledges that an individual's worldview is not superior to others' worldviews, respects differences, honors the lived experience of others (Hook et al., 2013), and requires stepping outside one's individual identity to honor the unique experience of others (McGee-Avila, 2018). Providers need to put the client experience into cultural context by questioning what in the environment may influence how the individual feels about self and others (Fisher-Borne et al., 2015). Cultural humility involves attending to power imbalances, partnering with clients, and advocating with them for changes (Tervalon & Murray-Garcia, 1998) and is in direct contrast to *implicit bias*—being unaware of having stereotypes or biased perceptions about a marginalized group (Sloane & Petra, 2021).

The recent update of the Educational Policy and Accreditation Standards (CSWE, 2022) recognizes the important role of social work educators to adopt models of cultural humility to effectively teach, model, and evaluate anti-racist and anti-oppressive social work practice. Social workers need to "demonstrate cultural humility by applying critical reflection, self-awareness, and self-regulation to manage the influence of bias, power, privilege, and values in working with clients and constituencies, acknowledging them as experts of their own lived experiences" (CSWE, 2022, p. 10).

Teaching From a Social Justice Perspective

Hackman (2005) postulates five key components in teaching from a social justice perspective: tools for content mastery, tools for critical thinking, tools for actions and social change, tools for personal reflection, and tools for awareness of multicultural group dynamics. Mastery of social justice content involves critical analysis of "factual information, historical contextualization, and a macro-to-micro content analysis" (p. 104). A broader representation of historical and factual information other than that presented in educational materials or mainstream media is essential. Based on these five key components useful in teaching from a social justice perspective, Kwong (2020) described and evaluated a set of reflective, experiential, and collaborative activities in an identity and social justice course designed for master-level social work students and found that students recognized the need to examine the social justice content with a critical perspective because historical and factual information is often written by members of dominant groups. Through class activities and discussion, students from privileged and dominant groups are encouraged to reflect on their privilege and power in the society and are made aware that they are often socialized not to see their privilege, not to see their life and its privileges as the "norms" for society, and that they have done nothing to earn such privilege (Hackman, 2005; Kwong, 2020). Students from subordinate or marginalized groups can reflect on and share how internalized oppression has impacted their lives and communities.

Social justice education helps students use the critical analysis of issues of oppression to provide both deep knowledge and a direction for the application of that knowledge in their lives (Hackman, 2005). Through brief lectures and class discussion, students learn how to use information to critique systems of power and inequality in society, understand who benefits from said systems, and consider what aspects of social structures keep those inequalities alive (Kwong, 2020). Instead of adopting a didactic model of teaching, the instructor facilitates an interactive and collaborative process that enhances student engagement, participation, and critical analysis of the subject matter and that represents a novel pedagogical approach, one different from the traditional approach of content mastery (Hackman, 2005). Students' responses and instructor's assessments showed that the educational tools proposed by Hackman (2005) could help students learn the concepts of race, racism, oppression, microaggression, power, privilege, intersectionality, and cultural humility and recognize the effects of racism, oppression, and other forms of bigotry on the physical and mental well-being of marginalized and vulnerable populations (Kwong, 2020).

Hamilton-Mason and Schneider (2018) suggest that incorporating a workshop-based learning approach may also be a viable way to expand social work education and allow students to learn the structures of racial oppression and how to advocate for oppressed populations on the individual and systemic levels, which are important educational goals for social work students. Such an approach demonstrates that cultivating an anti-racism stance in social work students is achieved by several major elements: activity-based learning, conversations with peers holding different experiences and perspectives, a discussion of White privilege, a focus on language, and the inclusion of concrete strategies and action plans (Hamilton-Mason & Schneider, 2018). Anti-racism is more effectively taught when taken beyond the classroom and into an intensive workshop environment so that it is not only integrated into the standard social work curriculum but also taught in a workshop format.

Conclusion

Anti-Asian racism, xenophobia, and discrimination negatively impacts Asian Americans' mental health, self-identity, and self-esteem, particularly among adolescents and young adults. To address the impacts of racism and xenophobia against Asian Americans, the GCER (Teasley et al., 2021) recommends several priorities and action steps: develop an anti-racist social work workforce, examine the social work profession to combat racist policies and practices, and expand social work education to address structural inequalities and White privilege and their impacts on marginalized communities.

In this chapter, several critical challenges impacting the development of an anti-racist social work workforce were reviewed. Creating pipelines within social work educational programs that recruit, train, and retain more members of minority racial-ethnic groups is essential for developing an anti-racist social work workforce. A significant gap exists in recruiting and training adequate number of both Asian and Hispanic/Latino social workers. For Black and African American students, significant differences were observed in their pass rates in social work licensing exams as compared with White test-takers. The pass rate disparities highlight possible challenges, constraints, and restrictions affecting test-takers from marginalized communities. The recruitment challenges facing Asian American social workers and low licensing exam pass rates among Black, Hispanic/Latino, or Native Americans/Indigenous peoples were a major concern affecting career options and advancement among them, resulting in a lack of licensed social workers from marginalized populations to serve their specific communities.

Minority students are motivated to become social workers because of their strong desire to serve poor and vulnerable populations and their belief in the profession as the most effective way to support their communities (Daniel, 2011). Social work is a dream career for many Asian Americans because of their idealism of the profession, a strong altruistic vision of social work, and their desire to serve their populations (Kwong, 2018b). However, low salaries and compensation and low occupational status have negatively affected many entering the field (Daniel, 2011; Moriarty & Murray, 2007). Many minority social work students and practitioners shared career-related concerns such as a lack of ability to effect change due to agency bureaucracy, negative views of minority clients living in poverty, and their experiences of prejudice and discrimination within the social work profession (Daniel, 2011). Among Asian American social workers, their perception of discrimination, a glass ceiling, and organizational unfairness may affect their perceived career prospects and their decisions to stay in the job (Kwong, 2018b). Because of these constraints and difficulties, many Asian and minority social workers experienced high levels of work-related stress, secondary trauma, and burnout that might cause them to consider a career change, resulting in increasing challenges in retaining them and causing further service gaps for minority populations (Kwong, 2018b). To enhance recruitment and retention of Asian American social work practitioners, career development and professional growth opportunities must be reflective of their personal needs and values, and professional experiences are very much needed. Adequate representation of an Asian American workforce and the inclusion of Asian Americans in social work literature is essential based on specific social work sectors such as health, mental health, gerontology, school social work, community organization, and policy and planning to serve the diverse needs of Asian American communities. Social workers need to be aware that Asian Americans continue to face discrimination and oppression as obstacles to their career advancement and be conscious of how structural and systemic racism and stereotypes, such as the model minority myth, create barriers for Asian Americans to access physical and mental health services.

Expanding the number and ranks of multilingual and multicultural social workers trained in anti-racist and anti-oppressive practice is critical in eradicating racism and anti-Asian violence. This includes more research and literature that centers race, racism, and White supremacy as major study constructs and explicitly discusses issues of inequity and racial disparities (Corley & Young, 2018; Woo et al., 2018). Schools of social work need to periodically assess the extent to which their curricular and educational content addresses racism, oppression, and racial equity (Teasley et al., 2021). Addressing disparities, inclusion, and anti-Asian racism in social work education can help promote students' active engagement in difficult dialogues about injustice, inequity, and oppression. Social work students who identified as Asian Americans and Asians often face common yet diverse challenges in social work education, including language, cultural identity, career-related stress, and professional development. To eradicate racism and anti-Asian violence, it is necessary for the social work profession to conduct critical self-reflection and raise self-awareness using both the cultural humility framework and social justice perspective that can address systemic racism and White supremacy, from both within the profession and in the larger society. To work toward social justice for Asian Americans, social work educators, scholars, and practitioners need to be aware of our own bias, assumptions, and values, as well as the power dynamics and hierarchies in our interactions with those with whom we work, whether in our research, education, or direct practice.

References

Arrington, P. (2008). *Stress at work: How do social workers cope?* NASW Membership Workforce Study. National Association of Social Workers.

Associations of Social Work Boards. (2022). 2022 ASWB exam pass rate analysis final report. https://www.aswb.org/wp-content/uploads/2022/07/2022-ASWB-Exam-Pass-Rate-Analysis.pdf

Benner, A. D., Wang, Y., Shen, Y., Boyle, A. E., Polk, R., & Cheng, Y.-P. (2018). Racial/ethnic discrimination and well-being during adolescence: A meta-analytic review. *American Psychologist*, 73(7), 855–883. https://psycnet.apa.org/doiLanding?doi=10.1037%2Famp 0000204

Budiman, A., & Ruiz, N. G. (2021). Key facts about Asian Americans, a diverse and growing population. Pew Research Center. https://www.pewresearch.org/fact-tank/2021/04/29/key-facts-about-asian-americans/

Byers, D. S., & Shapiro, J. R. (2019). Renewing the ethics of care for social work under the Trump administration. *Social Work*, 64(2), 175–180. https://doi.org/10.1093/sw/swz008

Chao, M. M., Chiu, C-Y., & Lee, J. S. (2010). Asians as the model minority: Implications for US government's policies. *Asian Journal of Social Psychology*, 13, 44–52. https://doi.org/10.1111/j.1467-839X.2010.01299.x

Corley, N. A., & Young, S. M. (2018). Is social work still racist? A content analysis of recent literature. *Social Work*, 63, 317–326. https://doi.org/10.1093/sw/swy042

Council on Social Work Education (CSWE). (2022). Educational policy and accreditation standards. https://www.cswe.org/accreditation/standards/2022-epas/

Daniel, C. (2011). The path to social work: Contextual determinants of career choice among racial/ethnic minority students. *Social Work Education*, 30(8), 895–910. https://doi.org/10.1080/02615479.2010.520121

Fisher-Borne, M., Cain, J. M., & Martin, S. L. (2015). From mastery to accountability: Cultural humility as an alternative to cultural competence. *Social Work Education*, 34(2), 165–181. http://doi.org/10.1080/026515479.2014.977244

Hackman, H. W. (2005). Five essential components for social justice education. *Equity & Excellence in Education*, 38, 103–109. https://doi.org/10.1080/10665680590935034

Hamilton-Mason, J., & Schneider, S. (2018). Antiracism expanding social work education: A qualitative analysis of the undoing racism workshop experience. *Journal of Social Work Education*, 54(2), 337–348. https://doi.org/10.1080/10437797.2017.1404518

Hook, J. N., Davis, D. E., Owen, J., Worthington, E. L., & Utsey, S. O. (2013). Cultural humility: Measuring openness to culturally diverse clients. *Journal of Counseling Psychology*, 60(3), 353–366. http://doi.org/10.1037/a0032595

Ghosh, A., & Fouad, N. A. (2016). Family influence on careers among Asian parent-child dyads. *Journal of Career Assessment*, 24(2), 318–322. https://doi.org/10.1177/1069072715580417

Gottlieb, M. (2021). The case for a cultural humility framework in social work practice. *Journal of Ethnic & Cultural Diversity in Social Work*, 30(6), 463–481. https://doi.org/10.1080/15313204.2020.1753615

Kwong, K. (2016). Understanding work-related stress and practice of professional self-care – An Innovative pedagogical approach. *International Journal of Higher Education*, 5(4), 41–51. http://dx.doi.org/10.5430/ijhe.v5n4p41

Kwong, K. (2018a). Career choice, barriers, and prospects of Asian American social workers. *International Journal of Higher Education*, 7(6), 1–12. https://doi.org/10.5430/ijhe.v7n6p1

Kwong, K. (2018b). Assessing secondary trauma, compassion satisfaction, and burnout: Implications for professional education for Asian-American social workers. *International Journal of Higher Education*, 7(5), 75–85. https://doi.org/10.5430/ijhe.v7n5p75

Kwong, K. (2020). Teaching microaggressions, identity, and social Justice: A reflective, experiential and collaborative pedagogical approach. *International Journal of Higher Education*, 9(4), 184–198. https://doi.org/10.5430/ijhe.v9n4p184

Kwong, K. (2022). 9.03. Special Populations: Asian. In G. J. G. Asmundson (ed.), *Comprehensive clinical psychology* (2nd ed., vol. 9, pp. 33–51). Elsevier. https://dx.doi.org/10.1016/B978-0-12-818697-8.00071-6.

McGee-Avila, J. (2018, June 23). Practicing cultural humility to transform healthcare [Blog post]. https://www.rwjf.org/en/blog/2018/06/practicing-cultural-humilityto-transform-healthcare.html

McMahon, A., & Allen-Meares, P. (1992). Is social work racist? A content analysis of recent literature. *Social Work, 37*, 533–539. https://doi.org/10.1093/sw/37.6.533

Miller, J. L., & Garran, A. M. (2017). *Racism in the United States: Implications for the helping professions.* Springer.

Moriarty, J., & Murray, J. (2007). Who wants to be a social worker? Using routine published data to identify trends in the numbers of people applying for and completing social work programs in England. *British Journal of Social Work, 37*(4), 715–733.

Nakayama, J. (2021). Joint statement – Social work's call to action against pandemic othering and anti-Asian racism. https://www.cswe.org/CSWE/media/News/Social-Work-Joint-Statement-on-Anti-Asian-Violence-and-Racism.pdf

National Association of Social Workers. (2021). NASW code of ethics. https://www.socialworkers.org/About/Ethics/Code-of-Ethics/Code-of-Ethics-English

Park, Y. (2008). Facilitating injustice: Tracing the role of social workers in the World War II internment of Japanese Americans. *Social Service Review, 82*, 447–483. https://doi.org/10.1086/592361

Poon, O. (2014). "The land of opportunity doesn't apply to everyone": The immigrant experience, race, and Asian American career choices. *Journal of College Student Development, 55*(6), 499–514. https://psycnet.apa.org/doi/10.1353/csd.2014.0056

Salsberg, E., Quigley, L., Mehfoud, N., Acquaviva, K. D., Wyche, K., & Silwa, S. (2017). Profile of the social work workforce. Health Workforce Institute and School of Nursing, George Washington University. https://hsrc.himmelfarb.gwu.edu/sphhs_policy_workforce_facpubs/16

Schmitt, M. T., Branscombe, N. R., Postmes, T., & Garcia, A. (2014). The consequences of perceived discrimination for psychological well-being: A meta-analytic review. *Psychological Bulletin, 140*(4), 921–948. https://doi.org/10.1037/a0035754

Sellers, L., & Hunter, A. (2005). Private pain, public choices: Influence of problems in the family of origin on career choices among a cohort of MSW students. *Social Work Education, 24*(8), 869–881.

Shen, F. C. (2013). The role of internalized stereotyping, parental pressure, and parental support of Asian Americans' choice of college major. *Journal of Multicultural Counseling and Development, 43*, 58–73.

Shih, K. Y., Chang, T. F., & Chen, S. Y. (2019). Impacts of the model minority myth on Asian American individuals and families: Social Justice and critical race feminist perspectives. *Journal of Family Theory & Review, 11*, 412–428. https://doi.org/10.1111/jftr.12342

Shrider, E. A., Kollar, M., Chen, F., & Semega, J. (2021). Income and poverty in the United States: 2020. US Census Bureau, Current Population Reports (P60-273). US Government Publishing Office. https://www.census.gov/content/dam/Census/library/publications/2021/demo/p60-273.pdf

Sloane H., & Petra, M. (2021). Modeling cultural humility: Listening to students' stories of religious identity. *Journal of Social Work Education, 57*(1), 28–39. https://doi.org/10.1080/10437797.2019.1662863

Sue, D. W., Rivera, D. P., Watkins, N. L., Kim, R. H., Kim, S., & Williams, C. D. (2011). Racial dialogues: Challenges faculty of color face in the classroom. *Cultural Diversity and Ethnic Minority Psychology, 17*(3), 331–340. https://doi.org/10.1037/a0024190

Teasley, M. L., McCarter, S., Woo, B., Conner, L. R., Spencer, M. S., & Green, T. (2021). Eliminate racism (Grand Challenges for Social Work initiative working paper no. 26). American Academy of Social Work & Social Welfare.

Tervalon, M., & Murray-Garcia, J. (1998). Cultural humility versus cultural competence: A critical distinction in defining physician training outcomes in multicultural education. *Journal of Health are for the Poor and Underserved, 9*(2), 117–125. http://doi.org/10.1353/hpu.2010.0233

Torpy, S. J. (2000). Native American women and coerced sterilization: On the Trail of Tears in the 1970s. *American Indian Culture and Research Journal, 24*(2), 1–22. http://dx.doi.org/10.17953/aicr.24.2.7646013460646042

Wilson, G., & McCrystal, P. (2007). Motivations and career aspirations of MSW students in Northern Ireland. *Social Work Education, 26*(1), 35–52. https://doi.org/10.1080/02615470601036534

Woo, B., Cano, M., & Pitt-Catsouphes, M. (2022). Research note: Equity and justice in social work explicit curriculum. *Journal of Social Work Education 58*(3), 611–618. https://doi.org/10.1080/10437797.2021.1895931

Woo, B., Figuereo, V., Rosales, R., Wang, K., & Sabur, K. (2018). Where is race and ethnicity in social work? A content analysis. *Social Work Research, 42*, 180–186. https://doi.org/10.1093/swr/svy010

Yoo, H., Miller, M., & Yip, P. (2015). Validation of the internalization of model minority myth measure and its link to academic performance and psychological adjustment among Asian American adolescents. *Cultural Diversity and Ethnic Minority Psychology, 21*, 237–246. https://doi.org/10.1037/a0037648

Zucker, H. A., & Greene, D. (2018). Potential child health consequences of the federal policy separating immigrant children from their parents. *Journal of the American Medical Association, 320*, 541–542. https://dx.doi.org/10.1001/jama.2018.10905

15
Service Access to Depression Treatment
Mental Health Help-Seeking Sources Among Asian Americans

Patrick Leung, Monit Cheung, and Carol A. Leung

Significance and Aim

Asian Americans represent the fastest-growing immigrant group in the United States (Pew Research Center, 2021), with a 96% increase from 10.5 million to 20.6 million between 2000 and 2020 (US Census Bureau, 2020). Despite this significant growth, Asian Americans have the lowest service utilization rate for mental health services, including psychotropic medications, outpatient and inpatient services, and professional consultation, compared to other racial groups (Center for Behavioral Health Statistics and Quality, 2021). Although recognizing the lack of research on Asian Americans, the National Institutes of Health (NIH) allocated only 0.17% of its budget to studying the needs of this minority group (Đoàn et al., 2019).

In the context of COVID-19, recent studies have explored the impact of cultural values, ethnic identities, racial discrimination, "model minority" stereotypes, and hate crimes on the unique health and mental health concerns of Asian Americans (Lee & Waters, 2021; Shahid et al., 2021). Yet research often focuses on specific Asian subgroups (e.g., Vietnamese) or isolated issues (e.g., acculturation stress), making it challenging to compare and analyze data across diverse Asian populations (Kim et al., 2021).

Although the model minority stereotype often portrays Asian Americans as a monolithic group, healthcare issues within the Asian Americans population have been a subject of research, recognizing that this population comprises individuals with cultural ties spanning more than 52 countries

---

Patrick Leung, Monit Cheung, and Carol A. Leung, *Service Access to Depression Treatment* In: *Addressing Anti-Asian Racism with Social Work, Advocacy, and Action*. Edited by: Meirong Liu and Keith T. Chan, Oxford University Press.
© Oxford University Press 2024. DOI: 10.1093/oso/9780197672242.003.0015

(Asian American Health Initiative, 2023). Acknowledging unique historical, social, and demographic factors, Yoshikawa et al. (2016) emphasized the importance of conducting large-scale and small-scale intersectional studies to understand Asian Americans populations. By examining ethnic variations in localized settings, researchers can gather diverse perspectives and comparative data that accurately represent the distinct experiences of different Asian American subgroups. This approach aims to inform practice implications that address the specific needs of individuals in particular locations.

Chapter Aim

This chapter provides an overview and analysis of six journal articles that adopt a comparative approach, utilizing data collected from the same study across six Asian ethnicities. While most studies on Asian Americans focus on a single ethnic group and selectively use data from a specific survey, the authors of these articles aimed to compare findings across the six ethnicities. The inspiration for this comparative analysis originated from a small-scale needs assessment study conducted in the Greater Area of Houston, Texas, the fourth largest city in the United States. Consequently, the data presented in this chapter represent a localized interethnic study. In 2018, the Asian population in Houston accounted for less than 6% of the total population (Houston, Texas Population, 2018). However, by 2023, Asian Americans had increased to approximately 6.87% of the city's population, with nearly 160,000 individuals residing there (US Census Bureau, 2023). It is important to note that ethnic breakdowns are only available from the 2000 Census, which indicated that Chinese comprised 23% and Vietnamese represented 31% of the Asian population in Houston (Infoplease, 2020).

With data from 1,840 Asian Americans expressing their mental health and service needs, we examine depression prevalences and service utilization preferences among diverse Asian American populations.[1] After examining mental health needs, this chapter presents significant survey findings regarding the prevalence of depression and service preferences among six distinct Asian American subgroups. The data were collected using the same methodology within the same timeframe to enable meaningful comparison. Based on the respondents' input, we discuss culturally responsive principles to enhance service accessibility and utilization for Asian Americans families.

Depression and Asian Americans

Prevalence. The Asian population in the United States comprises six primary ethnic origins, namely Vietnamese, Asian Indian, Chinese, Filipino, Korean, Japanese, and Pakistani, accounting for 87% of this population (Pew Research Center, 2023; US Census Bureau, 2022). However, when it comes to an understanding of the mental health status of Asian Americans, there is a lack of differentiation by specifical ethnicities within the diverse diaspora of Asian communities. This information gap leads to cross-sectional studies identifying factors attributed to the unique cultures and characteristics of Asian Americans ethnic groups in the United States. According to Lee et al. (2020), mental health stigma and shame often prevent Asian Americans from reporting depressive symptoms. For example, Leung and Cheung (2008) examined domestic violence rates across six ethnic groups. A common challenge in these studies is the difficulty in comparing depression prevalence data among Asian ethnicities due to low response rates focusing on mental health as a concern.

Contributing Factors. Sociocultural factors include social support, acculturative stress, marital status, financial status, education, gender, and age. For example, Leung et al. (2010) and Mui and Kang (2006) found that Vietnamese Americans ($n = 572$) and Asian American immigrants in general ($n = 407$) associated depression treatment with healthcare services. In other words, Vietnamese clients might hesitate to express challenges in adapting to a new country and often refrain from seeking help. In the case of Korean Americans, Jang et al. (2006) conducted a study with 230 participants and found a positive relationship between health perception and mental health status. Specifically, chronic illnesses were significant predictors of depressive symptoms (Jang & Chiriboga, 2011; Niti et al., 2007), and poorly perceived physical health was also associated with depression (Gautam et al., 2011; Ina et al., 2011). Ina et al. (2011) found that mobility acted as a health promoter for respondents from Korea ($n = 300$), while self-care activities were linked to a reduction in depressive symptoms, as shared by respondents from China ($n = 336$).

When Asian Americans are immigrants or first-generation immigrant parents, it is common to hear them express stress symptoms due to cultural adjustment challenges (Xu & Chi, 2013). When adjusting to a new environment, Asian immigrants with high acculturation levels experience more depressive symptoms than those with lower acculturation levels (Jang & Chiriboga, 2011; Kim, 2016). Jang and Chiriboga (2011) found that social activities were protective factors against depression, but solely promoting social participation might not yield positive outcomes even for highly acculturated individuals.

Access to Mental Health Services and Help-Seeking Behaviors. The Center for Behavioral Health Statistics and Quality (2021) reported data from 2015–2019 that Asian Americans populations had the lowest utilization rate of outpatient mental health services (5.9%), mental health medication (3.6%), and mental health inpatient services (0.6%) compared to other racial groups. Additionally, Asian Americans families often face challenges accessing resources due to language barriers, transportation difficulties, and mental health stigma. Additional barriers include service accessibility and preferences for informal and culturally relevant solutions/resources to mental health problems (Derr, 2016; Hechanova & Waelde, 2017). One study shows that 30.9% of Asian Americans do not consider themselves fluent in reading or speaking English, which contributes to low service utilization, mainly when translation services are not accessible (Schlossberg, 2021). Another study found (1) community mental health in proximity and (2) lack of culturally appropriate services as the main factors associated with Asian Americans' low utilization rate of mental health services (Augsberger et al., 2015).

In addition to the stigma surrounding mental health problems, Asian Americans often hesitate to seek mental health services due to various sociocultural factors. For example, Laditka et al. (2011) studied 62 Chinese and Vietnamese Americans who perceived the maintenance of cognitive health as burdensome for seniors (p. 1214). Many immigrants prefer traditional methods, such as acupuncture, herbal medicine, or religious consultation to heal pain, physically or emotionally. They choose alternative methods that entail less stigma or shame compared to therapeutic or pharmaceutical treatments (Aung et al., 2013; Hechanova & Waelde, 2017). Many Asian families rely on family and friend support even though they know mental health services are available (Lee & Chan, 2009; Picco et al., 2016).

Current research highlights the significant influence of sociocultural determinants on mental health outcomes. In the context of Asian American families, there is a tendency to attribute depression to personal misfortune or physical weakness (Yang et al., 2013). This belief can hinder the willingness to seek external help. To test the applicability of these statements across Asian Americans ethnicities, this chapter explores comparative data on depression prevalence among six distinct Asian Americans subgroups and their preferred sources of support. By integrating the prevalence data with practice implications, we aim to gain insights into help-seeking behaviors when faced with mental health concerns.

Methods

Six Asian Ethnicities in One Community Study

With internal review board (IRB) approval from the University of Houston, the authors conducted a needs assessment project in various Asian ethnic communities in Houston, Texas, the fourth-largest city in the United States. We recruited subjects by a convenience sampling method to hear the voice of the Asian population about the needs and concerns in their respective community.

In the United States, seven groups make up 87% of all Asian Americans: Chinese (24%), Asian Indian (22%), Filipino (16%), Vietnamese (10%), Korean (8%), Japanese (4%), and Pakistani (3%) (US Census Bureau, 2022). However, due to a low response rate from some Filipino communities, statistical data for this ethnic group could not be included in our analysis. Consequently, our statistical analyses focused on the remaining six ethnic groups, comprising more than 40 respondents in each group. Specifically, the ethnic subgroups included in our analysis, in descending order of respondent numbers, were Vietnamese, Chinese, Korean, Asian Indian, Pakistani, and Japanese. This chapter will summarize the findings presented and published in six articles, focusing on identifying similarities, differences, and the diverse cultural and ethnic characteristics of these findings.

It is helpful to understand the methods used in the survey study before summarizing the results for ethnic comparisons. Due to the Asian belief in collective participation, random sampling was not feasible. Therefore, we recruited subjects in cultural activities and Asian gathering places, festivals, and language classes. We invited community leaders as our honorary consultants to ask their members to participate in this assessment survey.

The recruitment goal of obtaining 1,500 respondents within a six-month data collection period was successfully achieved, in part due to the cooperation and support of respected university professors who acted as leaders in the study.

This convenience sampling procedure recruited a final sample of 1,840 respondents. These consented respondents completed an anonymous survey in English, Chinese, Korean, or Vietnamese. Before conducting the study, we worked with three bilingual researchers to pilot-test the translated versions with input from 340 respondents to validate the survey structure and wording. During the survey, bilingual research assistants were available to help fill out the survey; none of the respondents requested translation assistance.

The Instrument

This chapter used an interethnic comparative approach to analyze the contents presented in our articles with data collected from six Asian Americans subgroups from the same community survey (Cheung et al., 2011, 2013; Leung et al., 2010, 2011, 2012a, 2012b). These articles performed separate statistical reports from a dataset collected for a community survey to better understand six Asian ethnic subgroups: Korean, Japanese, Vietnamese, Chinese, Asian Indian, and Pakistani, respectively. Before conducting the study, we tested the survey's face and content validity in a prevalence study of partner abuse (Leung & Cheung, 2008). The survey had 24 questions on mental health concerns, a 25-item depression scale, 10 mental health helping sources, and the respondent demographics. With a 4-point scale (0 = None, 1 = Mild, 2 = Moderate, 3 = Serious) to indicate a concern or need, the answer measured the severity of each of the 24 mental health symptoms observed by someone the respondent knew. An average score was computed to indicate the respondent's mental health concern.

In terms of depression, Part II of the Hopkins Symptoms Checklist (HSCL-25), composed of 15 questions about depressive symptoms with a 4-point response scale (1 = Not at all, 2 = A little, 3 = Quite a bit, and 4 = Extremely) was used. The HSCL identified "symptomatic" depression when the average score was higher than or equal to 1.75 (Parloff et al., 1954). HSCL-25 has been verified as reliable when used with Asian populations (such as Cambodian, Chinese, and Vietnamese), with a coefficient alpha of

.89 for the Anxiety subscale and .92 for the Depression subscale (Lhewa et al., 2007; Silove et al., 2007). In Asian immigrant studies, HSCL-25 consistently shows a high correlation between the total scores and severe emotional distress of unspecified diagnoses (Hinton et al., 2004; Pernice & Brook, 1996).

Regarding mental health care sources, the survey had a multiple-response question identifying preferred help-seeking channels for mental health issues: "Who did you consult when facing difficulties or concerns mentioned previously?" Respondents could check one or more answers and provide additional helping sources they preferred.

Data Analysis Procedures

The six articles utilized Chi-square tests to analyze the relationship between "having symptomatic depression" (yes/no) and other categorical variables: gender (male and female), marital status (married and not married), employment (employed and unemployed), and educational level (high school or below, some college, bachelor's degree, master's degree, and PhD). We used independent t-tests to address the relationship between depression (yes/no) and the following interval/ratio-level variables: age, years lived in the United States, number of generations living in the household, and levels of concern. Concerns included access to medical care, language barriers, chronic pain, and anxiety symptoms. Significant variables were then entered into a logistic regression model to identify factors that might contribute to depressive symptoms.

To compare data across six Asian subgroups, we summarize findings from this cross-sectional community survey for two reasons. First, the survey is a comparative tool within the same timeframe using the same instruments (HSCL-25 and Care Access Checklist) to test the results from two variables across six ethnicities to study depression prevalences and service preferences. Second, the survey serves to identify individual and group data. As mentioned before, the computation score from the HSCL-25 measures each respondent's depression problem, which we use to compute each ethnic group's depression prevalence rate. The Care Access Checklist provided additional information on individual service preferences, enabling a comparison of preference ranking among the ethnic group. We used SPSS 27th edition to analyze the data and identified similarities and differences across the six ethnic groups.

Results

This community study included a convenience sample of 1,840 respondents. In this sample, 1,508 (82%) respondents provided both depression data and help-seeking preferences from six Asian subgroups: 572 Vietnamese, 516 Chinese, 205 Korean, 96 Asian Indian, 76 Pakistani, and 43 Japanese.

Among these respondents, the average length of residency in the United States was 13.28 years (standard deviation [SD] = 9.87). There were more females (55.0%) than males (43.6%), with 1.4% not indicating gender. They were about 43 years old (SD = 16.29). Their marital status included single (24.2%), married (63.5%), and divorced (3.2%). Most (65.5%) were employed, while almost one-third (32.1%) were not working (unemployed or not actively looking). Nearly half (48.2%) had a bachelor's degree or higher, and the other half (47%) had a high school education or less. Their median annual household income was at the $30,000–40,000 level. Almost half (44.7%) of the respondents lived in a household of four or more people, and 12.8% reported three or more generations residing together. On average, one child (mean = 1.37, SD = 1.64) lived with them.

Depression Prevalence in Six Asian Ethnic Subgroups

In this sample, 1,666 (90.5%) respondents provided answers on the depression scale with a prevalence rate of 25.3%. As reported by 1,508 respondents in the six identified Asian subgroups, the depression rate was 28.7%, ranging from 11.6% to 30.2% by ethnicity (see Table 15.1 and Figure 15.1).

Help-Seeking Preferences Among Six Asian American Subgroups

Regarding help-seeking behaviors, the data collected in this study pertained to respondents' help choices rather than actual service utilization. We used their preference rates to estimate potential service access. When facing a mental health crisis, they would think of accessing the following:

- Friends and relatives: 25% to 53.3%
- Physicians: 18% to 50.2%

Table 15.1 Comparing depression prevalences in six Asian ethnic groups

Asian ethnicity	Number of respondents	Depression prevalence (%)[a]
Vietnamese	572	30.2
Pakistani	76	26.3
Korean	205	18.5
Asian Indian	96	17.7
Chinese	516	17.4
Japanese	43	11.6
Total	1,508	28.7

[a]Depression rates in descending order

Depression Prevalences*: Six Asian Subgroups

Subgroup	n	Depression Rate of 2018
Vietnamese	572	30.2%
Chinese	516	17.4%
Korean	205	18.5%
Asian Indian	96	17.7%
Pakistani	76	26.3%
Japanese	43	11.6%

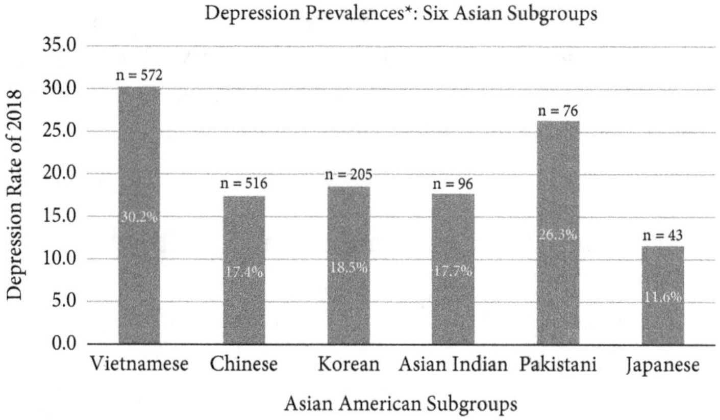

Figure 15.1 Depression prevalences.
Depression rates in descending order based on the number of respondents.

- Religious leaders: 5% to 39.5%
- Mental health professionals: 3.0% to 21.1%
- Herbalists: 1.9% to 20.3%

Notably, a portion of respondents in each ethnic group preferred doing nothing in response to their mental health issues, with percentages ranging from 5.2% to 23.3%.

As shown in Figure 15.2, after computing the scores based on the participants' expressed preferences, we determined the top six ranked helping sources by ethnicity. Results indicate that the participants' most preferred

SERVICE ACCESS TO DEPRESSION TREATMENT 279

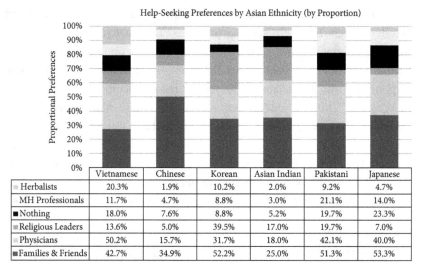

Figure 15.2 Help sources for family and relationship problems.

Table 15.2 Ranking of helping sources: preferences by Asian subgroups

Subgroups	Family & friends	Physicians	Religious consultation	Nothing	Mental health professionals	Herbalists
Vietnamese	2	1	5	4	6	3
Chinese	1	2	4	3	5	6
Koreans	1	3	2	6[c]	4	6[c]
Asian Indian	1	2	3	4	5	6
Pakistani	1	3[c]	5[c]	5[c]	3[c]	6
Japanese	1	2	5	3	4	6
Total Score	7	13	24	25	27	33
Rank[b]	1st	2nd	3rd	4th	5th	6th

Ranked preference of helping sources ($n = 1{,}508$)[a]

[a] From the most to the least preferred on a 6-point scale: 1 = Highly preferred to 6 = Least preferred.
[b] Rank is ordered from 1st = Highest preference score to 6th rank = Lowest preference score.
[c] Tied rank.

sources of help, in descending order, were family and friends, physicians, religious consultation, doing nothing, mental health professionals, and herbalists. Interestingly, the overall preference ranking system aligns with the responses from the Asian Indian subgroup, as demonstrated in Table 15.2.

Most respondents turned to extended families and friends for comfort or advice regarding help-seeking priorities. Data across these six ethnic subgroups show that more Vietnamese respondents preferred families and friends over other types of support. Pakistani, Asian Indian, and Vietnamese respondents saw physicians as the second most welcomed helping source. In contrast, Chinese and Korean Americans sought help from religious leaders. Additionally, herbalists were mentioned as a third-ranked source of assistance, particularly by Koreans and Asian Indians. These findings demonstrate the ethnic diversity in the responses, indicating that respondents from different subgroups have varied preferences and perspectives regarding mental health professionals as a potential choice for seeking help.

Statistical Results Connecting Help-Seeking to Depression

Using the survey data, we published six articles, separately for each of the subgroups indicated, with statistical findings related to depression and help-seeking preferences. These articles aimed to identify the strengths and barriers encountered in one of the six Asian Americans subgroups during mental health crises. Below is a summary of the significant results emphasizing predictive factors of depression.

Vietnamese Americans (Leung et al., 2010).

1. Vietnamese Americans with income loss were two times more likely to have depressive symptoms than those without a problem regarding income.
2. Compared to males, Vietnamese American females were 1.5 times more likely to have depressive symptoms.
3. An increase in family or relationship concerns increased the likelihood of depressive symptoms by 74%.
4. Increased health concerns and basic needs also increased the likelihood of depressive symptoms by 67.3% and 16.9%, respectively.
5. A one-year increase in age raised the likelihood of having depressive symptoms by 4.3%.
6. Vietnamese Americans who were employed and married could reduce the likelihood of having depressive symptoms by 50.4% and 70.2%, respectively.

7. Those who used religious consultation were 1.1 times more likely to have depressive symptoms than those who did not consult a spiritual leader.

Chinese Americans (Leung et al., 2012a).

1. Chinese Americans with anxiety symptoms were 24.8 times more likely to have depressive symptoms than people who did not have anxiety symptoms.
2. Chinese Americans who had acculturation concerns were 1.71 times more likely to have depressive symptoms than those who did not have acculturation concerns.
3. Chinese Americans who experienced domestic violence were 1.32 times more likely to have depressive symptoms than people who did not experience domestic violence.
4. Male Chinese Americans were more likely (53.5%) than female Chinese Americans (39.1%) to seek help from a physician.
5. Female Chinese Americans were more likely (84.2%) than male Chinese Americans (72.4%) to seek help from friends.
6. Those not employed were likelier than those with a job to think that their family problem would take care of itself or to seek help from herbalists, physicians, or friends.
7. Those with an annual income lower than $20,001 were more likely (29.3%) than those with higher income (8.3%) to seek help from herbalists.

Korean Americans (Cheung et al., 2011).

1. Korean Americans with depressive symptoms were significantly younger, more anxious, lower in educational levels, had less annual household income, and had more basic need concerns, family relationship problems, and health issues than those without depressive symptoms.
2. Korean Americans with anxiety issues were more likely to have depressive symptoms by 240 times than those without.

Asian Indian Americans (Leung et al., 2012b).

1. Asian Indians having depressive symptoms were more likely than Asian Indians without depressive symptoms to have faced health, social, and family relationship issues.
2. Asian Indians with anxiety problems were 11.344 times more likely to have depressive symptoms than those without anxiety problems.
3. Each additional unit in having family or relationship issues increased the likelihood of having depressive symptoms by 3.747 times.
4. Those currently employed were 90.9% less likely to have depressive symptoms than the unemployed.

Pakistani Americans (Leung et al., 2011).

1. Pakistani Americans with depressive symptoms had significantly more concerns about income loss, public financial assistance, and family issues than those without depressive symptoms.
2. Concerns about public financial assistance increased the likelihood of depressive symptoms by 4.67 times.
3. Each unit experiencing loss of income on the 4-point scale increased the likelihood of having depressive symptoms by 4.55 times.
4. Visiting physicians for mental health issues predicted an increased likelihood of having depressive symptoms by 3.18 times.
5. Each unit increase in family or relationship concerns on the 4-point scale increased the likelihood of having depressive symptoms by 1.43 times.

Japanese Americans (Cheung et al., 2013).

1. Japanese American women and those with health issues are more likely to seek help from religious leaders than their counterparts.
2. The overall statistical model shows significance when having health issues, anxiety symptoms, and a master's degree are included to predict depressive symptoms.

Table 15.3 and Table 15.4 summarize these depression prevalence findings and highlight three principles for assessing the mental health needs and concerns among Asian American clients by ethnic group. First, their

Table 15.3 Sociocultural variables and types of concerns: Significant predictive power toward depression

Predictive factors	Vietnamese	Chinese	Koreans	Asian Indians	Pakistani	Japanese
Age	Older +4.3%		Younger			
Education			Lower level			Master's degree
Employment	Unemployed	Unemployed		Unemployed		
Gender	Female ×1.5	Male				
Marital	Not married					
Socio-economic status	Lower	Lower	Lower			

Table 15.4 Concerns presented based on statistical analyses in six Asian ethnic subgroups

Type of concern	Vietnamese	Chinese	Koreans	Asian Indians	Pakistani	Japanese
Acculturation		High ×1.71				
Anxiety		High ×24.8	High ×240	High ×11.34		High
Basic needs		High +16.9%	High			
Domestic violence		High ×1.32				
Health issues	High +67.3%		High	High		High
Family/Relationship	High +74%		High	High ×3.75	High ×1.43	
Financial/Income	High ×2				High ×4.67	
Social/Community issues			High	High		

"+" indicates depression increased in percentage when the undesired intensity of this condition has increased by one unit.

"×" indicates the number of times depression is likely to increase when the undesired intensity of this condition increases by one unit.

sociocultural demographics helped professionals consider multicultural backgrounds before offering assistance. These variables include age, education, employment, gender, marital status, and socioeconomic status. Assessment should not be limited to these factors; the statistics supported them with diverse or inconsistent findings. For example, in an ethnic group (Vietnamese) advancing one year in age, the likelihood of having depression could rise by 4.3%, but in another subgroup (Korean), the finding was the opposite.

Second, even though Asian Americans may not seek external help, they respect professionals and recognize their wisdom and experience when interacting with them. Third, Asian Americans emphasize respecting multicultural values congruent with traditional cultures and religious beliefs. As a result, even when they do not turn to mental health services for help, it does not mean a lack of knowledge. Instead, they may prefer cultural or religious consultation aligned with their traditional values. Some may be concerned about showing their inability to access services or ask professionals questions. Different Asian ethnic groups may have unique perspectives to present their concerns, individually and collectively, based on their sociocultural background. However, we found from the statistical findings within the same study by ethnic differences that most respondents focused on finding solutions. Therefore, by approaching these findings from a collective viewpoint, we can gain insight into the essentiality of transforming problems into benefits for our clients. When we highlight the cultural importance of accessing services, clients become more open to learning about mental health and services.

Drawing from the experiences of these six Asian Americans groups, Table 15.5 provides valuable factors and depression predictors, underscoring the importance of internal and external perspectives from various sources. Consequently, the problems that led to depression can be turned into advantages when practitioners (1) collaborate with multiple professionals, (2) assist clients in developing a knowledge base about mental health for prevention before treatment becomes necessary, and (3) promote self-learning and self-care to mitigate the impact of stigma on patients and their caregivers. As a recommendation, practitioners may reframe underutilization as an opportunity to initiate addressing concerns and meeting needs. Establishing a motivational plan while collaborating with other professionals can contribute to the long-term sustainability of services.

Highlights of Practice Implications

We summarize the practice implications of these six subgroups concerning service access issues and help-seeking sources to treat mental health problems.

Table 15.5 Predicting factors and recommendations connecting to depression affecting six Asian subgroups

	Helpful factors (Reduced the likelihood of depressive symptoms)	Depression predictors (Raised the possibility of depressive symptoms)
Internal (personal and family)	- Being married - Being employed - Basic needs fulfilled	- Health issues - Family/Relationship concerns - Anxiety symptoms - Lower annual household income - Unemployed - Domestic violence
External (environmental factors)	- Collaborate with medical professionals - Remove stigma + encourage mental health awareness - Provide community education - Deliver multicultural training - Address underutilization of professional services - Design family-oriented services - Encourage spiritual support - Value traditional methods	- Basic needs concerns - Social/Community issues - Financial problems - Acculturation concerns

Vietnamese Americans (Leung et al., 2010).

- Most Vietnamese Americans chose not to use mental health services. Their emotional symptoms became an alerting sign for seeking spiritual support to improve their well-being.
- Since Asian American people value informal support, practitioners continued learning from Vietnamese clients to promote cultural humility and enhance treatment efficacy.
- Even though medical treatment was preferred, Vietnamese clients would see mental health practitioners if physicians or religious leaders referred them.

Chinese Americans (Leung et al., 2012a).

- Although Chinese Americans might not report depression or use mental health services, they know the connection between depressive symptoms and anxiety, domestic violence, and acculturation problems.

- Even though mental health service utilization and shame/stigma were closely related, Chinese Americans valued seeking advice from relatives and friends.
- There was an urgent need for advocacy and educational programs to promote mental health concepts in the Chinese American community. Community education must focus on dispelling the model minority myth, removing the stigma facing mental health patients and their families, and promoting healthy and positive mental health.
- Engaging physicians in the treatment process helps mental health professionals collaborate with healthcare professionals for mental illness prevention.

Korean Americans (Cheung et al., 2011).

- Korean Americans with lower annual household incomes, having concerns about health issues, and having anxiety were likely to exhibit depressive symptoms.
- Korean Americans would seek advice from friends or physicians for mental health problems.
- Most Korean Americans did not acknowledge the importance of psychological help or accept early intervention from mental health professionals. Thus, these professionals must provide educational information before making referrals.
- Culturally appropriate assessments that helped practitioners understand healthcare and income concerns were closely related to mental health service utilization.

Asian Indian Americans (Leung et al., 2012b).

- Asian Indian immigrants who did not seek professional help trusted physicians to help them reduce physical symptoms.
- Physicians and mental health professionals collaborate to help Asian Indian Americans access treatment options.
- It is essential to deliver culturally relevant practices to assess Asian Indian clients' belief systems and attitudes.

Pakistani Americans (Leung et al., 2011).

- Pakistani Americans visited physicians for mental health issues when these issues were related to family relationships and financial problems.
- Pakistani Americans saw depression from a symbolic perspective (i.e., as a physical weakness that required to medical attention). Helping them understand the importance of symptom reduction provided a concrete channel for them to reach appropriate mental health services.
- Even with high expectations for building family relationships, Pakistani clients discussed discord in arranged marriages and mismatched cultural expectations.
- Listening to clients' healthcare expectations helped Pakistani clients connect to culturally acceptable services.

Japanese Americans (Cheung et al., 2013).

- Attentive listening helped the Japanese develop positive attitudes toward professional help.
- Japanese Americans with a strong healthcare focus tended to minimize the impact of social stigma caused by their mental health disclosure. Therefore, community educators should collaborate with medical professionals to break down treatment barriers and raise public awareness about mental health.
- Mass media information could be a tool to help Japanese clients process the meaning of well-being, increase the importance of positive health, and improve treatment concordance.

Based on this comparative lens, practice implications based on data from these six ethnic-specific groups could be consolidated into eight helping tips to reduce risks and generate strengths. Table 15.6 lists these practice recommendations to promote clients' engagement in prevention and intervention when they share mental health challenges. These research–practice integrated strategies help practitioners and researchers use culturally relevant approaches to work with families and communities.

The objective is to foster a strong alliance between clients and workers while addressing barriers that may hinder the fulfillment of clients'

Table 15.6 Practice recommendations generated from statistical results from six ethnic groups

Mental health professionals emphasize their work to:	Vietnamese	Chinese	Koreans	Asian Indians	Pakistani	Japanese
Collaborate with medical professionals	✓	✓	✓	✓	✓	✓
Remove stigma and encourage mental health awareness	✓	✓	✓	✓	✓	✓
Address underutilization and provide cultural relevant services	✓	✓	✓	✓		
Provide community education	✓	✓	✓			✓
Deliver multicultural training	✓	✓		✓	✓	
Design family-oriented services	✓	✓				✓
Encourage spiritual support	✓	✓				
Value traditional methods	✓	✓				

priorities. By incorporating these priorities into the service delivery system, professionals can effectively collaborate with Asian American clients and their families to enhance service accessibility by establishing partnerships with medical professionals and promote prevention activities within various communities to combat mental health stigma. With these two types of worker-client-community collaborative effort, practitioners will not view Asian Americans' underutilization as a weakness but as an opportunity for clients to actively participate in their treatment, contribute to public education initiatives, and engage with their communities in addressing mental health concerns.

Discussions and Implications

In general, mental health services are not explicitly designed to tailor to the uniqueness of any particular Asian American group. Considering its population of more than 2 million, Houston is known for its cultural diversity, and it is crucial for the city to actively promote positive mental health while considering the racial and ethnic backgrounds of its residents in service delivery. This study reveals that the prevalence rate of depression among the six Asian American subgroups examined is higher (28.7%) compared to a range reported in another study of three subgroups (Southeast Asian, South Asians, and East Asians) in New York City (9–19%) (Misa et al., 2020). Similarly, a post-COVID study funded by the NIH encompassing all age groups and populations reported rates from 9.2% to 17.2% (Goodwin et al., 2022). A study by the Centers for Disease Control and Prevention involving US adults reported a rate of 18.5% (Lee et al., 2023). This study highlights the substantial demand for mental health services by examining the data presented in six articles to support the needs and service preferences among Asian Americans. It reveals that Asian American individuals do not prioritize help from mental health professionals. This study has a limitation due to its use of data from a community survey in the greater Houston area that may not be generalizable to other locations in the United States. However, these findings underscore the cultural diversity within Houston's Asian population and emphasize the urgent need for mental health services tailored to the city's reputation for ethnic diversity.

Problem-Solving Versus Help-Seeking

Encouraging problem-solving among clients can promote help-seeking behaviors. Mental health practitioners, including social workers, are crucial in guiding clients to initiate their needs to deal with personal challenges. This study suggests emphasizing the importance of family care as an effective solution. By shifting perspectives, individuals experiencing depressive symptoms may be more inclined to access mental health services for early intervention and prevention. Asian Americans, understanding the advantages of seeking help for preventive assessment, can perceive help-seeking as essential for their overall well-being. Professionals can effectively encourage help-seeking behavior by emphasizing the positive outcomes and the solutions provided by mental health services.

Another limitation of this study is its use of secondary data. Nevertheless, the integrated results from a cross-sectional community survey offer insights into Asian Americans' help-seeking in the context of familial depression. However, it is essential to acknowledge the limitations in the recruitment process, specifically concerning the underrepresentation of Filipino participants. As a result, we could not report the prevalence of service access for 26 individuals from the Filipino community in this chapter.

From Disparity to Inclusion: Navigating Service Underutilization and Accessibility

This community-based study revealed a range of depression prevalence rates, varying from 11.6% to 30.2% as measured by the HSCL-25. The assessment of depression in community settings may yield different prevalence rates compared to clinical settings. To enhance the utilization of social services, we recommend that professionals collaborate with community leaders to encourage Asian people's participation in self-care training. When preparing this training, mental health practitioners will discuss incorporating culturally responsive techniques to increase participants' engagement in knowledge exchange and design emotional regulation strategies.

A critical implication arising from this study is the role of social workers in supporting individuals who exhibit a lack of preference or express a state of inactivity despite their evident need for mental health care. This inquiry emphasizes the significance of culturally responsive interventions for social workers to develop and utilize appropriate skills in needs assessment. In addition, the study showcases that cultural responsiveness encompasses using research insights to effectively implement proactive outreach initiatives and actively engage with diverse Asian communities in preventive endeavors. Conversely, practice with cultural humility is vital in ensuring clients feel respected while accessing timely mental health services.

While the primary focus of this study was to gather data on perceived and actual needs within various Asian communities, it is also essential to consider other neighborhood characteristics. Factors such as hate crime rates, food deserts, and healthcare proximity play a significant role. By incorporating additional data, professionals can better understand how neighborhood factors may impact an individual's ability to establish familial relationships and foster community ties. This broader perspective can contribute to a comprehensive approach to addressing diverse communities' mental health needs.

Conclusion

In conclusion, the authors collected data through a community study to compare findings of depression prevalences and integrate multiethnic group results to understand how Asian American clients prioritized their sources of assistance when facing mental health concerns. The findings revealed an overall prevalence rate of 28.7%, ranging from 11.6% to 30.2% among the six subgroups identified. Nevertheless, it is crucial to gather supplementary data, particularly on service accessibility, to comprehend the service underutilization issues in mental health services. Previous research has criticized studies on depression among Asian Americans for their failure to explicitly address service utilization or account for ethnic heterogeneity (Kalibatseva & Leong, 2011). Helping professionals should remain attentive to intergroup differences in mental health concerns, recognizing that an aggregated prevalence rate for these six groups may not fully address the nuances required for effective treatment planning.

When medical practitioners assess a patient with mental health needs, they will also evaluate the types of care this patient may need and prefer. After considering the patient's history of care received and their priorities, practitioners can triage high-risk cases and refer them to mental health professionals for further assessment with informal support. The study respondents supported incorporating informal care into service prioritization to increase professional awareness in the referral system. When working with Asian clients' mental health concerns, it is crucial to prompt them to express viewpoints regarding the informal services available in their immediate vicinity before suggesting formal channels that may appear distant or unfamiliar. The proximity of services plays a significant role in ensuring user comfort and trust. Practitioners and educators catering to multicultural clients should evaluate service utilization patterns to foster a sense of value in clients and assist them in accessing support before, during, and after treatment.

This chapter highlights three principles derived from the needs assessment results of six Asian American subgroups. First, professionals must learn cross-cultural differences from their clients, including client–worker differences and sociocultural demographics within and across ethnicities. Second, educators should address influential factors that may help clients consider assistance from different sources. Last, practitioners must actively integrate research evidence into their practice to cater to clients' diverse needs. These principles shed light on improving service underutilization from a perspective that values clients' strengths and abilities to obtain benefits through various formal and informal networks.

Note

1. Survey participants who self-identified six Asian American ethnicities, starting from the largest sample size, were Vietnamese, Chinese, Asian Indian, Korean, Pakistani, and Japanese. Data from a few ethnicities (e.g., Filipino, Napalese) were not analyzed due to their nonsignificant sample size. No Native Hawaiians or Pacific Islanders were identified in the study results presented in this chapter based on six sets of statistical results published in refereed journals. As a result, the term "Asian Americans" is used in this chapter.

References

References marked with an asterisk indicate studies included in the review.

Asian American Health Initiative. (2023). Who are Asian Americans? http://www.aahiinfo.org/english/asianAmericans.php

Augsberger, A., Yeung, A., Dougher, M., & Hahm, H. C. (2015). Factors influencing the underutilization of mental health services among Asian American women with a history of depression and suicide. *BMC Health Services Research*, 15(1). https://doi.org/10.1186/s12913-015-1191-7

Aung, S. K. H., Fay, H., & Hobbs, R. F. (2013). Traditional Chinese medicine as a basis for treating psychiatric disorders: A review of theory with illustrative cases. *Medical Acupuncture*, 25(6), 398–406. https://doi.org/10.1089/acu.2013.1007

Center for Behavioral Health Statistics and Quality. (2021). Racial/ethnic differences in mental health service use among adults and adolescents (2015–2019) (Publication No. PEP21-07-01-002). Substance Abuse and Mental Health Services Administration. https://www.samhsa.gov/data/report/racialethnic-differences-mental-health-service-use

*Cheung, M., Leung, P., & Cheung, A. (2011). Depression symptoms and help-seeking behaviors among Korean Americans. *International Journal of Social Welfare*, 20(4), 421–429. https://doi.org/10.1111/j.1468-2397.2010.00764.x

*Cheung, M., Leung, P., & Tsui, V. (2013). Japanese Americans' health concerns and depressive symptoms: Implications for disaster counseling. *Social Work*, 58(3), 201–211. https://doi.org/10.1093/sw/swt016

Derr, A. S. (2016). Mental health service use among immigrants in the United States: A systematic review. *Psychiatric Services*, 67(3), 265–274. https://doi.org/10.1176/appi.ps.201500004

Đoàn, L. N., Takata, Y., Sakuma, K. K., & Irvin, V. L. (2019). Trends in clinical research including Asian American, Native Hawaiian, and Pacific Islander Participants funded by the US National Institutes of Health, 1992 to 2018. *JAMA Network Open, 2*(7), e197432. https://doi.org/10.1001/jamanetworkopen.2019.7432

Gautam, R., Saito, T., Houde, S. C., & Kai, I. (2011). Social interactions and depressive symptoms among community dwelling older adults in Nepal: A synergic effect model. *Archives of Gerontology and Geriatrics, 53*(1), 24–30. https://doi.org/10.1016/j.archger.2010.06.007

Goodwin, R. D., Dierker, L. C., Wu, M., Galea, S., Hoven, C. W., & Weinberger, A. H. (2022). Trends in US depression prevalence from 2015 to 2020: The widening treatment gap. *American Journal of Preventive Medicine, 63*(5), 726–733. https://10.1016/j.amepre.2022.05.014

Hechanova, R., & Waelde, L. C. (2017). The influence of culture on disaster mental health and psychosocial support interventions in Southeast Asia. *Mental Health, Religion & Culture, 20*(1), 31–44. https://doi.org/10.1080/13674676.2017.1322048

Hinton, D. E., Pham, T., Tran, M., Safren, S. A., Otto, M. W., & Pollack, M. H. (2004). CBT for Vietnamese refugees with treatment-resistant PTSD and panic attacks: A pilot study. *Journal of Traumatic Stress, 17*(5), 429–433.

Houston, Texas Population. (2018). Census 2010 and 2000 interactive map, demographics, statistics, quick facts. Census Reporter. https://www.census.gov/quickfacts/houstoncitytexas

Ina, K., Hayashi, T., Nomura, H., Ishitsuka, A., Hirai, H., & Iguchi, A. (2011). Depression, quality of life (QoL) and will to live of community-dwelling postmenopausal women in three Asian countries: Korea, China and Japan. *Archives of Gerontology and Geriatrics, 53*(1), 8–12. https://doi.org/10.1016/j.archger.2010.05.010

Infoplease. (2020). Demographic statistics: Houston, Texas. http://www.infoplease.com/us/census/data/texas/houston/demographic.html

Jang, Y., & Chiriboga, D. A. (2011). Social activity and depressive symptoms in Korean American older adults: The conditioning role of acculturation. *Journal of Aging and Health, 23*(5), 767–781. https://doi.org/10.1177/0898264310396214

Jang, Y., Kim, G., & Chiriboga, D. A. (2006). Health perception and depressive symptoms among older Korean Americans. *Journal of Cross-Cultural Gerontology, 1*, 91–102. https://doi.org/10.1007/s10823-006-9026-y

Kalibatseva, Z., & Leong, F. T. L. (2011). Depression among Asian Americans: Review and recommendations. *Depression Research & Treatment*. Article ID 320902, 1–9. https://doi.org/10.1155/2011/320902

Kim, J. H. J., Lu, Q., & Stanton, A. L. (2021). Overcoming constraints of the model minority stereotype to advance Asian American health. *American Psychologist, 76*(4), 611–626. https://doi.org/10.1037/amp0000799

Kim, Y. H. (2016). Different effects of acculturative stress and family life stress on depressive symptoms among married Vietnamese immigrant women in South Korea. *Asian Social Work and Policy Review, 10*(2), 225–236. https://doi.org/10.1111/aswp.12092

Laditka, J. N., Laditka, S. B., Liu, R., Price, A. E., Wu, B., Friedman, D. B., Corwin, S. J., Sharkey, J. R., Tseng, W., Hunter, R., & Logsdon, R. G. (2011). Older adults' concerns about cognitive health: Commonalities and differences among six United States ethnic groups. *Ageing and Society, 31*(7), 1202–1228. https://doi.org/10.1017/S0144686X10001273

Lee, B., Wang, Y., Carlson, S. A., Greenlund, K J., Lu, H., Liu, Y., Croft, J B., Eke, P. I., Town, M., & Thomas, C. W. (2023). National, state-level, and county-level prevalence estimates of adults aged ≥18 years self-reporting a lifetime diagnosis of depression – United States, 2020. *Morbidity and Morality Weekly Report*, Centers for Disease Control and Prevention. https://www.cdc.gov/mmwr/volumes/72/wr/mm7224a1.htm

Lee, E.-K. O., & Chan, K. (2009). Religious/spiritual and other adaptive coping strategies among Chinese American older immigrants. *Journal of Gerontological Social Work, 52*(5), 517–533.

Lee, H., Bhimla, A., Lu, W., & X, G., MA. (2020). Correlates of mental health treatment receipt among Asian Americans with perceived mental health problems. *Journal of Behavioral Health Services & Research, 48*(2), 199–212. https://doi.org/10.1007/s11414-020-09704-6

Lee, S., & Waters, S. F. (2021). Asians and Asian Americans' experiences of racial discrimination during the COVID-19 pandemic: Impacts on health outcomes and the buffering role of social support. *Stigma and Health, 6*(1), 70–78. https://doi.org/10.1037/sah0000275

Leung, P., & Cheung, M. (2008). A prevalence study on partner abuse in six Asian-American ethnic groups in the United States. *International Social Work, 51*(5), 635–649. https://doi.org/10.1177/0020872808093342

*Leung, P., Cheung, M., & Cheung, A. (2010). Vietnamese Americans and depression: A health and mental health concern. *Social Work in Mental Health, 8*(6), 526–542. https://doi.org/10.1080/15332985.2010.485092

*Leung, P., Cheung, M., & Cheung, A. (2011). Developing help-seeking strategies for Pakistani clients with depressive symptoms. *Asian Pacific Journal of Social Work and Development, 21*(2), 21–33. https://doi.org/10.1111/j.1468-2397.2010.00764.x

*Leung, P., Cheung, M., & Tsui, V. (2012a). Help-seeking behaviors among Chinese Americans with depressive symptoms. *Social Work, 57*(1), 61–71. https://doi.org/10.1093/sw/swr009

*Leung, P., Cheung, M., & Tsui, V. (2012b). Asian Indians and depressive symptoms: Reframing mental health help-seeking behavior. *International Social Work, 55*(1), 53–70. https://doi.org/10.1177/0020872811407940

Lhewa, D., Banu, S., Rosenfeld, B., & Keller, A. (2007). Validation of a Tibetan translation of the Hopkins Symptom Checklist-25 and the Harvard Trauma Questionnaire. *Assessment, 14*(3), 223–230.

Misa, S., Wyatt, L. C., Wong, J. A., Huang, C. Y., Ali, S. H., Chau, T-S., Islam, N. S., Yi, S. S., & Kwon, S. C. (2020). Determinant of depression risk among three Asian American subgroups in New York City. *Ethnicity & Disease, 30*(4), 553–562. https://doi.org/10.18865/ed.30.4.553

Mui, A. C., & Kang, S. (2006). Acculturation stress and depression among Asian immigrant elders. *Social Work, 51*(3), 243–255.

Niti, M., Ng, T., Kua, E. H., Ho, R. C. M., & Tan, C. H. (2007). Depression and chronic medical illnesses in Asian older adults: The role of subjective health and functional status. *International Journal of Geriatric Psychiatry, 22*, 1087–1094. https://doi.org/10.1002/gps.1789

Parloff, M. B., Kelman, H. C., & Frank, J. D. (1954). Comfort, effectiveness, and self-awareness as criteria of improvement in psychotherapy. *American Journal of Psychiatry, 111*(5), 343–352. https://doi.org/10.1176/ajp.111.5.343

Pernice, R., & Brook, J. (1996). Refugees' and immigrants' mental health: Association of demographic and post-immigration factors. *Journal of Social Psychology, 136*(4), 511–519.

Pew Research Center. (2021, April 29). Key facts about Asian Americans: A diverse and growing population. https://www.pewresearch.org/short-reads/2021/04/29/key-facts-about-asian-americans/

Pew Research Center. (2023, May 8). Diverse cultures and shared experiences shape Asian American identities. https://www.pewresearch.org/race-ethnicity/2023/05/08/diverse-cultures-and-shared-experiences-shape-asian-american-identities/

Picco, L., Abdin, E., Chong, S. A., Pang, S., Vaingankar, J. A., Sagayadevan, V., Kwok, K. W., & Subramaniam, M. (2016). Beliefs about help seeking for mental disorders: Findings from a mental health literacy study in Singapore. *Psychiatric Services, 67*(11), 1246–1253. https://doi.org/10.1176/appi.ps.201500442

Schlossberg, A. J. (2021). Confronting mental health barriers in the Asian American and Pacific Islander community. UCLA Health. https://www.uclahealth.org/news/confronting-mental-health-barriers-asian-american-and-2

Shahid, M., Weiss, N. H., Stoner, G. D., & Dewsbury, B. M. (2021). Asian Americans' mental health help-seeking attitudes: The relative and unique roles of cultural values and ethnic identity. *Asian American Journal of Psychology, 12*(2), 138–146. https://doi.org/10.1037/aap0000230

Silove, D., Manicavasagar, V., Mollica, R., Thai, M., Khiek, D., Lavelle, J., & Tor, S. (2007). Screening or depression and PTSD in a Cambodian population unaffected by war: Comparing the Hopkins Symptom Checklist and Harvard Trauma Questionnaire with the structured clinical interview. *Journal of Nervous and Mental Disease, 195*(2), 152–157.

US Census Bureau. (2022, May 25). Broad diversity of Asian, Native Hawaiian, Pacific Islander population. https://www.census.gov/library/stories/2022/05/aanhpi-population-diverse-geographically-dispersed.html#:~:text=20.6%20Million%20People%20in%20the,Native%20Hawaiian%20or%20Pacific%20Islander&text=There%20are%2020.6%20million%20people,according%20to%20the%202020%20Census

US Census Bureau. (2023). US Census Bureau QuickFacts: Houston City, Texas. Census Bureau QuickFacts. https://www.census.gov/quickfacts/houstoncitytexas

Yang, L. H., Purdie-Vaughns, V., Kotabe, H. P., Link, B. G., Saw, A., Wong, G. H., & Phelan, J. C. (2013). Culture, threat, and mental illness stigma: Identifying culture-specific threat among Chinese-American groups. *Social Science & Medicine, 88*, 56–67. https://doi.org/10.1016/j.socscimed.2013.03.036

Yoshikawa, H., Mistry, R. S., & Wang, Y. (2016). Advancing methods in research on Asian American children and youth. *Child Development, 87*(4), 1033–1050. https://doi.org/10.1111/cdev.12576

Xu, L., & Chi, I. (2013). Acculturative stress and depressive symptoms among Asian immigrants in the United States: The roles of social support and negative interaction. *Asian American Journal of Psychology, 4*(3), 217–226. https://doi.org/10.1037/a0030167

16
Promising, Culturally Sensitive Evidence-Based Interventions for Asian Americans

Dhrubodhi Mukherjee

Introduction

The term "Asian Americans" signifies persons with ancestry in China, India, the Philippine Islands, or other parts of Asia or the Indian subcontinent; on the other hand, Pacific Islanders signify individuals with ancestry in Hawai'i, Guam, Samoa, or other Pacific Islands. Often conflated together, the Asian American, Native Hawai'ian, Pacific Islander (AANHPI) population in the United States is a diverse and rapidly growing group representing numerous cultures, languages, and backgrounds. As of the most recent US Census data, they comprise almost 6% of the US population, with distinct communities. According to the US Census, the AANHPI group exhibited the most significant growth among immigrant people, increasing by 46% from 2000 to 2010 and 10% from 2010 to 2013, surpassing the growth rates of other racial groups nationally (US Census Bureau, 2022). A distinctive feature of the Asian American community is that 66% are foreign-born. Additionally, they stand out among immigrant and ethnic groups, with almost 77% of Asian Americans and Pacific Islanders speaking more than one language, including their native language, within their households (Kim & Tummala-Narra, 2022). The increasing numbers of the AANHPI population indicate a shift toward a critical mass, where their societal focus is likely to evolve from pursuing recognition to building a legacy.

The post–COVID-19 world has brought about exponential changes in attitudes toward mental health in societies around the globe; it has also brought about racism and prejudice in specific Asian American communities. Instances of violence against Asian Americans saw a 77% increase from 2019 to 2020. Between March 2020 and June 2021, more than 9,000 anti-Asian hate incidents were reported, although the actual numbers could be higher due to the community's tendency to underreport (US Census Bureau, 2022). During this period, 39% of Asian Americans experienced racism personally, and 51% reported that post–COVID-19 discrimination impacted their mental health. Healthcare systems need to consider these discriminatory experiences when providing trauma-informed care to Asian American patients. Delivering culturally and linguistically appropriate services (CLAS) is crucial in assessing patients' beliefs, practices, and languages (US Department of Health and Human Services, 2016). Mental health and healthcare practices for the AANHPI community should be trauma-informed and culturally sensitive, avoiding implicit biases and assumptions about Asian American patients. COVID-19 and the associated discrimination brought the mental health conditions of AANHPI communities to the forefront (Kim & Tummala-Narra, 2022). This chapter identifies the sociocultural context in which mental health conditions arose among the AANHPI community and discusses considerations for treatment foci.

Background and Presenting Problems

Historically, mental health practices have evolved, reflecting the changing values and presenting problems of given times. As American society grows more diverse, encompassing various cultural groups with intersecting values, beliefs, and morals, mental health practices have evolved to align with the cultural nuances of clients. Due to the pervasive stigma surrounding mental health and substance use in various cultures, the perception and acceptance of mental health issues vary significantly, leading to varied levels of treatment accessibility. Numerous instances of violent backlash mark the history of Asian Americans. For example, in 1871, many Chinese immigrants were tragically killed in Los Angeles. In 1877, the Chinatown in San Francisco faced extensive destruction and looting (Wu, 2014).

Additionally, following the 1906 earthquake, San Francisco failed to allocate resources to reconstruct Chinatown. These events underscore the challenges and hostilities faced by Asian American communities throughout history (Wu, 2014). Different cultural perspectives have historically influenced how mental health challenges are recognized and addressed, often limiting the availability of treatment options. The prognosis and treatment of mental illnesses are often incumbent upon the attitude of the clientele toward treatment. This attitude is often a combination of how clients perceive themselves and how the larger context of society perceives them. For Asian Americans, their immigration experience and their perception of themselves in the larger community played a pivotal role in their access to mental health (Chen et al., 2005).

Asian Americans have endured a challenging history in the United States, one marked by obstacles such as exclusion from naturalization, discrimination in employment, and enforced separation in living areas. During the 1960s, a fresh stereotype emerged, portraying Asian Americans as the "model minority." This concept set them apart from the White majority, depicting them as well-integrated, economically successful, politically unobtrusive, and distinctly separate from the Black community (Akutsu et al., 2010; Wu, 2014). This favorable stereotype resulted in Asian Americans internalizing these views, adapting themselves to align with the model minority image, which included adopting purportedly "Oriental" traits such as a natural inclination toward harmony and adaptability, a deep respect for family and education, and a relentless work ethic, all bolstering their pursuit of equality (Kendi & Schmidt, 2022; Said, 2003).

While positive stereotypes, such as the model minority myth, may initially seem like favorable depictions of a race, they can also perpetuate harmful societal views. This stereotype often contrasts Asian Americans with other racial groups, like Black or Latino communities, suggesting that Asian Americans are free from problems (Chan, 2020). Such societal perceptions can significantly impact Asian Americans' access to mental healthcare and recognition of mental health and substance issues because there is pressure to conform to this idealized image that misrepresents reality and hinders help-seeking behavior (Steele, 2010).

One of the key features of mental health includes overcoming a sense of "being trapped" in stereotypes, spaces, physical, psychological, traumatic, or perceptual, and attempts to escape from such traps (Steele, 2010; Van Der Kolk, 2014; Wasarhaley et al., 2017). The escaping mechanisms can take many forms: coping, defenses, adjustments, addictions, dissociations, anxieties, depression, suicidality, phobias, neurosis, psychosis, and the like. One common thread across all mental health conditions, when it comes to immigrant communities such as the AANHPI community, is a continuous negotiation between given social identities assigned to them as a group and the self-identities held by everyone. The social identities given to Asian Americans are contingent upon the ethnic and racial stereotypes that exist in the United States about them (Chan et al. 2020; Chan & Marsack-Topolewski, 2022). Genetic, biological, developmental, and environmental factors play a modulatory role in escaping from a specific trap that we struggle with in our interactions with our environments. The postpsychoanalytical mental health intervention practices came to the fore to deemphasize the prominence of "analysis" and emphasize the role of "treatment" and "interventions" in alleviating mental health conditions within a manageable timeframe, which was not the case with Freudian and even post-Freudian psychoanalysis (Lenz et al., 2017).

Stereotype Threats and Identity Contingencies. Social identities are shaped by how an environment organizes around and stereotypes Asian identities. The "stereotype threat" concept encapsulates the challenges arising from group stereotypes, representing a unique predicament linked to Asian American identity. It encompasses the issues of stigmatization, stigma pressure, and stereotype vulnerability, signifying the threat of being judged or mistreated based on one's group identity. This stereotype threat extends beyond personal limitations, reflecting a broader situational challenge tied to the individual's social identity within their environment. The concept of "contingency," as adapted from behaviorism by Steele (2010), refers to the specific conditions an individual must navigate within a particular environment to function effectively. Identity contingencies are unique to each person, shaped by their social identity, which influences perceptions of their intellectual abilities, trustworthiness, and mental acuity. These contingencies affect individuals, making them wary of stigmatization and vigilant about how they are perceived (Davis, 1983). They reflect how societal institutions, like banks, educational systems, and workplaces, interact with individuals based on their social standing and identity.

Identity Threat. An Asian American individual grappling with specific identity contingencies may constantly be alert in their social environment, acutely aware and sensitive to others' perceptions of them (Heller & LaPierre, 2012). This vigilance can be likened to being wary of an unseen, potentially dangerous snake—the threat may be unclear or uncertain, yet it looms large, ever-present in their mind. This pervasive sense of threat becomes a dominant part of their identity, influencing and dictating how they navigate and function in various social settings like auditoriums, classrooms, and workplaces. While they strive to blend in and appear unaffected, the preoccupation with this identity threat remains a central aspect of their experience. Even when they consciously dismiss or try to distance themselves from these threats, these concerns resurface, varying in intensity depending on their social context. This ongoing struggle with identity contingencies profoundly impacts their daily life and interactions. Long-term effects of identity threat could manifest in chronic health problems due to prolonged exposure to performative extra pressure.

Personality Lockdown. Personality lockdown, often triggered by identity contingencies and stereotype threats, occurs when individuals become highly vigilant and conceal their true selves behind a facade perceived as safer. Like a sudden freeze, this self-censorship stems from a diminished sense of self-worth (Lawson, 2017). Encountering symbols of the majority culture, such as legal institutions, law enforcement, prestigious educational settings, imposing architecture, and unfamiliar crowds can suppress one's natural personality due to a perceived sense of danger in these environments. In an attempt to navigate social interactions safely, individuals may excessively sanitize their behavior and speech. This prolonged period of personality lockdown, where one constantly treads carefully in their cultural adaptation process, can potentially lead to complex trauma.

Over-efforting. The phenomenon of over-efforting among Asian Americans and other minority groups facing negative stereotypes and identity contingencies is a significant psychological and social dynamic (Leong & Kalibatseva, 2010). Members of these groups often find themselves compelled to exert extra effort beyond what might be typically expected to counteract prevailing negative stereotypes and disprove the generalized assumptions made about their community. This additional effort is not merely about striving for personal success or excellence; it's driven by a need to prove to the majority community that they do not conform to the negative stereotypes associated with their group. Over-effort in can manifest in various ways, such as working longer hours, taking on additional responsibilities, or striving for perfection in tasks, all in an attempt to visibly demonstrate their capabilities and worth. However, this over-efforting comes with its own set of challenges and consequences. It can lead to immense pressure and stress as individuals feel they must constantly perform at an extraordinary level to be viewed as equal to their peers from the majority group. This relentless push to disprove stereotypes can lead to burnout, anxiety, and a range of other mental health issues.

Moreover, over-efforting can reinforce the idea that members of minority groups must "earn" their place or prove their worth, an expectation not typically placed on members of the majority group. This dynamic perpetuates a cycle where minority groups are continually held to higher standards, sustaining the very stereotypes they are trying to dismantle. Understanding this over-efforting is crucial in addressing the broader issues of racial stereotypes and identity contingencies. It highlights the need for more inclusive and equitable environments where individuals are valued and judged based on their unique abilities and contributions rather than being burdened with disproving harmful stereotypes (Mills, 2022; Steele, 2010).

Therapeutic Relationship and Cultural Competence

Understanding the parameters of someone else's experience is critical to forming a therapeutic relationship between therapists and clients. A power imbalance exists between the therapist and the patient in the therapeutic setting. A crucial early goal for the therapist is to relinquish this power, fostering a safe and trusting environment that allows the patient to let down their ego defenses (Cushman, 1995). These defenses typically stem from previous traumas and relational hurts and are shaped by cultural interpretations of values, ethics, and morals. Therapists working with AANHPI groups should possess a deep empathy and awareness of structural inequalities. They need to adopt an anti-deficit approach and maintain a critical consciousness of structural oppression, including privilege and systemic injustices. Therapists can align their goals with clients by advocating for social change and demonstrating a commitment to justice. This alignment fosters an equitable relationship, centering and unifying the therapist–client relationship around shared objectives.

Intake and Assessment

The intake process entails gathering descriptive, factual information about patients and screening for risk and protective factors associated with presenting problems. Suppose a presenting problem is lack of sleep: the intake screening process could screen for appetite, adverse childhood experiences (ACE), past sleep patterns, coffee intake, and the like. Given the background of Asian Americans and social identities, identity contingencies, and stereotype threats, working with these individuals would require an openness to understand the gamut of experiences that come with stereotype threats and intersectional identities. A strength-based approach to intake and assessment aims to capture the background and past experiences with identity contingencies and their impact on self-worth and self-evaluation, thus locating clients' patterns of coping with stereotype threats and understanding the processing of their self in the context of the larger "Asian" and non-Asian social spaces. When employing a strength-based approach for Asian American clients with mental health issues, objectives should focus on leveraging their inherent capabilities and the positive aspects of their cultural and personal experiences. Below is a list of such objectives.

1. *Identity and self-worth exploration*: Encourage clients to reflect on and articulate their experiences with identity contingencies, examining how these experiences have shaped their self-worth and self-evaluation.
2. *Coping mechanism identification*: Identify and reinforce clients' adaptive coping strategies, like exercise or participating in communal activities, while addressing and modifying maladaptive behaviors like substance use.
3. *Stereotype threat management*: Help clients recognize and understand their responses to stereotype threats and develop strategies to mitigate their impact.
4. *Social support systems analysis*: Facilitate discussions about their current social support networks, both within and outside the Asian community, and explore ways to strengthen these supports.
5. *Cultural and family dynamics understanding*: Encourage clients to share their family narratives and cultural backgrounds, understanding how these factors influence their mental health and coping strategies.
6. *Historical trauma acknowledgment*: Recognize and address the impact of historical trauma on their mental health, incorporating culturally sensitive approaches to healing and resilience.
7. *Identity perception evaluation*: Assist clients in exploring how they perceive their identities in various social contexts and the impact of these perceptions on their mental health.
8. *Resilience and strengths highlighting*: Identify and build upon the client's inherent strengths and resilience factors, highlighting how these can be used in their current mental health journey.

9. *Community connection enhancement*: Encourage engagement with cultural and community resources that reinforce positive identity and provide supportive networks.
10. *Personal empowerment focus*: Empower clients to take control of their mental health journey, emphasizing their agency in overcoming challenges and making positive changes.

Treatment Planning and Therapeutic Contract

One symptom of trauma is the learned behavior of seeing oneself through the perspective of others. In a traumatized childhood, a child often adopts the viewpoint of invalidating caregivers. This conditioning, over time, can lead to developmental trauma disorder that diminishes self-worth (Payant & Weiler, 2018). Traumatized children, constantly critiquing themselves through the lens of negative stereotypes imposed by their caregivers, adopt these stereotypes as a protective mechanism. Similarly, immigrant communities may experience a stereotype threat, internalizing mainstream cultural standards and perceptions about themselves. Therapy, particularly with Asian Americans, should focus on understanding and reshaping this sense of self, helping individuals move beyond these conditioned responses and stereotypes by outgrowing stereotypes.

Creating a treatment plan for Asian American psychotherapy clients should focus on addressing and limiting the impact of identity contingencies that are deeply rooted in cultural contexts. The purpose of treatment planning in the context of Asian Americans is to manage the challenges posed by stereotypes, discrimination, and prejudice. The plan revolves around two central questions: "Is this identity central to my functioning?" and "Is this identity central to my performance?"

1. Assessment and Exploration of Identity:
Conduct a thorough initial assessment focusing on the client's experiences with identity contingencies.
Explore how these contingencies have influenced their sense of self and interactions with others.
2. Understanding and Deconstructing Stereotypes:
Facilitate discussions to identify and understand the stereotypes impacting the client.

Work on deconstructing these stereotypes and their influence on the client's self-perception and behavior.
3. Enhancing Self-Awareness:
Engage in activities that increase self-awareness about the centrality of their identity in their daily functioning and performance.
Reflect on how identity contingencies impact their decision-making, relationships, and self-esteem.
4. Coping Strategies Development:
Develop coping strategies for handling situations involving negative stereotypes or discrimination.
Teach skills like assertiveness, boundary-setting, and self-advocacy.
5. Building Resilience and Empowerment:
Focus on building resilience to better cope with identity-related stressors.
Encourage empowerment by exploring and affirming the client's strengths and values.
6. Exploring Cultural and Racial Identity:
Facilitate exploration of the client's cultural and racial identity, fostering a positive connection with their heritage.
Address the complexities of 'passing' and expatriation and their impact on identity.
7. Social Support and Community Engagement:
Encourage the development of a supportive social network, including community groups or others who share similar experiences.
Discuss the role of social support in managing identity contingencies.
8. Continuous Evaluation and Adjustment:
Regularly evaluate the effectiveness of the treatment plan.
Adjust the plan based on the client's evolving needs and circumstances.
9. Goal Setting:
Collaborate with the client to set realistic and achievable goals related to their identity and how they navigate it in various contexts.

Interventions

The intervention aims to broaden the understanding of social identities and stereotype threats for Asian American clientele and bring empirical heft to that understanding. Following cognitive behavioral therapy (CBT) procedures, therapists can reframe this understanding and develop strategies to help clients navigate their challenges and improve functioning. Intervention strategies focusing on identity contingencies can be reformulated as follows:

1. *Modifying internal aspects of social identities* involves altering how clients experience their social identities internally. It includes shifting cultural perspectives, emotional responses, values, aspirations, and habitual behaviors. This strategy transforms these internalized aspects so they no longer dominate the client's psyche.
2. *Altering external influences on identity contingencies*: Instead of the client adapting to their environment, this strategy focuses on changing the external factors contributing to their identity contingencies by addressing and modifying the societal, cultural, or environmental determinants that shape them.

Psychoeducation

The understanding of mental health concepts like depression, anxiety, personality disorders, and attention deficit hyperactivity disorder (ADHD) varies significantly across cultures. While naming these experiences is crucial for comprehension, it is equally important to recognize that interpretations of mental health can differ widely. The assumption that concepts like depression or anxiety have a universal meaning is often misleading. Education and clarification about these differences are vital for effective intervention. For example, my perception of "depression" and "anxiety" in India differed from my current understanding. A Chinese friend of mine once told me that her parents thought that if White people, who are assumed to be privileged and up there, look for a job and cannot find it, they will get depressed (which in Chinese can be translated as "eating bitterness), while, as a Chinese person, if one cannot find a job, then they cannot get "bitter" or be depressed. They should keep looking until they find it. Such cultural bifurcation, which could be assumed as both a sign of stigma and a symbol of resilience toward mental health conditions, is very common in Asian cultures. Psychoeducation aims to develop a common language and framework regarding the mental health issue at hand. This shared understanding enables the therapist and the patient to gain insight into themselves, the therapeutic relationship, and the systems contributing to their stress.

Processing "Asianness"

Complex trauma manifests through unremarkable incremental encounters with traumatic experiences that are invalidating, hurtful, emotionally stressful, threatening, and micro aggressive. In the discussions of trauma literature, they are called *small t trauma*. A *big T trauma* is a product of a single remarkable traumatic and easily discernible event. The targeted mass shooting of Asian Americans in Atlanta in 2021, for example, is an example of a big T trauma; the direct and indirect survivors of such occurrences could experience posttraumatic stress disorder (PTSD) or PTSD-like symptoms. However, a prolonged experience with identity threat, racism, toxic stereotypes, and invalidations paves pathways for complex PTSD or developmental trauma disorders. The origin of such diagnoses is challenging to locate. Therefore, assessment of identity threats with Asian Americans could use both standardized assessment tools and combine them with therapeutic observational assessment using psychotherapy platforms.

Processing single or cumulative encounters with "Asian-ness" involves exploring identity contingencies, which are experiences one has to deal with that the social identity of being an "Asian" brings. The Asian social identity is not a chosen one and is not indigenous to the archetypes of the community. A social identity is assigned by society, and one has to negotiate with one's agency. Asian-ness is a stressor that Asian Americans have to encounter in their daily lives, a stressor not of their making. The constant anxiety of "one wrong move away" could cause Asian Americans to reduce their own sense of self. Identity contingencies lead to stereotype threats that "mystify" a group associated with arbitrarily assigned social identities. Then, every action they do fits into a stereotype before interpretation. The fragility of owning an autonomous identity leads to minority groups "performing" deflection of stereotypes. As an author (Steele, 2010) wrote, to deflect the stereotype threat that a Black man is violent and crime-prone, Black men often perform assuring deflections in their overt behavior to avoid these perceptions, such as "whistling Vivaldi" to appear culturally cultivated. Asian Americans wearing masks outdoors more excessively than any other communities is also a deflection technique from stereotype threat, allaying mainstream fear of causing and spreading the pandemic. The deflection strategies still don't work, depending on how entrenched the stereotype is in collective mainstream consciousness. Hence, an Asian person constantly has to deal with the persistent annoyance of weighing the "people could think" factor before navigating every activity they perform in a social space. The "people could think" factor is a stressor, compromising our sense of ourselves as autonomous individuals. For example, post-COVID, people wearing masks indoors or outdoors have been interpreted as belonging to "pro-mask" or "anti-mask" viewpoints for the general population. However, Asian people seen wearing a mask in more significant numbers are always met with an incriminatory interpretation that suggests that Asian people wearing a mask do not fall neatly into the pro- or anti-mask bandwagons. It is somehow a little different, as if they need to wear them to atone for their "deeds" of causing COVID in the first place.

Asian Americans themselves could be sensitive about the "people could think" phenomenon when it comes to mask-wearing (Kim & Tummala-Narra, 2022). *Allostatic load*, the accumulation of stress factors that weighs down one's ability to remain calm, relax, or perform executive functioning well by shifting brain activities to the limbic region, causes a constant flight-fight-freeze-like mood disposition that increases with stereotype threat. Post–COVID-19, it is crucial that Asian Americans recognize identity contingencies and stereotype threats as presenting problems and process them with competent therapists. Heightened allostatic loads acculturate communities with a language of fear that they cannot discern unless a therapist takes them to an intentional, objective point of view. For Asian Americans, the predicaments of stereotype threats have always been prevalent since model minority times; one shift in the content of the stereotype has been that from "good in math" (supposedly positive) to "the cause of the pandemic" (a negative stereotype). This causes the same stress increase, and the ever-present predicament of how to balance one's creed with these social assignments (Kendi & Schmidt, 2022; Steele, 2010; Wu, 2014). These stereotype threats and associated stress increase the allostatic load and, if not addressed, can contribute to chronic health conditions over time, such as heart disease, high blood pressure, cancer, and so on. The Adverse Childhood Experiences study has shown that the developmental presence of high allostatic stress load could be associated with the onset of chronic diseases and reduction in overall life expectancy in affected populations (Felitti et al., 1998). Within the Asian population, intracommunity intersectionality, such as one's gender identity, class identity, and ethnic identity, further adds to the stack of stressors.

Mental Health Recovery Model and Intersectionality of Asian Identities

The recovery model in psychotherapy and healthcare emphasizes recognizing how various identities intersect in an individual's life. This approach acknowledges that, alongside racial and ethnic identities, considerations of gender identities and mixed-racial identities are crucial in an identity-integrated healthcare setting. While race-matching between provider and client can be beneficial for some by allowing for shared experiences and understanding, it's also important to recognize that intraethnic stigma and shame about mental health issues might inhibit open communication with a provider from a similar cultural background. These dynamics are essential factors in determining the quality of the therapeutic relationship. For instance, in many Indian American families, and more broadly in Asian cultures, admitting to mental health struggles is often seen as a sign of weakness (Walker, 2013). Typically, mental health issues are only openly acknowledged when they escalate to a crisis. This can lead to a lack of empathy from many Asian American parents regarding mental health and intersectional identity challenges, such as those related to gender identity. Such cultural nuances are critical to understand and address in therapy for effective and compassionate mental health care.

The prognosis and treatment of mental health follow two primary approaches: the medical model and the recovery model. The *medical model* focuses on treatments, while the *recovery model* focuses on well-being that involves understanding persons' interactions with their environments and the stressors they produce (Marya & Patel, 2022). For immigrants and cultural minorities, the process of assimilation and accommodation to their adaptive environment creates barriers, challenges, and stressors that can negatively impact mental health. Treating mental conditions using pharmaceuticals and higher levels of medical intervention involving psychiatrists, doctors, nurses, physician assistants, and more is essential; the recovery model involves peer support, community health workers, employment counselors, and other social determinants of health to sustain treatment and prevent recurrence. The psychotherapist acts as a bridge between the medical and the recovery models. The difference between the medical and recovery models of treatment approaches to mental health is that in the recovery model, there is no negative prognosis. The holistic recovery model relies on hope, support, self-advocacy, and education toward mental well-being as opposed to just mental health.

The recovery model allows spaces for Asian Americans to receive contextualized mental health services that enable accommodations for cultural competence, stigma-related reservations, relapses, and utilizing existing family and kinship support (Morgan, 2019). Mental illnesses often co-occur with substance use disorder because maladaptive coping with mental health and trauma symptoms often leads to addiction. The recovery model of mental health treatment originated in the field of substance use treatment. The intersectionality of the stigma of both mental health and substance use complicates access and mars with collective shame and guilt that prevent patients from seeking services (Crenshaw, 2005). Moreover, a recovery community that upholds the values of "no negative prognosis" and works on the existing strength of patients is a critical recovery-related resources that Asian Americans can utilize in their network. The recovery model builds resilience by building relationships. If the medical model is a task-centered modality to mental health, then the recovery model is relational, which is more sustainable because it continues to engage with patients upon discharge. The medical model helps complement and enhance the impact of psychotherapy and recovery support services. The National Association for Mental Illness (NAMI) is an organization that has plenty of community-level resources and peer support opportunities that Asian Americans can utilize. The *Qian model*, rooted in Chinese philosophical traditions, offers a valuable framework for therapists practicing cultural humility, especially when working with diverse populations. The recovery model incorporates the individuation of the clientele without fetishizing them or dismissing their ethnocultural journey, and it is an excellent place to start mental health interventions with Asian American communities.

References

Akutsu, P., Tsuru, G., & Chu, J. (2010). Pre-intake attrition or non-attendance of intake appointments: At an ethnic-specific mental health program for Asian American children and adolescents. *AAPI Nexus, 8*(2), 39–62. 10.17953/appc.8.2.c37k5v6688j21247

Chan, K. (2020). The association of acculturation with overt and covert perceived discrimination for older Asian Americans. *Social Work Research, 44*(1), 59–71. https://doi.org/10.1093/swr/svz023

Chan, K. T., & Marsack-Topolewski, C. (2022). Ethnic and neighborhood differences in poverty and disability among older Asian Americans in New York City. *Social Work in Public Health, 37*(3), 258–273. https://doi.org/10.1080/19371918.2021.2000916

Chan, K. T., Zhou, S., & Marsack-Topolewski, C. (2020). Race differences in opioid misuse and adolescent suicidality. *Child and Adolescent Social Work Journal, 39* https://doi.org/10.1007/s10560-020-00721-0

Chen, H., Kramer, E., Chen, T., Chen, J., & Chung, H. (2005). The bridge program: A model for delivering mental health services to Asian Americans through primary care. *AAPI Nexus*, 3(1), 13–29. 10.17953/appc.3.1.u841n45526544687

Crenshaw, K. (2005). Mapping the margins: Intersectionality, identity politics, and violence against women of color (1994). In R. K. Bergen, J. L. Edleson, & C. M. Renzetti (Eds.), *Violence against women: Classic papers* (pp. 282–313). Pearson Education New Zealand.

Cushman, P. (1995). *Constructing the self, constructing America: A cultural history of psychotherapy*. Perseus.

Davis, A. Y. (1983). *Women, race & class*. Vintage Books.

Felitti, V. J., Anda, R. F., Nordenberg, D., Williamson, D. F., Spitz, A. M., Edwards, V., Koss, M. P., & Marks, J. S. (1998). Relationship of childhood abuse and household dysfunction to many of the leading causes of death in adults: The Adverse Childhood Experiences (ACE) study. *American Journal of Preventive Medicine*, 14(4), 245–258. 10.1016/S0749-3797(98)00017-8

Heller, L., & LaPierre, A. (2012). *Healing developmental trauma* (1st ed.). North Atlantic Books.

Kendi, I. X., & Schmidt, A. (2022). *How to be an antiracist*. One World.

Kim, J., & Tummala-Narra, P. (2022). Rise of anti-Asian violence and the COVID-19 pandemic for Asian Americans. *Asian American Journal of Psychology*, 13(3), 217–219.

Lawson, D. M. (2017). Treating adults with complex trauma: An evidence-based case study. *Journal of Counseling & Development*, 95(3), 288–298. 10.1002/jcad.12143

Lenz, A. S., Haktanir, A., & Callender, K. (2017). Meta-analysis of trauma-focused therapies for treating the symptoms of posttraumatic stress disorder. *Journal of Counseling & Development*, 95(3), 339–353. 10.1002/jcad.12148

Leong, F., & Kalibatseva, Z. (2010). Comparative effectiveness research on Asian American mental health: Review and recommendations. *AAPI Nexus*, 8(2), 21–38. 10.17953/appc.8.2.uq666pw4m5541735

Marya, R., & Patel, R. (2022). *Inflamed*. Penguin Books.

Mills, C. W. (2022). *The racial contract*. Cornell University Press. 10.1515/9781501764301

Morgan, O. J. (2019). *Addiction, attachment, trauma and recovery: The power of connection* (1st ed.). Norton.

Payant, E., & Weiler, L. (2019). *Unspoken legacy: Addressing the impact of trauma and addiction within the family*. Central Recovery Press. 10.1111/jmft.12380

Said, E. W. (2003). *Orientalism*. Penguin Classics.

Steele, C. M. (2010). *Whistling Vivaldi: How stereotypes affect us and what we can do*. Norton.

US Census Bureau. (2022). American Community Survey 1-year estimates, table GCT0101; generated by John Smith using American FactFinder. http://factfinder2.census.gov

US Department of Health and Human Services. (2016). National standards for culturally and linguistically appropriate services in health and health care: Compendium of state-sponsored national CLAS standards implementation activities.

Van Der Kolk, B. (2014). *The body keeps the score: Brain, mind, and body in the healing of trauma*. Viking Press.

Walker, P. (2013). *Complex PTSD: Surviving and thriving*. Azure Books.

Wasarhaley, N. E., Lynch, K. R., Golding, J. M., & Renzetti, C. M. (2017). The impact of gender stereotypes on legal perceptions of lesbian intimate partner violence. *Journal of Interpersonal Violence*, 32(5), 635–658. 10.1177/0886260515586370

Wu, E. (2014). *The color of success: Asian Americans and the origins of model minority*. Princeton University Press.

17

The Importance of Community-Based Solutions in Addressing Anti-Asian Racism

Clifford S. Bersamira, Sophia B. Lau, and Yeonjung Jane Lee

The phenomenon of anti-Asian racism is not limited to the COVID-19 pandemic. The United States has a long history of anti-Asian racism grounded in xenophobia and the racialization of health and social problems, and, subsequently, Asian American communities have addressed these inequalities through mutual support and advocacy for change. When committing to antiracist work, professional social workers can serve as natural partners with the Asian American community due to our profession's distinct emphasis on social justice and health equity, with attention paid to marginalized and underserved populations. Moreover, the social work profession addresses social determinants of health and assesses how built environments and social climates impact on the micro, meso, and macro levels. Although the foci and training of professional social workers are distinct from other helping professions, opportunities to address the challenges and needs of social workers and to support their capacity to engage as meaningful partners with the community are ever present. Therefore, this chapter covers the history and context of Asian American community advocacy, Asian American experiences with racially fueled hate, the challenges to and considerations in doing advocacy work, and the actions steps for engaging in community-based advocacy work.

History and Context of Community Advocacy

Before expanding on the community-based work that can be done to address anti-Asian racism, it is important to acknowledge the historical and contemporary legacy of Asian American community advocacy. In some instances, this intervention and advocacy were accomplished by Asian ethnic groups as a means to support their own communities, while in other instances, pan-ethnic Asian solidarity was leveraged to strengthen their voices, leading to a broader Asian American community identity in the 1960s. Furthermore, there are instances when Asian American individuals took collective action with other racial/ethnic groups through broader anti-racist coalition building. Below are examples of community resistance and collaboration, including in the development of Asian ethnic enclaves and leveraging of community mutual aid, through collective labor advocacy and strikes, in the development of Asian American Studies and in coalition-building efforts such as in the Civil Rights and Black Lives Matter movements. These examples highlight the challenges and discrimination faced by Asian American individuals in their migration to and settlement in the United States, the importance of shared community voice and mobilization to achieve shared goals for improved conditions and change, and the necessity for coalitions that may expand beyond how communities in the Asian diaspora have initially viewed themselves.

Ethnic Enclaves and Community Mutual Aid

In their migration to and settlement in the United States, Asian American immigrants were prone to settle in geographic locations where other individuals from their geographic places of origin had preceded them, creating ethnic enclaves such as Chinatowns, Japantowns, Koreatowns, Little Indias, Little Manilas, Little Vietnams, and more. These ethnic enclaves come in many sizes and configurations and range in taxonomy from traditional enclaves, such as those shaped before World War II, to satellite enclaves developing after the influx of immigrants following the 1965 Immigration Act, new enclaves shaped through contemporary immigrant and refugee arrival, and ethnoburbs shaped around suburban residential and business districts in larger metropolitan spaces (Liu & Geron, 2008). Debates exist as to the benefits and drawbacks of immigrants residing in ethnic enclaves.

Some have argued that ethnic enclaves are a source of strength for immigrant communities, as individuals benefit from the linguistic and cultural resources that aid in their adaptation and assimilation, while others have argued that these resources hinder the opportunity to connect with mainstream resources (Majka & Mullan, 2002). Historically, ethnic enclaves are often products of discriminatory housing policies restricting the locations in which Asian immigrants could reside (such as redlining) and thus obliging communities to develop their own labor markets and sources of support (Pascual, 1996). This benefitted members of these communities through improved earnings among Asian American male enclave workers and through increased education, English language ability, and labor experience (Zhou & Logan, 1989).

Many Asian American individuals developed their own mutual aid and benevolent organizations as a means of helping others in their community during times when local government social welfare systems and restrictive social policies fell short in providing aid in certain communities, including culturally and linguistically appropriate economic, social, and legal support. For example, Chinese Consolidated Benevolent Associations emerged in the mid-1800s, in parts of the United States with large Chinese immigrant communities, as a means of connecting together those from common Chinese regions and speaking similar dialects (Lai, 2004). In some instances, the development of mutual aid societies was by necessity because early Asian American immigrants could not receive support from government programs due to discriminatory policies and lack of linguistic access. More recently, such as among Southeast Asian refugees, government agencies have acknowledged the benefit of aid from members of these Asian refugee communities and have facilitated the development of such organizations (Majka & Mullan, 2002). Since the 1960s, urban Asian American enclaves have been most commonly mobilized as sites of community building and advocacy, where particular focus has been placed on issues pertaining to land use, affordable housing, and labor and community preservation (Liu & Geron, 2008).

Labor Movement and Strikes

The early migration of Asians to many parts of the United States, including the West Coast, Hawaiʻi, and Alaska, have historically been linked to labor and economic factors including the need for migrant agricultural workers on farms along the West Coast, in plantations in Hawai'i, and in fishing canneries in Alaska, among other sectors (Takaki, 2012). Examples of this labor migration and the struggles of migrant workers were captured in the fictional work of Filipino American laborer and writer, Carlos Bulosan in his 1946 seminal work, *America is in the heart* (2019), spotlighting the discrimination faced by Asian laborers and the hardships of daily living.

As various racial/ethnic groups arrived as laborers in Hawai'i and the West Coast, they were frequently met with difficult working and living conditions and cheated of fair wages. Plantation and farm owners would segregate racial/ethnic groups from one another, both in housing and in worksites, as a tactic to minimize the sharing of work grievances and potential alliances across groups. Labor unions representing particular racial/ethnic groups would go on strike, but these were often unsuccessful given the lack of solidarity among groups. This notion of solidarity would not come naturally given the differences in language and culture among workers, which was further perpetuated in racial/ethnic group isolation in living and work spaces.

In 1946, in Hawai'i, unions representing Filipino and Japanese sugar workers, respectively, successfully organized a 79-day strike shutting down 33 of the 34 sugar plantations in Hawai'i. This strike was among the first instances of multiethnic labor solidarity, in which participants learned from unsuccessful past efforts when single ethnic groups' unions acting alone would attempt to go on strike but would be sidelined and replaced by laborers from other racial/ethnic groups (University of Hawai'i West O'ahu Center for Labor Education and Research [CLEAR], n.d.). This multiethnic solidarity was also a product of—and further resulted in—the development of a local plantation culture intertwining the cultures of various plantation laborers.

In 1965, in Delano, California, the predominantly Filipino American Agricultural Workers Organizing Committee (AWOC), led by Larry Itliong, went on strike over poor pay and working conditions in the grape fields. Realizing the strike would more likely lead to concessions with a larger number of strikers, Itliong approached Cesar Chavez of the predominantly Mexican American National Farm Workers Association (NFWA) about joining the strike, and Chavez agreed after being convinced by others in the union, including Dolores Huerta. AWOC and NFWA combined to become the United Farm Workers of America (UFW). The legacy of Larry Itliong and the Filipino grape workers has only recently resurfaced as part of the narrative of California's labor history, often most associated with Chavez, who led the combined UFW (Delloro, 2009).

The Rise of Asian American Ethnic Identity and Asian American Studies

In the era of civil rights, it became quite evident in our society that learning about oneself and one's community was a means of empowerment and that systems of education in American society had historically been limiting—if not redefining—narratives in ways that perpetuated the oppression and marginalization of racial/ethnic groups, including Asian Americans. An Asian American pan-ethnic identity emerged in the 1960s, as a unifying political advocacy voice intended to protect the interests of a diverse group of Asian diasporic communities (Le Espiritu, 1992). The US Civil Rights Movement spotlighted attention on social and political inequalities in society, including the racism and oppression faced by African Americans dealing with the legacy of slavery in the American South. Social movements in this era followed, calling attention to the Vietnam War and the inequalities faced by women, LGBTQ+ peoples, Indigenous peoples, and other racial/ethnic minorities in the United States, including Asian Americans.

Asian American identity and Asian American Studies find their origins in student activism in the San Francisco Bay Area. At the time, radical students and community action called attention to a variety of sociopolitical issues; the emerging college-age generation, often including Asian Americans who were born in the United States, were leveraging their political voice through a shared new identity that was not embraced by their immigrant parents' generation (Chiang, 2009; Le Espiritu, 1992). At the University of California, Berkeley, graduate students Yuji Ichioka and Emma Gee, inspired by Black Power Movement, founded the Asian American Political Alliance as a way to unite Chinese, Japanese, Filipino, and other Asian students under the pan-ethnic identity of Asian Americans, as a strategic political label to combat shared experiences with racism (Kambhampaty, 2020). Through their coalition, the Third World Liberation Front, students from San Francisco State College (now University) demanded improvement to their education so that it would be more reflective of and relevant to their communities through the development of ethnic studies programs to meet the needs of

African American, Asian American, Chicano, Latino, and Native American students. The first College of Ethnic Studies at San Francisco State College and Department of Ethnic Studies at the University of California, Berkeley, with Asian American Studies programs, were established soon thereafter (Chiang, 2009). Fast forward to today, and another wave of Asian American student advocates and members of the Asian American and Pacific Islander (AAPI) Youth Rising have centered much of their work on vocalizing the need for untold Asian American stories and experiences to be taught in middle and high school curricula to promote a more equitable society and combat racism (AAPI Youth Rising, n.d.). The emerging development of and access to Asian American Studies curricula is important to the Asian American community because it offers an opportunity to not only learn identity, history, and cultural context, but also to solidify the fact that Asians are Americans.

Asian American Contributions to Anti-Racist Coalitions

Historically, a common experiential thread has involved Asian American coalition-building, whether among Asian American ethnic groups or with other racial/ethnic groups. Asian American political activists have mobilized alongside their counterparts for racial equality, social justice, and peace, such as Grace Lee Boggs alongside James Boggs; Yuri Kochiyama alongside Malcom X in pursuit of civil rights; and Thich Nhat Hanh alongside Martin Luther King, Jr. against the Vietnam War. More recently, Asian American individuals have mobilized in solidarity with the Black Lives Matter movement with the formation of Asian Americans for Black Lives.

Within the Asian American community, including among Asian American social workers, we observed community mobilization as a result of emerging anti-Asian hate at the start of the COVID-19 pandemic. Advocacy organizations such as Stop AAPI Hate developed with the intention of educating the community about the racist and violent acts taking place, and a call to action was made by a collective of social work organizations, including those representing Asian American social work practitioners and educators, condemning the "rise in discrimination, oppression, harassment, violence, and racism perpetuated against APIDA [Asian, Pacific Islander, and Desi American] people in the wake of the ongoing COVID-19 pandemic" and calling the profession to action (Joint Statement, 2021).

Limitations in Asian American Advocacy

Although Asian American ethnic groups have made strides in advocating for their community needs, one must also acknowledge the conflicts and limitations that exist in this advocacy. Pan-ethnic Asian American identity, intended to serve as a unifying voice, is commonly perceived as most aligned with East Asian American culture and identity, along with "model minority" stereotypes (MMS) of Western assimilation and socioeconomic success. This narrow consideration marginalizes the experiences of South Asian, Southeast Asian, working class, and other identities typically not considered in this scope (Yamashita, 2022). Recent coalitions (and simultaneous data collection efforts) have broadened even further to include Asian American and Pacific Islanders (AAPI), Asian American, Native Hawaiian, Pacific Islander (AANHPI), or Asian, Pacific Islander, and Desi American (APIDA). These coalition umbrellas can be powerful in their inclusion of a broader number and range of voices, but they can also be problematic when meaningful participation and representation of Native Hawaiians, Pacific Islanders, and South Asian Americans are not considered. Finally, community advocacy among Asian American ethnic groups and with other racial/ethnic groups has elucidated, both historically and contemporarily, the discrimination among particular Asian ethnic groups, intersectional biases, and anti-blackness and colorism that persists among some Asian American individuals (Liu, 2018) and that must be addressed in the Asian American community.

Experiences With Racially Fueled Hate and Discrimination

Given the history of the Asian American community's advocacy work, it is important to understand the current literature on the COVID-19 pandemic-fueled anti-Asian racism through the experiences of Asian American social workers, in particular. A growing number of Asian American individuals are interested in the field of social work. However, there are limited empirical investigations on Asian American social workers' experiences (and social workers' experiences in general) during heightened racist climates. The following section discusses the authors' empirical research investigating how Asian American social workers responded to escalated anti-Asian racism during the pandemic (Bersamira et al., 2024; Lau et al., 2023; Lee et al., 2023) as well as other scholars' empirical evidence. To the authors' knowledge, no other studies explore the experiences of Asian American social workers during the COVID-19 pandemic's anti-Asian hate climate.

The qualitative study was conducted by the authors of this chapter for the purpose of exploring Asian American social workers' experiences with and responses to anti-Asian racism (Bersamira et al., 2024; Lau et al., 2023; Lee et al., 2023). The authors of this study have argued the importance of raising Asian American social workers' visibility in the field by spotlighting their experiences and perspectives, which are underrepresented in literature. Exploring how Asian American social workers addressed racism during the pandemic can also inform practice, policy, and research strategies to better support social workers in their anti-racism work. Using thematic analysis, semi-structured interviews conducted from September to December 2021 were analyzed to identify the experiences and perceptions of Asian American social workers. A total of 17 individuals participated in interviews, all of whom received a social work degree from an academic institution accredited by the Council on Social Work Education (CSWE), were 18 years or older, and were living in the United States. Relevant findings from the qualitative study are integrated below, along with other empirical findings.

Marginalized Group Experiences With Anti-Asian Racism

Earlier, it was mentioned that ethnic enclaves mobilized to address challenges like lack of linguistic and cultural resources experienced in the community. These challenges are further corroborated in current literature as marginalized groups, such as people with limited English proficiency, immigrants, and older adults, have been underreporting unfair experiences (Lee, 2020; Ma et al., 2021). Similarly, in their qualitative study, Lee and colleagues (2023) found that Asian American social workers were concerned about the aging population. Most participants shared their perspectives on concerns about safety and discrimination, lack of service and support for older adults, and generational gaps as perceived barriers to advocacy to support the community (Lee et al., 2023). Despite the efforts to reduce ageism in society, the COVID-19 pandemic continued to confirm older adults' experiences with ageism (Morrow-Howell & Gonzales, 2020; Morrow-Howell et al., 2020). According to Lee et al. (2023), Asian American social workers expressed that they are particularly concerned about the safety of their older adult family members and/or clients in the community because of hate crime incidents in public transit, among other reasons. This is consistent with media coverage highlighting increased reported cases of hate crimes against older adults (Takamura et al., 2022). Moreover, the Asian American social workers' interviews highlighted the importance of understanding how intersectional identities can play a role in the well-being of the people they serve in the community. For instance, Asian American social workers were concerned about how older women and immigrants may experience greater barriers in seeking support when experiencing injustice. Takamura and colleagues (2022) indicated that the nature of anti-Asian hate is complex, and it requires collaboration from professionals to address the issue of intersectionality, especially those with intersecting identities of race, gender, and age. According to the Asian Critical (AsianCrit) Theory, Asian American individuals can be impacted by "intersectionality" as racism and other forms of oppression influence their life experiences. The recent qualitative study results on marginalized groups identified by Asian American social workers (Bersamira et al., 2024; Lau et al., 2023; Lee et al., 2023) echo the importance of supporting people with intersecting identities, as discussed in the AsianCrit Theory, who may be facing multiple forms of oppression. Thus, social workers working with the communities need to pay attention to the intersectional identities of their clients.

Identified Needs to Support Communities Experiencing Injustice

Asian American social workers shared the need for culturally and linguistically appropriate services and support when working with immigrants and the diverse aging population (Lee et al., 2023). The AsianCrit Theory indicates that Asian American individuals have often been homogenized despite their diversity (Iftikar & Museus, 2018; Museus & Iftikar, 2014). Language access is critical in empowering people experiencing injustice to raise their voices and protect their rights during difficult times. To do this, social workers and other professionals can work together to provide community-driven resources in different languages. An example of this is the work that Stop AAPI Hate, a US coalition founded in March 2020, is doing. They offer their reports and resources in 15 Asian and Pacific Islander languages other than English to serve those with limited English proficiency. Partnerships with organizations to properly educate Asian American communities are critical (Stop AAPI Hate, 2022).

Moreover, Asian American social workers raised concerns about the mental health challenges experienced among Asian American social workers and in Asian American communities. For instance, participants discussed their experiences with the MMS and how it impacted their relationships with colleagues and leadership in addition to their self-care practice (Lau et al., 2023). Another participant expressed not having enough mental health and aging services when these are much needed (Lee et al., 2023). Although strides have been made to support Asian American mental health, continued efforts must be made when developing, implementing, and evaluating culturally responsive mental health services.

Challenges and Considerations in Doing Advocacy Work

Community-based advocacy work for Asian Americans can be complex and nuanced; hence, the context within which social workers advocate cannot be disregarded. The following section discusses major challenges for consideration in doing advocacy work, including (1) leveraging the pan-ethnic Asian American identity while recognizing the diversity and heterogeneity among Asian American individuals, (2) foregrounding community-based work through collaborations, (3) developing skills to do advocacy work, (4) improving training and education to strengthen advocacy work, (5) promoting data disaggregation, and (6) doing advocacy informed by empirical evidence. In this section, we incorporate not only the qualitative study findings from the authors (Bersamira et al., 2024; Lau et al., 2023; Lee et al., 2023) but also discuss other evidence.

According to Bersamira et al. (2024), honoring the diversity and heterogeneity of Asian American communities is a critical step to strengthening coalition-building. As a racial category, the Asian American population is comprised of many ethnic groups, each with its own unique cultures and traditions, and it is important to acknowledge this diversity. Data aggregation results in the danger of having an unclear and inaccurate picture of the inequalities and injustices that Asian American individuals experience. Evidence shows that when data are disaggregated, Asian American communities show unique challenges and needs, such as those related to health and socioeconomic issues (Ahmad & Weller, 2014; Bhakta, 2022). The difficulty of capturing the diversity of Asian American individuals while honoring the pan-ethnic voice has been identified as a struggle in collaboration and advocacy work (Bersamira et al., 2024; Lau et al., 2023; Lee et al., 2023; Nadal, 2019; Nakano, 2013). Recognizing the heterogeneity among Asian American individuals can make advocacy work more effective by identifying interventions and resources unique to each group. Although "pan-ethnicity," defined as "the construction of a new categorical boundary through the consolidation of ethnic, tribal, religious, or national groups" (p. 211), can encourage diverse Asian groups to work together, the rhetoric of viewing Asians as a homogeneous group can result in the invisibility of different cultural and historical life experiences (Okamoto & Mora, 2014). Thus, community-based advocacy work for Asian American individuals must be nuanced. Recognizing the strengths of unifying voices to increase the impact of supporting Asian American communities while being aware of the right moment to engage in ethnic-specific advocacy is critical.

Another important consideration for advocacy work is to collaborate with Asian American community leaders and engage with other stakeholders to build stronger connections in addressing issues of racism. However, collaboration cannot be achieved without leveraging connections among different stakeholders, such as advocacy groups, students, scholars, and policymakers. According to Byon and colleagues (2023), activism in Black and Asian American communities is an example of how education coalitions and collaboration among advocacy groups play an important role. For example, Byon et al. (2023) discussed how the Maryland Historically Black Colleges and Universities (HBCU) Advocates coalition and Southeast Asia Resource Action Center (SEARAC), a national organization that advocates for Southeast Asian American communities, have been able to successfully move policy agendas forward by working with people in education, community leaders, students, and many other members and by offering advocacy training to educate the next generations of Southeast Asian American leaders who can make a political impact.

In these efforts, social workers served as catalysts in advocacy movements working with diverse groups of people. One of social work's core values is social justice. Social workers work to promote social justice and fight against injustices like racism and discrimination (National Association of Social Workers [NASW], n.d.). In a time of heightened anti-Asian racism and hate crime, social workers worked with communities to provide information, services, and resources. In the study focusing on interviews of Asian American social workers (Bersamira et al., 2024; Lau et al., 2023; Lee et al., 2023), social workers expressed feeling responsible for protecting the marginalized groups that were impacted during this time of anti-Asian hate. For instance, they shared their worries about the safety of older adults in the community as they were aware of various attacks rooted in hate that occurred. Social workers understand the impact of White supremacy and use their skills in addressing anti-racism (CSWE, 2022). They also understand how intersectionality can impact one's life experiences. Thus, they continue to engage in advocacy work to support marginalized populations. However, it is critical that appropriate resources, support, and opportunities are given to social workers so that they can continue to develop skills in doing advocacy work.

Although social workers have worked with the Asian American community to fight against anti-Asian hate, social workers expressed the need for further education and training on how social workers and the community can appropriately engage in advocacy work (Bersamira et al., 2024; Lau et al., 2023; Lee et al., 2023). Participants shared their experiences of lack of training and uncertainty about not knowing how to engage in advocacy work. As Bersamira et al. (2024) discussed, incorporating advocacy work in social work education and training would be critical in supporting social workers and other Asian American communities to stand against injustice and appropriately respond to issues like anti-Asian hate. As mentioned in the previous section regarding community work throughout history, learning from the history of advocacy may help address the current training and learning experience. As demonstrated in the development and work of Chinese Consolidated Benevolent Associations in the mid-1800s, the social work profession can be strengthened by educating future social workers to learn from past examples of why and how mutual aid and community support occurred. Current social work education does not comprehensively introduce the advocacy work examples and Asian American history as identified by Asian American social workers (Bersamira et al., 2024; Lau et al., 2023; Lee et al., 2023). Despite the historical examples of advocacy work among Asian American individuals, social workers may continue to encounter barriers in community advocacy work without a rigorous education in advocacy training.

The recent disaggregated data showed the differences in reported hate incidents by ethnicity. For instance, among 11,467 incidents between

March 2020 and March 2022, Chinese had the highest percentage (43%), followed by Korean (16%), Filipino (9%), Japanese (8%), and Vietnamese (8%) (Stop AAPI Hate, 2022). Another example demonstrating the importance of acknowledging disparities is the number of COVID-19 cases. As of May 3, 2023, in the state of Hawaiʻi, 31% of COVID-19 cases were identified as White, followed by Native Hawaiians (20%), Filipino (17%), and others (11%) (State of Hawaiʻi, Department of Health, 2023). Similarly, Lee et al. (2023), Bersamira et al. (2024), and Lau et al. (2023) discussed the power of understanding diversity among Asian American individuals. Data aggregation and the small sample sizes of Asian Americans in research findings continue to hinder the production of evidence to support specific Asian subgroups. Because social workers understand the impact of diversity and intersectionality in shaping cumulative life experiences, it is a struggle to continue to see research and science viewing Asian American communities as a monolithic group.

Finally, there is a challenge in conducting evidence-based practice and practice-informed research in social work. To effectively respond to anti-Asian racism, social workers must understand the empirical evidence and theoretical frameworks that can reinforce advocacy work and community collaboration. Another commonly experienced challenge vocalized by Asian American social workers (Bersamira et al., 2024) is that of using culturally responsive research approaches, like community-based participatory research (CBPR) in higher education institutions. CBPR engages researchers and community members to work together on all stages and aspects of research (Council on Social Work Education [CSWE], n.d.; National Institute on Minority Health and Health Disparities [NIMHD], n.d.) to strengthen the academic–community partnership and produce more clinically significant outcomes. Although it is ideal for social workers to perform CBPR, there are challenges, such as lack of education, lack of support, limited infrastructure, and feasibility of helping with the community relationship–building process.

Actions Steps for Engaging in Community-Based Advocacy Work

Social workers engaged in community-based advocacy are expected to integrate theoretical frameworks to understand and assess a problem's context and the related factors requiring change. The integration of theories further allows for a common language to be used by those advocates who maintain different backgrounds, worldviews, and assumptions. Additionally, social workers are trained to foster authentic relationships and effectively partner with systems when developing and strengthening empirically informed community-centered care responses to anti-Asian racism and other needs in the community. As emphasized earlier, six core challenges in doing advocacy work were discussed. Therefore, in this final section, theoretical and conceptual frameworks in addition to social work practices will be discussed that address the aforementioned challenges and that can support one's advocacy work.

Identifying Positionality in Social Work Advocacy Practice

As delineated earlier, Asian American lived realities with racism, sociopolitical discrimination, and health disparities have been historically misunderstood if not rendered invisible. Moreover, not only have community members taken the lead in addressing social and health concerns raised by group members, but advocacy work was noted to be fraught with challenges. Nevertheless, social workers have a responsibility to partner meaningfully with communities when engaging in advocacy work. Before we embark on responsible relationship-building with communities and relevant stakeholders, it should be emphasized that the work begins with us. Anti-racist work begins with each of us and requires accepting what may feel like a tumultuous process attached to gaining metacognition of one's own racial and ethnic identity, racism, and anti-racist stance. To begin, Pollock (2006) refers to a purposeful struggle with race talk and analysis as *race wrestling*, a conceptual framework that challenges people to consciously wrestle with normalized ideas that perpetuate racism and racial inequality. One such example of a *normalized* idea that is attached to the Asian American identity and experiences is the MMS, a misleading label externally imposed on the pan-ethnic Asian American identity since the 1960s and one that has influenced the lived realities of Asian American individuals, particularly those of East Asian descent (Lau et al., 2023). In addition to the behavioral mental health ramifications, internalizing the MMS has been shown to have lasting impacts on one's social health, fracturing relationships with other communities of color (Kim et al., 2021) and also discouraging Asian

American individuals from engaging in social activism relevant to their quality of life (Tran & Curtin, 2017).

When race wrestling, one is essentially interrogating one's personal ideologies based on a conceptualization of *self*. Social identity theory is relevant in this discussion and highlights perceived group belongingness as an explanatory framework underlying interpersonal relations. According to Hogg et al. (1995, p. 260), as "social identities have important self-evaluative consequences, groups and their members are motivated to adopt in-group/out-group comparisons and thus the self." These impacts on one's self-concept have been argued to encourage the individual to adopt characteristics and behaviors that maintain ingroup and outgroup comparisons and that promote ingroup favorability (Hogg et al., 1995). Let's take the internalization of the MMS as an example. If a self-identified Asian American believes this misleading label to be true, one outcome that can be experienced is pressured expectations to live up to the unrealistic standards established by the dominant group. In turn, this can result in the masking of existing health-related needs or experiences like discrimination and racism that can diminish the *face* of the group. Our responses to oppressive experiences like racism can range from intellectualization or emotional detachment to emotionalization or intense personal feelings (Smith et al., 2022). Therefore, when exploring one's own racial and ethnic identity and experiences with racism, social workers can organize their internal processing using strengths-based, empowerment approaches and counter narratives—the same frameworks used when servicing clients to gain a more accurate understanding of the impacts of race relations whether that be individually, in a group, or with a professional provider.

Scholars have acknowledged the specific role of one's social identity and its influence on individual and collective activism for social change (Van Zomeren et al., 2008; Yellow Horse et al., 2021). Therefore, we must hold ourselves accountable when race wrestling by monitoring and interrogating our own cognitive, affective, and behavioral responses throughout. The aforementioned psychological responses can be influenced by one's personal understanding of one's racial identity based on ancestry and color, among other intersecting identities like age, gender, sexual orientation, immigration status, and socioeconomic class. When acknowledging one's positionality across practice levels, we should remember that we all participate in oppression and move fluidly on the continuum as oppressor and oppressed. As part of our professional introduction and when facilitating anti-racist education, training, and research, we can aim to integrate other intersecting identities that influence our self-concept and worldviews at large. In this process and as a result of our individual work, we can raise the visibility of our unique ethnic Asian American identity and allow it to serve as a catalyst for strengthening connections with other ethnic group's experiences.

Education and Training: Using Theories to Center Lived Realities

Anti-Asian racism education and training opportunities should include theoretical frameworks to support the audience in understanding key concepts and the societal phenomena or the problem of interest. Education and training should remind learners that concepts like *racism* and *anti-racism* are multifaceted and complex, hence, the learning experience should reveal the realities of the psychological, social, and political impacts and be intentionally transformative for the recipient (Cane & Tedam, 2022). Furthermore, professional social workers should not only be aware of their positionality, but also possess the interpersonal skill sets needed to create and sustain a learning space that promotes vulnerability, metacognition, and critical reflection and that fosters humanity and transformation. Without in-depth and reflective teaching about race and racism, a concern is that *performative activism* may occur, where an individual's activism or allyship is not for the cause itself, but with the intention to self-serve and gain social capital.

Opportunities exist to strengthen the *interlocking* of single ethnic group and pan-ethnic Asian American groups' advocacy work (Nakano, 2013). When modeling vulnerability, critical self-interrogation, and reflection in the classroom setting, for example, anti-racism education should emphasize strengths-based and empowering narratives that historically were dismissed. These narratives can be shared by means of untangling and understanding the historical roots, an ethnic group's unique experiences, and the sociopolitical influences that result in racism, in addition to the social movements that underscored solidarity both within and between racial groups. Connections identified between racial/ethnic groups in pursuit of social justice and health equity can expand the pan-ethnic Asian American's identity to beyond East Asian American individuals and to experiences with racism as a collective. *Racial triangulation theory* can be integrated with these paradigm-shifting discussions with students in addition to serving as a precursor to a history lesson on cross-racial social justice movements. This theory was proposed to expand the incomplete White–Black binary racial stratification theories, which aim to explain racial relations by positing that Asian American individuals, categorized as either "honorary Whites" (e.g., East Asian American individuals) or "collective Blacks" (e.g., darker-skinned and/or Southeast Asian American individuals), are positioned in between White and Black populations (Bonilla-Silva, 2006). Although it has reported limitations, racial triangulation theory is viewed as helping push back against the racial relations discourse surrounding White supremacy's use of racial hierarchy to continue to ostracize Asian Americans and, ultimately, to discount systemic racism experienced by Black, Indigenous, and Other People of Color (BIPOC) communities, notably Black communities (Yellow Horse et al., 2021). As mentioned earlier, it is critical that appropriate resources, support, and opportunities are given to social workers so that they can continue to develop skills in doing advocacy work. In this respect, one must remember that a social worker's ethical responsibilities extend beyond their service recipients and include responsibilities to colleagues in practice settings as professionals, to the social work profession, and to the broader society. As such, social workers not only have the capacity to facilitate anti-racism training in the community, but also continuing education opportunities for other social workers at any stage in their careers to address the needs and challenges that can hinder advocacy work among professionals.

Bridging the Gap Between Research and Advocacy Practice

Professional social workers are expected to engage in advocacy informed by empirical evidence. When considering relevant theoretical frameworks in anti-Asian racism scholarship, Yoo et al. (2022) outline how to advance research with Asian American individuals using Asian critical race theory. In addition to applying the seven tenets of AsianCrit to promote Asian American psychology scholarship, the authors urge readers to remain cognizant of the traditionally excluded groups, including Brown Asian American individuals (e.g., South Asian, Southeast Asian, and Filipino), multiracial and multiethnic Asian American individuals, males, LGBTQ+ individuals, and religious minorities, among others (Yoo et al., 2022). Racial triangulation theory can further be considered to explore how Asian American individuals challenge White supremacy and to explain the reasons for complicity in racial color blindness, the MMS, colorism, and anti-blackness (Yoo et al., 2022).

Efforts have been made to address the misrepresentation and underrepresentation of Asians in research by disaggregating Asian American health data (Shah & Kandula, 2020). One must note that Brown Asian American individuals have been historically vocal about disaggregating health data as a way of combating the false notions of the prescribed model minority on Asian American individuals (Nadal, 2019). Despite these efforts, common challenges like small sample sizes continue to interfere with studies and result in publicly available datasets that include an aggregation of certain Asian American groups (Bacong et al., 2020). In response to the issue of aggregated data, Shah and Kandula's (2020) article included a recommendation for researchers to include statements and rationale for when disaggregated data is not provided or analyzed. Social workers can further consider the Public Health Critical Race Praxis (PHCRP) for future conduct of data disaggregation, which challenges researchers to (1) examine how racialization and racism operate within a study, (2) reflect on how racialization influences the production of knowledge and how reporting the results can perpetuate certain stereotypes attached to racial identity, (3) examine how health research conceptualizes race and ethnicity, and (4) engage with the moral implications of data collection (Bacong et al., 2020).

To facilitate community-driven research on anti-Asian racism and other important health scholarship that is focused on disparities, culturally anchored research approaches should be used to empower and sustain authentic partnerships with communities. Research teams can benefit from the trust established by long-standing partnerships among community systems and academic institutions to create culturally relevant research activities that can produce results of clinical significance (Hotz, 2011). CBPR is one such approach to research that is consistent with the social work profession's mission (Branom, 2012) and that maintains a social justice–oriented approach (Jacobson & Rugeley, 2007). Researchers should carefully consider CBPR's nine principles when deciding on its use: (1) recognizing community identity, (2) building on community strengths and resources, (3) developing systems in an iterative and cyclical process, (4) developing equitable involvement of all parties in all phases of the research, (5) engaging in co-learning and capacity building, (6) establishing mutually beneficial integration and balance of research and action, (7) addressing public health issues of local importance, (8) sharing participation in the dissemination and findings, and (9) committing to a long-term process of sustainability (Israel et al., 1998). Lessons learned when using CBPR to recruit Asian American participants included taking the time needed to build a trusting relationship before a research project begins, being mindful that investigators' shared identity does not equate having shared experiences with participants, maintaining transparency by reviewing informed consent to inform participants about the study's intentions and how data will be used, and using innovative ways to effectively reach hidden subgroups (Katigbak et al., 2016). In turn, assets-mapping, originally developed as part of *asset-based community development* (ABCD) for community capacity-building (Kretzmann & McKnight, 1996), is a participatory method that aligns with social work's strengths-based approach and involves the community in identifying assets (e.g., individual, institutional, economic, physical, and cultural) in addition to highlighting the relationships between assets (Lightfoot et al., 2014). In this process of producing an asset inventory and asset map, relationships with communities can be significantly enhanced (Lightfoot et al., 2014). As CBPR and participatory approaches align with social work values and have garnered support from communities who may be wary of research activities, careful consideration and implementation continue to be needed when planning and implementing the research to ensure that the essence of these research approaches is truly actualized.

Conclusion

This chapter provided an overview of Asian American advocacy history, challenges in advocacy work, and recommendations for Asian American social workers when engaging in community-engaged anti-Asian racism advocacy. Importantly, we have highlighted that advocacy work with the community has been vigorous and challenging. There are historical examples that guide us to working effectively together through pan-ethnic solidarity, but, at the same time, fostering and educating the social work profession and Asian American communities to respect the unique cultures and traditions of diverse subgroups can help marginalized Asian American groups gain accessible resources. Although social workers have been catalysts for advocacy work to promote justice in society, this cannot be done without the actions of others. In this regard, the community's inherent wisdom, practices, and advocacy work that have been historically disregarded or untold needs to be shared. This is stated with a recognition that combating racism cannot be done without systematic and macro-level changes. Educating social workers to engage in social justice and advocacy work at all levels of practice is critical. This is the new direction that the CSWE has announced in its 2022 Educational Policy and Accreditation Standards (EPAS). In particular, updated Competency 3, "Engage Anti-Racism, Diversity, Equity, and Inclusion (ADEI) in Practice," is relevant in supporting the educational and training needs of social workers.

References

AAPI Youth Rising. (n.d.). AAPI Youth Rising: About Us. https://aapiyouthrising.org/about/

Ahmad, F. Z., & Weller, C. E. (2014). Reading between the data: The incomplete story of Asian Americans, Native Hawaiians, and Pacific Islanders. Center for American Progress. https://cdn.americanprogress.org/wp-content/uploads/2014/03/AAPI-report.pdf

Bacong, A. M., Nguyen, A., & Hing, A. K. (2020). Making the invisible visible: The role of public health critical race praxis in data disaggregation of Asian Americans and Pacific Islanders in the midst of the COVID-19 Pandemic. *AAPI Nexus: Policy, Practice, and Community, 17*(1–2). https://escholarship.org/uc/item/38b5h7c8

Bersamira, C., Lau, S. B., Lee, Y. J., & Yamauchi, J. (2024). Anti-Asian hate's impact on Asian American social workers: Implications for professional training and education. *Social Work*. Forthcoming.

Bhakta, S. (2022). Data disaggregation: The case of Asian and Pacific Islander data and the role of health sciences librarians. *Journal of the Medical Library Association, 110*(1), 133–138. https://doi.org/10.5195/jmla.2022.1372

Bonilla-Silva, E. (2006). From bi-racial to tri-racial: Towards a new system of racial stratification in the USA. *Ethnic and Racial Studies, 27*(6), 931–950. https://doi.org/10.1080/0141987042000268530

Branom, C. (2012). Community-based participatory research as a social work research and intervention approach. *Journal of Community Practice, 20*(3), 260–273. https://doi.org/10.1080/10705422.2012.699871

Bulosan, C. (2019). *America is in the Heart*. Penguin Random House.

Byon, A. H., Preston, D. C., Assalone, A. E., & Elliott, K. C. (2023). The role of advocacy organizations in student activism: Black lives matter and stop anti-Asian hate. *New Directions for Student Services, 2022*(180), 71–81. https://doi.org/10.1002/ss.20449

Cane, T. C., & Tedam, P. (2022). "We didn't learn enough about racism and anti-racist practice": Newly qualified social workers' challenge in wrestling racism. *Social Work Education, 42*(8), 1563–1585. https://doi.org/10.1080/02615479.2022.2063271

Chiang, M. (2009). *The cultural capital of Asian American studies: Autonomy and representation in the university*. New York University Press.

Council on Social Work Education (CSWE). (2022). Educational policy and accreditation standards (EPAS). https://www.cswe.org/accreditation/standards/2022-epas/

Council on Social Work Education (CSWE). (n.d.). Community-based participatory research (CBPR). https://www.cswe.org/CSWE/media/Diversity-Center/3-Module-3_Community-Based-Participatory-Research.pdf

Delloro, J. (2009, March 31). Cesar Chavez Day and the forgotten Asian Americans. *LAP Progressive*. https://www.laprogressive.com/rankism/cesar-chavez-day-and-the-forgotten-asian-americans

Hogg, M.A., Terry, D.J., & White, K.M. (1995). A tale of two theories: A critical comparison of identity theory with social identity theory. *Social Psychology Quarterly, 58*(4), 255–269. https://doi.org/10.2307/2787127

Hotz, T. (2011). Identifying the challenges in community-based participatory research collaboration. *American Medical Association of Journal Ethics, 13*(2), 105–108. https://doi.org/10.1001/virtualmentor.2011.13.2.jdsc2-1102

Iftikar, J. S., & Museus, S. D. (2018). On the utility of Asian critical (AsianCrit) theory in the field of education. *International Journal of Qualitative Studies in Education, 31*(10), 935–949. https://doi.org/10.1080/09518398.2018.1522008

Israel, B., Schulz, A., Parker, E., & Becker, A. (1998). Review of community-based research: Assessing partnership approaches to improve public health. *Annual Review of Public Health, 19*(1), 173–202. https://doi.org/10.1146/annurev.publhealth.19.1.173

Jacobson, M., & Rugeley, C. (2007). Community-based participatory research: Group work for social justice and community change. *Social Work with Groups, 30*(4), 21–39. https://doi.org/10.1300/J009v30n04_03

Joint Statement. (2021). Social work's call to action against pandemic othering & anti-Asian racism. https://secure.sswr.org/social-works-call-to-action-against-pandemic-othering-anti-asian-racism/

Kambhampaty, A. P. (2020, May 22). In 1968, these activists coined the term "Asian American": And helped shape decades of advocacy. *Time*. https://time.com/5837805/asian-american-history/

Katigbak, C., Foley, M., Robert, L., & Hutchinson, M. K. (2016). Experiences and lessons learned in using community-based participatory research to recruit Asian American immigrant research participants. *Journal of Nursing Scholarship, 48*(2), 210–218. https://doi.org/10.1111/jnu.12194

Kim, J. H. J., Lu, Q., & Stanton, A. L. (2021). Overcoming constraints of the model minority stereotype to advance Asian American health. *American Psychologist, 76*(4), 611–626. https://doi.org/10.1037/amp0000799

Kretzmann, J. & McKnight, J.P. (1996). Assets-based community development. *National Civic Review, 85*(4), 23–29. https://doi.org/10.1002/ncr.4100850405

Lai, H. M. (2004). *Becoming Chinese American: A history of communities and institutions* (vol. 13). Rowman Altamira.

Lau, S. B., Bersamira, C. S., Lee, Y. J., & Yamauchi, J. (2023). Asian American social workers' experiences and perspectives on the anti-Asian hate. *Journal of Social Work, 24*(1), 21–39. https://doi.org/10.1177/14680173231206727

Lee, Y. J. (2020). The impact of the COVID-19 pandemic on vulnerable older adults in the United States. *Journal of Gerontological Social Work, 63*(6–7), 559–564. https://doi.org/10.1080/01634372.2020.1777240

Lee, Y. J., Lau, S. B., Bersamira, C. S., & Yamauchi, J. (2023). Anti-Asian racism and COVID-19 impact on older adults: The voices of social workers. *Journal of Gerontological Social Work*, 1–20. https://doi.org/10.1080/01634372.2023.2202240

Le Espiritu, Y. (1992). *Asian American panethnicity: Bridging institutions and identities* (vol. 231). Temple University Press.

Lightfoot, E., McCleary, J. S., & Lum, T. (2014). Asset mapping as a research tool for community-based participatory research in social work. *Social Work Research, 38*(1), 59–64. https://doi.org/10.1093/swr/svu001

Liu, M., & Geron, K. (2008). Changing neighborhood: Ethnic enclaves and the struggle for social justice. *Social Justice, 35*(2/112), 18–35.

Liu, W. (2018). Complicity and resistance: Asian American body politics in Black lives matter. *Journal of Asian American Studies, 21*(3), 421–451.

Ma, K. P. K., Bacong, A. M., Kwon, S. C., Yi, S. S., & Đoàn, L. N. (2021). The impact of structural inequities on older Asian Americans during COVID-19. *Frontiers in Public Health, 9*, 690014–690014. https://doi.org/10.3389/fpubh.2021.690014

Majka, L., & Mullan, B. (2002). Ethnic communities and ethnic organizations reconsidered: South-East Asians and Eastern Europeans in Chicago. *International Migration, 40*(2), 71–92.

Morrow-Howell, N., & Gonzales, E. (2020). Recovering from coronavirus disease 2019 (COVID-19): Resisting ageism and recommitting to a productive aging perspective. *Public Policy and Aging Report*, praa021. https://doi.org/10.1093/ppar/praa021

Morrow-Howell, N., Galucia, N., & Swinford, E. (2020). Recovering from the COVID-19 pandemic: A focus on older adults. *Journal of Aging & Social Policy, 32*(4–5), 526–535.https://doi.org/10.1080/08959420.2020.1759758

Museus, S. D., & Iftikar, J. (2014). Asian critical theory (AsianCrit). In M. Y. Danico (Ed.), *Asian American society: An encyclopedia* (pp. 95–98). Sage Publications and Association for Asian American Studies. https://doi.org/10.4135/9781452281889

Nadal, K. (2019). The Brown Asian American movement: Advocating for South Asian, Southeast Asian, and Filipino American communities. *Asian American Policy Review, 29*, 2–95.

Nakano, D. Y. (2013). An interlocking panethnicity: The negotiation of multiple identities among Asian American social movement leaders. *Sociological Perspectives, 56*(4), 569–595. https://doi.org/10.1525/sop.2013.56.4.569

National Association of Social Workers (NASW). (n.d.). Read the code of ethics. https://www.socialworkers.org/About/Ethics/Code-of-Ethics/Code-of-Ethics-English

National Institute on Minority Health and Health Disparities (NIMHD). (n.d.). Community-based participatory research program (CBPR). https://www.nimhd.nih.gov/programs/extramural/community-based-participatory.html

Okamoto, D., & Mora, G. C. (2014). Panethnicity. *Annual Review of Sociology, 40*(1), 219–239. https://doi.org/10.1146/annurev-soc-071913-043201

Pascual, R. (1996). Filipino towns. In Antalio C. Ubaldes (Ed.), *Filipino American architecture, design, and planning* (pp. 41–58). Flipside Press.

Pollock, M. (2006). Everyday racism in education. *Anthropology News, 47*(2), 9–10. https://doi.org/10.1525/an.2006.47.2.9

Shah, N. S., & Kandula, N. R. (2020). Addressing Asian American misrepresentation and underrepresentation in research. *Ethnicity & Disease, 30*(3), 513–516. https://doi.org/10.18865/ed.30.3.513

Smith, C. F., Aguilar, J. P., Kozu, S., D'Angelo, K. A., Keenan, E. K., & Monroe Tomczak, S. (2022). If anti-racism is the goal, then anti-oppression is how we get there. *Advances in Social Work, 22*(2), 758–778. https://doi.org/10.18060/24646

State of Hawaii, Department of Health. (2023). Race of COVID-19 cases, Hawaii 2023. https://health.hawaii.gov/coronavirusdisease2019/tableau_dashboard/race-ethnicity-data/

Stop AAPI Hate. (2022). Two years and thousands of voices: What community-generated data tells us about anti-AAPI hate. https://stopaapihate.org/wp-content/uploads/2022/07/Stop-AAPI-Hate-Year-2-Report.pdf

Takaki, R. T. (2012). *Strangers from a different shore: A history of Asian Americans* (updated and revised). eBookIt.com.

Takamura, J. C., Browne, C., Jeung, R., Yellow Horse, A. J., Kwok, D., & Howard, D. (2022). Asian American elders: Caught in the crosshairs of a syndemic of racism, misogyny, and ageism during coronavirus disease 2019. *Public Policy and Aging Report, 32*(3), 87–93. https://doi.org/10.1093/ppar/prac011

Tran, J., & Curtin, N. (2017). Not your model minority: Own-group activism among Asian Americans. *Cultural Diversity & Ethnic Minority Psychology, 23*(4), 499–507. https://doi.org/10.1037/cdp0000145

University of Hawai'i West O'ahu Center for Labor Education and Research. (n.d.). History of labor in Hawai'i. https://www.hawaii.edu/uhwo/clear/home/HawaiiLaborHistory.html

Van Zomeren, M., Postmes, T., & Spears, R. (2008). Toward an integrative social identity model of collective action: A quantitative research synthesis of three socio-psychological perspectives. *Psychological Bulletin, 134*(4), 504–535. doi:10.1037/0033-2909.134.4.504. PMID: 18605818.

Yamashita, L. (2022). "I just couldn't relate to that Asian American narrative": How Southeast Asian Americans reconsider panethnicity. *Sociology of Race and Ethnicity, 8*(2), 250–266.

Yellow Horse, A. J., Kuo, K., Seaton, E. K., & Vargas, E. D. (2021). Asian Americans' indifference to Black lives matter: The role of nativity, belonging and acknowledgment of anti-Black racism. *Social Sciences (Basel), 10*(5), 168–186. https://doi.org/10.3390/socsci10050168

Yoo, H. S., H. C., Gabriel, A. K., & Okazaki, S. (2022). Advancing research within Asian American psychology using Asian Critical Race Theory and as an Asian Americanist perspective. *Journal of Humanistic Psychology, 62*(4), 563–590. Doi:10.1177/00221678211062721

Zhou, M., & Logan, J. R. (1989). Returns on human capital in ethnic enclaves: New York City's Chinatown. *American Sociological Review*, 809–820.

18
Policy Initiatives on Eliminating Anti-Asian Racism

Meirong Liu, Yanfeng Xu, and Zhanjie Si

Introduction

Racism operates at institutional and individual levels, and the results of the oppressive ideologies are embedded in both policy and practice (Liu, 2023; Teixeira et al., 2021). Thus, to address the negative impact of racism, a macro lens is essential. A critical macro lens offers a perspective that shows the greatest challenge of racism is not the result of the broken social, educational, or criminal justice systems, but instead the result of these systems working as they were intended to work and for whom they were intended to work (Hayes-Greene & Love, 2018; Liu, 2023; Teixeria et al., 2021). The *policy practice approach* engages social workers in examining policies and advocating for changes at both meso and macro levels (Moyson et al., 2017), and it requires social work's involvement in policy analysis and advocacy to ensure that resources are allocated and collective actions can be taken (Padilla & Fong, 2016).

In fact, social workers have often been the key architects in developing major social policies, such as child welfare policies (Morris et al., 2018), immigration and refugee policies (Humphries, 2004), and mental health policies (Mullen, 2013). Scholars have also called for urgent institutional changes that address structural inequalities (Azhar et al., 2021; Corley & Young, 2018; Lee & Kim, 2022). Macro-practice methods to address racial injustice include social justice advocacy, general public education, professional training, media activism, and building alliances with other social justice organizations (Liu, 2023; Teixeira et al., 2021).

Foster and Advance Policies Eliminating Anti-Asian Racism

First, social workers need to foster and advance policies that work to protect vulnerable populations and end systems of oppression related to racism.

Federal Responses to Anti-Asian Racism

The increased violence targeting Asian Americans throughout the COVID-19 pandemic has motivated lawmakers at the local, state, and federal levels to act. On May 20, 2021, President Joe Biden signed the COVID-19 Hate Crimes Act to address hate crimes, with particular emphasis on the rising violence against Asian Americans throughout the pandemic (US Senate, 2021). The act mandates the Department of Justice (DOJ) to appoint an officer to expedite hate crime reviews. It also mandates the DOJ to guide state, local, and tribal law enforcement agencies to establish online hate crime reporting processes and collect data disaggregated by protected characteristics (e.g., race or national origin). Additionally, it mandates joint efforts between the DOJ and the Department of Health and Human Services (DHHS) to expand education campaigns and issue guidance aimed at raising awareness of hate crimes during the COVID-19 pandemic. Furthermore, the legislation authorized grants for states and local governments to implement the National Incident-Based Reporting System and to conduct crime reduction programs to prevent, address, or respond to hate crimes (US Senate, 2021). In addition, the act calls on the DHHS, in coordination with the COVID-19 Health Equity Task Force and Asian American, Native Hawai'ian, and Pacific Islander (AANHPI) community-based organizations, to issue guidance on best practices for mitigating racially discriminatory language when describing the COVID-19 pandemic. Finally, the law commits to building more inclusive, diverse, and tolerant societies by prioritizing language access and inclusivity in communication practices. It also aims to combat misinformation and discrimination that pose a threat to AANHPI communities (US Senate, 2021).

The enactment of the COVID-19 Hate Crime Act marks a crucial milestone in the federal government's commitment to address increasing anti-Asian discrimination and hate crimes. While addressing bias-motivated violence through legislation and law enforcement is a significant step, it is accompanied by several limitations and challenges. Based on research and expert and public testimony, the US Commission on Civil Rights issued a report assessing the federal role in preventing and enforcing penalties against anti-Asian hate crimes from 2019 through 2021. The assessment found that, first, hate crime data are underreported by victims and by law enforcement, are less likely to be reported to police compared to other types of crimes, and Asian Americans may be even less likely to report discriminatory behavior when it occurs. Second, language barriers are impeding the reporting of incidents. Third, many incidents that do not meet the legal criteria for hate crimes, such as racial slurs or being spat on, still evoke fear but go unaccounted for in official statistics. Fourth, the absence of adequate performance metrics poses a significant challenge in assessing the federal government's effectiveness in combating the surge in hate crimes against the AANHPI community (US Commission on Civil Rights, 2023). Additionally, while legislation can increase penalties, it may not effectively deter potential offenders because hate crimes are often driven by deep-seated biases not easily influenced by the threat of legal consequences. Finally, the evolution of hate crimes poses new challenges, with online hate speech and extremism requiring innovative approaches beyond legislation and law enforcement to address their root causes.

Other than the COVID-19 Hate Crime Act, there have been other efforts from the federal government to address anti-Asian racism. Examples of recent initiatives include the White House Executive Order 13985, issued on January 20, 2021, aimed at "Advancing Racial Equality and Support for Underserved Communities Through the Federal Government" (The White House, 2021, January 20). Subsequently, on January 26, 2021, Presidential Biden issued "Memorandum Condemning and Combating Racism, Xenophobia, and Intolerance Against AAPI in the US" to condemn and combat racism, xenophora, and intolerance against AANHPI communities. Another noteworthy action is Executive Order 14031, issued on May 28, 2021, which established the "White House Initiative on Asian Americans, Native Hawaiians, and Pacific Islanders" to advance equality, justice, and opportunity for AANHPI community. Additionally, it created the President's Advisory Commission on AANHPI within the DHHS to explore ways the public, private, and nonprofit sectors can work together to advance equity, justice, and opportunity for AANHPI communities (The White House, 2023, May 28). Beyond these government measures, the FBI has also initiated nationwide civil rights training to promote state and local law enforcement reporting of hate crimes. Furthermore, the National Science Foundation is making significant investments by supporting more than 100 grants nationwide to understand, address, and eliminate bias and discrimination against AANHPI communities (The White House, 2021, March 30).

Federal responses are critical in addressing the complex challenges posed by hate crimes. Yet addressing the multifaceted challenges of racism requires comprehensive actions that go beyond legislation and law enforcement. The policy and legal framework create the scope and legitimacy for social workers' anti-racist efforts. Social workers play important roles in fostering, supporting, assessing, and advancing policies and programs that eliminate anti-Asian racism.

Advocating for Policies Against Anti-Asian Racism

Social workers can engage in the local, state, and federal government's efforts to raise awareness and prosecution of hate crimes, expand outreach efforts, and support victims at all stages of prosecution (The White House, 2021, May 28). For example, the Delaware Department of Justice has proposed to strengthen its efforts in raising awareness and prosecuting hate crimes statewide by hiring a social worker and expanding outreach efforts. The social worker will support victims of hate crimes, from case intake through to trial preparation, trial, sentencing, and the seemingly unending appellate and pardon processes that often trigger their revictimization. Importantly, this social worker will receive training on effectively engaging with victims of hate and bias and best practices in confronting hate groups, hate symbols, and crimes based on discrimination. The social worker will also help to facilitate mediation in situations where hate activity has occurred but prosecution is not the best solution (Delaware Bureau of Justice Assistance, 2023). Macro-practice social workers can initiate and participate in such innovative strategies, evaluate their effectiveness, and advocate for nationwide implementation.

Research and Compiling and Reporting Data

A major barrier to understanding the severity and magnitude of anti-Asian hate crimes is the lack of comprehensive data. The US Commission on Civil

Rights (2023) emphasized that without national data collection and law enforcement training on accurately identifying and reporting hate crimes, the prevention of hate crimes is substantially challenging (US Commission on Civil Rights, 2023). Meanwhile, research shows that, after reporting, Asian Americans who have experienced racism have lower race-based traumatic stress (Stop AAPI Hate, 2021). This suggests that reporting is one important strategy for Asian Americans to cope with hate incidents (Stop AAPI Hate, 2021). Macro-level social work practice can actively advocate for the improvement of hate crime data collection through several key strategies. First, policy suggestions can be made at the federal level to make it mandatory for state and local law enforcement to submit hate crime data. Second, social workers can advocate for improving such data collection, offering support for the implementation process as identified in the US Commission on Civil Rights (2023) report, which points out challenges with implementing the National Incident-Based Reporting System. This support may involve allocating funds to state and local governments, including the purchase of new software and computers or training officers. Further recommendations can be made, including establishing a designated attorney in the prosecutor's office to prosecute hate crimes. It is also suggested that the tracking and reporting of both hate incidents and hate crimes be mandated, with an emphasis on ensuring that reporting forms facilitate easy identification of incidents or crimes as suspected hate-related. Macro-level social work practice should advocate for state and local officials to leverage FBI resources, publicity tools, forensic expertise, and experience in identifying and investigating hate-based motivations, even in cases where federal hate crime charges are not pursued. Last, macro practice should advocate for proper performance measurements to assess whether federal, state, and local governments are taking sufficient actions to combat the rise in hate crimes.

Advocate for Nondiscriminative Policies

Social workers should actively advocate for identifying and eliminating federal, state, or local policies that use racial profiling to disadvantage or burden AANHPI individuals and for advancing policies that raise awareness about increased racism and discrimination against AANHPI people.

Land Discrimination Laws

A recent law introduced in Florida (Florida Senate, 2023) and similar legislation proposed elsewhere, including in Texas and South Carolina, aimed to restrict the right to buy real properties for nationals from Russia, North Korea, Iran, and the People's Republic of China. These proposed pieces of legislation would establish a property-owning framework where Asian Americans and people of Asian descent will face unwarranted suspicion and racial profiling. While acknowledging the specific, legitimate threats posed by certain foreign governments and their state-owned enterprises to national security, banning individuals from purchasing land or properties because of their citizenship status, national origin, race, ethnicity, or immigration status is a blatant infringement on their civil rights and unconstitutional (Chu, 2023, May 25). Macro-practice social workers should advocate strongly to oppose such existing harmful and xenophobic legislation and mobilize support for legislation that will preempt such laws and practices (Chu, 2023, May 25).

Voting

Participating in voting is another important aspect of advocating for nondiscriminatory policies. Macro-practice social workers should also actively strive to eliminate barriers for AANHPI communities to exercise the right to vote in local, state, and national elections. For example, support can be extended to Section 203 of the Voting Right Act (VRA), which requires certain counties and jurisdictions to provide bilingual voting materials in communities with language minorities and limited English proficient residents (US Census Bureau, 2022). Additionally, advocating for Section 208 of the VRA, which permits voters needing assistance due to blindness, disability, language barriers, or other difficulties to bring someone into the voting booth to help them understand and cast a ballot, is crucial. Macro-practice social workers should also support legislation that safeguards democracy and voting rights, such as the John R. Lewis Voting Rights Advancement Act (117th Congress, 2021), which restores and modernizes the full protections of the VRA.

Bystander Training Policies

Macro-practice social workers should also advocate for policies and programs that incorporate bystander intervention training to disrupt anti-Asian racism whenever it is happening. By encouraging and preparing employees to act when they witness harassing and discriminating behavior, bystander intervention training helps remove the uncertainty of not knowing when or how to intervene, especially in uncomfortable work situations (Liu, 2023). Title II of the Civil Rights Act should be expanded to include retail stores and other businesses where discrimination occurs, to protect employees and customers from bias-based discrimination and harassment. In addition, businesses should be required to train employees on their responsibility to maintain a space that is free from bias-based harassment and discrimination, even if perpetrated by customers.

Advocating for Language Access Policies

Social workers play a crucial role in advocating for the development of a mandatory language access policy statement, which prohibits discrimination based on national origin and ensures equal access to federal programs and benefits to all individuals, including those with limited English proficiency (LEP). This advocacy should promote effective communication through interpreter services, document translation, and staff training. In the United States, 34% of the Asian American population has limited English-language skills. Language barriers continue to be a major barrier in reporting hate incidents and hate crimes, as well as in victims' access to services (US Commission on Civil Rights, 2023). Under the COVID-19 Hate Crimes Act, funding is provided for state and local incident reporting hotlines, and the DOJ also expanded its language services to be available in 18 of the most frequently spoken AANHPI languages across the nation. However, local reporting hotlines, victim services, and law enforcement were not accessible to victims with LEP, pointing to a discrepancy between federal and local resource availability (US Commission on Civil Rights, 2023).

Macro-practice practitioners should also actively collaborate with law enforcement agencies and social service agencies to identify critical deficiencies in LEP programs. Efforts also should be directed to expand reporting hotlines or in-person contact for those with LEP. Investment should be given to strengthen and expand community services for victims to report attacks, receive support services, and take safety training in their own language. Social workers should advocate for law enforcement agencies and victim services to assess their compliance with Title VI within Executive Order 13166 (US Department of Transportation, 2021). This order directs federal agencies to improve access to their services for individuals with LEP. Proactive steps must be taken to address any violations to ensure the provision of language access services, including the availability of interpreters and bilingual officers (US Commission on Civil Rights, 2023).

Campaign for Narrative Change

Furthermore, AANHPI individuals and communities continue to be predominately portrayed in stereotypical and negative roles in TV and movies. A most recent national survey found that prevalent stereotypes persist, depicting Asian American women in limited and often less desirable roles, such as Geisha, sex worker, maid/janitor, and depicting Asian American men as Kung Fu, criminals, or gangsters (Social Tracking of Asian Americans in the US Index Report, 2021). On the other side, the "model minority stereotype" reinforces color-blind ideologies, according to which racial barriers should not play a significant role in the lives of people of color (Museus, 2013). It masks significant inequalities within the racial group, fuels the misconception that Asian Americans are problem-free, and thus perpetuates assumptions that they do not require resources and support; furthermore, it renders them invisible in research, policy, and practice (Museus & Kiang, 2009). The myth constructs Asian Americans as honorary "Whites" who are not as good as individuals in the racial majority but are superior to other minority groups; it therefore fosters racial division rather than solidarity among people of color (Matsuda, 1990).

It is critical to dismantle the complexity of Asian American communities if we are to hear and address any community's issues, including but not limited to poverty, health and mental health, immigration, and discrimination. As Lee and Ramakrishnan (2021) pointed out, the majority group enjoys narrative plenitude, with most of the stories centering around them and being told from their perspective. In contrast, minority groups experience narrative scarcity, with relatively few stories focusing on them and even fewer told from a minority perspective. For example, the blockbuster movie *Crazy Rich Asians* featured an all-Asian cast and was a meaningful step toward greater representation of AANHPI individuals in leading Hollywood roles. Yet, because of narrative scarcity, Americans saw only a thin slice of Asian

American life and had no comparable opportunities to gain insight into the varied stories, experiences, and challenges of the diverse Asian Americans who are neither wealthy nor East Asian (Lee & Ramakrishnan, 2021). It is important to advocate for a change of narrative, shifting away from negative stereotypes and the model minority myth. Instead, the focus should be on narrating the life, experiences, and struggles of diverse AANHPI individuals and communities. Social workers can systematically design and conduct research, accurately convey narratives based on it, and, in the process, correct biased assumptions of Asian Americans and other minoritized populations. By doing this, social workers can actively push back against the one-dimensional narratives in which stereotypes, tropes, and dated assumptions about Asian Americans persist (Lee & Ramakrishnan, 2021). Some strategies are discussed below.

Strategy 1: Condemning Racism and Xenophobia

Actions and voices from leaders to condemn racism and xenophobia are needed to change the current atmosphere against racial minorities. Social workers should coordinate with policymakers, communication experts, and media outlets to condemn racism and xenophobia and stand in unity with communities that are targets of racial discrimination.

Macro-practice social workers can play a critical role in initiating and supporting efforts that call on cities and institutions to apologize for their histories of racism and discrimination targeting Asian Americans. In November 2021, San Francisco became the fourth city in California, following Antioch, San Jose, and Los Angeles, to apologize to its Chinese American community for "systematic and structural discrimination, targeted acts of violence, and atrocities." These included discriminatory statutes that prohibited Asian American students from attending public schools with White students and others that targeted Asian laundries, racially profiled and segregated the Asian American community, and restricted their civil liberties (Iovino, 2022). The effort was led by local college and high school students who saw a direct connection between the attacks on their community today and the history that they were beginning to learn. Historical injustice persistently shapes the present, and confronting anti-Asian hate and violence today begins with confronting the root causes of ongoing discrimination found in the past.

Strategy 2: Using Nonstigmatizing Language

Macro-practice social workers can actively promote nonstigmatizing language to not perpetuate xenophobia. During the pandemic, some misguided media and state government officials referred to COVID-19 as the "Chinese virus," "Kung Flu," and the "Wuhan virus," thus perpetuating negative views of Asian individuals and communities and leading to many Asian Americans feeling blamed. According to the World Health Organization (2020), social stigma associated with a disease can result in fear and social isolation for those affected. As observed during the pandemic, the usage of nonstigmatizing language can help to avoid scapegoating. In the context of the COVID-19 pandemic and beyond, it is important to avoid terms indicating locations, ethnicities, or cultures when referring to COVID-19 or any other diseases. This practice can help to prevent bias incidents and hate crimes.

Strategy 3: Launching Online Activism

Online activism is another strategy for changing narratives. It is defined as using online media, particularly social media, to state one's stance on a political issue or to further discuss a political issue (Robyn et al., 2019). It would allow community members to start a conversation on an issue, facilitate in-depth discussion, and further allow community members to provide support, organize activities, and challenge negative responses to their activities (Rúdólfsdóttir & Jóhannsdóttir, 2018). A recent example of online activism among the AANHPI community is actions through social media after the introduction of a bill that banned Chinese citizens from buying property in 33 states of the United States in Spring and Summer 2023 (Kindy, 2023). The introduction of this bill has affected millions of Chinese immigrants who temporarily live and work and/or hold permanent resident status in the United States. This bill even impacts Chinese Americans and other AANHPI members who share a similar Asian appearance. Leaders in the Asian American communities and social media writers posted millions of news articles and narratives on social media regarding this bill and its implications and mobilized community members to sign petitions, attend hearings, advocate policy changes, and march on the street via social media. All these online activities served as the first step to distributing the news, sending information for community sessions, creating a conversation on this issue, and educating community members on racism against Asian Americans and its implications on the community and the next generation.

Online activism could be used to fight against racism toward AANHPI community members and change any negative narratives about the AANHPI community. Social workers should play a more important role in promoting online activism against racism, particularly structural racism against AANHPI members. Social workers could partner with local organizations, communities, and media to identify racism or injustice in the community and facilitate conversations and activities against racism online and offline.

The Role of Social Work Organizations/Leaderships

It is essential that national leadership in the social work profession to speak out against anti-Asian stigma and coordinate an effective response (Misra et al., 2020). The National Association of Social Work (NASW), the largest membership organization of professional social workers, has a mission to "enhance the professional growth and development of its members, to create and maintain professional standards, and to advance sound social policies" (NASW, n.d.). On February 19, 2021, NASW released a formal statement denouncing anti-Asian crimes, which has served as a critical reminder of the profession's mission of promoting social and health justice and calls for social workers to maintain self-awareness and remain vigilant regarding Asian American challenges and needs (Lau et al., 2023; NASW, 2021). Other social work organizations, including the Academy for Social Work and Social Welfare, the Asian Pacific Islander Social Work Educators Association, Council on Social Work Education, and Society for Social Work Research (SSWR) also issued jointed statements on social work's call to action against othering and anti-Asian racism (Council on Social Work Education, 2020). NASW has also initiated work to get Congress to pass the No Hate Act to prevent hate crimes, improve data reporting, and expand community-centered responses (NASW, 2021).

Yet these efforts have been limited. Social work practitioners, researchers, and educational organizations are critical advocates for anti-racist policies and meaningful social change. For example, the NASW, with its 55 chapters around the country, can initiate and support interest groups, workshops, conferences, conversations, and webinars on eliminating anti-Asian racism and xenophobia, thus promoting culturally competent care for Asian American and Pacific Islanders that builds alliances and share struggles. Continuing education should cover topics on addressing anti-Asian racism in social work education, cultural competency, and understanding history and diversity, and in fostering critical reflection on anti-racist allyship. Moreover, social work organizations should also distribute studies, reports, standards, policy briefs, and position statements on eliminating anti-Asian racism, dismantling systems of oppression, and combating racism within social work profession. Critical conversations on eliminating anti-Asian racism, along with how current challenges and threats can be understood in the broader context of systemic racism, should be facilitated.

Furthermore, it is important to embrace and develop social workers' macro-practice approaches and competencies (Teixeria et al., 2021). Macro practice plays a critical role in the historical development of the social work profession and in addressing today's more complex social problems. However, it has not been paid enough attention or received sufficient support to develop social workers' macro-practice approaches and competencies (Mosley, 2017; Reisch, 2016). For instance, macro courses have been neglected or marginalized in school curriculum in social work education. Research on macro issues was downplayed because of a preference for the large federal grants available for micro practice research (Rothman & Mizrahi, 2014). To dismantle racism against the AANHPI community, it is necessary to apply the macro-practice framework, including case-to-cause, organizational management and leadership, community organizing, policy, and human rights advocacy, to advance social work's impact (Teixeria et al., 2021). Social workers serving AANHPI populations should be well-trained to analyze and identify the root causes of pressing problems, including racism. Using the case-to-cause framework, social workers not only need to provide direct services or make appropriate referrals but also analyze and address structural-level causes. Social workers also need to advocate for effective language interpretations if needed and increase cultural competency and humility in serving the AANHPI community. Macro interventions from the organizational management and leadership framework may include providing training to nonprofit organizations' workers to raise the awareness of anti-Asian racism, demystify the model minority illusion attached Asian Americans, and bring cultural humility to professionals working with AANHPI families. Employing a community organizing approach, social workers can foster and support the AANHPI community to support each other and advocate for a more inclusive community. At the policy practice level, social workers can advocate for policies to address the insufficient services available and to remove barriers to the AANHPI community by training more bilingual professionals, for instance. From a human rights perspective, social workers should assert that the rights and dignity of individuals should be assured and protected. Social workers are charged with elevating the voices of individuals and communities to advance policy that redresses inequality and improves well-being (Santiago et al., 2015). Social work's involvement in policy analysis and advocacy ensures that resources are equally allocated and collective actions can be taken in the face of anti-Asian racism (Padilla & Fong, 2016).

Build Coalitions With Social Justice Organizations

It is also critical for social workers to build alliances with other social justice organizations to combat racism. Stronger linkages across institutions and organizations can contribute to the development of collective wisdom for effectively addressing racism. This underscores the significance of our professional duties to intervene on a macro level as well and to persist in efforts in dismantling institutional racism (Corley & Young, 2018).

There has been an increasing political power in the Asian American community, unprecedented recognition of hate crimes against Asian Americans, growing solidarity across races, and increased determination to defeat White supremacy (Shah & Kauh, 2021). Social justice organizations—for example, Asian Americans Advancing Justice, the National Coalition for Asian Pacific American Community Development, and the Asian Youth Center—provide various anti-Asian racism resources to better inform Asian American communities and individuals experiencing anti-Asian harassment. Equally important, social workers need to closely cooperate and engage with community organizations, private practices, and grassroot and activist agencies.

In response to the current anti-Asian climate, Asian Americans have mobilized and continued to take actions on various types of support for their communities and allies. Many social justice organizations have been actively supporting the passage and implementation of legislation addressing anti-Asian racism. For example, Stop Asian American Pacific Islander Hate (Stop AAPI Hate) and the Congressional Asian Pacific American Caucus have played important roles in advocating for the passage of H.R. 3525 (Yellow

Horse et al., 2021). Stop AAPI Hate worked with elected officials to introduce the No Place for Hate California, which includes two bills. SB 1161 requires the largest transit operators to address hate-based harassment experienced by riders, and AB 2448 expands civil rights protections at large businesses, where 27% of reported hate incidents in the state occur (Yellow Horse et al., 2022). Make Us Visible, a coalition of students, parents, educators, and community members, led the effort to support the bills to include AANHPI history in K-12 curriculum in New Jersey. The Asian American Education Project offered free trainings and made more than 50 comprehensive lesson plans available online to support teachers in revising their course content to create a more inclusive learning environment while empowering Asian American students. Advocating Justice/Chicago also developed a professional workshop and has trained more than 1,300 teachers from across the United States how to teach Asian American history. Grassroots movements like this, in addition to top-down advocacy efforts like research and policy development, can combat anti-Asian racism by increasing education and awareness, which can result in policies and structural change (Lau et al., 2023).

Foster Communities to Get Involved in Civic Engagement and Policy Advocacy

It is crucial to further cultivate civic engagement among AANHPI members through various means. Strengthening civic involvement within the AANHPI community involves adopting diverse strategies, such as fostering engagement, disseminating information, and organizing initiatives (Alliance for a Better Community, n.d.). AANHPI members can actively participate in the community by staying informed through local news, volunteering, voting, running for offices, attending city council meetings, and supporting community-based organizations and local businesses (Garcia, 2020). Social workers, particularly AANHPI social workers, play a pivotal role in promoting civic engagement among community members. To do so, it begins with educating AANHPI individuals on the importance of civic participation. Implementing a Civic Education 101 course for AANHPI members, especially the younger generations, is imperative. Delivering this course through popular social media platforms like TikTok, Instagram, Facebook, and YouTube as concise videos would enhance accessibility.

Additionally, integrating this educational opportunity into AANHPI-oriented church Sunday schools, language schools (e.g., Chinese schools), and an educational session during AANHPI heritage month in public and private schools is essential. Social workers, particularly those of AANHPI descent, should create avenues for community volunteering and encourage AANHPI members to contribute to their communities as part of civic engagement. Collaborating with local AANHPI organizations, supporting cultural events, supporting local businesses, and actively participating in elections at various levels are crucial steps for social workers. For instance, Chinese Immigrants Associations in the United States routinely organize annual events for Moon festivals and the Lunar New Year; however, professional social workers' roles are very limited in these events. It is necessary for social workers to participate in such events and mobilize AANHPI members' civic engagement through these festive events. In addition, promoting civic engagement extends to supporting local businesses. Local businesses have substantial influence in various aspects in the community, including charitable contributions, community development, and even political elections. Social workers should play a vital role in advocating for local businesses to embrace civic engagement as an integral component of their corporate responsibility initiatives. Social workers should take a role in encouraging local businesses to actively participate in community volunteer opportunities, make donations, engage with elected officials, and contribute to the shaping of policies and legislation. Furthermore, social workers should act as facilitators, establishing meaningful connections between local businesses and the community, guiding and supporting businesses in their civic engagement endeavors. Fostering this partnership will lead to increased community well-being and unite more residents to civic activities.

Prior studies indicates that Asian Americans have among the lowest levels of voting participation, and this might be largely attributed to the large proportion of first-generation immigrants within the Asian adult citizen population, the lack of parental socialization into US political parties, limited exposure to American politics in Asian colleges, and lack of party contact and mobilization (Hajnal & Lee 2013; Lee & Ramakrishenan, 2021). Recognizing that not all AANHPI members are familiar with the political election process, social workers should take on the role of educators, providing information on voting procedures, candidate backgrounds and their visions, and the impact of elections on the community. Assisting with voter registration, conducting community information sessions, and even running for office are ways social workers can actively contribute to shaping policies and making change.

To have a larger positive impact on policy, macro social workers should also champion additional policy measures to increase the representation of AANHPI professionals in public service and civic leadership roles. For example, Asian Americans only make up 2% of police officers and 2% of teachers in public K-12 schools, while they constitute 7% of the US population (Chen & Contreras, 2021; Hussar et al., 2020). The underrepresentation of AANHPI professionals in these fields calls for policy initiatives that aim to recruit more Asian Americans into fields such as public service, education, policy-making, and social work.

It is equally important for social workers to empower the younger AANHPI generation by enhancing their leadership skills and community service involvement. Organizations like Asian American Advancing Leadership, which was founded in 2021 in South Carolina by a group of first-generation Asian Americans, exemplifies this effort by offering leadership development courses and services in the community to the next generation (Asian American Advancing Leadership, n.d.).

Ultimately, grassroots initiatives with a focus on leadership development will have the potential to significantly enhance civic engagement among AANHPI members, particularly the next generation, and eventually will foster positive changes and combat racism against this community.

Social workers can play a substantial role in fostering and facilitating civic engagement within AANHPI communities. However, the current scope of social workers' roles appears to be constrained, possibly caused by a shortage of AANHPI social workers or insufficient attention to the AANHPI community within the broader social work agenda in the United States. This limited focus may be attributed to societal unawareness of racism and discrimination against AANHPI individuals and a lack of macro practice and AANHPI-centered approaches in social work education and practice in the United States. This may be due to the predominant emphasis on clinical work over macro-level interventions (e.g., policy). Shifting this focus could empower social workers with the readiness to mobilize people in this community and make changes at the macro level. Moreover, social work educational programs need to elevate their attention to the AANHPI community, incorporating AANHPI-centered practices and policies into their curricula. By doing so, future social workers, particularly AANHPI social workers, will be better equipped to address the unique challenges faced by and opportunities within AANHPI communities and eliminate racism against the AANHPI community. By increasing awareness and mobilizing community members, social workers can actively contribute to positive changes at institutional and individual levels, thereby advancing the cause of equity and justice within the AANHPI community.

Promoting Policies and Programs on AANHPI History Education

In addition to the efforts we mentioned earlier, it is important that, through general education, we can systematically address prejudices, stereotypes, and biases that lead to misinformation, disinformation, bias, prejudices, and—ultimately—violence (Asian Americans Advancing Justice, n.d.).

Teaching of AANHPI History in Schools

The teaching of Asian American history remains largely absent in K-12 classrooms and in many college US history courses. Such an absence of Asian American history in classrooms lays the foundation for ignorance, hate, and violence. When entire communities and groups are erased, ignored, or dismissed as important members and actors in our shared history, their significance as contributors to the US today is also neglected. The lack of a comprehensive and truthful examination of America's extensive history of anti-Asian racism leads to characterizing contemporary hate crimes as random and isolated incidents, rather than acknowledging them as expressions of systematic racism specifically targeting Asian Americans (Lee, n.d.).

Macro social work practice can actively promote the teaching of Asian American history in public schools by providing testimony, introducing, and passing related bills. Oregon pioneered the requirement of ethnic studies for K-12 in 2017, with California subsequently becoming the first state to pass a statewide ethnic studies program in high schools in 2021 (Blume & Gomez, 2021). Illinois became the first state to require "a unit of instruction studying the events of Asian American history" in public schools the same year (Liu, 2023). A state representative stated, "Empathy comes from understanding. We cannot do better unless we know better. A lack of knowledge is the root cause of discrimination and the best weapon against ignorance is education"

(Davis-Marks, 2021). Other states have also taken steps. New Jersey, in January 2022, became the second state to mandate AANHPI history in K-12 schools. Connecticut became the first state to fund mandated instruction of AANHPI history and a coordinator position within the state department of education to oversee research and curriculum alignment in K-12 schools (Lau, 2022). Such legislation is a way to create a more inclusive and comprehensive understanding of Asian American history for students and their families and thereby contribute to the fight against anti-Asian racism and xenophobia.

Despite this progress, there have been limitations. The current teaching of AANHPI history is insufficient. Until January 2022, 18 states included zero content on Asian Americans in K-12 schools. In addition, most textbooks mainly focus on the Chinese Exclusion Act and Japanese American internment during World War II (Lee et al., 2022). Yet the nation's 22 million Asian American represent roots in more than 20 countries and many different faiths and traditions (Pew Research Center, 2021).

Furthermore, Asian American representation is quite limited and passive. Accomplishments are stated vaguely, and important historical Asian American figures are absent (Lee et al., 2022). Notably, in Florida, a new law mandated the teaching of AANHPI history in public schools yet at the same time limited the way race and gender would be taught in higher education institutions and no longer permitted public funding for diversity, equity, and inclusion efforts. Asian American history is intertwined and inextricably tied to others' experiences, challenges, and struggles. The greater context around race education can't be ignored (Yam, 2023). Recognizing Asian Americans—and all Americans—as equally integral to the nation's history and society is crucial to building solidarity and an inclusive future. Macropractice social workers should actively advocate for policies and programs that reform history curricula and support curriculum implementation. Ongoing efforts should be made together with educators to create activities and advance history curriculum to create a more inclusive history education (Asian Americans Advancing Justice, n.d.).

Teaching AANHPI History to the Public

Macro-level advocacy efforts are essential at the federal, state, and local levels to organize events that bring awareness to and educate the public on Asian American history. These initiatives should focus on the diverse culture, traditions, and contributions of AANHPI individuals and communities and the long-rooted history of anti-Asian racism and they should recognize the injustice and inequalities faced by various Asian American subgroups. A recent nationwide survey found that 58% of Americans were unable to name a prominent Asian American, 42% of Americans answered "don't know" when asked about significant events or policies related to the history and experience of Asian Americans (Asian American Foundation, 2023), and still nearly one-third of Americans are unaware that attacks against Asian Americans are increasing (Asian American Foundation, 2023).

In response to such a knowledge gap, several initiatives have been made to educate the public and recognize the history and culture of Asian Americas. For examples, H.R. 3525 was passed in 2022 to establish a commission to create a national museum of Asian Pacific American culture (The White House, 2022). New York State had recognized Asian Lunar New Year as a public school holiday (Chu, 2023). Lawmakers now are working toward making Lunar New Year a federal holiday, aiming to educate people on cultural practices and broaden experiences beyond one's individual heritage (Meng, 2022). Yet more needs to be done to recognize diverse Asian groups. In 1992, the US Congress passed a law designating May as Asian-Pacific American Heritage Month (Library of Congress, n.d.). Despite this recognition, efforts need to be made so that AANHPI Heritage Month highlights a broader array of the cultures and histories of Asian American subgroups, such as South Asians, Southeast Asians, Native Hawai'ians, and Pacific Islander. Macro-practice social workers can play a crucial role in advocating for policies and programs designed to bring such awareness and education directly to the public.

First Responders, Law Enforcement Officers, and Policymakers

Mandatory education or training programs on dealing with hate crimes should be implemented for first responders, law enforcement offers, and prosecutors in their respective jurisdictions. For instance, in the aftermath of the Atlanta killings, the shooter initially denied any racial motivation, claiming that his actions were driven by "sexual addiction." Authorities appeared to accept this claim and reiterated the suspect's claim that the spas represented "a temptation for him that he wanted to eliminate." However,

Asian American advocates quickly pointed to the historical sexualization of Asian women in the United States, emphasizing its role in perpetuating racist and sexist stereotypes and structures and leading to persistent racial and gender-based discrimination and violence. When the Congressional House Judiciary Committee held hearings on discrimination and violence against Asian Americans two days after the Atlanta shootings, advocates and scholars joined lawmakers to explain the deep roots of anti-Asian racism in the United States, condemn the use of racist terms, and urge Congress to take actions. Lawmakers were exposed to the realities of Asian American history when presented with evidence from the history of anti-Asian racism and discrimination (Lee, n.d.). Macro-practice social workers should actively support policies and programs that comprehensively educate first responders, law enforcement officers, and policymakers on the history of anti-Asian racism and "yellow peril" laws. Such programs are critical to contextualize the increased anti-Asian sentiment during the COVID-19 pandemic and to understand that the myth of the "perpetual foreigner" continues to play a role in understanding the rise of anti-Asian racism and discrimination.

Conclusion

In conclusion, macro social work is critical for system-level changes in eliminating the systemic, root causes of anti-Asian racism (Teixeira et al., 2021). Other areas that need actions from macro-practice social workers include pursuing a fair and accurate count of AANHPI communities in the US Census, increasing census research on improving outreach to Asian Americans, and working for redistricting efforts, such as developing and preserving communities of interest among Asian Americans. Through a variety of ways, macro social workers can take a broad range of concrete actions to advance policies and programs against anti-Asian racism, advocating for resources, bringing education and awareness, organizing and promoting anti-racism programs and initiatives, and fostering alliances with social justice organizations to address and prevent anti-Asian hate crimes and protect the well-being of AANHPI individuals and their communities. The Grand Challenge to Eliminate Racism urges the social work profession to focus on eradicating systemic racism and White supremacy (Teasley et al., 2021). Addressing the challenge requires social workers to embrace macro practice approaches and competencies (Teixeria et al., 2021). Social workers have the responsibility of elevating the voices of communities to advance policies that reduce inequality and enhance well-being (Zanbar & Itzhaky, 2018). Addressing the root causes of racism through the Grand Challenges takes a coordinated effort across all levels of social work practice. Given the institutional nature of racism, macro-level social work is much needed.

Acknowledgments

We would like to thank Tianpu Zhang and Keliang Zhu for their valuable contributions and insights that significantly enhanced the discussion of this chapter. Their expertise and dedication were instrumental in shaping the final content.

References

117th Congress. (2021). H.R.4 - John R. Lewis Voting Rights Advancement Act of 2021. Retrieved from https://www.congress.gov/bill/117th-congress/house-bill/4

Alliance for a Better Community. (n.d.). Civic engagement. https://afabc.org/what-we-do/civic-engagement/

Asian American Advancing Leadership. (n.d.). About. https://www.aaaleadership.org/about

Asian Americans Advancing Justice (AAJC). (n.d.). Education advocacy. https://www.advancingjustice-aajc.org/education-advocacy

Asian American Foundation. (2023). STAATUS Index 2023. https://www.staatus-index.org/

Azhar, S., Farina, A., Alvarez, A. R. G., & Klumpner, S. (2021). Asian in the time of COVID-19: Creating a social work agenda for Asian American and Pacific Islander communities. *Social Work*, swab044. Advance online publication. https://doi.org/10.1093/sw/swab044

Blume, H., & Gomez, M. (2021, October 8). California becomes first state to require ethnic studies for high school graduation. *Los Angeles Times*. https://www.latimes.com/california/story/2021-10-08/california-first-state-require-ethnic-studies-high-school-graduation

Chen, S., & Contreras, R. (2021, March 26,). Asian Americans are underrepresented in law enforcement. *Axios*. https://www.axios.com/2021/03/26/asian-americans-are-underrepresented-in-law-enforcement

Chu, I. (2023, September 13). Lunar New Year now a holiday for NY public schools. *The New York State Senate*. https://www.nysenate.gov/newsroom/in-the-news/2023/iwen-chu/lunar-new-year-now-holiday-ny-public-schools

Chu, J. (2023, May 25). Reps. Chu, Green introduce federal legislation to preempt discriminatory state land laws http://chu.house.gov/media-center/press-releases/reps-chu-green-introduce-federal-legislation-preempt-discriminatory

Corley, N. A., & Young, S. (2018). Is social work still racist? A content analysis of recent literature. *Social Work*, 63, 317–326. https://doi.org/10.1093/sw/swy042

Council on Social Work Education. (2020) Joint statement: Social work's call to action against pandemic othering and anti-Asian racism. https://www.cswe.org/CSWE/media/News/Social-Work-Joint-Statement-on-Anti-Asian-Violence-and-Racism.pdf

Davis-Marks, I. (2021, July 14). Illinois becomes first state to mandate teaching Asian American history. *Smithsonian Magazine.* https://www.smithsonianmag.com/smart-news/illinois-becomes-first-state-mandate-teaching-asian-american-history-public-schools-180978160/

Delaware Bureau of Justice Assistance. (2023, September 28). Hate crimes social worker & public outreach. https://bja.ojp.gov/funding/awards/15pbja-23-gg-05371-hate

Florida Senate. (2023). Interests of foreign countries. https://www.flsenate.gov/Committees/BillSummaries/2023/html/3145

Garcia, B. (2020). 5 ways civic engagement helps communities. Temboo. https://blog.temboo.com/5-ways-civic-engagement-helps-communities/

Hajnal, Z., & Lee, T. (2013). *Why Americans don't join the party: Race, immigration, and the failure (of political parties) to engage the electorate.* Princeton University Press.

Hayes-Greene, D., & Love, B. P. (2018). The groundwater approach: Building a practical understanding of structural racism. The Racial Equity Institute. https://www.racialequityinstitute.com/groundwaterapproach

Humphries, B. (2004). An unacceptable role for social work: Implementing immigration policy. *British Journal of Social Work, 34*(1), 93–107.

Hussar, B., Zhang, J., Hein, S., Wang, K., Roberts, A., Cui, J., Smith, M., Mann, F. B., Barmer, A., & Dilig, R. (2020). The condition of education 2020. https://nces.ed.gov/pubs2020/2020144.pdf

Iovino, N. (2022, February 1). San Francisco apologizes to Chinese immigrants for historic discrimination. *Courthouse News Service.* https://www.courthousenews.com/san-francisco-apologizes-to-chinese-immigrants-for-historic-discrimination/

Kindy, A. (2023, August 21). State laws on Chinese land ownership near military bases. *The Washington Post.* https://www.washingtonpost.com/politics/2023/08/21/state-laws-chinese-land-ownership-military-bases/

Lau, K. (2022). Investigating Asian American history and its roots in New England: A curriculum for secondary school students. *Holster Scholar Projects.* https://digitalcommons.lib.uconn.edu/srhonors_holster/38

Lau, S. B., Bersamira, C. S., Lee, Y. J., & Yamauchi, J. (2023). Asian American social workers' experiences and perspectives on anti-Asian hate. *Journal of Social Work.* https://doi.org/10.1177/14680173231206727

Lee, E. (n.d.). The necessity of teaching Asian American history. Organization of American Historians. https://www.oah.org/tah/asian-american-and-pacific-islander-history/the-necessity-of-teaching-asian-american-history/

Lee, J., Cho, H., & Orrego, J. (2022). Asian American representation in US History textbooks. *Journal of Student Research, 11*(3), 1–13.

Lee, J., & Kim, S. B. (2022). Standing against anti-Asian racism in America. *Health & Social Work, 47*(3), 157–159. https://doi.org/10.1093/hsw/hlac013

Lee, J., & Ramakrishnan, K. (2021). From narrative scarcity to research plenitude for Asian Americans. *RSF: The Russell Sage Foundation Journal of the Social Sciences, 7*(2), 1–20. https://doi.org/10.7758/rsf.2021.7.2.01

Lee, J. H. (2021). Combating anti-Asian sentiment: A practical guide for clinicians. *New England Journal of Medicine, 384*(25), 2367–2369. https://doi-org.proxyhu.wrlc.org/10.1056/NEJMp2102656

Library of Congress. (n.d.). Asian-Pacific American heritage month. https://cdn.loc.gov/project/lcnet/AsianPacificAmerMonth/#:~:text=In%201992%2C%20the%20official%20designation,Month%20was%20signed%20into%20law

Liu, M. (2023). Confronting the history of racism against Asian Americans in the United States. In M. L. Teasley, M. S. Spencer, & M. Bartholomew (Eds.), *Social work and the grand challenge to eliminate racism: Concepts, theory, and evidence-based approaches* (pp. 304–333).

Matsuda, G. (1990). "Only the beginning": Continuing the fight for empowerment. *Amerasia Journal, 16*(1): 159–169.

Meng, G. (2022). Meng reintroduces legislation to make Lunar New Year a federal holiday. House of Representatives. https://meng.house.gov/media-center/press-releases/meng-reintroduces-legislation-to-make-lunar-new-year-a-federal-holiday

Misra, S., Le, P. D., Goldmann, E., & Yang, L. H. (2020). Psychological impact of anti-Asian stigma due to the COVID-19 pandemic: A call for research, practice, and policy responses. *Psychological Trauma: Theory, Research, Practice, and Policy, 12*(5), 461.

Morris, K., Mason, W., Bywaters, P., Featherstone, B., Daniel, B., Brady, G., Bunting, L., Hooper, J., Mirza, N., Scourfield, J. & Webb, C. (2018). Social work, poverty, and child welfare interventions. *Child & Family Social Work, 23*(3), 364–372. https://doi.org/10.1111/cfs.12423

Mosley, J. E. (2017). Yes, macro practice matters: Embracing the complexity of real-world social work. *Human Service Organizations: Management, Leadership & Governance, 41*(1), 10–12.

Moyson, S., Scholten, P., & Weible, C. M. (2017). Policy learning and policy change: Theorizing their relations from different perspectives. *Policy and Society, 36*(2), 161–177. https://doi.org/10.1080/14494035.2017.1331879

Mullen, E. J. (2013). Outcomes measurement: A social work framework for health and mental health policy and practice. In A. Metteri, T. Kroger, A. Pohjola, & P.-L. Rauhala (Eds.), *Social work approaches in health and mental health from around the globe* (pp. 77–93). Routledge.

Museus, S. D. (2013). Asian Americans and Pacific Islanders: A national portrait of growth, diversity, and inequality. In *The misrepresented minority* (pp. 11–41). Routledge.

Museus, S. D., & Kiang, P. N. (2009). Deconstructing the model minority myth and how it contributes to the invisible minority reality in higher education research. *New Directions for Institutional Research, 2009*(144), 5–15. https://doi.org/10.1002/ir.292

National Association of Social Workers (NASW). (2021, June 29). NASW outraged by hate crimes against people who are Asian. https://www.socialworkers.org/News/News-Releases/ID/2280/NASW-outragedby-hate-crimes-against-people-who-are-Asian.

National Association of Social Workers (NASW). (2021). NASW calls for an end to hate, racism, and gun violence against Asian Americans. https://www.socialworkers.org/News/News-Releases/ID/2298/NASW-Calls-for-an-End-to-Hate-Racism-and-Gun-Violence-Against-Asian-Americans

National Association of Social Workers (NASW). (n.d.). About NASW. https://www.socialworkers.org/About

Padilla, Y. C., & Fong, R. (2016). Identifying grand challenges facing social work in the next decade: Maximizing social policy engagement. *Journal of Policy Practice, 15*(3), 133–144.

Reisch, M. (2016). Why macro practice matters. *Journal of Social Work Education, 52*(3), 258–268.

Robyn, K., Mallett, R. K., & Monteith, M. J. (Eds.). (2019). Confronting prejudice and discrimination: The science of changing minds and behaviors (pp. 319–335). Elsevier. https://doi.org/10.1016/B978-0-12-814715-3.00011-4

Rothman, J., & Mizrahi, T. (2014). Balancing Micro and Macro Practice: A Challenge for Social Work. *Social Work, 59*(1), 91–93. http://www.jstor.org/stable/23719548.

Rúdólfsdóttir, A. G., & Jóhannsdóttir, Á. (2018). Fuck patriarchy! An analysis of digital mainstream media discussion of the# freethenipple activities in Iceland in March 2015. *Feminism & Psychology, 28*(1), 133–151. https://doi.org/10.1177/0959353517715876

Pew Research Center. (2021, April 29). Key facts about Asian Americans, a diverse and growing population. https://www.pewresearch.org/short-reads/2021/04/29/key-facts-about-asian-americans/

Santiago, A. M., Rosenberg, B., Coulton, C., Bartle, E., Beck, E. L., Sherraden, M., & Chang, Y. (2015). Macro practice in social work: From learning to action for social justice. Frameworks for practice: Report of the Special Commission to Advance Macro Practice in Social Work.

Shah, M., & Kauh, T. J. (2021). How do we advance health equity for Asian Americans? Robert Wood Johnson Foundation. https://www.rwjf.org/en/insights/blog/2021/06/how-do-we-advance-health-equity-for-asian-americans.html

Social Tracking of Asian Americans in the US Index Report 2021. (2021). *LAAUNCH*. https://uploadsssl.webflow.com/5f629e7e013d961943d5cec9/6098a7be3d627168e03054da_staatus-index-2021.pdf

Stop AAPI Hate. (2021). Mental health report. https://stopaapihate.org/wp-content/uploads/2021/05/Stop-AAPI-Hate-Mental-Health-Report-210527.pdf

Teasley, M. L., McCarter, S., Woo, B., Conner, L. R., Spencer, M. S., & Green, T. (2021). The Grand challenges to eliminate racism. *Grand Challenges for Social Work*. https://grandchallengesforsocialwork.org/wp-content/uploads/2021/05/Eliminate-Racism-Concept-Paper.pdf

Teixeira, S., Augsberger, A., Richards-Schuster, K., Sprague Martinez, L., & Evans, K. (2021). Opportunities to "make macro matter" through the grand challenges for social work. *Families in Society, 102*(3), 414–426.

US Census Bureau. (2022, December 28). Redistricting & Voting Rights Data Office. Section 203 language determinations. cencus.gov. https://www.census.gov/programs-surveys/decennial-census/about/voting-rights/voting-rights-determination-file.html#:~:text=As%20enacted%20in%201965%20and,well%20enough%20to%20participate%20in

US Commission on Civil Rights. (2023). US Commission on Civil Rights releases report: The federal response to anti-Asian racism in the United States. https://www.usccr.gov/news/2023/us-commission-civil-rights-releases-report-federal-response-anti-asian-racism-united

US Department of Transportation. (2021). Title VI & Executive Order 13166. https://www.transportation.gov/civil-rights/civil-rights-awareness-enforcement/title-vi-executive-order-13166

US Senate. (2021). S.937 - COVID-19 Hate Crimes Act. Congress.gov. https://www.congress.gov/bill/117th-congress/senate-bill/937

The White House. (2021, January 20). Executive order on further advancing racial equity and support for underserved communities through the federal government. https://www.whitehouse.gov/briefing-room/presidential-actions/2023/02/16/executive-order-on-further-advancing-racial-equity-and-support-for-underserved-communities-through-the-federal-government/#:~:text=On%20my%20first%20day%20in,long%20been%20underserved%2C%20and%20addressing

The White House. (2021, March 30). President Biden announces additional actions to respond to anti-Asian violence, xenophobia and bias [fact sheet]. https://www.whitehouse.gov/briefing-room/statements-releases/2021/03/30/fact-sheet-president-biden-announces-additional-actions-to-respond-to-anti-asian-violence-xenophobia-and-bias/

The White House. (2021, May 28). Executive order on advancing equity, justice, and opportunity for Asian Americans, Native Hawaiians, and Pacific Islanders. https://www.whitehouse.gov/briefing-room/presidential-actions/2021/05/28/executive-order-on-advancing-equity-justice-and-opportunity-for-asian-americans-native-hawaiians-and-pacific-islanders/

The White House. (2022, June 13). Remarks by President Biden and Vice President Harris at Signing of H.R. 3525, the "Commission to Study the Potential Creation of a National Museum of Asian Pacific American History and Culture Act." https://www.whitehouse.gov/briefing-room/speeches-remarks/2022/06/13/remarks-by-president-biden-and-vice-president-harris-at-signing-of-h-r-3525-the-commission-to-study-the-potential-creation-of-a-national-museum-of-asian-pacific-american-history-and-culture/

Yam, K. (2023, May 17). DeSantis criticized for mandating Asian American history while banning courses on systemic racism. *NBC News*. https://www.nbcnews.com/news/asian-america/desantis-criticized-mandating-asian-american-history-banning-courses-s-rcna84972

Yellow Horse, A. J., Jeung, R., Matriano, R., & Tang, A. (2021). National report. *Stop AAPI Hate.* https://stopaapihate.org/wp-content/uploads/2021/08/Stop-AAPI-Hate-Report-National-v2-210830.pdf

Zanbar, L., & Itzhaky, H. (2018). Community activists from different cultures: Implications for social work. *Journal of Social Work, 18*(6), 732–751. https://doi.org/10.1177/1468017318757396

Conclusion

Hopes for the Future and Call for Action in Addressing Anti-Asian Racism

Keith T. Chan and Meirong Liu

This edited volume is a compilation from social work scholars, and it is a labor of love. The conceptualization of this volume began as a response to the tragic events that occurred during the COVID-19 pandemic and the rise of anti-Asian racism which impacted our communities. As many of us recoiled from the violence and hate we saw in the world, those of us who came together to contribute to the writing of this volume did so with hope in our hearts for a better world and a better future. Social work as a profession can play an enormous role in eradicating anti-Asian racism and hate, and, despite differences in cultures, backgrounds, and other intersecting identities and issues, we, as the contributors to this volume, believed in the power of working with other like-minded persons to achieve the goals of unity and social justice.

Although it is impossible to exhaustively address all intersections and marginalized identities related to anti-Asian racism within the diverse population of Asian Americans, we believe our volume can be an important step in infusing this content into social work curricula and our discipline. We hope to thread the needle and address the gap in knowledge to better understand and dismantle anti-Asian racism through efforts from the profession of social work through scholarship, research, policy action, and practice.

Keith T. Chan and Meirong Liu, *Conclusion* In: *Addressing Anti-Asian Racism with Social Work, Advocacy, and Action.* Edited by: Meirong Liu and Keith T. Chan, Oxford University Press. © Oxford University Press 2024.
DOI: 10.1093/oso/9780197672242.003.0019

Index

For the benefit of digital users, indexed terms that span two pages (e.g., 52–53) may, on occasion, appear on only one of those pages.

Tables and figures are indicated by an italic *t* and *f* following the page number.

AANHPI community. *See also* Asian American, Native Hawai'ian, and Pacific Islander (AANHPI) community
Aaron, Sofie Hana, storytelling, 238–41
Abeleda, Nikki, 159
Academic Search Ultimate, 206
Academy for Social Work and Social Welfare, 344
acculturation
    anti-Asian racism and mental health, 47
    becoming a US citizen, 43
    challenges for Japanese families adjusting to US, 132–34
    discrimination and health, 41–42
    diversity, 140
    equity, 141
    inclusion, 140–41
    Japanese families navigating anti-Asian racism in US, 134–36
    Japanese immigrant and temporary residents, 130–31, 141–42
    Japanese supplementary schools, 137–40
    language, 42
    process, 129–30
acculturative stress, 132
Adverse Childhood Experience study, 301–2, 306–7
advocacy. *See* community advocacy
advocacy work
    action steps for engaging community-based, 323–29
    challenges and considerations, 320–23
    collaborating with Asian American community leaders, 321
    hate incidents by ethnicity, 322–23
    identifying positionality in social work advocacy practice, 324–26
    pan-ethnicity, 320–21
    social workers as catalysts for, 321–23
    See also community advocacy
Advocating Justice/Chicago, 346–47

affirmative action
    AANHPI individuals, 83
    Korean Americans, 120
African Americans, social work journals, xx
AgeLine, 206
Agricultural Workers Organizing Committee (AWOC), 314–15
Alcoholics Anonymous, 179–80
Ali, Muhammad, 100
allostatic load, stress factors, 307
"Amerasians," children of Korean women and US servicemen, 64–65
"America First," promotion by Trump administration, 33
America is in the heart (Bulosan), 313–14
American Citizens for Justice (ACJ), 50–51
"American Dream," Asian Americans and, 3–4
American Identity Development Model, 160–61
anti-Asian hate crimes
    COVID-19 pandemic and, 236
    research and compiling/reporting data, 337–38
anti-Asian racism, 243
    advocating for language access, 340–41
    advocating for policies against, 337
    campaign for narrative change, 341–44
    community-based solutions, xxiii–xxiv
    COVID-19 pandemic and, 252, 359
    federal responses to, 335–37
    history in United States, 4
    history of, xix
    impact on mental health since COVID-19 pandemic, 47–48
    impact on overall health, 42–43
    implication for advocacy, policy, and practice, 50–51
    incidents in United States, xxi
    Japanese families navigating in US, 134–36
    Korean Americans, 111–12
    literature on, xx

anti-Asian racism (*cont.*)
    marginalized group experiences with, 318–19
    mental health and, 45–47
    past response from social work scholarship, CPS1
    phenomenon of, 311
    physical health and, 43–45
    policies eliminating, 335–40
    trauma and, 48–50
    United States, 41–42
    See also campaign for narrative change; community advocacy; policies eliminating anti-Asian racism
anti-Asian violence, revisioning social work education to eradicate, 261–64
anti-Chinese violence, institutional complicity, 15–16
Anti-Defamation League (ADL), 239
anti-Islamic bigotry
    religion and spirituality as buffers to impact of, 178–82
    in United States, 173–74
anti-miscegenation laws, 58–59
anti-racism, 326
anti-racist coalitions, Asian American contributions, 316
anti-Semitism, rise in, 63–64
anxiety, mental health concept, 305
APA PsycArticles, 206
APIDA (Asian, Pacific Islander, and Desi American), 316
Arab Americans, violence against, 17
Asian, word, 230
Asian, Pacific Islander, and Desi American (APIDA), 317
Asian American
    concept, 248
    racism education and training, 326–27
    term, 95–96, 248
Asian American, Native Hawai'ian, and Pacific Islander (AANHPI) community, xix, 227–28, 317, 335–37
    COVID-19 pandemic and, 3–4
    discrimination against, 77–78
    personal narratives, xxiii–xxiv
    population in US, 296
    therapeutic relationship and cultural competence, 301
Asian American, Native Hawai'ian, and Pacific Islander (AANHPI) populations
    model minority stereotype and impact on health and wellbeing of, 79–80
    research gaps, 66–67

"Asian American, Pacific Islander, and Desi Americans" (APIDA), 69–70
Asian American Advancing Leadership, 349
Asian American and Pacific Islander (AAPI), 317
    relative valorization as "honorary Whites," 17–18
    Youth Rising, 315–16
Asian American and Pacific Islander-Serving Institutions (AAPISIs), 87
Asian American assimilation theory, reevaluation of, 4
Asian American Education Project, 346–47
Asian American Legal Defense and Education Foundation, 83
Asian American Muslims, xxii–xxiii, 168–69
    cultural background of, 171–72
    migration to United States, 170–71
    religion and spirituality as buffers to impact of bigotry, 178–82
    role of religion and spirituality on, 170
    United States, 169–72
Asian American Muslim youth, 168–69
    acculturation stressors, 168–69
    bullying and, 176
    California survey on bullying of, 175
    coping mechanisms, 179
    discrimination and, 175–78
    educational settings, 174–75
    hijabs, 174–75, 177
    impact of anti-Islamic bigotry on, 174–78
    mental health outcomes, 175–78
    recommendation for social work advocacy, 182–83
    striving for Americanness, 175
Asian American Political Alliance, 248, 315–16
Asian American psychotherapy, creating a treatment plan, 303–4
Asian Americans
    background and presenting mental health problems, 297–301
    communities honoring diversity and heterogeneity, 320–21
    COVID-19 pandemic, 19
    culturally and linguistically appropriate services (CLAS), 296–97
    employment discrimination and World War II, 49
    literature on racism experiences of, xxi
    model minorities for "American Dream," 3–4
    as monolith, 16
    "othering" of, 7
    population growth, xix

post-COVID-19, 296–97
processing "Asianness," 306–7
social work journals, xx
social work practice, 67–69
status of minorities, 18
subgroups of, 274, 275
term, 296
US Census and, 41–42
valorization and civic ostracism of, 18
See also mental health services
Asian Americans Advancing Justice, 346
Asian American studies, rise of, 315–16
Asian American Studies curriculum, United States, 68
Asian and Black communities
  collaboration with Civil Rights movement, 95–96
  creating racial solidarity, 96–97
  histories of similar oppression, 103–6
  history of, 95
  history of colonial oppression, 98–99
Asian and Pacific Islander Women and Family Safety Center (APIWFSC), 244–45
Asian communities, civic-political threat, 10–11
Asian Critical (AsianCrit) Theory, 318–20, 327–28
Asian Exclusion act (1924), 4, 14
Asian identities
  citizenship/immigrant status, 58–59
  diversity of, in America, 56–57
  intersectionality, 308–9
  mental health recovery model, 308–9
  multiracial and biracial, 64–66
  racism and intersection of, in US, 57–62
  religiosity/spirituality, 62–64
  research, 66–67
  sexism, 59–60
  sexual orientation/gender identity, 61–62
  social work practice, 67–69
Asian immigration, United States (1850s), 103–4
Asian Indian Americans
  concerns based on statistical analyses, 283t
  connecting help-seeking to depression, 282
  depression prevalence, 278f, 278t
  help-seeking preferences among, 279f, 279t
  practice implications, 286, 288t
  sociocultural variables and types of concerns, 283t
  See also mental health services
Asian Lesbians of the East Coast, 61
Asian nation, violence against Japan, 17
Asianness, processing, 306–7

Asian Pacific Environmental Network, 101
Asian Pacific Islander Social Work Educators Association, 344
Asian population, United States, 272
Asian Solidarity Collective (ASC), 86–87
Asian women, as colonial sex objects, 243–44
Asian Youth Center, 346
Asiatic Barred Zone Act (Immigration Act of 1917), 58, 248
asset-based community development (ABCD), 328–29
Association of Social Work Boards (ASWB), 255–56
Atlanta Spa Shooting, Spring 2021, xix, 5
attention deficit hyperactivity disorder (ADHD), mental health concept, 305
Awareness of Stereotype Internalization on Asian Narratives and Preventing Racism and Identity Distancing through Empowerment (Asian Pride), 85

babaylans, 147–48
  Philippines, 147–48
  role in Indigenous communities, 148
bakla
  Filipino, 148–49
  term, 148–49
"bamboo ceiling," phrase, 82
Bao Dai (Emperor), 98
barkadas, kinship relationships, 157–58
Batayola, Maria, 244
Biden, Joe, 27, 335
big T trauma, 306
biracial identities, Asians, 64–66
Black, Indigenous, and Other People of Color (BIPOC), 159, 227–28, 326–27
  mental health screening, 65
Black communities. *See* Asian and Black communities
Black Lives Matter (BLM), 29, 95, 103
  movement, 101, 312
Black Lives Matter Foundation, 102–3
Black Power (Ture and Hamilton), 95–96
Black Power movement, 69–70, 248, 315–16
  Detroit's, 100–1
Black Veterans of the Vietnam War, 100
Blackwell, Susana, 242, 244
Bloody Sunday, 102
Bo, Saum Song, 12–13
Board of Health of Honolulu, burning down Chinatown, 10
Boggs, Grace Lee, 100–1, 316

Boggs, James, 316
British Empire, 98
Brown v. Board of Education (1954), 99
bubonic plague
　case study of Hawai'i, 10
　outbreak in California, 10
Bulosan, Carlos, 313–14

California, Chinese in 1870 labor force, 8
California Alien Land Law (1913), 13–14
California Constitution (1879), 10
California Department of Social Services (CDSS), 88
California Health Interview Survey (CHIS), 44–45, 208–12
campaign for narrative change, 341–44
　condemning racism and xenophobia, 342
　launching online activism, 343–44
　using nonstigmatizing language, 343
Cannery Workers Union, 244–45
Care Access Checklist, 276
Catague, Emma, 244
Catholicism, 148
　Filipinx American LGBTQ+, 150, 151, 152–53
Catholics, 170
Cendana, Gregory, 86–87
Center for Behavioral Health Statistics and Quality, 273
Centers for Disease Control and Prevention (CDC), 289
Central Pacific Railroad, employing Chinese laborers, 8
Central Pacific Railway, Chinese immigration, 7–8
Chavez, Cesar, 314–15
Chen, Judy, 244
Chin, Vincent
　killing of, 32–33
　murder of, 50–51, 101, 231
China dolls, Asian women as, 60
Chinatown, San Francisco, 297–98
"China virus"
　term, 33–34
　Trump referring to COVID-19 as, 31–32
Chinese Americans
　concerns based on statistical analyses, 283*t*
　connecting help-seeking to depression, 281
　depression prevalence, 278*f*, 278*t*
　espionage charges of, 14–15
　hate incidents, 322–23
　help-seeking preferences among, 279*f*, 279*t*
　perceived discrimination, 44–45
　practice implications, 285–86, 288*t*
　sociocultural variables and types of concerns, 283*t*
　See also mental health services
Chinese Consolidated Benevolent Association, 313, 322
Chinese Exclusion Act (1882) (CEA), 10, 12–13, 30–31, 58, 77–78, 104, 105, 351
Chinese immigrants, 4
　economic and public health scapegoating, 9–10
　as economic threat, 7–8, 9
Chinese Immigrants Associations, 347–48
"Chinese invasion," proliferation in 1880s, 11
Chinese laborers
　leprosy as "Chinese disease," 8
　as threat to "true Americans," 11
Chinese miners, murder of, 15
"Chinese virus," 343
　coronavirus as, 6
Christianity, 169, 181–82
CINAHL, 206
citizenship, Asians in United States, 58–59
City of Austin, Asian American Quality of Life (AAQoL), 208–12
Civic Education 101 course, 347–48
civil engagement, community involvement, 347–50
Civil Liberties Act, 14
Civil Rights Act (1964)
　Title II of, 339–40
　Title VII of, 219
Civil Rights Act (1965), 50
Civil Rights movement, 95–96, 99–103, 248, 312, 315
Civil War, 8
"claiming space," multiracial Asian Americans, 65–66
Cochrane Library, 206
Code of Ethics, social workers, 84
Codependency Anonymous, 179–80
cognitive behavioral therapy (CBT), 162–63
collectivism, Korean culture, 113
colonialism, 229, 243
　legacy of, 243
Commission on Asian and Pacific Islander American Affairs (CAPIAA), 88
community advocacy
　Asian American contributions to anti-racist coalitions, 316
　community mutual aid, 312–13
　ethnic enclaves, 312–13

experiences with racially fueled hate and discrimination, 317–20
history and context of, 312–17
identifying needs for communities experiencing injustice, 319–20
labor movement and strikes, 313–15
limitations of Asian American, 317
marginalized group experiences with anti-Asian racism, 318–19
rise of Asian American identity and studies, 315–16
See also advocacy work
community-based advocacy work
action steps for engaging in, 323–29
bridging the gap between research and advocacy practice, 327–29
education and training, 326–27
identifying positionality in, 324–26
community-based participatory research (CBPR), 323, 328–29
community mutual aid, 312–13
community organizing, model minority stereotype, 86–87
Confucianism
Asian immigrants, 129–30
group harmony of, 129–30, 131
Korean culture, 114
Congressional Asian Pacific American Caucus, 346–47
contingency, concept of, 299
Coolie Trade Prohibition Act (1862), 9–10
coping
definition, 188
strategies, 188–89
Coronavirus Research Database, 206
Council on Social Work Education (CWSE), 120–21, 227–28, 255, 318, 344
COVID-19 Hate Crimes Act (2021), 3, 27, 36, 140, 335–36, 340
COVID-19 Health Equity Task Force, 335
COVID-19 pandemic
anti-Asian racism and, 41, 359
anti-Asian racism and impact on mental health, 47–48
anti-Asian racism and intensified nationalism, 31–34
anti-Asian racism and violence during, 5–7
anti-Asian violence and discrimination, 25–27
Asian American, Native Hawai'ian, and Pacific Islander (AANHPI) community, 3–4
Asian American communities, 19, 24
Asian American hate and, 252

Asian Americans during, xxi–xxii
fear and mistrust by communities of color during, 178–79
hate crimes during, 131
Korean Americans and, 112, 115, 116–18, 119
mental health risks among Asian Americans, 27–29
"model minority" stereotype, 220
psychosociological perspectives on scapegoating and discrimination, 29–31
racism, xenophobia and violence against Asian Americans, 30–31
seeking answers to pandemic-fueled AANHPI hate, 6
theory of "othering," 6–7
White supremacy as root of racial hierarchy, 34–35
Crazy Rich Asians (movie), 341–42
Crenshaw, Kimberle Williams, 189
critical race theory (CRT), 248
dismantling the model minority stereotype (MMS), 80–84
CRT. *See* critical race theory (CRT)
Cullors, Patrisse, 102–3
cultural genocide, 229
cultural humility
definition, 262
principles of, 262
raising reflection and self-awareness using, 262–63

Deferred Action for Childhood Arrival program, 59
depression
Asian Americans and, 272–74
Asian Indian Americans, 282
Chinese Americans, 281
connecting help-seeking to, 280–84
Japanese Americans, 282
Korean Americans, 281
mental health concept, 305
Pakistani Americans, 282
predicting factors and recommendations for subgroups, 284, 285*t*
prevalence in Asian ethnic subgroups, 277, 278*f*, 278*t*
Vietnamese Americans, 280–81
See also mental health services
depression and Asian Americans, 272–74
access to mental health services, 273–74
contributing factors, 272–73
help-seeking behavior, 273–74
prevalence, 272

Diabetes Among Indian Americans (DIA) study, 208–12
Diagnostic and Statistical Manual of Mental Disorders (DSM-IV), 175–76
Dill, LeConté, 181
Dinh, Tam, 245–47
   storytelling, 245–47
discrimination
   psychosociological perspectives on, 29–31
   See also older Asian Americans
diversity, acculturation, 140
Dizon, Phoebe, 242, 244
Doctrine of Overwhelming Force, Powell, 100
Domaguin, Daniel, 159
"Dotbusters" attacks, South Asians in New Jersey, 11
Douglass, Frederick, 96
dragon ladies, Asian women as, 60
Dred Scott decision, US Supreme Court, 104–5
Du, Soon Ja, 235
Duterte, Rodrigo, 153–54

Edmund Pettus Bridge, 102
education
   AANHPI individuals, 81–82
   anti-Asian racism training and, 326–27
   Filipinx American LGBTQ+, 153
   first responders, law enforcement and policymakers, 352–53
   promoting AANHPI history, 350–53
   teaching AANHPI history in public, 351–52
   teaching AANHPI history in schools, 350–51
   See also social work profession
Educational Policy and Accreditation Standards (EPAS), 253, 262–63, 329–30
egalitarianism, 50
Eid al Adha, 171, 181
Eid al Fitr, 181
Eid ul Fitr, 171
Enriquez, Virgilio, 162–63
equity, acculturation, 141
ethnic and racial identity (ERI), Korean Americans, 102, 116–17
ethnic enclaves, community advocacy, 312–13
ethnic identity, rise of Asian American, 315–16
ethnic identity pride (EI-Pride), Korean Americans, 116–17
Everyday Discrimination Scale (EDS), Williams and colleagues, 44
exposure hypothesis, 43, 47

Facebook, 347–48
familism, Filipinx American LGBTQ+, 151
Family & Society Studies Worldwide, 206
fearmongering, anti-Asian, 49
Federal Bureau of Investigation (FBI), 5
   Hate Crime Statistics, 62–63
   prejudice of Chinese heritage, 15
Feng, Daoyou, 241–42
fictive kinship, 157–59
Filipino(s)
   hate incidents, 322–23
   perceived discrimination, 44–45
   violence against, 16
   See also LGBTQ+ Filipinos
Filipino American Decolonization Experience (FADE), 162–63
Filipino and Filipinx American LGBTQ+
   access to mental health services, 156–57
   deaths of, 153–54
   identity, xxii–xxiii
   issues and outcomes, 153–57
   mental health of sexual minorities in Philippines, 154–55
   microaggressions and mental health outcomes, 155–56
Filipinx American LGBTQ+
   conducting research with, 160–61
   culturally responsive and queer affirming mental health interventions, 162–63
   education, 153
   familism, 151
   fictive kinship, 157–59
   identity formation, 150–53
   immigration and migration, 152–53
   peer-based mental health support, 161–62
   providing inclusive clinical services to, 161–63
   race and ethnicity, 151–52
   religion, 150
   resistance of, 157–59
   social support and advocacy in contemporary Filipina/o American organizations, 159
Firebaugh, E. J., 16
Floyd, George, death of, 4, 101–3
Forbes (magazine), 6
Fowler, James Bonard, 101–2
Fox News, 6
France-Vietnam War, 98
Freud, Sigmund, 181–82

Garza, Alicia, 102–3
Gay Asian and Pacific Islander Men of New York, 61
Gay/Trans Panic Defense, 153–54

INDEX   367

Geary Act (1892), 13
Gee, Emma, 315–16
Geisha, Asian women as, 60, 341
gender identity, Asian identities, 61–62
gender neutrality, precolonial
    Philippines, 147–48
Gentleman's Agreement (1907), 13–14
Go, Michelle Alyssa, 26–27
Gold Rush of 1849, 7–8
government sanctions
    Chinese Exclusion Act (1882) (CEA), 12–13
    economic and public health domains, 9–10
    espionage charges of Chinese
        Americans, 14–15
    exclusion of other Asians post-CEA, 13–14
    incarceration of Japanese Americans during
        WWII, 14
    neutralizing threat via civic-political
        ostracism, 11–15
Grand Challenges for Social Work, xxi, 264–65
Grand Challenge to Eliminate Racism (GCER),
    252–53, 353–54
    pipeline issues in developing anti-racist
        social work workforce, 255–56
    priorities of, 254–55
    reasons and challenges to pursue social work
        career among minority students, 256–57
    social work, 253–57
    See also social work profession
Grant, Hyun Jung, 241–42
Great Depression, 16
greater power
    search for clarity, 195
    search for healing, 195
gurdwara, Sikhs murdered in, 62–63

hāfus, biracial Japanese children, 64–65
Hamilton, Charles V., 95–96
hapa, Kānaka Maoli usage, 64–65
Harlins, Latasha, 115, 235
Hate Crimes Analysis and Review Act of New
    York (2021), 27
hate incidents, by Asian ethnicity, 322–23
Hawai'i
    case study of bubonic plague, 10
    marriages in, 64–65
health
    anti-Asian racism and impact on
        overall, 42–43
    anti-Asian racism and mental, 45–47
    anti-Asian racism and physical, 43–45
    impact of model minority stereotype on
        AANHPI populations, 79–80

healthcare system, silence of Asian
    Americans, 234
Health Source: Nursing/Academic
    Edition, 206
Hebrew Immigrant Aid Society (HIAS), 238
heterogeneity, AANHPI individuals, 80–81
Hinduism, 170
Hindus, minority religious group, 63
Hispanic Americans, social work
    journals, xx
Hispanic-Serving Institutions (HSIs), 87
Historically Black Colleges and Universities
    (HBCUs), 87, 321
Hitler, Adolph, 63–64
HIV/AIDS Prevention Balls, LGBTQ+ Filipinx
    Americans, 157
Hmong older adults, xxii–xxiii
    children supporting, 193
    community-based programs, 199–200
    community support for, 194
    coping mechanisms, 197–98, 200
    data collection and analysis, 190–92
    escaping loneliness through activity, 195–96
    greater power for coping with
        loneliness, 194–95
    limitations and implications of study,
        199–200
    loneliness among, 186–87
    migration out of Laos, 187
    recruitment and participants, 190
    relatives as social support, 193
    residing in United States, 187
    romantic companion and, 194
    sociodemographic characteristics of study
        participants, 191*t*
    spouses support for, 192–93
    See also loneliness
Hochul, Kathy, 27
Holocaust, 239
Hong, Cathy P., 234, 237, 245
Hopkins Symptoms Checklist (HSCL-25),
    275–76, 290
Huerta, Dolores, 314–15
Human Behaviors in Social Environment, xxi

Ichioka, Yuji, 95–96, 315–16
identity contingencies, mental health, 299
identity threat, mental health, 299–300
immigrant(s)
    Asians' status in US, 58–59
    CEA definition of, 14
    civic-political threat, 10–11
    as public health scapegoats, 8–9

immigration, Filipinx American LGBTQ+, 152–53
Immigration Act (1965), 146–47
Immigration Act of 1917 (Asiatic Barred Zone Act), 13–14, 58, 248
Immigration and Customs Enforcement, 59
Immigration and Nationality Act (1965), 77–78, 112–13
Immigration and Naturalization Act (1965), 3–4
imperialism, United States, 60
implicit bias, 214–15, 219, 262, 296–97
"inassimilable Orientals," 13
inclusion, acculturation, 140–41
inclusive policies, Asian Americans advocating, 69
Indigenous land dispossession, 229
individual racism, definition, 204
In re: Ah Yup (1878), 10, 12
Instagram, 347–48
institutional complicity, racialized violence and, 15–17
internal review board (IRB), 274
International Bibliography of the Social Sciences (IBSS), 206
intersectionality
  Asian identities, 308–9
  framework, 189
  racial identity and follower of Islam, 178–79
  term, 57
interventions
  Asian American clients, 304–7
  cognitive behavior therapy (CBT), 304–5
  processing "Asianness," 306–7
  psychoeducation, 305
Irish Potato Famine, 7–8
Islam, 170
Islamic belief
  intermittent fasting, 180
  pillars of practice, 179–80
Islamophobia
  anti-Islamic bigotry, 168
  impact on Muslim youth, 168–69
Itliong, Larry, 314–15
Ito, Alice, 244

Jackson, Jesse, 101
Jackson, Jimmy Lee, 101–2
Japanese American Redress Movement, 244–45
Japanese Americans
  concerns based on statistical analyses, 283*t*
  connecting help-seeking to depression, 282
  hate incidents, 322–23
  help-seeking preferences among, 279*f*, 279*t*
  incarceration during World War II, 14
  practice implications, 287, 288*t*
  sociocultural variables and types of concerns, 283*t*
  See also mental health services
Japanese immigrants
  acculturation of, and temporary residents, 130–31, 141–42
  diversity, 140
  equity, 141
  inclusion, 140–41
  Japanese supplementary schools, 137–40
  parents' socialization practices, 137–40
Japanese supplementary schools, socialization practice, 137–40
Jews of color, United States, 63–64
John R. Lewis Voting Rights Advancement Act, 339
Johnson, Lyndon B., 100, 102
Johnson-Reed Immigration Act (1924), 58

kabaklaan, concept of, 148–49
Kandi, DJ Kuttin, 86–87
Kang, Hye-Kyung, storytelling, 241–45
Keller, George Frederick, 11
Kim, Claire, 4
Kim, Suncha, 241–42
King, Martin Luther, Jr., 100, 101–2, 316
King, Rodney, 115, 235
Kochiyama, Yuri, 100–1, 316
konketsuji, children of military men and Japanese women, 64–65
Korean Americans, 111, 122
  anti-Asian racism, 111–12
  collectivism, 113
  concerns based on statistical analyses, 283*t*
  Confucianism, 113, 114
  connecting help-seeking to depression, 281
  COVID-19 pandemic and, 115
  depression prevalence, 278*f*, 278*t*
  hate incidents, 322–23
  help-seeking preferences among, 279*f*, 279*t*
  Korean culture, 113–14
  Korean immigration to UN, 111
  Los Angeles Riots (1992), 115
  model minority myth and risk of mental health problems, 114–15
  policy implications, 120–21
  practice implications, 118–20, 286, 288*t*
  racial discrimination among, xxii–xxiii

racial discrimination and coping
    strategies, 116–18
  research implications, 121–22
  sociocultural variables and types of
    concerns, 283t
  US Census, 112–13
  US history and characteristics of Korean
    immigrants, 112–13
  See also mental health services
Korean immigrants
  story of Jane J. Lee, 232–41
  See also Lee, Jane L.
Korean War, 99
  "Amerasians," 64–65
Ku Klux Klan mob violence, Filipino
  Americans, 4
"kung flu," 77–78, 343
  coronavirus as, 6, 59
  term, 33–34
K. W. Lee Center for Leadership, 235

labor movements and strikes, 313–15
Ladlad Partylist, 149
Lambda Legal Defense and Education
  Fund, 61
land acknowledgment, 229
land discrimination laws, 339
Laude, Jennifer, murder of, 153–54
Laureta, Veronica, 242, 244
Leadership, Education, Activism, and Dialogue
  (LEAD) Filipino, 159
League for the Independence of Vietnam, 98
Le Duan, 98
Lee, Jane J.
  father's headaches, 233
  hate and its complications, 236
  healing of Los Angeles riots, 237–38
  Los Angeles riots of April 29, 1992, 234–36
  mother, Jeong, 237
  staying silent in healthcare system, 234
  storytelling by, 232–41
  See also storytelling
Lee, Marie Myong-Ok, 243
leprosy, as "Chinese disease," 8
lesbian, gay, bisexual, transgender, queer plus
  (LGBTQ+). See LGBTQ+
LGBTQ+
  Asian Americans, 61–62
  mental health screening, 65
  See also Filipino and Filipinx American
    LGBTQ+; Filipinx American LGBTQ+
LGBTQ+ Filipinos
  contemporary, 148–49

gender, sexuality, and *babaylan*, 147–48
  history of, 147–49
  precolonial history, 147–48
  Spanish colonization and gender binary
    introduction, 148
  See also Filipinx American LGBTQ+
loneliness
  children as sources, 193
  control and avoidance, 196–97
  coping, 188–89
  data collection and analysis, 190–92
  escaping through activity, 195–96
  greater power for coping, 194–95
  Hmong community as support, 194
  intersectionality framework, 189
  limitations and implications of study,
    199–200
  methods for study, 190–92
  older adults and, 186–87
  recruitment and participants, 190
  relatives in support for coping, 193
  romantic companion for supporting, 194
  seeking social support and
    community, 192–94
  sociodemographic characteristics of
    participants, 191t
  spouses as key support, 192–93
  See also Hmong older adults
Long, Robert Aaron, 242
Los Angeles Riots (1992), 115, 234–36,
    237–38

machismo, Spanish gender norms, 148
McNamara, Robert, 100
mail order bride, 242–43
Make Us Visible, 346–47
Malcolm X, 97, 316
marianismo, Spanish gender norms, 148
Martin, Trayvon, 102–3
masjid, neighborhood gathering place for
  Muslims, 169–70, 171, 172–73
Mau rebellion, 97
medical model, mental health treatment, 308
Medline, 206
mental health
  access to services of Filipinx
    Americans, 156–57
  anti-Asian racism and, 45–47
  anti-Asian racism and impact on, since
    COVID-19, 47–48
  discrimination and Asian American Muslim
    youth, 175–78
  escaping mechanisms, 298–99

mental health (cont.)
  identity contingencies, 299
  identity threat, 299–300
  intake and assessment, 301–3
  objectives for working with clients, 302–3
  over-efforting, 300
  pandemic-related risks among Asian Americans, 27–29
  peer support for LGBTQ+ Filipinx Americans, 161–62
  personality lockdown, 300
  processing "Asianness," 306–7
  recovery model, 308–9
  sexual minorities in Philippines, 154–55
  stereotype threats, 299
  therapeutic relationship and cultural competence, 301
  treatment planning and therapeutic contact, 303–4
mental health practices, background and presenting problems, 297–301
mental health services
  Asian American groups, 289
  Asian ethnicities in community study, 274–75
  Care Access Checklist, 276
  community study, 291
  concerns based on statistical analyses in Asian subgroups, 283t
  data analysis procedures, 276
  depression and Asian Americans, 272–74
  help-seeking behavior and access to, 273–74
  help-seeking preferences among Asian American subgroups, 277–80, 279f, 279t
  Hopkins Symptoms Checklist (HSCL-25) for depression, 275–76
  interethnic comparative approach for analysis, 275
  methods for study, 274–76
  navigating service underutilization and accessibility, 290–91
  practice implications, 284–88, 288t
  problem-solving vs. help-seeking, 289–90
  significance and aim of research, 270–74
  sociocultural variables and types of concerns, 283t
  utilization rates for Asian Americans, 270, 271
  See also depression
mestizos, children of mixed marriages, 64–65
Mexican-Cuban War, 99
microaggressions, 50
  LGBTQ+ Filipina/o Americans, 155–56

migration, Filipinx American LGBTQ+, 152–53
Minor Feelings (Hong), 234, 245
minorities, Asian Americans as, 18
Minority Serving Institution (MSI) program, 87
minority strengths model, LGBTQ+ Filipinx American, 160–61
minority stress theory, racism and sexism of Asian Americans LGBTQ individuals, 61–62
misogyny, 243
Miss Saigon (play), 61
model minority
  Asian Americans as, 50
  concept, 298
  myth of, 17
  stereotype, 35, 50
  term, 78
  transgression of, 63–64
"model minority myth"
  Asian Americans, 265–66
  concept, 298
  Korean Americans' risk of mental health problems, 114–15
  storytelling pushing against, 228–29
  term, 78
  unmet service needs and, of Asian Americans, 258–59
model minority stereotype(s) (MMS), xxi–xxii, 270–71, 317, 341
  Asian Americans, 3–4
  Asians, 129–30
  California's Stop the Hat Fund, 88
  disrespecting Black people and Asians, 105–6
  historical context of, 77–79
  impact on health and well-being of AANHPI populations, 79–80
  macro level, 87–89
  meso level, 85–87
  micro level, 85
  social workers dismantling MMS, 84–89
  social work research with AANHPI individuals, 89
  using critical race theory to dismantle, 80–84
model of racism-related stress and well-being (MRSW), 122
Muhammad, Elijah, 97
multiracial identities, Asians, 64–66
Muslims
  Asian American, xxii–xxiii
  masjid as gathering place, 169–70
  minority religious group, 63
  in United States, 168, 169–72

violence against, 17
See also Asian American Muslims
Muslim youth, impact of Islamophobia, 168–69
Myers, June, 244
My Lai, 100

Nadal, K. L., 163
Narasaki, Diane, 244
narrative change. *See* campaign for narrative change
narrative therapy, 228–29
NASW, 344–45
National Association for Mental Illness (NAMI), 309
National Association for the Advancement of Colored People, 101
National Association of Social Work (NASW), 344
National Coalition for Asian Pacific American Community Development, 346
National Farm Workers Association (NFWA), 314–15
National Incident-Based Reporting System, 335, 339–40
National Institutes of Health (NIH), 66, 270
 AANHPI population, 84
 interest in epidemiologic studies in AANHPI, 66–67
nationalism, intensified, during coronavirus pandemic, 31–34
National Latino and Asian American Study (NLAAS), 44–45, 46–47, 208–12
"nationals," Philipinx as American, 81
National Science Foundation, 336–37
Nation of Islam, Malcolm X, 97
Native Americans, social work journals, xx
nativism, 10–11
Naturalization Act (1870), 11–12
New York City, Asian American woman pushed to path of subway train, 26–27
New York Sun (newspaper), Bo's letter to, 12–13
New York Times (newspaper), 6, 17
New York Times Magazine, 78–79
Ngo Dinh Diem, 98
Nguyen Van Thieu, 98
Nixon, Richard, 100
NLAAS. *See* National Latino and Asian American Study (NLAAS)
No Place for Hate California, 346–47

older adults
 risk for loneliness in, 186–87
 See also Hmong older adults

older Asian Americans
 challenges of, 203–4
 comprehensive overview of documented experiences of racism, 215–17
 conceptual model of relationship between racism and psychosocial well-being, 216f, 216–17
 consort chart of article selection process, 208f, 208–12
 data collection and extraction, 207
 ethnic groups of, 203
 healthy aging within context of racism, 204–6
 implications for practice and policy, 218–20
 implications for research, 217–18
 life expectancy, 203
 methods of study, 206–7
 practice and policy strategies addressing racism/discrimination, 214–15
 racism and, 204
 relationship between age and experience of discrimination/racism, 212–13
 relationship between racism/discrimination and psychosocial well-being, 213–14, 220
 research aims, 205–6
 search method, 206–7
 study characteristics, 207, 208f
online activism, changing narratives, 343–44
Organizing Asian Communities, 101
Orientalism, sexism and, 60
Osaka, Naomi, 65–66
"othering"
 Anti-Asian discrimination and xenophobia, 19
 Asian Americans, 7
 fight against racial, 36
 process of, 7
 strategy for coping with unknown, 32–33
 theory of, 6–7
"outgroup," Asian Americans as, 30–31
Overeaters Anonymous, 179–80
over-efforting, mental health, 300

Page, Wade Michael, 62–63
Page Act (1875), 12, 60
Pakistani Americans
 concerns based on statistical analyses, 283t
 connecting help-seeking to depression, 282
 depression prevalence, 278f, 278t
 help-seeking preferences among, 279f, 279t
 practice implications, 287, 288t
 sociocultural variables and types of concerns, 283t
 See also mental health services

pan-ethnicity, definition, 320–21
Park, Soon Chung, 241–42
Pemberton, Joseph Scott, 153–54
"people could think" factor, 306–7
People's Collective for Justice and Liberation, 86–87
People v. Georg Hall (1854), 11–12, 103–4
perceived discrimination
    Chinese, Filipino, and Vietnamese, 44–45
    foreign-born Asian older adults, 47
perceived threat, context of, 19
Peregrino, Ellis, 16
performative activism, 326
"perpetual foreigner" stereotype, 3–4
    anti-Asian sentiment reinforcing, 59
    Korean Americans as, 111–12, 113
    othered as, 7
    stereotype, 30–31
"perpetual outsiders" stereotype, 35
personality disorders, mental health concept, 305
personality lockdown, mental health, 300
Pettersen, William, 78–79
Pew Research Center, 168
Philippine American war (1898–1902), 96–97, 146–47
Philippines
    African American/Black soldiers in World War I and II, 97
    American colonization of, 81
    gender neutrality in precolonial, 147–48
    introduction to gender binary, 148
    mental health of sexual minorities in, 154–55
    Spanish colonization, 148
    Spanish gender norms, 148
physical health, anti-Asian racism and, 43–45
Plessy v. Ferguson (1896), 104–5
policies eliminating anti-Asian racism
    advocating for language access, 340–41
    advocating for nondiscrimination policies, 338–40
    bystander training, 339–40
    federal responses, 335–37
    land discrimination laws, 339
    research and compiling/reporting data for, 337–38
    social workers advocating for, 337
    voting, 339
    See also anti-Asian racism
policy advocacy, community involvement, 347–50

policy practice approach, 334
Pompeo, Mike, 6
Population-Based Study of Chinese Elderly (PINE), 44–45
Population Study of Chinese Elderly (PINE) Study, 208–12
posttraumatic stress disorder (PTSD), 45, 306
Powell, Colin, 99
Powell Doctrine, 99
Preferred Reporting Items for Systemic Reviews and Meta-Analyses (PRISMA), 206
ProQuest, 206
Pryce, Jonathan, 61
psychoeducation, mental health concepts, 305
psychosocial well-being
    conceptual model of relationship between racism and, 216f, 216–17
    older Asian Americans, xxii–xxiii
    relationship between racism/discrimination and, 213–14
psychotherapy, creating a treatment plan, 303–4
PsycINFO, 206
public health crisis, racism as, 27
Public Health Critical Race Praxis (PHCRP), 328
public health scapegoats, immigrants with diseases, 8–9
Publicly Available Content Database, 206

Qian model, 309
quality of life, intersectionality framework, 189
Queer Lakbay Summit, 159
Queer Pin@y Conference (QPC), 158–59
Quran, dealing with discrimination stress, 179

race, conceptual boundaries of, 49
race and ethnicity, Filipinx American LGBTQ+, 151–52
race wrestling, 324–25
racial discrimination, Korean Americans, 116–18, 121–22
racial/ethnic lumping, 4
racial hierarchy, White supremacy as root of, 34–35
racial imposter syndrome, term, 65
racialized violence
    institutional complicity and, 15–17
    other Asian ethnic groups, 16–17
racially fueled hate and discrimination
    experiences with, 317–20
    identifying needs for communities experiencing, 319–20
    marginalized group experiences, 318–19

racial microaggressions, definition, 155
racial objectification, 65–66
racial solidarity, creating, 96–97
racial triangulation theory, 326–28
racism, 326, 334
　AANHPI individuals, 83
　anti-Asian, during pandemic, 31–34
　characteristics of, 204
　diverse practice and policy strategies addressing, 214–15
　microaggressions, 50
　relationship between age and experience of, 212–13
　relationship between psychosocial well-being and, 213–14
　revisioning social work education to eradicate, 261–64
　See also older Asian Americans
Rainbow Coalition, 101
Ramadan, 181
Reagan, President, 14
recovery model, mental health treatment, 308
religion
　Asian American Muslims, 172–73
　buffering impact of anti-Islamic bigotry, 178–82
　greater power for coping with loneliness, 194–95
religiosity, Asian identities, 62–64
research, racism and marginalization of Asian populations, 66–67
resilience, Korean Americans, 116–17
Revolutionary War, 99
Roman Catholic religion, Filipinx American LGBTQ+, 150
Roosevelt, President, 14

Sales, Jaxon, 154
Sandford, John, 104–5
San Francisco, Chinatown, 10, 297–98
San Francisco Chronicle (newspaper), 11
San Francisco State College (now University), 315–16
scapegoating
　definition, 29–30
　psychosociological perspectives on, 29–31
Scopus, 206
Scott, Dred, 104–5
Scott Act (1888), 13
Seattle Rape Relief, 242
self, concept of, 325

Selma to Montgomery (Alabama), peaceful march, 101–2
September 11, 2001
　discrimination on Muslims following attacks of, 173–74
　Islamophobia, 168
sexism, Asian identities, 59–60
sexual orientation, Asian identities, 61–62
Sexual Orientation and Gender Identity or Expression Equality (SOGIE) Bill, Philippine House and Senate, 149
Sharify, Denise Tung, 244
Sikh(s)
　violence against, 17
　violence against community, 62–63
　United States, 62–63
Sikh Coalition, 62–63
Sinophobia, 28, 29–30
　American nationalism, 33
small t trauma, 306
Smith, Anna Deavere, 234–35
social change, individual and collective activism, 325–26
Social Identity Approach, 30
social justice organizations, building coalitions with, 346–47
social justice perspective, teaching, 263–64
Social Science Abstracts, 206
social support
　coping with loneliness, 192–94
　Korean Americans, 117–18
Social Welfare Policies and Programs, xxi
social well-being. *See* older Asian Americans
social work
　essential role in addressing hate, 227–29
　leadership role of organizations, 344–46
　research on AANHPI individuals, 89
　roles of racism, xenophobia, discrimination and violence, 247–49
　See also storytelling
social workers, 249
　as catalysts for advocacy movements, 321–23
　Code of Ethics, 84
　community organizing, 86–87
　developing policies, 334
　direct services, 88
　dismantling MMS (model minority stereotype) at macro level, 87–89
　dismantling MMS at meso level, 85–87
　dismantling MMS at micro level, 85
　education of, 85–86

social workers (cont.)
    expanding number and ranks of multilingual/multicultural, 266
    fostering and facilitating civic engagement, 349–50
    intervention services, 88
    prevention services, 88
social work practice
    advocacy for Asian American Muslim youth, 182–83
    advocating for inclusive policies, 69
    increasing education and awareness, 68
    intersectional racism for Asian Americans, 67–69
    strengthening responsive practices and community partnerships, 68–69
Social Work Practice with Diverse Populations, xxi
social work profession
    career-related stress and concerns among minority students and practitioners, 257–61
    challenge to eliminate racism, 253–57
    cultural humility framework in, 262–63
    lack of inclusion of race and ethnicity in research, 259–61
    minority students pursuing a career in, 256–57, 264–66
    model minority myth and unmet service needs of Asian Americans, 258–59
    pipeline issues in developing anti-racist workforce, 255–56
    revisioning education to eradicate racism and anti-Asian violence, 261–64
    teaching from social justice perspective, 263–64
Society for Social Work Research (SSWR), 344
socioeconomic well-being, AANHPI individuals, 82
Sociological Abstracts, 206
South Asian, violence against, 17
South Asian community, violence against, 16
Southeast Asia Resource Action Center (SEARAC), 321
Southern Christian Leadership Conference (SCLC), 101–2
South Pacific Railroad, 10
Spencer, Michael S., storytelling, 230–32
spirituality
    Asian American Muslims, 172–73
    Asian identities, 62–64
    buffering impact of anti-Islamic bigotry, 178–82
    greater power for coping with loneliness, 194–95
Statue of Liberty, cartoon of, 11
stereotype(s)
    Asian women, 243–44
    mental health threats, 299
    See also model minority stereotype(s) (MMS); "perpetual foreigner" stereotype; "yellow peril" stereotype
Stop AAPI Hate, xix, 5, 59–60, 316, 319–20, 346–47
Stop AAPI Hate Reporting Center, 29
Stop Asian American Pacific Islander Hate. See Stop AAPI Hate
Stop the Hate Fund, California's, 88
storytelling
    Aaron, Sofie Hana, 238–41
    Dinh, Tam, 245–47
    Kang, Hye-Kyung, 241–45
    Lee, Jane J., 232–41
    role in addressing hate, 228–29
    Spencer, Michael S., 230–32
    Verdugo, 248
    See also Lee, Jane J.
Study of Older Korean Americans (SOKA), 208–12
successful aging, definition, 204–5
systemic racism, definition, 204

Takao Ozawa v. United States (1922), 14
Tan, Xiaojie, 241–42
therapeutic relationship, cultural competence and, 301
Thich Nhat Hanh, 316
Third World Liberation Front, 315–16
TikTok, 347–48
Tobera, Fermin, 16
tomboy, term, 148–49
Tometi, Opal, 102–3
training, anti-Asian racism education and, 326–27
trauma
    anti-Asian racism and, 48–50
    big *T* trauma, 306
    small *t* trauma, 306
Treaty of Paris (1898), 146–47
Tribal Colleges and Universities, 87
Trump, Donald J., 6
    administration's "America First" promotion, 33
    COVID-19 as "China virus," 31–32
    election of, 34–35
Truth, Sojourner, 57

INDEX 375

Ture, Kwame, 95–96
Turner, Henry M., 97
Twilight: Los Angeles (Smith), 234–35
Twitter, 6
Tydings-McDuffie Act (1935), 58

United Farm Workers of America
  (UFW), 314–15
United States
  acculturation challenges of Japanese families
    in, 132–34
  anti-Asian racism in, 41–42
  anti-Asian racism phenomenon, 311
  anti-Islamic bigotry in, 173–74
  Asian Americans and US Census, 41–42
  Asian population in, 272
  history of anti-Asian racism in, 4
  imperialism, 60
  Japanese families navigating anti-Asian
    racism in, 134–36
  Muslims in, 169–72
United States v. Bhagat Singh Thind (1923), 14
University of California Berkeley, 78–
  79, 315–16
University of California Los Angeles
  (UCLA), 158–59
University of Houston, 274
US Census Bureau
  AANHPI population, 296
  race and ethnicity categories, 64
US Commission on Civil Rights, 335–
  36, 337–38
US Constitution
  13th Amendment, 104–5
  14th Amendment, 104–5
US Supreme Court, Dred Scott decision, 104–5

Vietnamese Americans
  Black Americans and, 97
  concerns based on statistical analyses, 283*t*
  connecting help-seeking to
    depression, 280–81
  depression prevalence, 278*f*, 278*t*
  hate incidents, 322–23
  help-seeking preferences among, 279*f*, 279*t*
  perceived discrimination, 44–45
  practice implications, 285, 288*t*
  sociocultural variables and types of
    concerns, 283*t*
  violence against, 17
  See also mental health services

Vietnam War, 97, 98, 99, 100, 315, 316
Visiting Forces Agreement (VFA), 153–54
voting participation
  AANHPI communities, 339
  Asian Americans, 348–49
Voting Rights Act (1965), 102, 339

Wall Street Journal (newspaper), 6
War Bride Act (1945), 60
Washington Times (newspaper), 6
Wasp, The (magazine), 8
Watsonville Riot (1930), 16
Web of Science, 206
Wells, Ida B., 97
Westmoreland, William, 100
White nationalism, 231
  xenophobia and, in US, 96
Whiteness, xenophobia and construction
  of, 34
White society, relative valorization of AAPIs as
  honorary, 17–18
White supremacy, root of racial
  hierarchy, 34–35
Williams Everyday Discrimination Scale
  (EDS), 44
workforce, AANHPI individuals, 82
World Health Organization, 343
World Population Review, 56
World War I, 97, 99
World War II, 97, 99, 170
  fear of Asian immigrants during, 77–78
  Japanese internment camps, 14, 30–31, 49,
    131, 351
"Wuhan virus," term, 6, 343

xenophobia, 19
  Asian immigrants in United States, 58
  othering, 19
  violence against Asian Americans, 49
  White nationalism in US, 96

"yellow peril" stereotype, 3, 15, 35
  Asian immigrants as, 77–78
  "assimilating others" from, 49
  Japanese as, 13
  marginalized status of Asian
    Americans, 18–19
  othered as, 7
  stereotype, 3, 15, 35
YouTube, 347–48
Yue, Yong Ae, 241–42